SHIP MANAGEMENT

SHIP MANAGEMENT

THIRD EDITION

by

MALCOLM WILLINGALE
V Ships (UK) Limited

CONTRIBUTORS

DAVID FAVRE
Chartered Information
Systems Practitioner

OTTO FRITZNER
Stolt Parcel Tankers Inc.

HARRY GILBERT
Wallem Group Limited

DOUGLAS LANG
Denholm Ship Management (UK) Limited

HEREWARD M. P. LAWFORD
UK P&I Club

DAVID RODGER
Acomarit (UK) Limited

LLP

LONDON   HONG KONG
1998

LLP Reference Publishing
69–77 Paul Street
London EC2A 4LQ
Great Britain

EAST ASIA
LLP Asia
Sixth Floor, Hollywood Centre
233 Hollywood Road
Hong Kong

First published in Great Britain 1990
Second edition 1994
Third edition 1998
© John Spruyt, 1990, 1994
© Malcolm Willingale 1998

British Library Cataloguing in Publication Data
A catalogue record
for this book is available
from the British Library

ISBN 1 85978 835 1

Whilst every effort has been made to ensure that the
information contained in this book is correct neither the
editor and contributors nor LLP Limited can accept any
responsibility for any errors or omissions or for any
consequences resulting therefrom.

Are you satisfied with our customer service?

These telephone numbers are your service hot lines for questions and queries:

Delivery:	+44 (0) 1206 772866
Payment/invoices/renewals:	+44 (0) 1206 772114
LLP Products & Services:	+44 (0) 1206 772113

e-mail: Publications@LLPLimited.com or fax us on +44 (0) 1206 772771

*We welcome your views and comments in order to ease any problems
and answer any queries you may have.*

LLP Limited, Colchester CO3 3LP, U.K.

Text set in 10/12 Times by
Interactive Sciences Ltd
Gloucester
Printed in Great Britain by
MPG Books
Bodmin, Cornwall

PREFACE TO THE THIRD EDITION

"I have worked with different shipmanagers over the years and I know every trick in the book. Ship management is a game where the shipowner must keep a close eye on what his manager is up to."

(Extract from a conversation with an experienced shipowner's representative 30,000ft over Central Europe.)

"In general terms a manager would expect to provide the owner with a ship that operated safely, reliably, efficiently and cost effectively . . . However, as we know there are sections of the market that are operating on very short time horizons and if the revenue is not there then expenses must be curtailed to maintain a positive cashflow at all times. This may result in some hard decisions that could impact on safe operation, could reduce the reliability factor and affect the efficient operation. Whilst relatively short periods of such curtailment may be possible, ultimately the impact will be such that the ground cannot easily be regained and the minimum standards set by the manager or by statute may be compromised."

(Extract from a speech presented to the LSM 7th International Ship Management Conference in September 1996 by David Sterrett MD and CEO of ASP Ship-Management.)

Ship management is a subject which divides opinion. To many people involved in shipping, shipmanagers are a necessary but not necessarily welcome development. Others, however, including a growing body of opinion within the insurance and chartering communities, recognize the considerable efforts that ship management companies have made in recent years to improve standards of operation by readily embracing the safety and quality management disciplines which many shipowners have (and still are having) problems getting to grips with.

The main aim of this book is to provide a clear insight into independent ship management—a sector of the international shipping industry which has experienced significant growth over a relatively short space of time. It looks at the services which shipmanagers provide, some of the problems they face and possible future directions amongst other aspects and, hopefully, provides the reader with an appetite for further knowledge.

When I was asked by LLP to produce the third edition of John Spruyt's authoritative work on ship management I was at first very reluctant. My mind was changed, however, for two reasons. Firstly, ship management is an extremely dynamic sector of an industry which is undergoing considerable change. Much has happened therefore since publication of the second edition and I felt that there was a definite need to update John Spruyt's previous work. Secondly, since I joined the ship management sector in 1990 I have become increasingly aware of the lack of research on the subject of ship management and the need to explain why and how the sector is developing. Thirdly, and most importantly, my decision was influenced by a number of leading spokesmen in the ship management sector agreeing to contribute articles on specialist aspects of the business and by a number of other people who were willing to assist in the task. While the contributors are named in the book I would also like to thank my colleague at V Ships Paul Kerr (now exiled to our Singapore office) and to Ian McLean of Hanseatic whose comments on the draft text have been extremely helpful.

In compiling the third edition I have tried to provide a strategic view of the ship management business. I have done so in the belief that ship management has become a significant sector of international shipping despite its relatively short history and that ship management companies must do more to train future generations of office and sea staff rather than rely on the efforts of others.

Deepest Suffolk   MALCOLM WILLINGALE
1 December 1997

ABOUT THE CONTRIBUTING AUTHORS

The contributors to this book were selected on the basis of their specialist knowledge of the subject-matter they were asked to write about and because they are all actively involved in the market and, therefore, aware of latest developments.

OTTO FRITZNER (CHAPTER 5)

Otto Fritzner has extensive experience of many aspects of ship operation having held senior management positions in a number of respected shipowning and ship management companies.

After graduating with an MSc in naval architecture and marine engineering, Otto's initial experience in the shipping industry was with Det Norske Veritas—a path trodden by many of his fellow-countrymen. During his time with DNV he worked in Japan and Hong Kong before returning to Norway as a senior surveyor in the mid 1970s.

Otto joined the long-established Norwegian shipowner L. Gill-Johannessen & Co. as Technical Director in 1977 where he oversaw all technical and operational matters until he left to join Bergen-based Kristian Gerhard Jebsen in 1986 as General Manager of the Fleet Management Division and VP of open hatch bulk carrier specialist Gearbulk.

He then joined Limassol-based Columbia Ship Management, one of the world's largest independent ship management companies, in 1988 as Director. During his period with Columbia he was instrumental in the formation of the International Ship Managers' Association in 1991 where he was a member of the Executive Board and acted as one of the association's principal spokesmen especially on matters regarding ISMA's Code of Shipmanagement Standards.

Otto currently holds the position of Executive VP and General Manager of Stolt Parcel Tankers Inc.—the world's largest chemical tanker owner and operator. He is based in Houston and is responsible for all aspects of fleet management including the supervision of new buildings and insurance matters. He is also a member of Intertanko's Executive Committee and General Council, a Director of GARD and Steamship Mutual Underwriting Association.

Having had experience of shipowning and independent ship management Otto is well qualified to write on the subject of shipmanager selection.

HEREWARD LAWFORD (CHAPTER 6)

Herry Lawford graduated in law from Southampton University and joined Thomas Miller, the managers of the UK P&I Club, the TT Club and ITIC in 1967.

He spent the next 17 years handling shipowners' P&I and Defence claims, and travelled widely, particularly in the Far East. He was also Secretary of the International Group of P&I Clubs for six years.

In 1984 he was the first Chairman of the managers of Transport Intermediaries Mutual, the Miller club insuring the professional negligence risks of ship agents, ship brokers, shipmanagers, correspondents and surveyors. He then oversaw the merger of this Club with CISBA in 1992 to become International Transport Intermediaries Club (ITIC).

In 1993 Herry returned to the UK P&I Club as Service Director where he is responsible for the delivery of the Club's services worldwide.

His specialist knowledge includes third party ship management, the ISM Code, STCW, Port State Control and safety issues. He is also Chairman of Signum Services, Miller's fraud investigation unit.

DOUGLAS LANG (CHAPTER 7)

Douglas Lang graduated as a naval architect from the University of Strathclyde in 1980 and spent the first ten years of his career with DNV in Oslo specializing in R&D. He complemented his technical expertise by gaining an MBA from Strathclyde in 1988.

Douglas joined Denholm Ship Management in 1990 taking responsibility for the development of the company's quality assurance system based on the ISO 9002 standard and the ISMA Code. He was a member of ISMA Code Committee during its formative years.

Douglas has broadened his experience at Denholms into business development and IT: he is currently head of Denholms crew management business.

Douglas has written a number of papers on ship management and spoken at various conferences. In 1996 he presented a thought-provoking paper on QA as the David Underwood Memorial Lecture.

DAVID FAVRE (CHAPTER 8)

David Favre is a Chartered Information Systems Practitioner and Member of the British Computer Society having been actively involved in the international Information Technology (IT) and communications industry since the mid 1960s. Since the mid 1980s, he has specialized in the application of IT systems in the marine industry.

Currently, David runs his own consultancy business which specializes in advising senior management in the strategic application of IT to meet individual company requirements. He is a well-known writer and speaker on IT and communications systems. In association with the Cambridge Academy of Transport, David provides specialist seminars for senior management on all aspects of IT development and application.

As an independent consultant he is well placed to provide an objective view on all aspects of IT in the marine industry especially matters relating to strategic management.

DAVID RODGER (CHAPTER 9)

David Rodger started his career at sea with Anchor Line joining P&O in 1960 where he rose to the rank of Chief Officer coming ashore as Personnel Training Officer in the Passenger Division.

During his service with P&O, he graduated B.Sc (Economics) from London University; he is a Fellow of the Institute of Charterered Shipbuilders and a past member of the Controlling Council of the Institute.

He joined Denholm Ship Management as a Marine Superintendent in 1972. During a career with Denholms spanning 18 years, David held senior management positions in the UK and Hong Kong. He gained line management experience during this period in ship management as personnel, consultancy, technical services and agency.

David left Denholms in 1990 to run his own consultancy business before joining Acomarit where he currently holds the position of Group Personnel & Training Executive. He is responsible for the recruitment, training and administration of Acomarit's 8,000 seafaring staff of various nationalities.

HARRY GILBERT (CHAPTER 10)

Harry Gilbert is a well-known figure in the ship management sector and is now one of its leading spokesmen. He started his career as a marine engineer serving on ships owned and managed by Sir R. Ropner & Co., Manchester Liners and Denholm Ship Management before broadening his experience in the offshore industry where he worked on semi-submersible rigs and dynamically positioned diving support vessels.

Having spent some time in the Middle East as a superintendent engineer with Gray Mackenzie, Harry came ashore in 1981 as a superintendent engineer with Denholms where he served in a number of management positions including MD of the Glasgow group's ship management Division.

In 1994 Harry Gilbert left Denholms to take up his current position as MD of the Wallem Group of Companies based in Hong Kong. Wallem is one of the world's largest shipping services groups with interests in the fields of agency and shipbroking as well as ship management.

Harry is a member of the Institute of Marine Engineers and was elected as President of ISMA in 1997. He is a board member of the International Transport Intermediaries Club and the Liberian Shipowners' Council.

He is a regular contributor of articles, is a conference speaker and holds strong views on the future of independent ship management.

CONTENTS

CHAPTER 3. DEVELOPMENT

CHAPTER 4.   MARKETING SHIP MANAGEMENT

CHAPTER 5.   WHICH SHIPMANAGER?

CHAPTER 6.   WHO IS RESPONSIBLE? WHO IS LIABLE?

CHAPTER 7.   THE QUEST FOR SAFETY AND QUALITY MANAGEMENT

CHAPTER 8.   THE IT REVOLUTION

CHAPTER 9.   THE HUMAN ELEMENT

CHAPTER 10.   TOMORROW'S SHIPMANAGERS

LIST OF ILLUSTRATIONS

LIST OF TABLES

LIST OF ABBREVIATIONS

AME   Automated Message Exchange
ASCII   American Standard Code for Information Interchange
ASTM   American Society of Testing Materials
BIMCO   The Baltic and International Maritime Council
C/E   Chief Engineer
C/O   Chief Officer
COBOL   Common Business-Orientated Language
COLREGS   Collision Regulations
DF   Direction Finding
DFM   Dobson Fleet Management
DIS   Danish International Ship Register
DNV   Det Norske Veritas
DOC   Document of Compliance
FD&D   Freight, Demurrage & Defence
FFA   Fire Fighting Appliances
FLASH   Feeder for Lighter Aboard Ship
FOC   Flag of Convenience
FPSO   Floating Production Storage & Offloading
FSA   Formal Safety Assessment
FSO   Floating Storage and Offloading
FSU   Former Soviet Union
GIS   German International Shipregister
GMDSS   Global Maritime Distress Safety System
H&M   Hull and Machinery
HSC   Hanseatic Shipping Company
IACS   International Association of Classification Societies

IAME   International Association of Maritime Economists
ICF   Image Capture Facility
ILO   International Labour Office
IMEC   International Maritime Employers' Committee
IMO   International Maritime Organisation
Inmarsat   International Maritime Satellite Organisation
INS   Inertial Navigation System
ISIT   Integrated Shipboard Information Technology
ISM   International Safety Management
ISM Code   International Safety Management Code
ISMA   International Ship Managers' Association
ISMA Code   International Ship Managers' Association Code of Shipmanagement Standards
ISO 9002   International Standards Organisation: Quality Standard 9002
IT   Information Technology
ITC Hulls   Institute Time Clauses Hulls
ITF   International Transport Workers Federation
ITIC   International Transport Intermediaries' Club
LNG   Liquefied Natural Gas
LOC   Launch Operation Centre
LOF   Lloyd's Open Form (of salvage agreement)
LOH   Loss of Hire
LSA   Life Saving Applicances

REFERENCES AND FURTHER READING

BAJPAEE, RAJAISH, Eurasia Group, Hong Kong: "New Marketing Strategies: How to Face the Competition". 7th International LSM Ship Management Conference, Limassol, Cyprus, 12–13 September 1996.

BALTIC MAGAZINE: Shipmanagement. Special Issue, September 1996.

BARNEY, MICHAEL, Marine Management Systems Inc. USA: "Hardware and Software Selection". LLP Strategies in Shipping Conference, London, UK, 20–21 February 1997.

BASCOMBE, ADRIAN: "Playing the Management Game". *Containerisation International*, July 1995.

BASCOMBE, ADRIAN: "The Changing Role". *Containerisation International*, July 1995.

BERGANTINO, ANGELA and MARLOW, PETER: "Factors Influencing Choice of Flag". International Association of Maritime Economists (IAME) Conference, London, UK, 22–24 September 1997.

BRIGHTMAN, RICK, BP Shipping UK: "The Unstoppable Revolution". LLP Strategies in Shipping Conference, London, UK, 20–21 February 1997.

BROOK, KEITH, Lloyd's Register of Shipping, UK: "The Electronic Future for Managing Ship Condition Data". Nor-Shipping Conference, Oslo, Norway, 11–13 June 1997.

DONALDSON, LORD: "Safer Ships, Cleaner Seas". Report of Lord Donaldson's Inquiry into the Prevention of Pollution from Merchant Shipping, HMSO, May 1994.

FAIRPLAY: *Shipmanagers Guide*, May 1997.

FAVRE, DAVID, Information Technologist: "IT in Shipping". Lloyd's Shipping Economist Supplement, September 1996.

FAVRE, DAVID: "IT: Strategic Approach". *Inmarsat-Ocean Voice*, July 1996.

FILANOWSKI, MARK, MTL Ship Management, New York, US: "On Quality: Views of a Major Ship Owner". 5th International LSM Ship Management Conference, Limassol, Cyrpus, 19–20 September 1994.

FINANCIAL TIMES: Property Facilities Management Survey, 24 May 1996.

GALLAGHER, BRENDAN (Editor). Inmarsat, UK: *Never Beyond Reach*, Inmarsat 1989.

GILBERT, HARRY, Wallem Shipmanagement, Hong Kong: "The Future of the Industry". 5th International LSM Ship Management Conference, Limassol, Cyprus, 19–20 September 1994.

GILBERTSON, DAVID, LLP Ltd: "How Shipping can Benefit from Internet Services". Nor-Shipping Conference, Oslo, Norway, 11–13 June 1997.

HOGAN, BRIDGET and others: *The Gold Book: A Guide to Safety and Quality in the Maritime Industries*, Making Waves Publishing Ltd, 1996.

INDUSTRIAL BANK OF JAPAN: *Quarterly Survey*, Japanese Finance and Industry, No. 96, Vol. IV, 1993.

INMARSAT, International Maritime Satellite Organisation: *Inmarsat Maritime Communications Handbook*.

ISMA: *A Profile of the International Ship Managers' Association*, August 1994.

KERR, PAUL, V Ships, Monaco: "Developing New Management Business". 5th International LSM Ship Management Conference, Limassol, Cyprus, 12–13 September 1996.

KOCH, EBERHARD, Osterreichischer Lloyd Ship Management: "One view of the future is clear . . . Is this what the industry wants?". 5th International LSM Ship Management Conference, Limassol, Cyprus, 12–13 September 1996.

LANG, DOUGLAS, W., Denholm Ship Management Ltd, Glasgow, UK: "Is Ship Management Walking Upright? The Evolution of Quality Assurance". The David Underwood Memorial Lecture, Cambridge Academy of Transport, October 1996.

LEE, CARL, J. E. Hyde & Co. UK: "Why Shipping Must Grasp the IT Nettle". Nor-Shipping Conference, Oslo, Norway, 11–13 June 1997.

LLOYD'S LIST: Ship Management Supplement, March 1993.

LLOYD'S LIST: "Ship Registers". Feature article, 19 September 1997.

LLOYD'S LIST: Green Tanker Guide & Directory, Special Supplement, 29 September 1997.

LLOYD'S SHIP MANAGER: "Building Business by Bolstering Commercial Skills", March 1987.

LLOYD'S SHIP MANAGER: ISMA: Managing the Future. Supplement, October 1995.

LLOYD'S SHIP MANAGER: "Guide to International Ship Registers and Ship Management Services". 1996.

LLOYD'S SHIPPING ECONOMIST: "Jury out on QM benefits". November 1995.

OCEAN PRESS AND PUBLISHING LIMITED: The Shipmanager's Register, 1997 Edition.

PANAYIDES, PHOTIS: "Profit from 'Relationship Marketing'". 5th International LSM Ship Management Conference, Limassol, Cyprus, 12–13 September 1996.

PANAYIDES, PHOTIS M. and GREY, RICHARD, Institute of Marine Studies, University of Plymouth, UK: "A Relationship Approach for Marketing the Professional Ship Management Service". Universities Transport Studies Conference, Bournemouth University, 6–8 January 1997.

PANAYIDES, PHOTIS M. and GREY, RICHARD, Institute of Marine Studies, University of Plymouth, UK: "An Investigation of Professional Ship Manager-Client Relationships". International Association of Maritime Economists (IAME) Conference, London, UK, 22–24 September 1997.

PARKER, LOCK, Acomarit Group, Geneva, Switzerland: "Profit from a Ship Manager's Experiences". 5th International LSM Ship Management Conference, Limassol, Cyprus, 19–20 September 1994.

PARKER, LOCK, Acomarit Group, Geneva, Switzerland: "IT Applications to Maintain and Enhance Quality Management Systems". LLP Strategies in Shipping Conference, London, UK, 20–21 February 1997.

THE TIMES: Facilities Management Supplement, 22 March 1996.

THE TIMES: Facilities Management Supplement, 8 April 1997.

SEATRADE REVIEW: Ship Management & Crewing Report, August 1996.

SEATRADE REVIEW: Ship Management & Crewing Report, February 1997.

SLESINGER, PATRICK, Wallem Group. "Corporation Systems—What is the Key Objective?". LLP Strategies in Shipping Conference, London, UK, 20–21 February 1997.

STAMFORD RESEARCH GROUP. "Market Attitudes to V. Ships and the Ship Management Industry".

STERRETT, DAVID, ASP Shipmanagement, Australia: "What Size will best Guarantee Success: Small, Medium or Large?". 7th International LSM Ship Management Conference, Limassol, Cyprus, 12–13 September 1996.

STOPFORD, MARTIN: Maritime Economics. 2nd edition, Routledge, 1997.

STOPFORD, MARTIN: "Lessons From a Century of Shipping Cycles". International Association of Maritime Economists (IAME) Conference, London, UK, 22–24 September 1997.

STORY, EUGENE D., Marine Management Systems, US: "The Application of IT to Ship Safety and the Protection of the Environment". SNAME, 14–15 May 1997.

STORY, EUGENE D., Marine Management Systems, US: "The Application of a Standard IT Platform to New Ship Design". AISE, 9–11 September 1997.

STORY, EUGENE, D., Marine Management Systems, US: "Entering the Next Generation". *Lloyd's Shipping Economist*, March 1997.

THORSTENSEN, OLAV, Thome Ship Management, Singapore: "Quality: A Way to Profit". 7th International LSM Ship Management Conference, Limassol, Cyprus, 12–13 September 1996.

UNDERWOOD, T. DAVID, Denholm Shipmanagement, Glasgow, UK: "Quality Assurance and Liability Issues". Anatomy of Shipping, Cambridge, UK, 16 September 1992.

VARDAKIS, ACHILLES N., Shipmanagement Expert Systems, Greece: "ISM Code Compliance". LLP Strategies in Shipping Conference, London, UK, 20–21 February 1997.

WHITE, ROBERT and JAMES, BARRY, Lucidus Ltd: *The Outsourcing Manual*. Gower 1996.

WILLINGALE, MALCOLM, V Ships Group, Monaco: "Ship Management: Seven Things You Always Wanted to Know". Anatomy of Shipping, Cambridge, UK, 1992–1997.

WILLINGALE, MALCOLM, V Ships Group, Monaco: "Crewing and Training" Anatomy of Shipping, Cambridge, UK, 1994–1997.

INTRODUCTION

1.1 A PERSONAL VIEW

I joined the marketing department of V Ships, one of the world's largest ship management companies, in 1990 at a time of uncertainty for the sector. The optimism of the late 1980s was beginning to evaporate with renewed concerns about the shipping industry's deep-rooted structural problems especially its ageing fleet and worsening manpower shortages. The downturn in business confidence at that time was also demonstrated by the end of a phase which had seen fresh equity attracted into the shipping industry *via* a number of public funds and the Norwegian K/S market—two important, albeit relatively short-lived new sources of business for shipmanagers.

The early 1990s saw growing fears about falling professional standards in ship operation. Shipmanagers and the classification societies became the industry's favourite "whipping boys" especially among the chartering and the insurance communities. While class surveyors were criticized for turning too many blind eyes to vessel technical problems, shipmanagers were accused of being too good at cutting corners and keeping bad shipowners (and, therefore, ships) in business. Given these criticisms it was hardly surprising that there was a growing belief that the movement away from integrated to independent ship management would soon be reversed and that the days of the third party shipmanager were numbered.

In the event the worst fears proved to be unfounded for two main reasons. Firstly, many ship management companies, rather than sit back and absorb criticism, seized the initiative and started to invest in quality assurance (QA) programmes. Considerable resources were dedicated to establishing formal management systems based on safety and quality management disciplines in an effort to prove that third party ship management was not synonymous with low standards. In doing so, many shipmanagers decided to plough their own furrow while others decided to pursue the "holy grail" of QA *via* membership of the International Ship Managers' Association (ISMA)—the sector's first trade association which was formed in April 1991.

Secondly, in addition to QA, shipmanagers proved once again to be good at exploiting new opportunities in the marketplace. New markets began to emerge in the early 1990s notably *via* the breakdown of the Soviet bloc: a process which was to deliver a vast reservoir of well-trained manpower badly needed by Western shipowners, as well as ships for third party management as Former Soviet Union (FSU) shipowners sought to flag out ships in order to raise the Western bank finance sorely needed for fleet renewal. Shipmanagers were quick to seize the opportunity offered albeit on the understanding that time and resources were needed to establish long-term relationships.

The 1990s, therefore, while not witnessing the strength of demand growth seen in the 1970s and 1980s, have not proved to be as difficult for shipmanagers as initially feared. Currently, as the end of the decade approaches, there are real grounds for optimism within the ship management sector provided that a number of major challenges can be met. These are:

1 How will a people business like ship management continue to find, train and motivate sufficient office and seastaff?
2 How will the best use be made of information technology without wasteful use of precious resources?
3 How will the increasing regulatory demands of ISM and STCW continue to be met at a time when oversupply of ship management services continues to depress management fees to the extent that clients demand more services for less than they were paying in real terms 15 years ago?

Given the track record of the ship management sector to date I am confident that answers will be found to these and any other challenges. Moreover, I believe that despite these difficulties the experiences of other industries may point the way to even greater opportunities for growth for shipmanagers in the future.

The examination of manufacturing and service industries, particularly in the US and the UK, shows an increasing trend towards outsourcing. This is a process whereby a manufacturer or a service company focuses on its core competencies by contracting out or outsourcing non-core activities to specialist suppliers of support services which are able to supply such services in a cost effective, reliable and consistent manner. This process had developed to the extent that it is now seen by many companies as an important initiative in gaining a sustainable competitive advantage.

The trend towards outsourcing has been brought about by increasing management confidence in its ability to regulate contractual relationships, greater use of quality assurance techniques to control contracted-in services which form an essential part of business processes and a growth in the number of specialist suppliers leading to greater choice and price competition. These suppliers or facilities managers have experienced strong demand growth in the US and selected European countries and are now turning their attention towards opportunities in the developing world. By the year 2000, according to forecasts produced by Johnson Controls as quoted in the *Financial Times* in May 1996, the EU(12) facilities management market could be worth some US$1.3b. Accompanying this growth is the process of globalization as marked by the development of multinational facilities management companies able to provide a client's offices or plant with a diverse range of services beyond the traditional catering, security, cleaning, and repair and maintenance services such as purchasing, IT and the production of company system and procedure documentation.

Driving this whole process is the continuing need to keep down costs and to achieve flexibility—two powerful forces which have been prevalent in the shipping industry for many years now and which have spawned the development to date of "floating" facilities managers.

So what do the experiences of other industries tell us about the role of the shipmanager within the shipping industry in the future?

Will we see, for example, the widespread development of what may be described as "virtual" shipowners. Not the short-term asset players of the 1980s but companies committed to shipping long-term which concentrate on strategic initiatives, risk hedging, investment appraisal and marketing while delegating all other functions to specialist service suppliers according to long-term contracts?

Will we also see that, by the same token, the average size of contracts will increase as will the sophistication of how contracts are awarded? Hand-in-hand with this greater sophistication, will we also witness much more stringent performance monitoring of service suppliers as suggested by John Ellis, Chairman of the Facilities Management Association in a special facilities management supplement published by *The Times* in April 1997:

"The industry is maturing. We have moved away from everyone just diving into the market to outsource services. Clients have become more sophisticated. They want to be charged a competitive price, but are now looking at the track record and reputation of the companies that are taking over their non-core activities. Executives are taking a far greater interest and are including facilities in the company strategy and policy making."

Ship management, despite its relatively short history, is a maturing market in many respects. The ship management companies of the late 1990s have a strategic rather than a transient role to play in the development of the international shipping industry. However, they also face no let-up in the intensive competition which has marked the growth of the ship management sector to date with little or no prospect of any significant increase in management fees. For this reason, the key to future success is the shipmanager's ability to deliver a high standard of service on a consistent basis at a highly competitive price. Achievement of this will, in turn, be dependent on the ability to source, train and motivate competitively-priced staff offering a varied skills base and to make the best use of information technology and formal safety and quality management disciplines to enhance productivity—themes which are recurrent throughout this book.

1.2 OBJECTIVES AND CONTENT OF THE THIRD EDITION

In accepting that the shipmanager of the future will have a strategic role to play in the future development of the shipping industry, it must also be accepted that shipmanagers must adopt a strategic approach to the recruitment and training of their office and shipboard staff. In the past, shipmanagers have not done enough to train and educate the personnel needed to manage the shipping industry ashore and afloat as it was all too easy to hire staff from shipowning companies which, due to recession, were either unwilling or unable to provide long-term employment. Things have now changed, however, and the shipmanagers of the 1990s must do a lot more than their predecessors in the field of training.

It is hoped that the third edition of this book will help to address one aspect of this training need i.e. the need to provide newly-recruited staff to the office side of a ship-management organization with a basic grounding in the diverse nature of ship management. It is hoped that, in particular, the book will prove to be a useful reference for people looking to acquire not only detailed knowledge of one designated area but also a broader knowledge of different areas be it crewing, technical management, insurance, purchasing or safety and quality management. It will, perhaps, also stimulate the reader to take an interest in where the ship management sector is heading in the next century and the challenges which await.

With this objective in mind, the remainder of this chapter previews the content of the various chapters which set out to explain:

1 how the ship management sector has developed to date including an insight into the various factors which have shaped this development;
2 where the sector stands today; and
3 what the future might have in store.

Preview of Chapter 2

To ensure that the reader is familiar with the basic terminology used throughout the book, Chapter 2 explains what is meant by the term ship management. No apology is made for doing so given that ship management is an umbrella term which can cover many different services and virtually all aspects of day-to-day vessel operation. The chapter also makes the point that no two relationships between a shipowner and a shipmanager will be exactly the same and that these relationships can only be understood when the respective risk and reward profiles of the contracting parties are fully appreciated.

Chapter 2 also examines the miscellaneous services which a shipowner can choose from when entering a management agreement. The three groupings presented: technical, crewing and commercial management, are each broken down into various service elements which are, in turn, seen to comprise various tasks which describe what a ship management company does on a daily basis. Time is also spent looking at the various ancillary services which certain ship management companies now offer.

The chapter also makes the point that no two ship management companies will work or be organized in exactly the same way. Nevertheless, the chapter looks at four commonly used tools of the shipmanager's trade—the management agreement, the vessel operating budget, the vessel operating report and safety and quality management to provide a further insight into standard practice. Moreover, in spite of the differences often evident, the chapter argues that the future may well see fewer and fewer differences due to the use of common IT systems and the greater emphasis placed on the basic principles of safety and quality assurance.

Preview of Chapter 3

Having set the scene, Chapter 3 examines the history of how the independent ship management market has developed since the late 1950s. In doing so, four distinct phases of development are identified with each one characterized by a growth driver or set of drivers which include the continuing desire by shipowners to contain or reduce vessel operating costs with the help of a ship management company. Each phase is, in turn, related to the general cycles which have characterized the shipping industry in the post-war era.

Chapter 3 takes a closer look at these various growth drivers including the flagging out process. It argues that while the desire by shipowners to pursue this cost-cutting initiative has ebbed and flowed in recent years, and in spite of the recent revival in interest in the use of national and second registers, the use of an open flag which maximizes vessel operating flexibility is still the preferred option of the majority of ship-owning companies and in all likelihood will continue to be so.

The chapter demonstrates that the ship management market has reached a state of maturity in terms of the diversity of ship types which shipmanagers now serve, the broad geographical spread from which ship management services are offered and the intensive competition which has characterized the market in recent years as evidenced by little or no increase in management and manning fees.

By contrast, the maturity of the ship management market is called into question by the continuing lack of detailed statistics on who manages what. The chapter identifies the main reasons why accurate market data continues to be elusive i.e. due to the secrecy which still pervades the shipping industry and due to definitional problems. Nevertheless, by examining three sources of published information an idea of the size of the demand and the supply side of the ship management market is provided. In the former case, the maximum size of the total fleet under third party management (manning as well as full management vessels) is put at approximately 8,000 ships. In the latter case, the number of *bona fide* ship management companies is put at some 150 to 250 companies which range from a small number of large-size players offering a comprehensive product range from various office locations to a large number of small, single-office companies serving a fleet of perhaps less than ten ships controlled by one or maybe two owners.

Finally, the chapter takes a closer look at the supply and demand side of the ship management market equation. In the former case, a three-tier pyramid shaped structure is described and reasons are suggested as to why there has been little apparent change in this structure in recent years despite the generally adverse trading conditions prevailing. In the latter case, demand side trends are highlighted by an examination of three sectors of the ship management market—the tanker sector in which shipmanagers have played a prominent role for many years; container shipping which is a market sector where shipmanagers have made only relatively limited inroads, and the cruise market which is a new sector offering good growth potential but one where only a small number of shipmanagers offering the relevant skills are likely to be successful.

Preview of Chapter 4

Chapter 4 looks at how shipmanagers sell themselves in an intensely competitive marketplace. In particular, the chapter identifies the specific service requirements of the shipowning clients and how these requirements have changed over time, together with the different elements of a shipmanager's marketing strategy and the sales process itself.

Importantly, the chapter examines the question of differentiation i.e. how individual managers are able to set themselves apart from their competitors. It does so by identifying the opportunities which have been available to shipmanagers in recent years—notably the challenge of introducing safety and quality management disciplines and, more recently, the use of information technology in service delivery.

On the one hand, the chapter draws attention to the fact that the process through which a shipmanager is selected by a client is becoming a more rigorous and objective one. This is in many ways an inevitable development given the increasing regulatory pressures on shipowners and the need to ensure that a shipmanager is capable of consistently delivering a highly professional service not only on a day-to-day basis but as and when problems, including major incidents, occur.

On the other hand Chapter 4 also stresses the continuing importance of personal and subjective factors in shipowner–shipmanager relations. The chapter concludes by stressing that personal factors will continue to serve as a powerful tool in winning new business since they are, perhaps, the only way that a shipmanager can achieve sustainable competitive advantage.

Preview of Chapter 5

In picking up some of the themes introduced in Chapter 4, Otto Fritzner in Chapter 5 addresses the important question—which shipmanager? He does so by looking at some of the main selection criteria which influence shipowner decision-making. Aside from a shipmanager's competence, the ability to find good crew, the influence of company size and office location, particular attention is paid to the question of cost. The chapter examines how a shipowner attempts to assess the cost information supplied by competing shipmanagers at various stages in the decision-making process.

The chapter also takes a closer look at the selection process and illustrates how and why this process may vary from one decision to another in terms of the degree of formality adopted by the shipowner. Otto Fritzner does this by presenting the example of a typical tendering process which is becoming more evident in the ship management sector. Five stages of a typical tendering process are identified and some of the shortcomings of this method are discussed.

Further "colour" is added through the identification of a number of "golden" rules which may or may not be followed by a shipowner when choosing a shipmanager. These include the fairly basic principles such as the importance of the shipowner actually visiting the office of its prospective manager in order to meet key staff to the less obvious which include the need to dig deeper into a shipmanager's safety and quality management system in order to assess its effectiveness in controlling key day-to-day tasks which make up overall service delivery.

Chapter 5 concludes by looking at an equally important aspect of shipmanager selection—post selection management. The importance of maintaining good channels of communication is stressed as is the importance of avoiding certain pitfalls including the shipowner's tendency to micro-manage its shipmanager.

Preview of Chapter 6

Herry Lawford tackles the thorny question of shipmanager responsibilities and liabilities in Chapter 6. He does so by explaining how and why the contractual relationship between the shipowner and the shipmanager has been brought into sharper focus in recent years as the shipmanager has been forced to become more accountable for his actions—a further reason why many shipmanagers have made a conscious effort to introduce safety and quality management disciplines since the late 1980s as a way of achieving higher professional standards.

Chapter 6 spends some time looking at the two BIMCO standard agreements —SHIPMAN and CREWMAN—which are being increasingly used. The principal clauses of both documents are reviewed and discussed as are the ways in which they are being revised at the time of writing.

Herry Lawford also addresses two other aspects of shipmanager liabilities. Firstly, the types of insurance cover used by shipmanagers are identified and the pros and cons of co-assurance discussed. Secondly, the legal implications of the ISM Code are explored—an aspect which has commanded considerable attention in the past two years since Herry first drew attention to the potential problems that a shipmanager faced when complying with the Code's various requirements.

Preview of Chapter 7

Chapter 7 provides an interesting view of the relatively short history of the application of safety and quality management disciplines to the shipping industry in general and the ship management sector in particular. It is written by a true practitioner: Douglas Lang of Denholms was responsible for overseeing the development and implementation of his company's quality management systems based on the ISMA Code and contributed to the development of ISMA in its formative years.

The chapter compares and contrasts the relative merits of the various quality and safety codes which have been used by different shipowners, ship operators and shipmanagers over the past decade. It also includes a separate section on Total Quality Management (TQM)—the non-standard based route to quality which has so far been adopted by numerous manufacturing and service companies particularly in the US and Japan but by very few shipping companies.

Douglas Lang touches on a number of aspects of safety and quality management worthy of special mention. One of these, which struck a familiar chord given my own experience with quality management, was the difficulty in interpreting the ISO 9002 standard in the early 1990s when quality assurance was very new to shipping. At that time many so-called experts were actively seeking to sell advice to unwary shipowners and shipmanagers. Particularly frustrating was the fact that too many consultants were very good at pointing out where a client was failing to comply but less forthcoming when a possible solution was asked for. Whether to use an external consultant is, therefore, a difficult question to answer. In certain companies they may well get in the way and contribute little of tangible benefit. In many others, however, a consultant can serve a useful purpose i.e. as a catalyst to change as senior management is often prepared to listen to external advice if not the views of its own staff. Regardless of whether an external consultant is used the end result must be the same i.e. a clear and simply documented system that is "owned" by staff ashore and afloat. Unfortunately, this objective is often lost sight of as panic sets in and the temptation to add additional instructions just to be on the safe side cannot be resisted. What the company ends up with is an impractical and bureaucratic system. However, all is not lost if a company in using the systems gradually streamlines and refines the system into a much more practical management tool.

Chapter 7 also examines why certain companies are able to successfully implement a formal safety and quality management system and others find it extremely difficult. Aside from the obvious reason i.e. a total lack of senior management commitment who fail to lead by example, the cultural question is addressed. Douglas Lang questions the wisdom of trying to pose the culture of an office organization onto an increasingly migrant seastaff.

Chapter 7 really whets the appetite for further knowledge and underlines the fact that the shipping industry has still much to learn about the benefits of implementing safety and quality management disciplines. Hopefully, over the next few years more and more companies will be able to share experiences of what they have achieved including better measurement of performance which is generally lacking in the industry at present as many shipowners are preoccupied with meeting the first of the ISM compliance deadlines.

Preview of Chapter 8

David Favre attempts to answer the question as to how shipmanagers can get the most out of information technology. It is both a timely and a thought-provoking appraisal. Timely, because it stresses the fact that the pace of change in IT continues to outpace our ability to manage change. Thought provoking, because it advocates that senior management must not, as is all too often the case, delegate their decision-making responsibility in the use of IT to meet their business information needs, but, rather, play an active role.

After reading this chapter a clear impression is left of the need to fundamentally understand how ship management companies function in a dynamic marketplace. It advocates the need to take a strategic and infrastructural rather than the all too frequently seen piecemeal applications approach to IT. It does so in the belief that only in this way will a company achieve an attractive payback on its investment and not lose sight of its basic business information objectives.

Another argument in favour of this approach is the need to comply with the IMO's ISM Code. These guidelines provide an extremely useful functional framework for a ship management company encompassing the entire shipboard and shore-based organization. Indeed, David Favre bravely suggests that shipmanagers should consider themselves lucky in so far as the mounting regulatory and commercial pressures within the sector have come at a time when IT is on hand to help! But how many shipmanagers will firstly decide to take advantage of this opportunity and, more importantly, adopt the right approach is open to question.

Preview of Chapter 9

David Rodger looks at the all-important human element of ship management. While, like any other service business, a shipmanager is heavily reliant on its people capital, David also highlights at the outset the peculiarity of the ship management structure which necessitates close cooperation and communication between the office and the ship side of the management equation. Imbalance and conflict can, of course, have disastrous consequences.

Chapter 9 examines both the quantitative and qualitative aspects of crewing. In the former case, David makes reference to the widely cited BIMCO/ISF study originally produced in 1990 but updated in 1995. In doing so the imbalance between supply and demand areas for maritime labour is highlighted as is the global shortage of officers particularly those offering specialist skills and experience.

When addressing the quality aspect, Chapter 9 examines the substantial changes in the regulatory environment which are currently in progress. The far-reaching implications of the ISM, STCW (95) and the two ILO conventions (147 and 180) are discussed including the impact of crewing costs.

Reflecting some of the points discussed in Chapter 5, David Rodger looks at how a shipowner selects a particular type of crew and stresses the need for close cooperation between the shipowner and its manager in this matter. The relative importance of the various selection criteria which are taken into consideration are assessed including the importance of continuity within a fluid labour market.

An overview of crew training is also provided including a useful reminder of the need to have clear objectives rather than the desire just to meet latest regulations. The chapter concludes by identifying some of the future challenges which must be faced including the importance of developing long-established sources rather than a headlong rush to unearth new and hopefully cheaper supplies. Allied to this train of thought is the importance of maintaining high crew retention levels by addressing some of the key causes which persuade seafarers to give up on the sea.

Preview of Chapter 10

In the final chapter Harry Gilbert paints a very positive view for the future of independent ship management. His optimism is based on the belief that the ship management sector has come of age by being accepted as a well established and mature part of the shipping industry and also because of the way in which various challenges faced by the shipping industry in recent years, notably increasing legislation and the use of information technology, have not only been met by ship management companies but also seen as an opportunity to differentiate themselves.

Harry Gilbert casts a seasoned eye over the various factors which will determine the future shape of the ship management sector. For example, in reviewing the question of size he concludes that there is room for both the big companies managing extensive fleets of diverse ship types and the smaller niche players able to offer expertise and experience in specialist areas.

Chapter 10 also considers the important question as to who will own the ship-managers of the future. Despite the obvious maturing of the sector, there has been surprisingly little merger and acquisition activity for two particular reasons cited by the author—the difficulty in valuing a ship management business and the potential post-acquisition/merger trauma among existing clients of the consenting parties. However, given that most commentators believe that greater concentration will emerge on the supply as well as the demand side of the ship management market equation in the future, will this mean that the sector will witness its first significant acquisition among the major players?

SHIP MANAGEMENT DEFINED

2.1 SHIP MANAGEMENT—WHAT IS IT?

As explained in previous editions of this book, answering this question is not a straightforward task. Ship management is an umbrella term which comprises various types of management services covering all aspects of daily vessel operations. For this reason, no two management contracts signed between a shipowner and a shipmanager are exactly the same.

In an effort to keep things simple, it is useful to take, at the outset, a shortened version of the definition used by John Spruyt in the previous edition of this book: "The professional supply of a single or range of services by a management company separate from the vessel's ownership" where: "professional supply" means that the supplier (shipmanager) provides service(s) to the user (shipowner) according to contracted terms and in return for a management fee. In doing so the shipmanager is required to ensure that the vessel always complies with international rules and regulations, is run in a safe and cost efficient manner without threat to the environment and is maintained so as to preserve as far as possible its asset value.

The shipmanager must also take responsibility for its actions—a point which is discussed at greater length later in this chapter.

"A single or range of services" means that the shipowner selects to use a comprehensive range or just one service from a number offered by the shipmanager. These services break down into three main groups: technical management, crew management and commercial management (see section 2.2).

"Management company separate from the vessel's ownership" means that the supplier of the services is independent from the user working with its own staff and from a separate office. This office may be located several thousand miles away from where the shipowner is domiciled and in a completely different time zone to where the vessel in question normally trades. The term separate, in the strictest sense, means that there is no common shareholding interest between the shipowner and the manager. In practice, such shareholding interests exist in many instances, although in every case the manager will function as a separate cost centre and will provide equitable services to all clients according to a well defined contract and detailed budget agreed between the two main contracting parties.

So far so good. However, in reality this simple definition does not reflect the complexity of the relationship which often exists between the shipowner and the shipmanager for a number of reasons.

Spruyt (1994) illustrates this complexity by providing a number of specific examples of what can be described as hybrid shipowner–shipmanager relationships. These include situations where:

1 The shipowner elects to retain control over a number of critical functions in the management of its ships, including the selection of senior officers, safety auditing and the negotiation and management of drydockings, while outsourcing the remaining day-to-day ship management activities.

2 The shipowner retains a technical department to run a "core" fleet of, say, bulk carriers, but in acquiring a fleet of specialist vessels, such as parcel tankers or reefers, uses a shipmanager that is able to provide the requisite skills in technical management including the maintenance of tank coatings or of refrigeration equipment, as well as the sourcing of seastaff with the specialist skills and experience relevant to the ship type(s) in question.

3 The shipowner does not have the inhouse technical and personnel staff to handle an unforeseen increase in its fleet, perhaps *via* an opportunistic purchase. In this particular situation a shipmanager will be used only until the shipowner recruits additional staff to cope with the additional workload.

4 A shipmanager has a shareholding position in a vessel under management or has some kind of equity association with the shipowner i.e. both companies are part of the same group.

Other examples of hybrid relationships include instances where the shipowner seconds staff to the shipmanager's office to control certain functions and where the shipowner "imports" selected systems and procedures from the shipmanager as part of a consultancy agreement which also includes staff training.

Spruyt (1994) describes such relationships as representing a new frontier for ship management. Furthermore, he draws attention to the potential problems which may be encountered in trying to make them work and makes clear who the dominant partner is. He states:

"So a new frontier is established—within the overall partnership between owner and manager each designs his organization to provide what is appropriate to particular pressures and specific business. Adjustment to such a new definition and division of authority takes some experience to work smoothly—there is a danger of overlap of authority, or contradiction of instructions. This needs patient handling to avoid frustration on both sides. But in the ship management business the owner is king and the adaptability of the manager to client's needs is the secret of his survival."

Scenarios of the kind identified above can blur the relationship between the shipowner and the shipmanager. In reality, this relationship can only be brought into sharp focus when the risk and reward profile of the vessel in question is apparent. In its purest form this relationship is clear where the shipowner is the risk taker whose primary objective and success is dependent upon its ability to find profitable employment for the ship and/or to realize a profit from the vessel's resale for demolition or further trading. By contrast, the shipmanager's aim is to supply a service or services to assist the shipowner in return for a fixed management fee. This is not to say that the shipmanager is without risk. For example, the risk of non-payment if the shipowner runs into financial problems or the damage that may be suffered to reputation (among charterers and/or suppliers) through problems caused by insufficient funding. Nevertheless, the key to understanding the relationship between the shipowner and the shipmanager is the degree of risk which each party takes on board.

In exploring this relationship further and at the risk of over-complicating the previously-used definition, one further aspect of ship management should, therefore, be added:

"Ship management is: 'The professional supply of a single or range of services by a management company separate from the vessel's ownership in support of the primary objectives of the shipowner' where: 'in support of the primary objectives of the shipowner' makes clear that the shipmanager's and the shipowner's main objectives are different."

This important addition can be explained further by breaking down the various constituent parts of a shipowning company into core and non-core activities. The result of such an exercise is presented as Table 2.1. Of the 14 elements shown, five can be identified as typically core and the remainder as non-core. It is the non-core activities which are the subject of the outsourcing or contracting-out process referred to in Chapter 1 and, by the same token, the activities targeted by ship management companies.

Table 2.1: Breakdown of shipowning functions

Function	Core	Non-core
Corporate Strategy	×	
Marketing	×	
Accounting	×	
Personnel		×
S&Q Management		×
Purchasing		×
IT		×
Repair & Maintenance		×
Certification		×
Cargo Procurement	×	
Financing	×	
Insurance		×
S&P	×	
Bunkering	×	

NOTE: Many of the functions listed can be subdivided further. For example, the personnel function comprises the selection and recruitment of seastaff, welfare, training, payroll, performance appraisal, etc.

Once again, however, this exercise oversimplifies matters in so far as certain elements or functions are in reality split between the owner and the manager albeit with the degree of decision-making authority delegated by the former to the latter clearly spelt out. For example, in the case of commercial management, which will be explained more fully in section 2.2, the manager acts in accordance with the shipowner's instructions in terms of approving alternative charter opportunities, sale and purchase options and in the appointment of agents. In similar vein, accounting is split into at least two parts with the shipmanager focusing on the day-to-day management of vessel accounts (although in certain cases the shipmanager may well also look after the corporate accounts of a single shipowning company controlled perhaps by a private investor).

Having spent some time defining the literal meaning of the term ship management it is important to add some colour to this rather plain canvas. As Bajpaee (1996) and others have pointed out, ship management is an international business of many characteristics including low margins, relatively low (albeit rising) barriers to entry, heavy paperwork, intense competition, high risks (if things go wrong) and a need to provide services 24 hours a day. It is also a business where the shipmanager must be capable of tailoring the services to the differing needs of individual clients while retaining efficiency and cost effectiveness in service delivery and trying to treat all clients equitably. Indeed, a straw poll taken among shipmanagers would almost certainly show that ship management is a problem intensive and often difficult business characterized by low profitability and a need to diversify activities into higher yielding areas. Nevertheless it continues to attract new companies lured by market growth potential.

2.2 SHIP MANAGEMENT—WHAT SERVICES?

We have already established ship management as an umbrella term encompassing miscellaneous types of services. Essentially, these services comprise three main groups—technical management, crew management and commercial management —plus a fourth group of what can be termed ancillary services. These different groups are depicted as a "family tree" in Figure 2.1. Where technical and crew management services are provided (with or without commercial management) then the contract between the shipowner and the manager is referred to as full management. Technical- and crewing-only contracts are typically termed part management (or manning-only) contracts in the case of the latter.

2.2.1 Technical Management

The primary objective of technical management is safe, pollution-free and cost-efficient vessel operation in accordance with international rules and regulations and where due consideration is given to the protection of asset value. As Figure 2.1 shows, technical management is subdivided into various service elements. These different elements are, in turn, made up of individual tasks which are conducted by designated office and seastaff with defined levels of authority and responsibility who follow company procedures and work instructions. The various tasks are also interrelated and interdependent. For example, regular vessel inspections by a superintendent provides an input and serves as an output for other service elements including purchasing, reporting, certification, maintenance and budgeting. In similar vein, purchasing has a bearing on vessel inspection, safety and quality management and maintenance.

To illustrate the individual tasks which make up the various service elements three examples are presented below.

Purchasing: involves arranging the supply of all victuals, spares, stores, lubricants, chemicals and the miscellaneous other products and services which are required by the vessel on a day-to-day basis together with inventory control and the control of suppliers, subcontractors and supply contracts. Though part of technical management, purchasing is a profession in its own right and as such may be offered as a separate service to a shipowning client willing to contract out this essential activity to a management company offering stronger buying power and specialist skills and contacts. Purchasing managers work very closely with other technical staff in the office and with the master and departmental heads on board ship who are given the authority to initiate purchase orders. Efficient and cost effective purchasing, like other services, is dependent on good planning and attention to detail to ensure that what is required on board is delivered at the right place at the right time and according to specification.

Vessel Inspection: the primary objectives of regular visits by the designated superintendent to a vessel are: to monitor the technical condition of the ship's structure and equipment and the vessel's performance; to ensure ship's staff compliance with company policies and operational procedures; and to assist ship's staff resolve any technical and operational problems. Typically, visits are conducted two to five times a year depending on a vessel's trading pattern in relation to the managing office, with each visit of two to five days' duration.

Whenever possible, visits are preplanned and conducted according to a systematic procedure in order to maximize the benefit of time spent on board. This necessitates the use of a standard vessel inspection report a typical format of which is presented as Table 2.2. These reports can serve as the basis of ongoing checks that reported defects are followed up and as effective previsit plans. The information contained in the inspection report will also serve as the basis of regular reports to clients (see section 2.3).

Despite efforts to plan and systematize visits, unforeseen circumstances dictate that visits, occasionally, must be arranged at short notice in response to particular problems which require the attendance of the superintendent and/or specialist support staff.

Vessel Drydocking: given that the periodic drydocking of a vessel in accordance with class and the owner's requirements invariably involves heavy expenditure, the shipmanager must be able to offer its clients good planning, negotiating and cost management skills as well as technical expertise. In essence the shipmanager must be able to coordinate all predocking activities, including the preparation of a

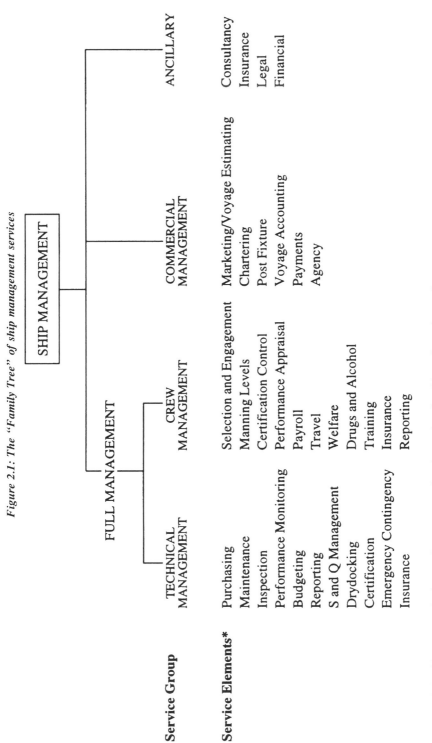

Figure 2.1: The "Family Tree" of ship management services

Service Group				
	FULL MANAGEMENT			ANCILLARY
	TECHNICAL MANAGEMENT	CREW MANAGEMENT	COMMERCIAL MANAGEMENT	

Service Elements*

TECHNICAL MANAGEMENT	CREW MANAGEMENT	COMMERCIAL MANAGEMENT	ANCILLARY
Purchasing	Selection and Engagement	Marketing/Voyage Estimating	Consultancy
Maintenance	Manning Levels	Chartering	Insurance
Inspection	Certification Control	Post Fixture	Legal
Performance Monitoring	Performance Appraisal	Voyage Accounting	Financial
Budgeting	Payroll	Payments	
Reporting	Travel	Agency	
S and Q Management	Welfare		
Drydocking	Drugs and Alcohol		
Certification	Training		
Emergency Contingency	Insurance		
Insurance	Reporting		

* As explained in text, each element in turn comprises interrelated and interdependent tasks detailed specification based on information on the vessel's performance and technical condition supplied by the master and the C/E in the form of drydock work lists, assess the many factors which influence the shipowner's selection of a repair yard, including price, terms of payment, delivery and redelivery costs, and project manage the drydock operation including the assessment of any unbudgeted items and approval of the work carried out.

Table 2.2: Content of a Vessel Inspection Report

1 CONTROL SHEET

– circulation list and guidelines to usage

2 EXTERNAL CONDITION*

– including prop., rudder, funnel structure, superstructure, bridge front, spare prop., accommodation ladders, draught markers, anchors and cables etc.

3 DECK CONDITION*

– including mooring ropes, masts and fittings, winches, windlass, deck scupperplugs, deck rails, hatch coamings/covers/seals/closing devices (as applicable), cargo/ballast lines, hose derricks/cranes (as applicable) etc.

4 INTERNAL HULL STRUCTURE*

– including aft/fore peak, chain locker, storage rooms, hold/tank ladders, cargo holds/tanks, pipe tunnels, fuel tanks etc.

5 ACCOMMODATION/SUPERSTRUCTURE*

– including outer decks, rails, fittings, storage spaces, alleyways, stairways, washrooms, monkey island, wheelhouse, chartroom, radio room, officer/ crew cabins and lounges etc.

6 NAVIGATION AND RADIO EQUIPMENT*

– including steering controls, DF equipment, speed log, radars, GMDSS equipment, echo sounders, satnav/gps, whistle etc.

Table 2.2 cont.

7 ENGINE ROOM*

– including general appearance, ME, auxiliary generators, main and auxiliary boilers, UMS, compressors, piping and valves, etc.

8 CARGO EQUIPMENT*

– including cargo winches/motors, hydraulic lines, lashing gear, wires, cargo blocks, cleaning equipment, heating equipment, cargo pumps, loadicators etc.

9 SEP EQUIPMENT*

– including alarms, vent fan flaps, oily water separators, LSA (Life Saving Appliances), FFA (Fire Fighting Appliances) and oil spill containment and clean up equipment

10 SEP RECORDS*

– including deck log, official log, garbage disposal log, oil record book, PMS records, inventories, charts and publications etc.

11 CREW PERFORMANCE

12 SHIP PERFORMANCE RECORDS

– including average laden/ballast speeds, ME consumptions, auxiliary consumption, lub consumption etc.

13 PENDING STORES AND SPARES

14 DEFECT LIST

– summary of deficiencies requiring corrective action.

NOTES: * denotes standard format showing details of condition, planned action (as applicable), who is responsible for implementation (ship's staff, riding squad, shipyard, subcontractor etc.) and time scales.

The miscellaneous items listed are often coded for ease of identification, recording and followup purposes in subsequent reports.

Table 2.2 cont.

Defect lists show main items and timeframes for corrective action (as a recap of the individual sections). This list may be used for recording followup action.

Reports are signed and dated by the superintendent, master, C/E and C/O.

Photographic evidence of standard shipboard views may be attached as an addendum to demonstrate technical condition/physical appearance and before/after scenarios.

To illustrate one of the individual drydocking tasks, Table 2.3 provides an example of a typical spreadsheet analysis of alternative repairyard proposals—in this particular case as applicable to the proposed docking of a modern multipurpose vessel where the work to be conducted includes removal and repair of the bow-thruster and extensive bottom blasting and repainting. A spreadsheet analysis of the kind presented as Table 2.3 serves as the basis for the yard selection process which will also involve the shipmanager providing the shipowner with advice of intangible factors such as yard reliability. If the shipmanager was also providing commercial management (see section 2.2.3) then information on the opportunity cost of loss of hire would also be provided so that the owner is fully informed of all the technical and commercial facts influencing repair yard selection.

2.2.2 Crew Management

The primary objective of crew management is the provision of well trained and suitably experienced crew of the nationality required by the shipowner to a vessel to ensure safe and efficient operation according to international regulations. As in the case of technical management, crew management is made up of different service elements (and, in turn, individual tasks). Dealing primarily with the "humanware" as opposed to hardware, service delivery requires a different approach and set of skills to technical management. Indeed, harmonization between the technical and personnel departments in a ship management company can be hard to achieve but, nevertheless, is essential if the overall "product" delivered to the client is to be of an acceptable standard.

The various crewing service elements identified in Figure 2.1 comprise many different tasks. For example, crew selection and engagement involve relief planning, the management of large amounts of data and paperwork including personnel records, application forms, training records, employer history and medical records as well as people-vetting skills. In addition, there must be close liaison between different staff who are involved in the sourcing of seastaff at various locations—typically, the master, the crew manager at the shipmanager's office and the recruitment officer located in the source country, as well as other interested parties including port agents, medical practitioners, government agencies etc.

A further example of service delivery in crew management is provided by performance appraisal the basic objectives of which are to assess the performance of seastaff during their period of employment, the identification of training needs and the determination of career development (in both a positive and negative sense). Once again, different office and seastaff are involved including the staff responsible for conducting appraisals—typically the master (or designated head of department) immediately prior to disembarkation, and the superintendent (or crew manager)

Table 2.3: Spreadsheet analysis of drydocking quotations

Vessel:	YARD A	YARD B	YARD C	YARD D	YARD E
Total repair days	13	11	11	9	37
Included drydock days	13	11	11	9	15
Total (repairs + fixed costs) $	442,990	579,828	480,586	505,324	357,848
Cheapest yard for repairs (1),	*1.24*	*1.62*	*1.34*	*1.41*	*1*
Dollar yardtime cost @ $10,000/d	130,000	110,000	110,000	90,000	370,000
Total repairs + timecost	572,990	689,828	590,586	595,324	727,848
Least expensive yard overall	*1*	*1.20*	*1.03*	*1.04*	*1.27*
Services	23,876	37,913	32,272	27,855	45,108
Drydocking	25,466	49,347	33,497	28,477	25,041
Cleaning and painting	116,880	162,745	152,347	127,926	51,871
Drydock work	68,378	74,270	64,115	74,821	33,218
Deck	65,289	84,874	84,804	133,245	81,091
Engineroom	26,523	40,558	34,945	36,147	25,487
Navigation	2,217	4,217	2,147	4,095	5,203
Subtotal repairs (1)	328,629	453,934	404,127	432,566	267,019
Contingency @ 10%	32,863	45,393	40,413	43,257	26,702
Subtotal repairs + extras (2)	361,492	499,327	444,540	475,823	293,721
Ranking for repairs only	*1*	*1.38*	*1.23*	*1.32*	*0.81*
Discount	0	0	44,454	50,000	29,372
Subtotal repairs + extras – discount	361,492	499,327	400,086	425,823	264,349
Fixed costs					
Paint supply	45,000	45,000	45,000	45,000	45,000
Class fees	25,000	25,000	25,000	25,000	25,000
Agents	6,500	5,500	5,500	4,500	18,500
Navigation equipment	5,000	5,000	5,000	5,000	5,000
Subtotal fixed costs (4)	81,500	80,500	80,500	79,500	93,000
Total repairs	442,992	579,827	480,586	505,323	357,849

NOTE: Modern multipurpose vessel: work includes removal/repair of bowthruster, comprehensive bottom blasting/repainting blasting and painting holds and hatch covers.

during a regular visit. Once again the documentation plays a key role i.e. standardized report forms and personnel record databases. Moreover, performance appraisal is interdependent on other service elements notably crew training, selection and recruitment, and control of drugs and alcohol.

2.2.3 Commercial Management

Commercial management involves the provision of miscellaneous shipbroking services relating to the employment of a vessel according to instructions laid down by the shipowner. Specifically, the commercial manager represents the interests of the shipowner by way of the following services:

- The marketing of a vessel on the voyage, time or bareboat charter market including the provision of market data and voyage estimating to assist the owner to select the most advantageous employment.
- Once the chosen employment has been selected, the commercial manager negotiates the required terms and conditions and instructs the vessel master accordingly.
- Post fixture services including the maintenance of vessel accounts, receipt of freight income, appointment of agents, checking of invoices and settlement of same according to owner's instructions.
- Resolution of any claims and disputes involving the charter.

For this package of services the commercial manager typically receives the standard 1.25 per cent commission on gross freight income which is deducted on receipt. In addition to the above, the commercial manager may also provide sale and purchase broking services to assist the owner in the sale or acquisition of tonnage for which an additional (normally 1 per cent) fee on the sale or purchase price is payable.

In providing the various services described above the commercial manager is seeking to maximize the vessel's earning power and, in the case of the S&P function, acquire and dispose of tonnage at the most competitive price. To do so, the commercial manager must liaise very closely with other parties involved in day-to-day operations. In many instances, shipmanagers provide commercial management to vessels which are owned by or associated within the parent company in some way. Commercial management is a growth area for shipmanagers but problems can arise if, for example, commercial management is provided to ship "A" in direct competition to ship "B" for which the shipmanager provides technical management services.

2.2.4 Ancillary Services

Given that the delivery of technical, crewing and commercial management services requires a multidisciplinary skills base, it is hardly surprising that many of the larger ship management companies have sought to broaden the range of services they offer in the marketplace. The key areas for diversification have been: consultancy, financial services and insurance services. Each of these areas is described below:

Consultancy: this has been the most popular target with a number of the large shipmanagers going to the extent of setting up separate consultancy companies as independent cost/profit centres. The consultancy services offered have tended to focus on the management of technical projects—primarily vessel newbuilding, conversion or upgrading works.

In recent years, however, with the advent of increasing regulation including the implementation of the ISM Code (see Chapter 7), a whole new market has opened up whereby shipmanagers have been able to sell their expertise and experience in designing, implementing and maintaining safety and quality management systems to small shipowners of limited resources.

Arguably, these services are not strictly impartial as they can be viewed as a "means to an end" i.e. efforts to increase core business. Nevertheless, the advice is in the main pragmatic rather than theoretical and based on sound practical experience.

Typically, shipmanagers seek daily fees for the provision of consultancy services in the region of $500/day—possibly more depending on the seniority of the staff involved and the specialist nature of the advice provided.

The future is likely to see greater efforts by shipmanagers to sell their expertise although the potential to realize the value of inhouse expertise and experience is often thwarted in the case of existing clients who invariably view consultancy services as benefits which should be provided free (*gratis*) as part of the management fee.

Financial Services: in spite of the increasing availability of competitively-priced debt finance in recent years, there is a growing market for the provision of financial broking services to shipowners lacking an understanding of and contacts with the banking lending community. FSU shipowners have been an important source of business in this area as they have sought to raise the funds needed for fleet renewal by mortgaging existing vessels flagged out to open registers. A small number of shipmanagers were able to spot this growing need and have positioned themselves as debt finance brokers for which, typically, a 1 per cent fee is payable.

Despite the increasing availability of debt finance it is likely that a number of shipowners will continue to use the services of an intermediary. Shipmanagers will compete for this business with a number of independent finance boutiques on the strength of existing client relationships. Allied to services provided to borrowers, shipmanagers are also in a position to advise lenders on credit risks and technical matters particularly in the case of non-performing loans.

Insurance Services: there is an analogy with financial services in so far as soft insurance markets in recent years have lowered the cost of securing insurance cover. Moreover, there is no shortage of specialist insurance brokers available to place insurance and provide claims-handling services on behalf of shipowners. Once again, however, the strength of existing relationships with clients may enable the insurance department of a ship management company with extensive contacts with the insurance community to provide advisory services in certain instances.

2.3 THE TOOLS OF THE TRADE

Having spent some time describing the diverse services which shipmanagers offer to their clients, attention is now turned towards how these services are actually delivered i.e. the processes involved. While it is true to say that no two ship management companies will work in exactly the same way, common work practices are evident and can be described in terms of a number of key instruments of modern ship management. These are:

– the Management Agreement;
– the Vessel Operating Budget;
– the Vessel Operating Report;
– the Safety and Quality Management System.

2.3.1 The Management Agreement

The management agreement governs the relationship between the shipmanager and the shipowner. The various terms and conditions it contains determine the roles and responsibilities of the respective parties. Typically, management agreements are based on the law of agency as interpreted under English law where the shipmanager does not conduct business in its own right but acts as an agent on behalf of a principal (the shipowner).

Aside from the individual terms and conditions which are discussed in greater detail below and in Chapter 6, management agreements vary in the following main ways:

1 Agreements are either prepared by the ship management company itself, based on its own experience over time and in consultation with legal advisors, or a standard format is utilized. The latter is provided in the form of BIMCO's SHIPMAN which was introduced in 1988 as the first attempt to standardize the terms and conditions on which ship management contracts are negotiated.

   Similar in format to the other standard forms produced by BIMCO's documentation committee, SHIPMAN is presented in two parts: Part I sets out basic information including the services to be covered by the agreement and bears the signatures of the owner and the shipmanager; Part II explains the various clauses relating to the agreement (as applicable to the services selected for inclusion). Further discussion of the merits of using SHIPMAN including recent efforts to revise its content is presented in Chapter 6.

2 Agreements vary in terms of the range of services they encompass. Essentially, there are two main types: the ship management agreement which

covers a comprehensive range of technical and crew management i.e. full management services plus ancillary services as required; the crewing or manning agreement which is limited to the provision and management of crew (either full complement or in part).

3 Agreements also vary in terms of the method of charging for the services provided. The most widely used is the costs plus agreement whereby the shipowner pays or undertakes to reimburse the shipmanager for all costs incurred in the provision of services to the vessel plus a separate (usually fixed price) management fee. Alternatively, a lump sum agreement (more popular in the case of crew management) is used. This type of agreement is based on the payment of a single, all encompassing sum out of which the shipmanager pays all the costs of service provision and takes a management fee without further recourse to the shipowner unless exceptional circumstances prevail. These include crew changes which are requested by the shipowner, any overtime worked by the crew over and above contracted amounts (for example 120 hours/month), or any exceptional work conducted in addition to normal duties.

Regardless of the type of agreement used it is invariably subject to detailed and often lengthy negotiations over specific terms and conditions including fees payable. With the shipowner aware that it is a buyer's market for ship management services, given the large number of ship management companies who invariably chase any one contract, this situation is hardly surprising.

By way of illustration, Table 2.4 presents the main terms and conditions which are presented in a typical ship management agreement which should be read in conjunction with the following comments:

1 Service delivery
An owner may insert a clause in the agreement which specifies that the services which are provided by the manager must comply with a specified safety and/or quality standard and that the shipmanager must maintain accreditation to that standard throughout the duration of the agreement. The standards cited can either be voluntary (ISO 9002, DNV's SEP or ISMA Code) or mandatory (ISM Code for certain ship types from July 1998).

2 Warranties
Certain warranties relating to the manager's performance may be written into the agreement. For example, if the manager fails to provide properly qualified and suitably experienced officers and ratings then the manager will be forced to replace the crew or implement other corrective action at its expense. Similarly, in certain circumstances, an owner may try to secure a performance guarantee from a shipmanager which is forfeited if the manager breaches its contractual obligations and fails to remedy the breach within an agreed period.

3 Termination Rights

Aside from a winding-up order or liquidation of the owner, the manager is typically entitled to terminate the agreement if monies payable by the owner as demanded by the manager remain unpaid after a certain period (15 days is normal); if any of the requirements of the insurance clause are not fulfilled; if the owner does anything to harm the reputation of the manager or the manager's commercial interests; if the budget is not agreed within a specified period and, of course, if the vessel is lost, sold or otherwise disposed of.

4 Financial

Financial reporting and accounting practices contained in a management agreement can also vary significantly. For example, budgets may be submitted and approved according to different time scales, cash advances may be made by the owner on the basis of more detailed, ship specific working capital projections and the methods of chasing up late payments and penalties incurred may vary. For this reason, addenda may be added to a standard agreement describing the owner's specific financial reporting and accounting requirements. Typically, the accounts maintained by the shipmanager are US dollar denominated although other currencies can be used at owner's request.

5 Law and Arbitration

Typically, for the reasons already specified, ship management agreements are based on English law. The arbitration process to be adopted in the event of a dispute is based on the Arbitration Acts of 1950, 1979 and 1996.

6 Management Fees

Last but not least management fees vary according to the type of and age of the vessel(s) involved, the location of the shipmanager's office, the number of ships managed for the owner (generating a volume discount) and any special considerations. Due to the intense competition for ship management contracts previously referred to, however, management fees typically fall within fairly closely defined bands which have not increased in real terms for many years. For a bulk carrier, these fees range from $75,000 to $100,000/year, while tanker management fees range from $90,000 to $150,000/year depending, primarily, on the size of the ship. Specialist ship types can command higher fees with cruise vessels representing the top of the market commanding fees for full management including the hotel operation in the region of $400,000/year reflecting the complexity of the management operation and the number of crew involved.

Table 2.4: Content of a typical Ship Management Agreement: Example

PREAMBLE

– Names and addresses of parties to the agreement
– Description of vessel(s) (name/type/flag/etc.)
– Commencement date
– Identification of applicable services
– Definitions of terms used

MANAGER'S POWERS

– Confirmation of manager's appointment to act as an agent on behalf of the owner using best endeavours to deliver the services to enable safe and efficient management of the vessel(s)
– Right (subject consultation with the owner) to appoint any agent, broker, consultant to provide support services
– Right to open and operate bank accounts and to endorse and pay bills on the owner's behalf
– Right to bring or defend actions affecting the manager and to seek legal advice in relation to disputes

INSURANCE

– Confirmation that:
  vessel(s) are insured at not less than full market value against fire and usual marine risks, protection and indemnity risks (including pollution) using first class insurers
  insurances on the vessel(s) name the manager (and any of the third parties appointed by the manager as referred to under MANAGER'S POWERS) as co-insured, and that written proof is provided and the manager is not liable for any unpaid calls
  the insurers waive rights of subrogation against the manager and third parties and endorse the policies of the insurers with appropriate cross-liability waiver

ACCOUNTS, BUDGETS AND REPORTING

– The manager keeps proper accounts and shall make same available to owner for inspection and audit on reasonable notice
– The manager submits a budget showing estimated expenses and fees to the owner prior to commencement of agreement

Table 2.4—cont.

- The manager delivers a revised budget three months prior to the end of each budgeting period (as defined in the agreement) and the owner has the right to object within one month of receipt
- The owner pays the manager on the first banking day of each month the relevant monthly amount specified in the budget and any additional expenses incurred subject to receipt of bank statements
- The manager submits to the owner monthly financial statements including a statement of receipts, expenses and disbursements paid or to be paid together with supporting invoices upon the owner's request, and a trial balance itemizing all account entries
- The manager provides quarterly and annual statements of expenses and disbursements comprising actual expenses and accruals
- The manager provides a vessel operating report including a full description of technical condition on a quarterly basis

REMUNERATION AND REIMBURSEMENT

- The manager will account to the owner all price discounts and rebates due to the vessel by third parties
- The owner pays the manager an annual management fee in advance in equal monthly instalments
- The owner pays or reimburses all costs incurred by the manager in the provision of management services including but not limited to:
  1 expenses incurred in the provision or supervision of maintenance, inspections, drydockings and surveys;
  2 wages and associated costs including travelling, pension, insurance and training to ship's staff;
  3 disbursements and expenses for victualling, provisioning, bunkering and insuring the vessel (as applicable);
  4 communication costs incurred by the manager;
  5 all fines, penalties incurred by the vessel;
  6 pre-takeover expenses including riding crew costs and initial crew movements
- the owner pays to the manager the management fee for a period of three months after termination of the agreement to cover work involved in vessel handover including the settlement of all outstanding accounts

LAW AND ARBITRATION

- The governing law of the agreement
- The arbitration process to be followed in the event of a dispute
- Identification of a named party to accept service of all proceedings on behalf of the owner

Table 2.4—cont.

DURATION

– Commencement date and period of notice (typically 90 days)
– Terms of entitlement to terminate the agreement by either party
– Confirmation that any termination does not prejudice the accrued rights of either party

INDEMNITY FOR THIRD PARTY CLAIMS

– Confirmation that the owner shall indemnify the manager and its employees and agents against all claims, actions and proceedings in connection with the performance of the agreement and against and in respect of all losses, damages and costs (including legal expenses)

FORCE MAJEURE

– Confirmation that the manager shall not be under any liability for any failure to perform under this agreement of any cause beyond its reasonable control

LIABILITY TO OWNER

– Confirmation that the manager shall not be held liable to the owner for any loss or damage unless the same has resulted from negligence, gross negligence or wilful default by the manager or agents
– The manager's liability for each incident giving rise to a loss is limited to ten times the annual management fee

2.3.2 The Vessel Operating Budget

Determination of vessel operating budgets is an important task performed prior to vessel takeover and at regular intervals thereafter. The initial vessel operating budget is prepared on the basis of certain assumptions and is submitted as a quotation to a potential shipowning client. This quotation is then refined after a pre-takeover inspection to determine the actual condition of the vessel and factors such as the level of stores and spares on board and any outstanding technical and/or operational items requiring extraordinary expenditure. The revised budget is then submitted to the potential client for further discussion and, as necessary, revision.

The end result of this initial budgeting process is the creation of a 12-month budget forecast which is agreed with the shipowner. The budget is usually divided into quarters to serve as the database for vessel accounting and budget control. In effect, this database is a yardstick against which the performance of the vessel and the shipmanager is measured, with a report submitted by the shipmanager (usually on a quarterly basis) to explain any significant positive and negative variances (see section 2.3).

Three months prior to the end of the budget period, the shipmanager prepares a new annual forecast which takes into consideration any ship specific information regarding past and future performance as well as macro-inflationary trends. Depending on their familiarity with the vessel, the master and senior officers are required to submit their projections regarding future expenditure to increase their involvement in and accountability for cost control.

The typical format of a vessel operating budget is presented as Table 2.5. This table presents the summary sheet showing the main budget categories which are in turn broken down into individual cost items. For example, the engine stores category comprises paints, chemicals, packings, electrical and general stores as separate items while the lubricants category is made up of cylinder oils, crankcase oils, generator oils, hydraulic oils and other oils and greases.

Given the volume of data involved and the need to update and, as necessary, amend budgets on a regular basis, budget generation is computerized.

The outputs are a function of calculations applied to a database of basic parameters including crew wages and associated costs, travel expenses, prices of stores, spares and bought in services and insurance premiums. For example, total crew travel expense is a function of the number and nationalities of the crew on board, average length of contract, projected airfares, travel routeings and miscellaneous other travel costs.

Table 2.5: Format of a Vessel Operating Budget

Vessel	Built	Type		DWT: 34,900	
All figures in US$	QI	QII	QIII	QIV	TOTAL
Total Crew Wages	85,100	85,100	85,100	85,100	340,400
War Bonus	0	0	0	0	0
Crew Travel	33,500	33,500	33,500	33,500	134,000
Victualling	12,800	12,800	12,800	12,800	51,200
Total Crew Costs	131,400	131,400	131,400	131,400	525,600
General Insurance	0	0	0	0	0
Club Calls	0	0	0	0	0
Total Insurances	0	0	0	0	0
Deck Stores	9,925	9,925	9,925	9,925	39,700
Engine Stores	8,050	8,050	8,050	8,050	32,200
General Stores	6,300	6,300	6,300	6,300	25,200
Cabin Stores	2,000	2,000	2,000	2,000	8,000
Rentals	0	0	0	0	0

Table 2.5—cont.

Vessel	Built	Type		DWT: 34,900	
All figures in US$	QI	QII	QIII	QIV	TOTAL
New Equipments	0	0	0	0	0
Fresh Water	500	500	500	500	500
Total Purchasing	26,775	26,775	26,775	26,775	107,100
Total Lubricants	13,800	13,800	13,800	13,800	55,200
Drydock	0	0	0	0	0
D/D Reserve	0	0	0	0	0
Survey Exp	4,500	4,500	4,500	4,500	18,000
R&M	17,750	17,750	17,750	17,750	71,000
Spares	23,500	23,500	23,500	23,500	94,000
Total R&M	45,750	45,750	45,750	45,750	183,000
Registrations Exp.	0	0	0	0	0
Management Fees	25,500	25,500	25,500	25,500	102,000
General Exp.	4,000	4,000	4,000	4,000	16,000
Total Adm. Costs	29,500	29,500	29,500	29,500	118,000
Grand Total	247,225	247,225	247,225	247,225	988,900

Daily Rate = US$2709

Notes: The above is a summary sheet which is supported by more detailed breakdowns for each of the six major cost items shown. For example, crew costs would include:
  (i) proposed crew list showing rank, nationality, ITF or non-ITF conditions, basic wages, leave pay, special bonus, overtime, social contribution, training costs etc.;
  (ii) average period on board, number of crew moves/year, crew travel ratings, fares, recruitment costs, P&I irrecoverable;
  (iii) crew victualling cost per man/day.

2.3.3 The Vessel Operating Report

A ship management company must be able to provide its clients with timely and up-to-date information on all technical, financial and operational aspects of the vessels under management. Typically, such detailed information is provided on a quarterly basis in the form of a Vessel Operating Report. Such reports are presented in a standardized format so that the shipowner can monitor the performance of its ship in a consistent way over time.

The format and content of a typical vessel operating report is presented as Table 2.6. This shows that comprehensive financial, technical and operational information is provided including, importantly, any significant variances in actual expenditure compared with budget together with the underlying reasons and estimates as to whether such variances are short- or long-term in nature. Quarterly reports also contain information regarding the technical condition and performance of the vessel over time based on information supplied by the master and his senior officers.

Such information is provided in the form of standard report forms sent to the office on a weekly, monthly, quarterly, six-monthly or annual basis together with the findings of any inspections undertaken during the report period by the vessel's superintendent.

Table 2.6: Content of a typical Vessel Operating Report

SECTION 1: EXECUTIVE SUMMARY

– End of period accounts by main budget items
  (actual and accrued expenditure against budget)
– Explanation of positive and/or negative variances
– Estimated expenditure for next period and to end year

SECTION 2: CONDITION REPORT*

– Report on navigational equipment, hull, deck and fittings, accommodation, cargo gear, tanks/hold/hatches, steering gear, piping, valves, main engine, generators, boiler and safety equipment
– Major works in progress

SECTION 3: OPERATIONAL PERFORMANCE

– Port and sea time, average speed and consumption (main engines, auxiliaries [laden and ballast conditions]
– Offhire report (if applicable)

SECTION 4: PERSONNEL REPORT

– Planned and actual crew changes
– Performance of master and senior officers

SECTION 5: INSURANCE REPORT

– Reports of accidents and incidents leading to H&M or P&I Claims

* Supported by copies of reports sent by ship's staff, vessel inspection reports and/or photographic evidence

2.3.4 Safety and Quality (S&Q) Management

Whereas management agreements, vessel operating budgets and vessel operating reports are long-established instruments which have been refined by ship management companies over many years of usage, safety and quality management systems are more recent phenomena. The earliest usage really only dates back to the late 1980s when shipmanagers were among the first ship operating companies to recognize the potential benefits to be derived from implementing formal management disciplines designed to enhance the safety and quality of ship operation.

At that time a number of different "routes" to safety and/or quality management were followed by ship management companies (see Table 2.7). Of the various alternatives, the International Ship Managers' Association's (ISMA) Code of Shipmanagement Standards proved to be the most popular among the ship management community due in part to its applicability to the specific needs of a ship management company. Nevertheless, the ISMA Code did not gain universal acceptance. Certain shipmanagers, notably Acomarit, opted for alternative routes (in its case DNV's SEP Rules and ISO 9002) on the grounds that it focused on safety and environment protection rather than the all embracing nature of the ISMA Code (Parker 1994).

The early 1990s were, in fact, characterized by considerable debate about the relative merits of the different standards (and, indeed, on whether a standard should be used at all). Although this debate did not result in a conclusive answer, it is true to say that many ship operating companies and shipmanagers, having started with the aim to introduce an all embracing safety and quality management system, refocused their attention on safety especially since the IMO's adoption of the International Safety Management (ISM) Code in 1994 as a mandatory requirement for ship operating companies from 1998 onwards. (This debate is analysed in much more detail in Chapter 8.)

Although different approaches have been followed by ship management companies, all safety and/or quality management systems display common elements or hallmarks which can be summarized as follows:

Internal Auditing i.e. systematic and independent checks that a company's S&Q procedures are being followed by office and shipboard staff and that S&Q objectives are being met.

Non-Conformities i.e. the identification of problems or potential problems with an S&Q system (either during an internal audit or by way of day-to-day reporting by staff). When a non-conformity is raised a corrective action is determined in order to rectify the problem in question within a specified period of time and to prevent recurrence. Determination of corrective action is therefore critical to the continuous improvement of the S&Q system and must be based on the detection and thorough understanding of the root cause of the problem in question. A corrective action may involve a change to the S&Q system itself or further training of staff to ensure compliance with system requirements.

Management Review i.e. a systematic review of the S&Q system by senior

Table 2.7: Different "routes" to Safety and Quality management

---

STANDARD-DRIVEN INITIATIVES

1 ISO 9002
   - the tried and tested quality standard used by many manufacturing and service industries worldwide. ISO 9002 needs to be interpreted from the ship operations viewpoint to make it "shipping friendly".
2 ISMA CODE
   - detailed and comprehensive quality code written specifically for ship management (and, latterly, crew management) companies including safety and environmental protection requirements. The ISMA Code incorporates the basic principles of ISO 9002 and Resolution A741(18)—see below.
3 HYBRIDS
   - blended ISO 9002 and IMO Resolution A647(17) prepared by Class. For example, DNV's Safety & Environmental Protection (SEP) Rules widely used by Norwegian shipowners and shipmanagers.
4 IMO ISM CODE
   - Resolution A741(18) focusing on safety and environmental protection issues. The only mandatory as opposed to voluntary standard.

NON-STANDARD DRIVEN

5 TQM
   - Total Quality Management is based on the principles of continuous improvement and the empowerment of *all* company employees so that they can contribute to improving the product or service provided to a client. TQM does not follow any set rules imposed by an external party; it is up to the individual company to decide on the policies and objectives to be adhered to.

---

management (including masters) to provide feedback on what is and is not working together with recommendations for improvement.

Planning i.e. allocation of resources to ensure where possible that problems are prevented in order to exert greater control over critical tasks affecting safety and quality.

Responsibility and Authority i.e. the definition of clear levels of authority and reporting lines within an organization and the designation of suitably qualified and experienced staff to take responsibility and hold authority for key tasks and decision making. As part of this process, thorough training is provided to ensure staff are familiar with their own responsibilities within the S&Q system and where necessary action is taken to rectify any deficiencies.

Records i.e. disciplined record keeping to demonstrate that key tasks are being performed according to the policies and procedures set out in the S&Q system.

Figure 2.2: A documented S&Q Management System in theory

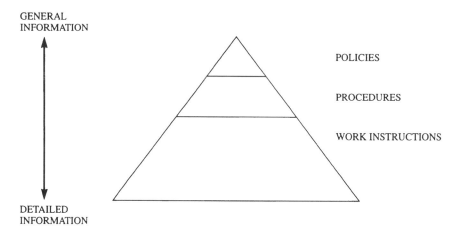

* The classic pyramid structure
* POLICIES are implemented by PROCEDURES which are made to work
  by WORK INSTRUCTIONS
* The system is <u>integrated</u>

Emergency Response i.e. the preparation and deployment of a contingency plan as and when circumstances dictate. The plan must define key responsibilities, ensure that office, ship and external staff work in unison and provide for sufficient resources to be made available.

Similarities also exist between different S&Q management systems in terms of structure and documentation. Figures 2.2 and 2.3 display the typical structure and documentation used by a ship management company's S&Q management system. Both the theoretical and the practical aspects are portrayed. In the former case, the classic pyramid structure shows three levels or tiers of information whereby company S&Q policies (at the top tier) are implemented by procedures (in the middle) which are made to work by work instructions (at the lowest tier). The relative size of the three tiers also reflects the volume of documentation presented at the different levels.

This point is made clear when attention is paid to the practical case. This shows the shape and extent of a typical S&Q documented system. A company policy manual is presented at the top tier, a number of operating manuals at the middle tier and miscellaneous work instructions (manuals, forms and check lists, etc.) at the lowest tier. While this diagram shows a typical case, variations do, of course, exist. For example, because the volume of documentation used is largely left to the individual company to decide, the size of the system can vary enormously. The decision regarding how many manuals and the degree of detail presented within each is influenced by the structure of the organization in question and the skill and

Figure 2.3: A documented S&Q Management System in practice

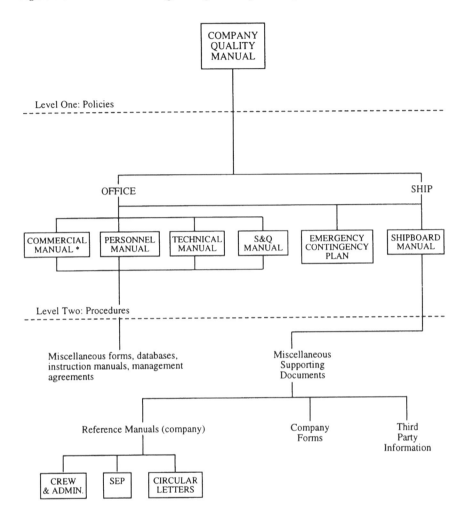

Level One: Policies

Level Two: Procedures

Level Three: Supporting Documentation (Work Instructions)

* Accounts, Administration, Marketing, Insurance etc.

experience of the labour force i.e. the more extensive the skills and experience the lesser the need to "write things down".

Variations will also exist in terms of what information is written where in the system. For example, responsibilities and authorities of key staff appear in the top tier or the middle tier documentation (and may or may not be reinforced at the lowest). Also, variations exist to the extent that a company may decide to present all of the system to all of its staff or restrict distribution strictly according to need i.e. so that shipboard staff are not "burdened" with information relating to office procedures and *vice versa*. In the case of restricted distribution the company policy manual may be the only manual distributed throughout the organization.

2.4 OFFICE ORGANIZATION AND STAFFING

Just as different ship management companies use different systems, procedures, work practices and documentation in service delivery they are also organized in different ways albeit with common traits evident. Commonality is due to three main factors which influence organization and management structure:

(1) traditional practice;
(2) pressures to control overheads (particularly staffing levels and costs); and
(3) the need to comply with increasing regulatory demands especially the requirements of the International Safety Management (ISM) Code.

A fourth factor, which is becoming increasingly influential, has a bearing on the other three i.e. the impact of labour-saving IT offering substantial productivity gains.

Figure 2.4 presents a typical organizational structure for a medium-sized ship management company. It shows the basic management hierarchy and reporting lines for 28 staff responsible for the management of 24 vessels (full management contracts). Of particular note is the subdivision of the total number of vessels into three (eight-ship) fleets.

Each fleet is managed on a day-to-day basis by a fleet support group or cell comprising four staff—two superintendents (each designated to supervise four vessels) who are assisted by two support staff responsible for purchasing and administrative matters. Together the fleet support group works as a team and relates with other departmental staff on a daily basis.

Assuming that each superintendent makes three visits a year to each vessel under his supervision and each visit lasts, on average, five days, then 60 days are spent by each superintendent out of the office (excluding vacations). In reality, lengthy periods spent at drydock and supervising repairs means that the office to shipboard time of the "normal" superintendent is nearer the 50:50 mark—on occasion considerably more. Periods of absence necessitate the designation of a back-up person to supervise the work of the "missing" superintendent.

Of course there are variations to the typical case described above and in Figure 2.4. For example, the fleet support group may be smaller in size if the purchasing function is performed by a separate department. Conversely, the group may be larger if the fleet accountant and/or the crew manager are part of the team.

Another variation may occur in the form of a two 12-ship rather than three eight-

Figure 2.4: Organization of a "typical" ship management company

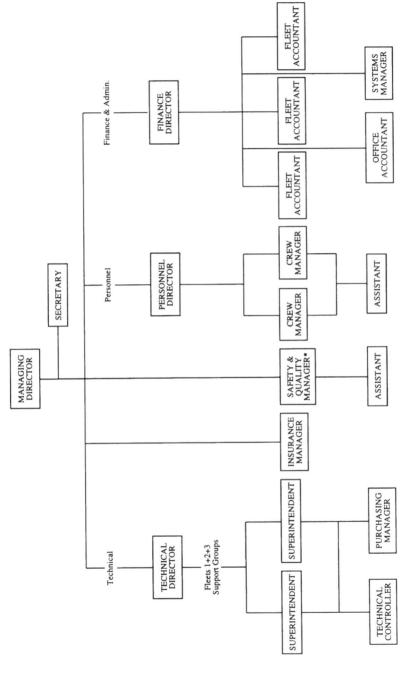

NOTE: Total staffing = 28 persons   total fleet = 24 ships (ratio staff : ship = 1.2 : 1)
* Designated Person Ashore (ISM) + Management Representative (ISO)

ship fleets configuration with an additional level of management added in the form of a fleet manager. The fleet manager will perform some of the duties of superintendents, notably budget preparation and management.

Regardless of the number of ships allocated to a fleet support group, the number of ships looked after by each superintendent is typically limited to a maximum of five given the need for the superintendent to have a thorough working knowledge of the performance of each vessel in his care.

In the case of larger ship management companies specialist support services may be provided in-house, for example in the form of a drydock estimator, contracts manager, projects manager, electrical superintendent or naval architect—areas of specialization which are otherwise provided by subcontractors. As an alternative, a company may be able to call on part-time staff to handle special projects or to help cope with periods of heavy workload which occur at particular times of the year including the preparation of annual budgets and quarterly reports. If senior seastaff are seconded for this purpose then a double benefit is derived in so far as an understanding of office work practices is provided. Whichever option is taken, the ability to have flexibility in the availability of manpower resources is an important asset given that a ship management company's ability to generate a profit on a consistent basis is determined to a large extent by maintaining a lean staffing level in relation to the size of the managed fleet.

Looking ahead it is likely that organizational structures will continue to evolve. In recent years the overall cost of service delivery has increased due to the need to employ additional specialist staff to oversee the company safety and quality management system. Typically, this requirement has been covered by way of retraining existing staff with suitable office and seagoing experience or, in a small number of cases, specialists have been brought in from other industries.

In similar vein, the desire to make the best use of computerization has created the need for a full time Systems/IT manager to ensure that computer networks and applications function properly and are adapted to perform additional tasks. This, in turn, has reduced the volume of clerical and secretarial work which has enabled staff savings to be made.

As an example, superintendents are now expected to carry laptop computers as part of their personal "toolkits" to enable them to generate inspection reports while the are away from the office as opposed to passing on rough notes to a secretary for typing on return to the office. In this way benefits are derived from speedier production of vessel inspection reports although this new work practice has not been enthusiastically embraced in all cases.

As well as a reduction in clerical/secretarial staff, ship management companies are likely to continue to strive for flexibility in the provision of staff resources. In addition to the ability to call on part-time staff, multi-skilling enables staff to be reallocated between different tasks as workload dictates. The most forward-thinking shipmanagers are beginning to implement training programmes to achieve this flexibility which will also help to break down traditional rivalries between different departments.

DEVELOPMENT

3.1 DEVELOPMENT TO DATE

The origins of independent ship management can be traced back to the 18th century. Since then this specialized sector of the shipping industry can be seen to have passed through a number of phases of development each one characterized by a distinctive growth driver or set of drivers. Common to each phase has been the consistent role of the shipmanager as an enabling vehicle i.e. as a provider of flexibility in vessel operation. This flexibility can be viewed as one of a number of important ingredients which have contributed to the successful development of the shipping industry including cargo demand growth, capital, technological innovation and debt financing.

Little has been written about the various drivers and development phases which have characterized the growth of independent ship management. David Underwood, however, the late CEO of Denholms, one of the pioneering ship management companies, presented a brief history of the sector's development in the modern (post-war) era in a paper presented to the Cambridge Academy of Transport's Anatomy of Shipping Course in 1992 (Underwood 1992). The various phases identified by David Underwood are summarized in Table 3.1 and discussed below.

Table 3.1: The evolution of the ship management market

Phase	Period	Drivers
1 SLOW GROWTH	Late 1950s to late 1960s	Entry of entrepreneurial shipowners
2 MARKET TAKE OFF	1970s–mid 1980s	Flagging out commences and gathers momentum Bank foreclosures LOC shipowners contract in Asset players "Birth" of many shipmanagers Erosion of margins
3 MARKET MATURITY	Late 1980s	Concern over role of shipmanagers Implementation of safety and quality management New markets emerge Intensive competition
4 RENEWED SELECTIVE GROWTH	Mid 1990s onwards	Pre- and post-ISM growth

The initial phase of development in the modern era of ship management commenced in the late 1950s with the establishment of a new breed of entrepreneurial shipowners bringing much needed equity into the shipping industry.

These new entrants spotted opportunities to benefit from building and operating vessels in certain countries different to their country of domicile. These benefits included tax breaks, investment allowances and subsidies which were accessible if a ship management company was used in the source country. During this initial phase, the total fleet controlled by shipmanagers increased slowly to reach only a few hundred ships after a period of ten years.

From the late 1960s onwards, demand for independent ship management grew for two reasons. Industrial corporations looking to shelter profits in the shipping industry utilized the services of an independent shipmanager able to provide the necessary ship operating expertise. This period also saw the start of flagging out—a process which above all others has been a consistent driver of demand. This process involved shipowners domiciled in high (labour) cost countries of Europe using what Underwood described as the cosmetic timecharter to transfer day-to-day operation to a shipmanager able to achieve substantial cost savings through the employment of crew without union or national flag legislative restriction.

The 1970s also witnessed the birth of a number of ship management companies including several set up by shipowners seeking to sell their core competencies to third party owners out of choice or necessity. Of the shipmanagers established during this period, three established in Asia in close proximity to new sources of maritime labour were Wallem (which was born out of long-established Hong Kong shipping and trading interests in 1971); Univan (a fellow Hong Kong shipowner established in 1973) and Thome (which was established in Singapore in 1976 by Scandinavian shipowning interests).

Wholesale flagging out gathered momentum in the 1970s and became the major growth driver in the 1980s as cyclical downturns in the freight markets forced shipowners to cut costs by changing the registration of their ships to flags of convenience and second registers which permitted the employment of Third World, especially Indian and Filipino, seafarers at significantly reduced cost. The same cyclical downturns were also responsible for bringing two new breeds of financial shipowner into the industry. On the one hand foreclosures by banks on non-performing loans saw the banks acquire tonnage which they chose to operate with the assistance of ship management companies rather than immediately sell at auction at distressed prices on depressed secondhand markets. On the other hand, the lure of spectacular appreciation in secondhand prices attracted asset players into the shipping industry (particularly the tanker sector) in the shape of investors looking to own tonnage only until a significant gain could be realised through resale. Hence the use of a ship management company rather than the employment of in-house staff.

The 1980s also witnessed the emergence of shipowning companies in the developing countries which needed to import the technical expertise from established shipowning and ship management companies. A notable source of such business was derived at the time from Arab shipowners who also needed to access foreign seastaff—officers from Europe and ratings from Asia.

In the second half of the decade, new investors were attracted to shipping *via* tax shelter schemes—notably Norway's K/S partnerships—which granted high earning individuals the opportunity to defer income tax payments by utilizing depreciation allowances on newbuildings and secondhand vessels.

These partnerships proved to be yet another significant source of new business for shipmanagers willing themselves to commit a small amount of equity to shipping investment schemes in return for ship management contracts. Regrettably, however, as widely reported at the time, the early phase of K/S market growth saw shipmanagers take ageing bulk tonnage in poor states of repair into management.

Bringing the ship management story up to date, the 1990s has also proved to be a decade of new business opportunity for shipmanagers. Aside from the opening up of new markets including South America, the US and, latterly, Japan, where shipowners were for many years reluctant to use shipmanagers despite the obvious cost savings, Eastern Europe became the single most important source of new business for shipmanagers.

This new market grew as a direct result of the breakdown of the Soviet order in the Comecon pact countries which, in turn, resulted in rapid and far-reaching change in Russia and its former satellites.

With the loss of long-term vessel employment "contracts" controlled by intergovernment trade pacts, these monolithic shipowning groups employing many thousands of staff were forced to redeploy tonnage on Western markets at commercial rates. Furthermore, with the need to replace ageing fleets using Western bank finance instead of state funding, the Former Soviet Union (FSU) shipowners sought the assistance of Western shipowners and notably shipmanagers who enabled the wholesale transfer of tonnage to offshore régimes and open flags required by the lending banks for mortgage security purposes.

In these circumstances, shipmanagers served as the enabling vehicles for many such transfers and also provided expert help by way of the transfer of modern ship operating practices needed to enhance competitiveness. Shipmanagers have also looked to source well trained and competitively priced crews from FSU countries which have been used in great numbers by many shipowners since the early 1990s.

By the mid-1990s, independent ship management had reached a sufficient size, had achieved extensive linkages, had obtained an extensive client base and had achieved a global presence to be categorized as a mature sector of the international shipping industry. But what of the future?

As discussed in other parts of this book, shipmanagers have not been without their critics particularly in the early 1990s when the shipping industry passed through a period of great uncertainty due to growing concerns over falling standards of vessel operation.

At that time, shipmanagers were singled out with classification societies as being two of the main culprits responsible for falling standards: criticism which forced both sectors to invest considerable resources in formal management systems based on safety and/or quality management disciplines.

This process has in the case of the independent ship management sector enabled many shipmanagers to recapture the high ground as far as new standards of ship operation based on safety and quality management disciplines are concerned. Indeed, shipmanagers, having improved their internal organizations ashore and afloat, are now in a position to capture a new source of business.

Mandatory compliance of shipowners and ship operating companies to the IMO's International Safety Management (ISM) Code from July 1998 (earlier in the case of passenger ferry companies regularly trading to EU ports and later in the case of owners of less sensitive ship types) is putting smaller shipowning companies under immense pressure to commit the magnitude of resources needed to achieve the necessary documents of compliance (DOCs) and Safety Management Certificates (SMCs) ahead of the deadlines laid down.

Shipmanagers are already actively marketing their experience and expertise in the implementation and maintenance of safety and quality management systems and, at the time of writing, were beginning to expand their client base accordingly—particularly as further pressure has been put on shipowners in the light of the 1995 revisions to STCW (the Standards of Training, Certification and Watchkeeping Convention) which governs how seastaff are trained.

At the time of writing, therefore, the ship management sector could be seen to be entering a new phase of development reflecting a general mood of optimism in certain sectors of shipping including, significantly, the tanker sector. However, this is not to say that there are no clouds on the shipmanager's horizon.

Challenges still have to be faced in how best to deal with worsening shortages of skilled and experienced staff and how to get the best out of new technology ashore and afloat. Shipmanagers need also to exercise caution when deciding whether or not to accept ISM-derived new business if the motive behind the contracting-out process is driven by the shipowner's desire to avoid the commitment of adequate funds to safety. Also the marked consolidation of vessel ownership particularly evident in the liner and the tanker sectors could reduce the potential size of the overall potential client base to which shipmanagers offer their services.

The impact of these and other factors is hard to predict. What can be foreseen with much greater certainty is that shipping will continue to be an extremely dynamic industry and also a market of opportunity for shipmanagers.

Any attempt to quantify the development process outlined above in terms of the size of world managed fleet controlled by ship management companies is fraught with difficulties for reasons explained in section 3.3. A useful "snapshot", however, is provided by an independent research study conducted by UK consultants Riley Williams Associates (RWA) on behalf of a major UK shipowning group in 1985/86.

The findings of this study, which were reviewed in an article appearing in the March 1997 issue of *Lloyd's Ship Manager* (LSM 1997), highlighted the following:

1 The value of the market was estimated at around US$2b. with total fee income of approximately US$200m.

2 In mid 1986, "well over" 200 companies were involved in the supply of ship management services of which around one third were UK-registered with Hong Kong and Japan representing other major centres.

3 Some 20 different services were provided although "very few" companies were able to supply the full range from in-house resources.

4 The total fleet numbered some 2,200 vessels—up from approximately 1,700 in 1985—which was estimated to equate to around 4 per cent of the total market of 1,000grt plus vessels. The managed fleet in 1985 was owned by some 450 companies.

5 In 1985, 59 per cent of ship management companies provided services purely to third party shipowners, 31 per cent to both in-house and third party and the remaining 10 per cent to parent company controlled ships only.

6 The supply side of the ship management market was fragmented in 1985. Although approximately 20 per cent of the total fleet was controlled by five shipmanagers, the remaining 80 per cent was distributed across some 180 companies.

According to the RWA study, by the mid-1980s the ship management sector, having grown steadily over the initial 20 years of development, was beginning to see impressive growth and build up a significant share of the world market. The snapshot provided by RWA is brought up to date in section 3.3 which examines the current market.

3.1.1 Where in the Cycle?

Before looking at the various growth drivers in greater detail it is interesting to compare how the various phases of development identified in Table 3.1 relate to the general cyclical movements in world freight markets over the post-war period.

Table 3.2 portrays four distinct periods of development as identified by Stopford (1997). In a paper entitled "Lessons from a Century of Shipping Cycles", Stopford:

(a) identifies seven distinctive development phases during the period 1896 to 1997 and ranks each period according to the relative prosperity offered to shipowners i.e. 1 = Best Phase, 7 = Worst Phase. Stopford also describes the main characteristics of each phase;

(b) the four phases shown in Table 3.2 relate to the post-war period (and the modern era of ship management). It is interesting to note that this period witnessed both the best and the worst phases for shipowners;

(c) the modern era of ship management commenced as the best phase was drawing to a close in the mid-1950s i.e. a phase marked by slow growth demand but limited supply due to the marked shortage of shipbuilding in the immediate post-war era;

(d) ship management market take-off only really began once the worst phase was underway i.e. depressed market conditions triggered by the 1973 oil crisis, falling world trade and chronic overcapacity which forced many shipowners to cut costs etc. *via* flagging out (see section 3.2);

(e) Stopford's current phase, which is characterized by slow demand growth and expanding supply, giving rise to more competitive market conditions, coincides with a period which has seen the maturing of the ship management market.

Table 3.2: Ship management and shipping cycles

Period	Demand Growth Trend	Supply Tendency	General Market Tone	Rank*	Phase as per Table 3.1
1945–1956	VERY FAST	SHORTAGE	PROSPEROUS	1	*"Birth" of modern era of ship management*
1956–1973	VERY FAST	EXPANDING	COMPETITIVE	3	*Market take off*
1973–1988	FALLING	OVER-CAPACITY	DEPRESSED	7	*Continual growth*
1988–1997	SLOW	EXPANDING	COMPETITIVE	4	*Slower growth*

NOTE: * 1 = BEST CYCLE; 7 = WORST CYCLE
Source: After Stopford (1997)

3.2 THE GROWTH DRIVERS

Having presented a brief overview of the modern era of ship management it is useful to further explain the various factors which have driven the growth of the ship management market. These factors or growth drivers have acted in isolation or as complementary forces in persuading shipowners to either switch from in-house management or to start new ventures with ship management companies.

Over time, the relative significance of the various growth drivers has changed in response to cyclical changes in the freight markets and/or for political reasons.

Spruyt (1994) examined the various factors which can be broadly categorized into three principal shipowner needs:

1 the need to reduce costs;
2 the need to "import" expertise;
3 the need for flexibility.

By understanding these three basic needs the reader goes a long way towards understanding the different types of shipowning clients who use the services of ship management companies. These various types are examined more fully in section 3.5.

3.2.1 The Need to Reduce Costs

The need for shipowners to cut or contain costs has been addressed by a number of commentators in recent years as have the various cost-cutting/containing initiatives pursued by them in an effort to improve competitive standing. Interest in the subject heightens at times when certain shipping sectors, notably the tanker and bulk carrier markets, experience strong cyclical downturns in freight rates to the extent that vessel break-even levels are breached and strong remedial measures are needed to ensure shipowner survival. While it is not the intention to revisit the subject in any great depth (the 2nd edition presents a very detailed review), it is useful to address seven specific questions which are particularly relevant to the ship management sector as they throw light on the supporting role that shipmanagers have played in achieving cost savings on behalf of their clients. These questions are:

(a) Why do shipowners need to reduce costs?
(b) How can a shipowner reduce costs?
(c) Why do shipowners flag out?
(d) What is flagging out?
(e) What are the cost savings achievable?
(f) How does the shipmanager fit in?
(g) Will shipowners continue to flag out?

(a) Why do shipowners need to reduce costs?

Shipowning is no different to many other businesses where inflationary pressures on the cost of producing a product or delivering a service (including wage rates and associated costs, raw materials, insurance premiums and general overheads) combine from time to time with competitive pressures in the marketplace which depress the volume of sales revenue and/or the price a business can command for its products or services. Shipowning is special, however, in that shipowners employ their assets in markets which can be highly volatile. The forces of supply and demand are strongly cyclical, particularly where overtonnaging conspires with a sharp and unexpected weakening in the demand for transportation. The net effect is falling vessel employment levels and severely depressed freight rates. Furthermore, shipowners are exposed to volatile currency markets which can, for example, exert considerable pressure if an owner's local currency weakens against the US dollar—the denomination of most earnings.

These circumstances have been examined by a number of commentators including Morel (1991). In a paper entitled "The erosion of margins through rising vessel operating, maintenance and repair costs", which he presented to the Lloyd's Shipping Economist Ship Finance Conference in November 1991, Morel took the example of a mid-1970s-built handy size bulk carrier operated under an open flag with European senior officers and Asian juniors and ratings and employed on the timecharter market to demonstrate the difficulties experienced by owners of this type of tonnage during the 1980s. His analysis showed how a sharp fall in timecharter rates during the first half of the 1980s i.e. from US$9,000 to approximately US$3,000/day in 1986 combined with a steady increase in running costs from around US$1,700 to US$2,400/day over the same period served to virtually wipe out operating margins by the mid-1980s. At that time many dry bulk carrier shipowners were operating vessels at less than break-even and, were, therefore unable to meet debt finance commitments. Enforced sales of tonnage at depressed prices ensued.

(b) How can a shipowner reduce costs?

Having established that there is a real need to reduce costs when trading conditions deteriorate, it is useful to examine the various ways in which shipowners/operators attempt to improve their financial position. In simple terms, efforts can be made to enhance the revenue side of the shipowning equation and/or initiatives can be pursued on the costs side.

In practice, the shipowner's scope for enhancing revenues and for reducing costs is dictated by a number of factors including, importantly, the standard of service which the shipowner must offer in a competitive marketplace and the sector in which the vessel in question is deployed. Certain sectors of the shipping industry are more sensitive to service quality than others. The particularly demanding sectors are the parcel tanker trades, car carrying, reefer shipping and, notably, the cruise market where "talking cargo" is extremely sensitive to any changes in service delivery and where the owner must do its utmost to provide a value for money service on a consistent basis.

As a compensatory factor, the scope that a shipowner has to enhance or at least protect revenue is, in general, greatest in certain specialized trades. For in these trades, which are marked by high barriers to entry in terms of capital and operating skills, the ownership of capacity tends to be concentrated. Shipowners can, therefore, exert greater influence in their own right or work in unison (to the extent permissible by regulatory actions laid down by governments) to limit supply as an effective way of correcting any imbalance between supply and demand. In contrast to the tanker and bulk carrier markets characterized by fragmented ownership which dictates that shipowners have far fewer options (notably slow steaming or lay up), owners of specialized ships in concert with other shipowners can rotate vessel deployment opportunities, floor prices (freight rates fixed) can be agreed or special agreements such as vessel pooling or slot sharing in the case of the container markets be entered. If depressed trading conditions are expected to persist, then stronger measures such as rationalization can be pursued.

A notable example of the kind of initiative is provided by the merger in 1996 of two of the world's largest container shipping companies, P&O and Nedlloyd (to form P&O Nedlloyd Container Line). This initiative is expected to achieve combined savings of US$200m.

(c) Why do shipowners flag out?

While in certain specialized sectors shipowners can (*via* collective actions) take various steps to exert influence over the revenue side of the market equation, such actions may not be sustainable or have limited impact and depend on a high degree of cooperation among shipowners used to competition. Therefore, inevitably, the shipowner focuses on the costs side of the equation to examine ways to reduce the cost of service delivery.

A simplified flow chart of the process through which this is achieved is presented as Figure 3.1. In broad terms, shipowners can attack financial costs and/or vessel operating costs.

FINANCIAL COSTS
Refinancing debt may be an effective way of reducing cost pressures. A shipowner can work with its banks to reschedule or postpone principal payments on outstanding loans in the hope that an upturn in market trading conditions will create better employment opportunities and higher revenues. Alternatively, a shipowner may seek a more tax efficient operating structure.

OPERATING COSTS
Figure 3.1 shows the relative importance of the main vessel operating cost components. Although the percentages shown vary according to ship type, age of vessel, development, size and other factors and they vary over time (for example, insurance premiums are a function not only of the age and performance of the ship and the reputation of its owners but also as a function of the underwriting capacity in insurance markets and the performance of other (non-marine) sectors of the insurance market). Likewise, shipowners can try to reduce technical costs and purchasing costs but these tend to be of short-term benefit. Expenditure on non-essential maintenance can be deferred but only to the detriment of safety margins and at the risk of a detrimental impact on the asset value (see Chapter 5).

As Figure 3.1 clearly shows, the manning cost is invariably the biggest cost element and, therefore, the area which owners see as offering the greatest scope for cost reduction. Potential savings in this area can be realized either by reducing the number of crew employed and/or by reducing the wages and associated benefits paid. While in the 1970s and 1980s considerable efforts were made by shipowners

Figure 3.1: Simplified model of the flagging out process

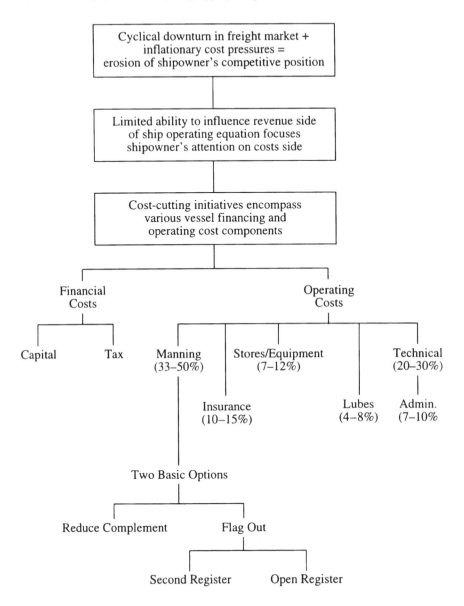

Note: figures in parentheses denote typical percentages of total vessel
    operating costs incurred by this component

to reduce crew complements through the introduction of automation and labour-saving equipment, this course of action is now widely seen as offering very limited further potential. This belief is reflected by Miles (1993) CEO of containership operator Canada Maritime who was quoted in Lloyd's List as stating:

"We have reached the limits on pushing down crew sizes. There are diminishing returns and it is more cost effective to have maintenance done with a slightly higher than minimum crew."

While crew downsizing has now largely run its course, especially in an era of greater regulatory control, the possibility of reducing crew costs *via* substituting crew paid on a high wage scale and associated benefits with a cheaper, more flexible alternative has endured. The principal method through which this is achieved is by way of changing a vessel's flag—a process commonly referred to as flagging out.

(d) What is flagging out?

Flagging out has commanded considerable attention since the process was first used in the 1950s. In simple terms, flagging out is the process through which the shipowner seeks to reduce the cost of operating a ship by switching from a high cost, national flag to a lower cost open or second register. Spruyt (1994) in the previous edition of this book, presented a very thorough appraisal of the relative advantages of selecting one flag in favour of another. These advantages are summarized as Table 3.3 which presents profiles for the four main types of shipping register that a shipowner can select—traditional, dependent, second or open.

Table 3.3: Shipping register profiles

A TRADITIONAL

Strictly regulated, national flag registers where vessels are crewed solely or largely by national seafarers trained/certified by the flag state. Vessel operations are higher cost as shipowners must ensure full compliance with all maritime conventions and pay higher wages to unionized seafarers. Traditional registers are associated with cargo protection and vessels are subject to military requisition by governments at times of hostilities.

The size of the traditional registers has diminished over the past 30 years as more and more shipowners have flagged ships out to open, dependent and second registers (see below). However, efforts have been made to improve the competitiveness of traditional registers through the granting of limited concessions of payment of employment subsidies.

Examples: USA, UK, Japan, Greece, Norway

Table 3.3—cont.

B DEPENDENT

Mainly associated with the former British colonies where British shipowners were permitted to change to the flag of a dependent territory offering greater freedom in terms of crew nationality and tax. Dependent registers are subject to the British Merchant Shipping Acts.

Examples: Isle of Man, Gibraltar, Bermuda, Cayman Islands.

C OPEN

Flag of Convenience (FOC) registers which grant freedom to shipowners in terms of crew nationality and terms/conditions of employment, tax exemption, regulatory control and company disclosure requirements. The standards of surveillance by the different FOC flag state administrations vary substantially from those which regularly inspect ships bearing their flag to ensure compliance with the major maritime statutory requirements to those which pay little attention to such matters.

Examples: Liberia, Panama, Cyprus, Bahamas.

D SECOND OR PARALLEL

Registers set up since the 1980s by governments granting certain national flag shipowners access to less stringent crew employment regulations *via* a second or parallel register. These registers were set up to arrest the flight of national flag shipowners to the open registers and to encourage shipowners who had already made this move to flag in.

Examples: NIS (Norwegian International Shipregister), DIS (Danish), GIS (German), Kerguelen (France), Madeira (Portugal), Netherland Antilles (The Netherlands).

While shipowners flag out ships for a number of reasons, the principal reason is to reduce crew costs. This point is made clear in a recently published paper by Bergantino and Marlow (1997). This paper which presents the preliminary findings of an investigation of shipowner decision-making in flag selection includes a review of 26 quantitative research projects conducted between 1976 and 1996 from which they conclude that:

"We share the belief that crew costs can be considered as the main financial reason behind the shipowner's decision to flag out. The cost of manning a ship can be considered the easiest variable to influence when compared to other ship costs which appear to be mostly fixed internationally, especially in the short run. Moreover, flagging out satisfies the shipowners' attempt to lower operating outlay and to bypass rigid labour market regulations."

Table 3.4 shows the relative importance of the various factors as provided by Bergantino and Marlow's literature review of which reductions in crew costs and associated costs and the reduced control exerted by the flag state administration are seen as the most influential. By contrast, little significance is attached to the attitude of the shipowners' lending banks or the question of crew productivity.

(e) What are the cost savings achievable?

Numerous examples of the magnitude of savings achievable *via* flagging out have been cited by shipowners and their representative bodies in recent years. The following are notable examples:

JAPAN

Figures produced by the Japanese Shipowners' Association in 1993 as published in the Industrial Bank of Japan's *Quarterly Survey* showed annual labour costs for a vessel manned with 22 Japanese crew to be US$2.75m. (US$7,534/day)—a figure nearly 80 per cent higher than a comparable vessel manned with a mixed crew of nine Japanese and 14 South East Asian (Filipino) crew. The comparable cost for a full Filipino crew was just US$530,000 (US$1,452/day).

GERMANY

The German Shipowners' Federation (VDR) claimed in March 1997 that the annual crew cost for operating a 1,500 teu containership under the national flag was DM3m. compared with DM1.1–1.2m. under the German International Register and DM0.8m–0.9m. under an open flag.

FINLAND

The Finnish Shipowners' Association in August 1997 claimed that the employment of a Finnish crew was on average approximately Fm2m. (US$364,000/year) more expensive than compared with an international crew.

SWEDEN

In 1997 Swedish shipowner Bylock & Njordsjofrakt (B&N) switched several vessels from the Swedish national register to the Norwegian International Ship Register (NIS) to achieve estimated annual savings of US$260,000 per vessel even though the Swedish government subsidizes its owners (US$3,850/man) to compensate for higher social costs.

BRITAIN

In early 1996 Shell announced its decision to transfer the employment contracts of more than 600 of its British seafarers to offshore terms in order to save "millions of pounds" in national insurance contributions.

In addition to these specific examples, Tables 3.5A, 3.5B, 3.5C and 3.5D provide further illustrations of the cost savings achievable.

Table 3.5A provides comparative costings for three vessel types (a Suezmax tanker, Panamax bulker and Containership derived from an OECD study prepared in

Table 3.4: A review of quantitative research on flagging out 1976–1996

VARIABLES	CREW COSTS	OTHER COSTS	PRODUCTIVITY OF LABOUR	MANNING RULES	HIGHER PROFITABILITY	FISCAL REASONS	CONTROL	ECON. AND POLITICAL FACTORS	ATTITUDE OF FINANCIAL INSTITUTION
1. Metaxas/Dogaris '76	*	*	*		*		*		
2. EIU (1979)	*	*	*	*	*		*		
3. Metaxas (1985)	*	*		*	*	*	*	*	*
4. Goss (1985)	*								
5. Drewry (1980)	*	*	*		*	*	*	*	*
6. Unctad (1981)	*			*		*	*		
7. Merc (1985)	*	*				*	*		
8. B.M.L. (1985)	*				*	*	*	*	
9. Tolofari et al. (1986)	*				*	*	*		
10. H.O.C. [a] (1987)	*	*		*	*	*	*	*	
11. H.O.C. [b] (1989)	*	*		*	*	*	*	*	
12. M.C.F. [a] (1986)	*				*		*	*	
13. M.C.F. [b] (1988)	*				*				
14. Yanropoulos (1988)	*	*	*	*			*		
15. McCuskey (1988)	*			*					
16. Lusted (1988)	*	*	*	*	*		*	*	

Table 3.4—cont.

VARIABLES	CREW COSTS	OTHER COSTS	PRODUCTIVITY OF LABOUR	MANNING RULES	HIGHER PROFITABILITY	FISCAL REASONS	CONTROL	ECON. AND POLITICAL FACTORS	ATTITUDE OF FINANCIAL INSTITUTION
17. Tolofari (1989)	*				*	*	*		
18. Vogel (1993)	*					*	*		
19. Slema Holste (1993)					*			*	
20. P.R.C. (1994)						*			
21. Petitt (1996)						*			
22. Tae-Woo Lee (1996)	*	*		*	*	*	*		*
23. OECD (1996)	*	*		*			*		
24. N.S. Ass (1996)	*	*		*		*	*	*	*
25. Conficanna (1996)	*	*		*		*	*		
26. Cubirane Robertshaw (1996)	*	*		*		*	*		
TOTALS	23:26	14:26	5:26	13:26	13:26	16:26	19:26	9:26	4:26

1994). This study showed that significant savings can be realized by shipowners as illustrated by the following scenarios:

Suezmax tanker

1A: Crew Complement = 27
     (four seniors/seven juniors/16 ratings, all Indian)
     Management Level = Common Practice
1B: Crew Complement = 28
     (As 1A plus 1 extra rating, five British seniors + Indian juniors and ratings)
     Management Level = Good Practice

where 1B offers a US$1,057/day saving over 1A.

Panamax bulk carrier

2A: Crew Complement = 24
     (four seniors/seven juniors/13 ratings, all Indian)
     Management Level = Good Practice
2B: Crew Complement = 24
     (As 2A, all Ukrainian)
     Management Level = Good Practice

where 2B offers a US$883/day saving over 2A.

Containership

3A: Crew Complement = 21
     (four seniors/seven juniors/10 ratings, all Indian)
     Management Level = Common Practice
3B: Crew Complement = 21
     (As 3A, Polish seniors/Filipino juniors/Indian ratings)
     Management Level = Good Practice

where 3A offers a US$204/day saving over 3B.

Table 3.5B presents some comparative costings for selective senior and junior officer ranks and for three ratings positions. The six selected crew nationalities once again show the major differences between, in this particular case, European, Russian and Asian seafarers with, for example, in the case of the C/E rank, the most expensive nationality (British) being over twice as expensive as the least (Russian).

Table 3.5C presents eight different manning budgets for a 1988-built products tanker trading on a worldwide basis as prepared by Precious Associates. Each budget is based on a total crew complement of 23 persons comprising nine officers and 14 ratings. Five of the eight budgets are based on ITF terms. The figures show that the most expensive budget D (British officers plus Chinese ratings) at US$63,200/month (US$758,400/year) is over twice as expensive as the

Table 3.5A: Comparative vessel operating costs (All figures US$/Year)

	Vessel Type 1		Vessel Type 2		Vessel Type 3	
	Scenario 1A	Scenario 1B	Scenario 2A	Scenario 2B	Scenario 3A	Scenario 3B
Crew Wages	590,000	747,200	514,000	320,800	472,800	444,400
Crew Travel & Victualling	178,400	193,800	145,600	179,600	128,400	131,600
Total	768,400	941,000	659,600	500,400	601,200	576,000
Insurance	424,500	424,500	389,000	225,900	204,100	204,100
Purchasing	120,000	163,200	104,000	104,000	77,600	89,500
Lubricants	137,100	166,800	83,700	83,700	48,000	70,000
Technical	305,900	433,900	240,000	240,000	176,000	220,800
Administration	128,000	140,000	120,000	120,000	91,000	112,000
Total	1,883,900	2,269,400	1,596,300	1,274,000	1,197,900	1,272,400
US$/Day	5,161	6,218	4,373	3,490	3,282	3,486

Notes: Vessel Type 1 = Suezmax Tanker (150,000 dwt/90,000 grt/Built 85/23000 BHP/Insured Value US$20m.)
Vessel Type 2 = Panamax Bulker (75,000 dwt/36,000 grt/Built 85/17400 BHP/Insured Value US$15m.)
Vessel Type 3 = Containership (800 teu/12700 dwt/Built 85/9260 BHP/Insured Value US$10m.)
The crewing arrangements for each scenario are described in the accompanying text.

Source: OECD, 1994

Table 3.5B: Crew costs compared for selected positions

	SENIOR OFFICERS		JUNIOR OFFICERS		RATINGS		
	MASTER	C/E	3rd/OFFICER	ELECTRICIAN	BOSUN	OILER	C.COOK
BRITISH	6,975	6,606	3,628	4,308			
SPANISH	5,683	5,479	2,681	2,681	1,868	1,703	1,868
INDIAN	4,194	4,117	2,095	2,332	1,104	864	1,159
FILIPINO	3,470	3,378	1,888	2,166	1,260	969	1,315
RUSSIAN	3,422	3,272	1,670	1,790	1,262	1,143	1,322
BURMESE	3,760	3,445	1,176	1,480	782	623	848

Note: Figures include basic wages, leave and guaranteed overtime in US$/Month (mid-1990s rates).

Table 3.5C: Manning Budgets compared

Example: 1998 Built Products Tanker, WW Trading, GMDSS. Manning Scale = 23 (Master, C/O, 2/O, 3/O, C/E, 2/E, 3/E, 4/E, Electrician, Bosun, Pumpman, Fitter × 2, AB × 3, OS × 2, Motorman, Wiper, CC, 2/C, Messman).

Budget	Nationality	Basis	US$ Monthly[1]	Rank[2]
A	9 Polish officers & 14 Filipino ratings	ITF Clear	39,200	5
B	Full Ukrainian	Non ITF Clear	28,600	8
C	Full Croatian	ITF Clear	56,700	3
D	9 British officers & 14 Chinese ratings	Non ITF Clear	63,200	1
E	4 Senior British, 5 Indian juniors + 14 Filipino ratings	ITF Clear	57,600	2
F	Full Indian	ITF Clear	43,500	4
G	Full Filipino	ITF Clear	36,500	7
H	British Master + C/E & Sri Lankan officers + ratings	Non ITF Clear	38,300	6

1. Includes wages, leave pay & guaranteed overtime.
2. 1 = Most expensive; 8 = Least expensive.

Table 3.5D: A comparison of crewing costs

Example: 35,000 DWT, 10-year-old bulk carrier trading worldwide

	OPTION 1	OPTION 2	OPTION 3
CREW COMPLEMENT			
– Senior Officers	26	26	26
– Junior Officers	4	4	4
– Ratings	6	6	6
	16	16	16
CREW NATIONALITY	INDIAN	INDIAN OFFICERS/ FILIPINO RATINGS	UKRAINIAN
Contract Length (Months)	9	9(Indian)/10 (Filipino)	6.5
Number of Crew Moves/yr	69	65	96
Crew Transfer	Mumbai/Sing./Rott.	AS 1 + Manila/Sing./Rott.	Odessa/Sing./Rott.
Cost per Crew Move (Average)	US$890	US$855	US$750
Victualling Cost (Crew+2)	US$5/Day/Man	AS 1	AS 1
Monthly Overtime (Hours)	6,294	5,322	9,919
Total Wages	349,600	361,200	179,200
Total Overtime	64,000	75,600	119,200
Social	14,400	14,400	26,000
Travel	111,300	103,000	123,480
Training	26,800	23,200	16,000
Victualling	51,100	51,100	51,100
Grand Total	617,200	628,500	514,980
= $/Day	1,691	1,722	1,411

cheapest, budget B (the full Ukrainian complement) at US$28,600/month (US$343,200/year).

Table 3.5D presents three different crewing options for a handy size bulk carrier including a breakdown of the total vessel manning costs applicable to each by the main cost elements. This comparison shows that in spite of higher overtime, social and travel costs, the latter necessitated by shorter contract length, the full Ukrainian crew presented as Option 3 works out the cheapest by offering a US$280/day saving over the full Indian crew (Option 1) and more than US$300/day over the combined Indian/Filipino crew (Option 2).

(f) Where does the shipmanager fit in?

Having discussed the shipowner's need to reduce costs and the potential savings available, it is relevant to ask where does the shipmanager fit in? In simple terms, a shipowner does not need to use the services of a shipmanager in flagging out. Indeed, the flagging out process has been pursued on numerous occasions by owners working individually.

However, a shipmanager will be used by a shipowner if added value can be achieved. For example, this added value might simply be in terms of the convenience that a shipmanager offers, for example, through its experience in working with vessels manned by different (mixed) crew nationalities and operated under an FOC. In other instances, flagging out may form part of a broader cost reduction programme implemented by a shipmanager.

To illustrate the principal flags used by shipmanagers, Table 3.6A presents the top five flags used by seven leading ship management companies. Based on the LLP database as at March 1997 (see section 3.3), this table shows the prominence of Liberia, Bahamas and to a lesser extent Singapore. To illustrate the main crew nationalities used by shipmanagers, Table 3.6B presents a breakdown of the 35,000 seamen employed by the ISMA member companies in 1994. This table shows the prominence of Indian and Filipino crew.

(g) Will shipowners continue to flag out?

This final question relating to the flagging out process is the hardest one to answer. The reason for this is that shipping is a dynamic industry influenced by many socio-economic and political factors which can create an uncertain environment for decision-making. All that can be done, therefore, at any particular point in time, is to state the case for and against continued flagging out and indicate which argument is holding the upper hand.

The case against flagging out in general and the use of certain open flags (FOCs) in particular was stated in an article appearing in a *Lloyd's List* special feature on ship registers on 19 September 1997. The article, entitled "Fightback starts against flags of convenience", cited two reasons for this belief. Firstly, the effect of increasing regulation, particularly the need for shipowners to comply with ISM and the revised STCW requirements, is causing many owners to think more carefully

Table 3.6A: Leading flags of selected shipmanager fleets

Rank	Acomarit	Anglo-Eastern	Columbia	Denholm	Univan	V Ships	Wallem
1	Liberia	Hong Kong	Cyprus	Singapore	Panama	Bahamas	Panama
2	Singapore	Bermuda	Antigua	IOM	Philippines	Hong Kong	Singapore
3	Bahamas	BRB	Liberia	Bahamas	Liberia	Liberia	NIS
4	Saudi Arabia	Philippines	Marshall Islands	Liberia	NIS	Panama	Liberia
5	Malta/Panama	Bahamas	Bahamas	NIS/Bermuda	Hong Kong	Saudi Arabia	Bahamas

Source: LLP database March 1997

Table 3.6B: Seamen employed by ISMA members

Crew Nationality	Full Management Officers	Full Management Ratings	Crew Management Officers	Crew Management Ratings	Total Officers	Total Ratings
Western Europe[1]	1,271	483	745	344	2,016	827
Eastern Europe[2]	985	1,042	329	367	1,314	1,409
US and Canada	98	179	1	0	99	179
Indian	2,667	2,216	720	837	3,387	3,053
Filipino	1,817	4,833	1,833	6,101	3,650	10,934
Chinese	20	120	4	60	24	180
Burmese	400	278	30	61	430	339
Bangladesh	0	0	0	179	0	179
Others[3]	3,145	3,513	87	278	3,232	3,791
TOTAL	10,403	12,664	3,749	8,227	14,152	20,891

GRAND TOTAL =   70,086 + 15,000 retained or on paid leave

Notes: 1 = EC & EFTA countries; 2 = ex Soviet and former Yugoslavia; 3 = Brazil, Colombia, Croatia, Indonesia, Israel, Jamaica, Japan, Peru, Trinidad & Tobago (and unspecified).

Source: A Profile of the International Ship Managers' Association, August 1994.

about which flag they select given that certain FOCs could well be targeted by port state control (PSC) and P&I Clubs if they are perceived to harbour substandard shipowners. Secondly, certain national registers have increased their attractiveness to shipowners and, as a result, lessened the cost advantages held by the open registers. The efforts made by the Dutch government in allowing Dutch shipowners to use non-national officers on Dutch flag vessels and similar measures by the Greek and Swedish governments are notable examples of the efforts being made to persuade European shipowners to remain on national registers and indeed, to flag in. In the case of the Greek flag, for example, the government announced its decision to relax national manning requirements in July 1997 from 100 per cent of officers and 60 per cent of ratings to five to seven senior officers and three to four junior officers plus 60 per cent of ratings. In similar vein, the second registers such as Norway's NIS and Denmark's DIS can justifiably claim that they have achieved their aim after a period of ten years to have stemmed the exodus of national shipowners to open registers by offering a truly competitive alternative. As at July 1997, some 700 vessels totalling 30.5 million were NIS registered.

Nevertheless, the pressures on shipowners to use FOCs persist. Shortages of European senior officers particularly for certain vessel types means that shipowners must continue to look further afield for experienced crew. Moreover, inflationary pressures continue to drive a rise in vessel operating costs. A report published in March 1997 by independent consultants Drewry, for example, predicted a 16.5 per cent rise in operating costs during the period to 2000 including crew costs if the supply sources are not expanded and training programmes do not increase.

Against this background, the outlook in 1997 was that open registers would continue to hold their appeal compared with national and second registers as evidenced by leading chemical tanker owner, Stolt-Nielsen which was to switch six of its vessels from the NIS to the Cayman Islands in October 1997 because of the continuing nationality requirements for masters, and speculation surrounding Delmas' expected decision to flag out ten ships from the French flag with the loss of 450 French seafarer jobs. These and other instances strongly suggest that flagging out will remain an important cost-cutting initiative, which will provide business opportunities for shipmanagers, for many years to come.

3.2.2 The Need to Import Expertise

A shipmanager will be used to provide expertise under certain circumstances. In the case of a new entrant owner lacking the basic skills or desire to directly control the day-to-day management of a vessel, the need for the supply of specialist services is obvious. Established shipowners may also chose to use a shipmanager at the start of a diversification into a new market sector or sectors.

While these and other examples have provided new business for shipmanagers on an occasional basis in the past, the impending mandatory requirement to comply with ISM has given rise to a more widespread source of business. At the time of writing, many shipmanagers were receiving a string of enquiries from shipowners increasingly desperate to get to grips with ISM. In certain cases, such new business was being turned down because of fears that the shipmanager would be taking on a contract only for a short period where the primary motive was to jump the ISM barrier i.e. without any commitment on the shipowner's part to meet the safety and environmental protection requirements spelt out in the code.

3.2.3 The Need for Flexibility

This basic need is allied to the previous requirement. The timing of an investment decision is very critical in such a strongly cyclical business as shipping where a shipowner may wish to move quickly out of or in to a particular market sector without having to consider how to reduce staffing levels or hire staff. In the former case, downsizing will be expensive in certain countries with strict employment protection. In the latter, the difficulty of finding well trained and suitably experienced technical staff, particularly superintendent engineers, may well persuade many more owners in the future to call on the services of shipmanagers as opposed to funding training programmes which only yield results after a number of years. It is likely, therefore, that ship management companies will have to take on more responsibility for training tomorrow's office managers as well as senior officers and seastaff as opposed to relying on shipowners to fulfil this basic role.

3.3 THE CURRENT MARKET

For the various reasons already described, independent ship management has grown to become a sizeable and vibrant part of the shipping industry. Ship management companies today control a substantial fleet of vessels comprising diverse ship types including some of the most technically sophisticated and unusual ships afloat. While the former category includes parcel tankers and LNG carriers, the latter includes a floating rocket launch installation (Barber) and a floating prison (Denholm).

In spite of such impressive growth, the availability of accurate statistics is limited. The databases which do exist are incomplete and can be misleading unless they are used with a degree of caution and scepticism. Consequently, it is difficult to obtain a clear idea of who manages what, the relative size of and market shares held by individual ship management companies and how fast the market is actually growing.

The problem of inadequate statistics was discussed at length by Spruyt in the previous edition of this book. The author clearly expressed his frustration at the fact that in spite of the obvious and growing need for quantification, information regarding the size and structure of the ship management market was still impressionistic and based on guestimates.

Others, including Panayides and Gray (1997), have also referred to the problems caused by inadequate statistics in this case in respect to the difficulties in basing research on sampling. It should be noted that, the RWA study referred to in section 3.1 (which has not been updated), remains the only significant independent survey of the ship management market.

Spruyt identified two main reasons why accurate statistics are difficult to obtain: the difficulty in defining ship management and lack of information disclosure.

3.3.1 Definition

For reasons already described in Chapter 2, defining ship management and by the same token a shipmanager, is no easy task. Deciding on which companies and which vessels to include in any analysis is somewhat subjective and judgemental dependent on the extent to which the individual company is seen to offer services on an independent basis and is reliant on third party tonnage for its livelihood. Unfortunately, the picture is further complicated by the fact that certain ships can justifiably be ruled out of consideration if only a limited number of services are provided (perhaps only certain officers).

Furthermore, depending on the analyst's view as to the strictness of the definition to be used, ships are ruled out if a significant shareholding interest in a vessel is held by the shipmanager either directly or *via* an associate company or if a vessel is owned by a shipmanager's parent company (so-called captive vessels as included in the managed fleets of many of the larger shipmanagers including Columbia, Barber, V Ships, Wallem and the Schulte group member companies).

Taken together, these various factors explain why any in-depth analysis is problematic and why each managed vessel must be judged on an individual basis.

3.3.2 Disclosure

The problems outlined above are compounded by the fact that the analyst has only limited information readily available. Although the shipping industry is becoming more transparent, due in large part to the efforts of the major charterers (particularly the oil companies) to vet tonnage and to exchange information *via* the establishment of databases (notably OCIMF's SIRE), shipping is still a secretive business where information on the ownership and management of a ship is distributed on a need-to-know basis. Secrecy is still a hallmark of the relationship between a shipmanager and its clients to the extent that information is only given out to third party sources on the express permission of the owner.

To a certain extent, discretion is also due to the fact that shipmanagers do not wish to make life easy for their competitors by freely distributing fleet lists. And to make matters harder still, it should be remembered that ships move into and out of the ship management sector and between shipmanagers on a daily basis.

Regrettably, therefore, any analysis of published sources today, some four years since the publication of the second edition of this book, would show that there has been no significant improvement in the usefulness of available statistics. Nevertheless, on the basis that the published databases readily available in the marketplace are the same ones used by the ship management sector, albeit to a fairly limited extent, to analyse market trends and competitive standing, it is useful to examine three of the main sources. By combining this with some detective work a useful picture of the ship management market can be built up.

The three sources examined below are Lloyd's Ship Manager's Guide to International Ship Registers and Ship Management Services (1996 edition), the Ship Manager's Register (1997 edition) produced and published by Ocean Press and Publishing, and LLP's database of shipowning and ship operating companies (an extract was taken from this database in March 1997). The basis of the analysis conducted and the principal findings are set out below.

3.3.3 LSM Analysis

Lloyd's Ship Manager's Guide is produced annually in association with the International Shipping Federation. It is based on responses to a questionnaire survey asking for information concerning office location, contact personnel and services offered. For the last category, 10 separate services are listed: crewing; insurance; accounting, sale and purchase; bunkering; technical management; freight management; chartering; provisioning, and operations. Companies offering one or a number of these services are listed individually by country.

The results of an analysis of LSM's 1996 Guide are presented as Table 3.7. The 515 companies located in 61 different countries listed in this table reflect the apparent vastness of the supply side of the ship management market and its international nature. Not surprisingly, the greatest number of companies can be found in Western Europe which accounts for approximately half of the world figure. Within this region the UK and Norway are prominent—the latter increasing in importance along with the growth of the Norwegian International Shipregister (NIS) from the late 1980s. Cyprus, where many international shipowners and shipmanagers (especially of German origin) have set up offices, Greece and the Netherlands are also important supply centres. Outside of Western Europe, Hong Kong, Singapore and the Philippines command attention.

A closer examination of the database, however, reveals that of the 515 companies listed, only 314 offer technical management and 359 crew management as the core services of the ship management sector. Also of important note is the fact that the total population of ship management companies is reduced further if intercompany relationships are examined. For example, many of the larger ship management groups are represented more than once including Barber (six times), Acomarit (five) and Denholm (five).

Table 3.7: Analysis of Ship Management Sector (I)

	Country	Companies	TM	CR	INS	AC	SP	BU	FM	CH	PR	OPS
1	Australia	5	3	3	0	2	1	2	0	2	2	3
2	Austria	1	1	1	1	1	0	1	1	1	1	1
3	Bangladesh	2	1	2	0	0	1	0	2	2	0	1
4	Belgium	3	2	3	2	2	1	1	1	0	3	2
5	Bermuda	2	1	1	1	1	0	1	0	1	1	1
6	Brazil	4	1	1	0	0	0	0	0	0	0	1
7	Bulgaria	1	0	0	0	0	0	0	0	0	0	0
8	Canada	6	5	3	1	4	2	3	3	4	2	4
9	Chile	2	1	2	2	2	1	0	0	0	0	0
10	Croatia	2	0	1	0	1	0	0	0	1	0	0
11	Cyprus	21	19	19	16	17	13	13	14	12	13	14
12	Denmark	8	5	4	5	6	7	4	4	5	3	6
13	Egypt	3	1	1	1	1	2	0	1	2	2	2
14	Estonia	2	1	1	0	0	1	0	1	0	0	1
15	Finland	3	1	2	1	1	2	1	2	2	1	3
16	France	3	1	1	1	1	1	0	0	0	1	0
17	Germany	16	11	11	9	9	12	9	7	11	8	12
18	Ghana	1	1	1	0	0	0	1	1	1	0	1
19	Gibraltar	2	0	0	1	0	1	1	1	1	1	1
20	Greece	24	10	13	8	9	7	8	8	9	8	10
21	Hong Kong	42	27	32	22	23	24	12	11	17	18	29
22	India	17	11	14	2	2	5	1	1	5	6	9
23	Indonesia	2	2	2	1	0	1	1	1	2	0	1

Table 3.7—cont.

	Country	Companies	TM	CR	INS	AC	SP	BU	FM	CH	PR	OPS
24	Iran	1	0	0	0	0	0	1	1	0	0	1
25	IOM	11	7	8	6	8	4	4	2	4	4	7
26	Italy	4	3	3	1	3	2	4	2	2	2	3
27	Japan	6	2	2	2	2	2	2	2	2	2	2
28	Korea	18	12	15	3	1	7	7	5	4	8	3
29	Kuwait	1	0	0	0	0	0	0	0	0	0	0
30	Latvia	3	1	2	1	1	2	1	1	1	1	1
31	Luxembourg	3	2	1	3	1	1	1	0	1	0	2
32	Malaysia	2	2	2	2	2	1	0	1	1	1	1
33	Maldives	4	2	4	2	2	3	2	3	4	3	4
34	Malta	7	4	5	2	2	4	3	1	3	2	0
35	Mauritius	2	1	1	0	1	0	0	0	0	1	0
36	Monaco	4	3	3	3	3	3	2	2	3	2	3
37	Morocco	1	0	1	1	0	0	0	0	1	0	0
38	Myanmar	1	1	1	0	1	0	0	0	0	0	1
39	Netherlands	20	13	14	8	13	8	5	5	7	8	12
40	Neth. Antilles	5	5	5	2	5	2	0	1	4	0	2
41	New Zealand	5	5	5	1	2	2	1	2	4	2	5
42	Norway	40	25	21	22	22	12	9	15	14	18	23
43	Pakistan	3	3	3	1	0	2	0	1	2	0	2
44	Panama	1	1	1	1	1	0	0	0	0	1	0
45	Philippines	20	4	11	2	7	4	3	0	3	7	6
46	Poland	2	2	2	1	1	1	1	1	1	1	1
47	Portugal	1	1	1	0	0	1	1	0	0	0	0
48	Russia	4	1	1	0	0	2	0	0	0	0	0
49	Singapore	35	25	26	15	18	13	15	9	11	19	19
50	South Africa	1	1	1	1	1	1	1	1	1	1	1
51	Spain	8	3	5	5	4	2	2	2	1	5	4
52	Sri Lanka	21	7	18	4	7	7	17	10	9	15	14
53	Sweden	6	6	5	6	6	4	3	0	2	4	3
54	Switzerland	7	5	5	6	5	4	5	2	4	4	5
55	Thailand	1	0	0	0	0	0	0	0	0	0	0
56	Trinidad	1	1	1	1	1	1	1	1	1	1	1
57	Turkey	1	0	0	0	0	0	0	0	0	0	0
58	Ukraine	3	0	2	0	0	1	1	2	2	0	0
59	UAE	2	1	1	0	0	0	0	0	1	0	1
60	UK	68	50	53	30	33	25	21	18	25	30	38
61	USA	20	10	12	10	10	11	6	7	10	9	12
Total		**515**	**314**	**359**	**216**	**245**	**214**	**178**	**156**	**206**	**221**	**279**

Source: LSM Guide to International Ship Registers and Ship Management Services 1996.

Note: TM = Technical Management; CR = Crewing; INS = Insurance; AC = Accounting; SP = Sale and Purchase; BU = Bunkering; FM = Freight Management; CH = Chartering; PR = Purchasing; OPS = Operations.

3.3.4 Ocean Analysis

The Ship Manager's Register is published twice yearly by London-based Ocean Press and Publishing Ltd. Like the LSM Guide, it is based on questionnaires requesting information on office location and the type of services offered. In addition, information is sought on company shareholding as well as the number and types of ships to which services are provided.

The data is collected and collated by Ocean and cross checked against other published sources. In addition, Ocean imposes a qualification requirement in so far as entries are only permissible from companies providing five or more of the following services: commercial management/vessel operations; crewing/manning; newbuilding supervision; marine purchasing; superintendency; insurance; budget/cost control; financial administration; training/management consultancy; reactivation; shipbroking/agency; alternative flag options; chartering, and technical management. Strenuous efforts are also made by Ocean's research team to check the authenticity of responses and in certain instances information is excluded.

For the purposes of analysis, the author included only those companies claiming to offer services to a fleet of 10 or more vessels (128 companies were identified as managing fleets of nine or fewer ships).

The results of this analysis are presented as Table 3.8 which lists 187 companies meeting the qualification requirement. Collectively these companies control a managed fleet of 7,816 vessels. In deriving this figure it should be noted that:

(a) while the publishers make every effort to encourage comprehensive and accurate responses, the Ocean database is, nevertheless, incomplete. For example, many companies listed in the register do not specify how many ships served are wholly-owned as opposed to third party tonnage;

(b) where the breakdown between wholly-owned and third party is declared, companies are included only if a significant minority of their managed fleet is third party;

(c) not all companies listed specify how many ships are managed under full management contracts, crew management contracts or technical-only contracts;

(d) companies which are primarily crew managers are included but all ships declared as commercial management only contracts are discounted.

Table 3.8   Analysis of Ship Management Sector (II)

	Company Name	Full MGMT.	Crew Num.	Tech. Num.	Fleet Total	Vessel Types
1	Accord Ship Mgmt.	8	5	0	13	L.STOCK; CHEM.TANK; CAR CARR; BULK CARR; PROD.TANK; GCC.
2	Acomarit Services	na	na	na	140	CRD; PROD; GAS & CHEM TANK; BULK; REEF; GCC; RO; CONTAIN; PASS./CRUISE.
3	Adriatico	2	78	0	80	CRD; PROD.TANK; BULK; GCC; PASS./CRUISE
4	Ahlers Maritime	na	na	na	29	GCC; RO; GAS, CHEM. GAS TANK; CONTAIN; DRILL.GCC

Table 3.8—cont.

	Company Name	Full MGMT.	Crew Num.	Tech. Num.	Fleet Total	Vessel Types
5	Ahrenkiel Shipping	na	na	na	110	CRD; PROD.TANK; GAS & CHEM.TANK; BULK; REEF; GCC; RO; CONTAIN
6	Amer Ship Mgmt.	na	na	na	35	GCC; REEF; CHEM. TANK; PROD.TANK; CONTAIN; BULK; GAS; RIGS
7	American O/Seas Marine Corp.	16	0	0	16	GCC; RO
8	Anders Utkilens	12	0	0	12	CHEM.TANKS
9	Andhika Lines	na	na	na	27	GAS & CHEM.TANKS; BULK; GCC; PROD. TANK
10	Andrew Weir	0	0	15	15	GCC; CONTAIN; RO.
11	Anglo Eastern	79	2	0	81	BULK; CONTAIN; GCC; OBO; GAS/LPG TANK; CRD; S/LOAD; MULTI.
12	Anthony Veder	10	0	5	15	GAS TANK; CONTAIN; REEF; BULK
13	Asia Mgmt.	0	36	0	36	BULK; CONTAIN; GCC; S/LOAD; RO
14	ASP Ship Mgmt.	21	1	0	22	BULK; OBO; PROD. TANK;
15	Atlantic Marine	6	25	0	31	CRDE; GAS & CHEM. TANK; PROD.CONTAIN. TANK
16	Avin Int.	20	na	na	20	
17	B+B Shipping	na	75	na	75	CONTAIN; RO; COASTAL; BULK; OBO; REEF; GCC
18	Baltic Internat.	na	na	na	360	CRDE; PROD.TANK; GAS & CHEM. TANK; MULTI; REEF; GCC; RO
19	Baltic Uniservice	na	20	na	20	—
20	Barber Ship Mgmt.	na	na	na	170	CRDE; PRO; CHEM. TANK; BULK; REEF; GCC; SUPPLY; RO; CONTAIN; VEHICLE; L/STOCK.
21	Beeline Shipping	8	23	8	39	CRDE; PROD; BULK; GCC; SUPPLY
22	Bereincua Herman	na	40	na	40	CHEM. & GAS; VLCCs; CEMENT
23	Bergen Ship Mgmt.	na	na	10	10	CRDE; PROD TANK; GAS & CHEM.TANK; BULK
24	Berry Interoceanic	na	20	na	20	CONTAIN; CRDE; PROD. TANK
25	Bibby Internat.	na	na	na	64	GAS & CHEM.TANK; GCC; OBO; RO; O/SHORE SUPPORT; CRDE
26	Blue Star Line	19	na	na	19	CONTAIN; REEF
27	Bona Shipping	na	na	na	31	CRDE; BULK; OBO

Table 3.8—cont.

	Company Name	Full MGMT.	Crew Num.	Tech. Num.	Fleet Total	Vessel Types
28	BR/BR Marine	4	10	10	14	GAS & CHEM.TANK; PROD.
29	BSR Ship Mgmt.	2	42	2	46	BULK; OBO; GCC; REEF; CONTAIN; CRDE; GAS & CHEM.TANK; PROD; PASS/CRUISE.
30	Bumi Laut (PT)	12	na	na	12	TANK; GCC
31	Campbell Maritime	13	na	na	13	TANK; DRY CARG
32	Canada Steamship	17	na	na	17	S/LOAD; DRY BULK
33	Celtic Marine	16	153	na	169	CRDE; PROD; GAS & CHEM.TANK; BULK; CONTAIN; RO; REEF; FERR; COASTAL
34	Celtic Pacific	10	105	na	115	CRDE; PROD; CHEM. TANK; BULK; GCC; RO; CONTAIN; AHS/ O/SHORE; PASS/CRUISE
35	Chemikalien	11	2	na	13	GAS TANK; OBO; PROD. TANK
36	Chokwang Shipping	na	22	na	22	CHEM.TANK
37	C-Link Netherlands	na	76	na	76	COAST; CONTAIN; GAS & CHEM.TANK; PROD.
38	Columbia Ship Mgmt.	85	174	na	259	REEF; CONTAIN; CRDE; PASS/CRUISE; BULK; OBO; GCC; GAS & CHEM.TANK; PROD; RO
39	Consulmar	na	na	na	39	GCC; GAS/CHEM.TANK; REEF; CONTAIN; PASS/ CRUISE; RO; HEAVY LIFT
40	Cosmos Maritime	5	10	3	18	CRDE; CHEM.TANK; GCC
41	Crescent Ship Mgmt.	11	na	1	12	RO; GCC; SPEC.TANK; GCC; OBO
42	Dammers	na	na	na	18	BULK; GCC; REEF; RO
43	Denholm Ship Mgmt.	na	na	na	100	CRDE; PROD.TANK; GAS/ CHEM. TANK; BULK; REEF; GCC; RO; CONT. PASS/CRUISE
44	Donji Marine	2	11	na	13	CRDE; LPG; RO; GEN. CARG; FERRY; PASS/ CRUISE
45	Dong Jin Shipping	2	40	na	42	BULK; CHEM.TANK
46	Dorchester	8	51	4	63	CRDE; GAS/CHEM. TANK; GCC; PROD; CONTAIN; FPSO; BULK; RO; DSV
47	Dortech Engineer	9	na	3	12	GAS/CHEM.TANK; BULK; OBO; CRDE; CONTAIN.
48	DS Marine	7	10	2	19	BULK; GCC; BULK; OBO
49	Elite Shipping	na	na	na	41	GCC; M/PURPOSE; CONTAIN.
50	Erik Thun	na	na	na	17	GCC; OBO; PROD.TANK; GAS/CHEM.TANK.

Table 3.8—cont.

	Company Name	Full MGMT.	Crew Num.	Tech. Num.	Fleet Total	Vessel Types
51	Eurasia Shipping	22	16	na	38	BULK; OBO; CRDE; VLCC; PROD; CONT CONTAIN; RO; GAS/ CHEM.TANK
52	Euroship Services	10	1	na	11	RO; BULK; CRDE
53	Everard	22	na	9	31	BULK; PROD.TANK; PCC
54	Fairmont Shipping	23	12	na	35	GCC
55	Fayza	na	na	na	21	GCC
56	Ferm International	na	26	26	26	PROD.TANK; GAS/ CHEM.TANK; GCC; BULK; OBO
57	FG Shipping	25	na	na	25	RO; BARG; RO/PASS; BULK; PUSH; GCC; RAIL; TUG
58	Feronia	na	na	na	41	OFFSHORE; RESEARCH
59	Fisser/Doornum	na	na	na	17	BULK; GAS/CHEM. TANK
60	Five Stars Shipping	22	na	na	22	TANK; BULK
61	Fleet Mgmt.	20	na	na	20	BULK; OBO; GCC
62	Fort Shipping	na	13	na	13	REEF; GAS/CHEM.TANK
63	France Ship Mgmt.	23	na	na	23	CRDE; BULK
64	Freeship	2	58	na	60	PROD.TANK; GAS/ CHEM.TANK; BULK; RO; PASS/CRUISE; SUPPLY
65	FG Shipping	25	0	0	25	RO/RO; BARGE; RO/ ROPASS; BULK; PUSHERS; GCC; RAILFERRY; TUG.
66	Gemarlux	20	na	na	20	CRDE; PROD.TANK; BULK; REEF; GCC; RO; CONTAIN; PASS/CRUISE; VEHICLE; SAILING
67	Gen. Ship & Chartering Service	0	na	na	20	BULK; MINIBULK; CONTAIN.
68	Glahr & Co	11	na	na	11	CONTAIN; RO
69	Globtik Express	0	na	na	18	CONTAIN; PROD.TANK; CHEM.TANK CRDE; LPG/ LNG; BULK; RO
70	Griffin Shipping	13	na	na	13	BULK; GCC; CONTAIN.
71	Hanseatic Shipping	42	91	na	133	GAS/CHEM.TANK; CONTAIN; CRDE; BULK; OBO; COASTAL; PROD.
72	Harmstorf S/M	na	na	na	36	GCC; PROD; CONTAIN
73	Herald Maritime	10	20	10	30	PROD; BULK; OBO; CRDE; GCC; CONTAIN; GAS/CHEM.TANK
74	Hoegh Fleet	na	na	na	31	BULK; VEHICLE; GCC; GAS TANK; REEF
75	Howard Smith	19	na	na	19	OIL TANK; CHEM. TANK; BULK; RO; RESEARCH

Table 3.8—cont.

	Company Name	Full MGMT.	Crew Num.	Tech. Num.	Fleet Total	Vessel Types
76	Iberian Ship Mgmt.	na	56	na	56	GCC; CHEM.TANK; LPG
77	Ibernor	1	71	1	73	GAS/CHEM.TANK; GCC; CRDE; BULK; OBO; RO; PROD; VEHICLE; FERRY; REEF; CONTAIN; CRUISE; OTHER
78	IMC Shipping	41	1	na	42	BULK; OBO; GCC; CONTAIN; PROD; CRDE
79	IMS Marine	3	25	2	30	TANK; BULK; GCC
80	IMS Ship Mgmt.	8	80	na	88	CRDE; BULK; CONTAIN; PROD; GAS/CHEM. TANK; M/PURPOSE
81	Int. Corp. Mgmt. of Bermuda	na	30	na	30	BULK; LUX.YACHT
82	Interocean Ugland	na	na	na	55	ALL CLASSES
83	Interorient Greece	na	11	na	11	BULK; CRDE; CONTAIN; GAS/CHEM.
84	Interorient Philippines	na	134	na	137	TANK; BULK; GCC
85	Interorient Navig.	30	90	na	120	BULK; REEF; GCC; RO; CONTAIN; VEHICLE; PASS/CRUISE; HEAVY LIFT VESSEL
86	Island Ship Mgmt.	8	na	2	10	BULK; GCC; SUPPLY; PASS/CRUISE
87	Jadroplov S/M	15	2	0	17	BULK; CONTAIN.
88	Jardine Ship Mgmt.	48	88	na	136	CRDE; PROD; CHEM. TANK; BULK; REEF; GCC; RO; CONTAIN; M/PURPOSE; CAR; FOREST PRODS
89	Jebsens (inc. Aboitiz)	45	38	4	87	BULK; GCC; CHEM. TANK; CRUISE; FERRY; WINE TANK; OBO.
90	Kapal Mgmt.	na	na	na	20	PROD; BULK; GCC; RO; CONTAIN; PASS/CRUISE; BUNK BARGE
91	Kent Line	6	na	6	12	PROD; CONTAIN; GCC; RO.
92	Knud I Larsen	46	na	na	46	CHEM.TANK; PROD; GAS/CHEM.TANK; CONTAIN
93	La Cross Cons.	na	12	na	12	BULK; GCC; GAS/CHEM. TANK; FERRY; FISH FAC
94	Lasco Shipping	23	na	1	24	BULK; CONBULK
95	Leohardt & Blumberg	26	na	na	26	BULK; CONTAIN; REEF
96	Lipolar Maritime	10	na	na	10	TANK; GCC
97	Lundqvist-Rederierna	na	na	na	12	CRDE; RO
98	Lydia Mar	2	46	4	52	BULK; OBO; CONTAIN
99	Marcons Ship Mgmt.	na	12	na	12	TANK; BULK; MULTI

Table 3.8—cont.

	Company Name	Full MGMT.	Crew Num.	Tech. Num.	Fleet Total	Vessel Types
100	Mare Maritime	3	na	13	16	GAS/CHEM.TANK; CRDE; PRODUCT; BULK; OBO
101	Marin Ship Mgmt.	na	13	na	13	MINIBULK; GCC
102	Marine Chartering	25	3	2	30	BULK; REEF; GCC; CONTAIN
103	Marine Service	14	na	na	14	LNG/LPG TANK; BULK; OBO
104	Marine Transport	4	19	0	23	RO; GAS/CHEM.TANK; CRDE; GCC; VEHICLE
105	Maritima Fullman	na	na	na	32	GAS/CHEM.TANK; CRDE; RO; PRODUCT; OBO; VEHICLE; BULK; PASS/ CRUISE; FERRY
106	Maritime Mgmt.	34	33	na	67	CRUDE; PRODUCT; GAS/ CHEM.TANK; BULK; OBO; REEF; GCC; RO; CONTAIN
107	Marlow Navigation	na	97	0	97	BULK; LPG; CONTAIN.
108	Martime-Gesellschaft	5	na	7	12	CONTAIN; GAS/CHEM. TANK
109	Mayflower S/M	5	na	35	40	REEF; BULK; CRDE; CONTAIN.
110	Med Crew	na	38	na	38	GCC; CONTAIN; RO; REEF
111	Middle East S/M	na	17	3	20	BULK; REEF; GCC; CONTAIN.
112	Midocean S/M	9	76	na	85	BULK; OBO; GCC; REEF; CONTAIN.
113	MTM Ship Mgmt.	12	na	na	12	GAS/CHEM.TANK
114	Naess	5	15	0	20	PROD; REEF; CRUDE
115	Navigo Mgmt.	na	na	na	60	CRDE; PROD; LPG/LNG; GCC; BULK; SALVAGE; REEF; CONTAIN; RO; COASTAL; HEAVY LIFT; BACO
116	Norbulk Shipping	30	50	na	80	REEF; PRODUCT; CRDE; CHEM.TANK; BULK; CONTAIN.
117	Nordic Oriental	18	26	na	44	TANK; WOODCHIP; OBO
118	Northern Marine	29	21	na	50	CRDE; O/SHORE; RO; DRILL; PROD; FERRY; CRUISE
119	Northsouth S/M	16	na	na	16	BULK; PRODUCT; CRDE; CHEM.TANK.
120	Novoship	na	na	na	20	PRODUCT; OBO; RO.
121	Oak Maritime	na	na	na	16	BULK; WOODCHIP
122	Ocean Tramping	48	na	na	48	BULK; GCC
123	Oesterreichischer	38	na	na	38	BULK; OBO; MULTI; CONTAIN; REEF; GCC
124	Orient Ship Mgmt.	na	na	na	52	TANK; CHEM.TANK; BULK; OBO; REEF; GCC; CONTAIN; RESEARCH; APTV

Table 3.8—cont.

	Company Name	Full MGMT.	Crew Num.	Tech. Num.	Fleet Total	Vessel Types
125	Oyster Ship Mgmt.	0	62	2	64	COAST; CRDE; PRODUCT; GCC; GAS/CHEM.TANK; BULK; OBO; RO.
126	Pacific Int.	47	na	5	52	CONTAIN.
127	Pacific Ship Mgmt.	na	na	na	19	BULK; OBO; GAS/CHEM. TANK; PROD.
128	Pacnav	4	25	3	32	PROD; GAS/CHEM. TANK; BULK; OFFSHORE
129	Pentagon Shipping	na	43	2	45	TANK; BULK; CONTAIN; PASS./CRUISE
130	Pertamina Shipping	na	na	na	87	CRDE; PRODUCT; LPG; CHEM.TANK; ASPHALT
131	Peter Dohle	na	na	na	25	CONTAIN; BULK.
132	Polish Manning	na	32	na	32	CRDE; PRODUCT; CHEM. TANK; LPG; BULK; COMBI; RO; CONTAIN; REEF; SEISMIC RESEARCH; ARCTIC RESEARCH
133	Promarinha	na	16	na	16	SUPPLY; CONTAIN.
134	Ravenscroft	17	na	na	17	BULK; OBO; CRDE; GCC; PRODUCT; COAST; GAS/CHEM.TANK
135	Red Band	na	14	0	14	CRDE; BULK; OBO
136	Red Sea Marine Serv.	14	18	na	32	TUG; PRODUCT; CRDE; CHEM.TANK; STORAGE; BUNKER
137	Rederiaktiebolaget	11	1	na	12	REEF; RO.
138	Richfield Ship Mgmt.	na	22	na	22	CONTAIN; BULK; OBO; CRDE; AS/CHEM.TANK VEHICLE; PRODUCT; REEF
139	Rota Shipping	12	na	na	12	GCC; OBO; BULK
140	Russochart Shipping	14	na	na	20	BULK; COAST.
141	Samrat Ship Mgmt.	na	67	na	67	CRDE; BULK; OBO; REEF; PRODUCT; CONTAIN; VEHICLE; GAS/CHEM.TANK
142	Samsun Corporation	18	na	na	18	BULK; OBO; GCC
143	Scorpio Marine	na	21	na	21	GCC; CONTAIN; BULK; OBO; CRDE
144	Seaarland	10	na	na	10	PRODUCT; CRDE; BULK; OBO
145	Seacon Mgmt.	na	11	0	11	RO; BULK; OBO; CONTAIN.
146	Sealion Shipping	17	na	na	17	O/SHORE; SAFETY STANDBY; U/WATER SUPP.
147	Seascot Ship Mgmt.	36	na	na	36	GCC; BULK; OBO; RESCUE; DREDGE.
148	Seatrade Groningen	51	na	na	51	REEF; BULK; OBO

Table 3.8—cont.

Company Name	Full MGMT.	Crew Num.	Tech. Num.	Fleet Total	Vessel Types
149 Seatrade Ship Mgmt.	na	na	na	12	VEHICLE; CONTAIN; GCC; OBO; BULK
150 Sejin Lines	1	14	na	15	BULK; CHEM.TANK; REEF; CONTAIN.
151 Sembawang S/M.	16	29	na	45	GAS; BULK; VEHICLE; CRDE; LIVESTOCK; REEF; CRUISE; CEMENT.
152 C F Sharp	18	14	4	36	CRDE; PRODUCT; GCC; REEF; CHEM.TANK; COAST; PASS/CRUISE; BULK; OBO
153 Shipco Marine	4	6	na	10	GCC
154 Ship-Control	18	na	na	18	CONTAIN.
155 Shiserco	3	6	3	12	BULK; LPG; LNG
156 Singa Ship Mgmt.	21	75	na	96	PRODUCT; GAS/CHEM. TANK; BULK
157 Southern Ship Mgmt.	15	na	na	15	CONTAIN; VEHICLE; GCC; REEF
158 Spa-Tsm Ship Mgmt.	na	na	na	25	PRODUCT; CRDE; GAS/ CHEM.TANK
159 Split Ship Mgmt.	22	1	na	23	GCC; BULK; OBO; CONTAIN; REEF; RO; FERRY
160 Star Ship Mgmt.	25	na	na	25	TANK; PRODUCT; VEHICLE; RO; PUSH; BARGE
161 Stephenson Clarke	10	na	2	12	SHORTSEA COASTAL
162 Stirling Ship Mgmt.	14	na	5	19	O/SHORE; FERRY
163 Suisse-Atlantique	na	na	na	11	BULK
164 Swire Pacific S/M	na	na	na	48	CRDE; RO; CONTAIN; O/SHORE
165 Taiyo Sangyo	na	na	na	40	BULK; REEF; GCC; OBO; VEHICLE; GAS/ CHEM.TANK; PRODUCT; RO
166 Team Ship Mgmt.	na	na	na	16	CRDE; PRODUCT; CHEM.TANK
167 Tecto	50	4	1	55	GAS/CHEM.TANK; PRODUCT; CRDE; CONTAIN; OBO; REEF
168 Terra Marine S/M	10	30	na	40	TANK; BULK; GCC; REEF
169 Thome Ship Mgmt.	na	28	37	65	PRODUCT; CRDE; GAS/ CHEM.TANK; BULK; OBO; GCC; COAST
170 Transit-Express	1	41	2	44	GCC; BULK; OBO; COAST; CONTAIN; PRODUCT; REEF; RO; CRDE; CHEM.TANK; CRUISE
171 Transocean S/M	74	na	na	74	CEMENT; GAS/CHEM. TANK; CONTAIN; GCC; BULK; OBO; ALL CLASSES; TANKS

Table 3.8—cont.

	Company Name	Full MGMT.	Crew Num.	Tech. Num.	Fleet Total	Vessel Types
172	Ugland	2	10	na	12	VLCC; ULCC; LPG; TANK; RO; PASS/CRUISE
173	Unicom Mgmt.	68	na	na	68	CRDE; GCC; BULK; OBO; PRODUCT; CONTAIN; TIMBER; PASS/CRUISE
174	Unicorn Lines	8	1	1	10	BITUMEN/VEGOIL TANK; MULTI; CONTAIN; PRODUCT; VEHICLE; CELLULAR CONTAIN
175	Unimar Ship Mgmt.	20	na	2	22	DRY BULK
176	Uniteam Marine	5	23	na	28	CONTAIN; BULK; OBO; COAST; REEF; GCC
177	United Ship Mgmt.	na	20	0	20	MULTI DRY; BULK; OPEN HATCH + GANTRY CRANES
178	United Shipping	na	na	na	13	BULK; OBO; CRDE; PRODUCT
179	Unitramp	30	na	na	30	BULK.
180	Univan Ship Mgmt.	63	0	0	63	CRDE; BULK; CONTAIN; GCC; PRODUCT; VEHICLE; CHEM.TANK; WOODCHIP; REEF; RO; TUG
181	Vermilion Overseas	55	na	na	55	BULK; OBO; CONTAIN
182	V Ships	na	na	na	180	CRDE; PRODUCT; GAS/ CHEM.TANK; BULK; REEF; GCC; RO; CONTAIN; VEHICLE; PASS/CRUISE
183	Wagenborg Shipping	31	47	na	78	TANK; BULK; GCC; CONTAIN; RO.
184	Wah Tung	24	0	0	24	BULK; CONT; RO; GCC
185	Wallem Group	148	25	3	176	TANK; BULK; OBO; CONTAIN; MULTI; RO; PASS/CRUISE; WOODCHIP; GCC; REEF; CHEM./GAS TANK; PRODUCT
186	Westfal-Larsen	16	na	na	16	GCC; GAS/CHEM.TANK
187	Westfleet Mgmt.	na	0	0	53	GCC; OBO; PRODUCT
187	**COMPANIES**	**2,356**	**3,089**	**274**	**7,816**	

Source: The Ship Managers' Register, 1997 edition

3.3.5 LLP Analysis

LLP (formerly Lloyd's of London Press) manages the world's largest maritime database of commercial trading vessels. In addition to basic technical details of the ships, flag of operation and vessel movements, information is maintained on ownership and, where known, on how the vessel is managed.

In March 1997 the author requested a computer run from LLP's Colchester office to identify all vessels listed on the database operated by a ship management company. The computer run selected 6,508 vessels to which the following qualification requirements were applied:

1 companies listing ten or more managed vessels;
2 companies serving at least two shipowners;
3 companies managing solely specialist vessels (fishing, research, offshore supply) were excluded.

The results of this analysis are presented as Table 3.9 which shows that just 43 companies qualified for inclusion. Collectively, these companies control a fleet of 1,170 vessels with an aggregate dwt of 56.6m. This table shows that 14 of the 43 companies listed manage five or more ship types under five or more flags and that 18 companies serve a managed fleet of over 1m. dwt (nine over 2m. dwt).

Table 3.9: Analysis of Ship Management Sector (III)

Company	Rank	Fleet No.	Dwt (m.)	Flags/Ship Types	Market Share Vsls.	Dwt
Acomarit	1	90	7.888	MISC./MISC.	7.69	13.94
Barber	=2	81	4.679	MISC./MISC.	6.92	8.27
V Ships	=2	81	2.904	MISC./MISC.	6.92	5.13
Wallem	4	71	5.398	MISC./MISC.	6.07	9.54
Columbia	5	58	1.191	MISC./MISC.	4.96	2.11
Anglo Eastern	6	55	2.243	MISC./MISC.	4.70	3.97
RMS	7	42	0.110	MISC./GCC; CON; RO.	3.59	0.19
Denholm	8	38	1.972	MISC./MISC.	3.25	3.49
Univan	9	34	1.860	MISC./MISC.	2.91	3.29
Seascot	=10	30	0.264	MISC./MISC.	2.56	0.47
Poseiden	=10	30	0.351	RUS; LBR; CYP; VCT/BULK	2.56	0.62
Thome	12	29	2.181	MISC./TANK; BULK	2.48	3.86
MMS	13	28	1.071	MISC./MISC.	2.39	1.89
Jardine	14	27	0.831	MISC./MISC.	2.31	1.47
Everard	15	26	0.073	GBR; BHS/COAST; SS	2.22	0.13
Interocean	=16	25	3.588	MISC./TANK; BULK	2.14	6.34
Laiez	=16	25	0.438	LIB; DEU; MLT/MISC.	2.14	0.77
Jebsens	18	24	0.200	MISC./BULK; GCC; CHEM, TANK	2.05	0.35
Hanseatic	19	23	1.088	MISC./MISC.	1.97	1.92
ASP	20	22	1.002	AUS/MISC.	1.88	1.77
Northern Marine	21	20	4.088	MISC./RO; TANK	1.71	7.23
Split	22	19	0.381	MISC./GCC; BULK; CON.	1.62	0.67
Aboitiz	23	17	0.144	PHL; HK; PAN/GCC; FERRY BULK	1.42	0.25
Ahrenkiel	=24	16	0.285	MISC./MISC.	1.37	0.50
Gie	=24	16	2.670	MISC./TANK; TUG; RO.	1.37	4.72
Neptune	=24	16	0.703	SGP; MYS/CON; TANK	1.37	1.24
Norbulk	=24	16	0.275	PAN; LIB; MLT; SAV/TANK/REF.	1.37	0.49
Unicom	=24	16	0.168	PAN; CYP; MLT/GCC; PASS; TANK	1.37	0.30
Coeclerici	=29	15	0.596	IT; ANT;/BULK; BARGE	1.28	1.05

Table 3.9—cont.

Company	Rank	Fleet No.	Dwt (m.)	Flags/Ship Types	Market Share Vsls.	Dwt
Northsouth	=29	15	0.670	PANINIS/NOR; PHL; BULK; TANK	1.28	1.18
Ahlers/Euro.	=29	15	0.242	MISC./MISC.	1.28	0.43
Souter	=32	13	1.546	HK; MHL/BULK	1.11	2.73
Singa	=32	13	1.099	NIS; MLT; BHS./TANK; BULK; CON; LPG.	1.11	1.94
Transocean	=34	12	1.230	PR; PMD; LBR; GAB/TANK; BULK; CHEM.	1.03	2.17
Lino	=34	12	0.921	SGP; LIB; JAP; PAN/MISC.	1.03	1.63
Far Etc.	=34	12	0.291	PAN; LIB/MISC.	1.03	0.51
Cambell	=34	12	0.046	GBR; BHS/TANK; GCC.	1.03	0.08
Eurasia	=38	12	1.219	GBR; BHS/TANK; GCC.	1.03	2.15
Ravenscroft	=38	11	0.277	PAN; VUT/BULK; TANK; BARGE; TUG	0.93	0.49
Ferm	=38	11	0.100	SWE; NIS; BHS/CHEM; TANK; GCC.	0.94	0.18
Eastern Car. L.	=38	11	0.097	MISC./RO; GCC	0.94	0.17
Fisher, T.	=38	11	0.070	GIB; LIB/TANKER	0.94	0.12
Marlow	=38	11	0.041	CYP; ATG/BULK; GCC	0.94	0.07
Crescent	43	10	0.077	MISC./RO; GCC; SLUDGE	0.85	0.14
TOTAL		**1,170**	**56.568**			

Notes:

Qualification criteria = 10 or more ships in managed fleet; >1 owner; specialist tonnage excluded (fish factories, tugs, offshore support/anchor handling vessels) unless included in fleet with "mainstream" ship types. Misc. = five or more flags or ship types.

Ship Types:

GCC = General Cargo Carrier; Tank = Tanker; Bulk = Bulk Carrier; Ro = Roll-on/Roll-off; Con = Container Ship; SLVOGE = Sludge Carrier; Chem = Chemical Tanker

Flags:

PAN = Panama; LIB = Liberia; CYP = Cyprus; SGP = Singapore; MYS = Malaysia; PHL = Philippines; MLT = Malta; IT = Italy; ATC = Antigua; BHS = Bahamas; VUT = Vanuatu; JAP = Japan.

Source:

LLP database. Computer run listing 6,500 vessels where manager cited as at 24th March 1997.

It is also interesting to note that the average size of the vessels under management is 48,000 dwt with the average for three of the "big ship" shipmanagers, Northern Marine, GIE and Interocean 204,000 dwt, 167,000 dwt and 144,000 dwt respectively. By contrast, three of the "small ship" shipmanagers listed are Everard, RMS and Far Etc. averaging just 3,000–4,000 dwt.

Table 3.9 also shows the fragmented nature of the supply side of the ship management market. Only four shipmanagers (Acomarit, Wallem, Barber and V Ships) held a market share in excess of 5 per cent in terms of dwt and number of ships.

So what are the principal conclusions which can be drawn from the analyses of the three different databases? Firstly, the most reliable publicly available database (as opposed to questionnaire-based information) only provides partial coverage. If the numbers specified in Table 3.9 are compared with the number of managed ships the shipmanagers themselves declare, then the coverage would appear to be around 60 per cent to 70 per cent. In most cases, the shortfall would appear to be due to the exclusion of part-managed tonnage.

The most optimistic picture is presented by Ocean which suggests a total market of over 8,000 ships (if the vessels managed by the small ship management companies are included and if vessels under part-management contracts are included). This figure equates to around 25 per cent of the world fleet and suggests that the total fleet controlled by ship management companies has nearly quadrupled since the RWA study conducted in 1986—a compound annual rate of nearly 15 per cent. If captive tonnage and ships for which only one or two crew are discounted (together with a measure of double counting) then the total third party market is probably never half of the total suggested by Ocean, i.e. approximately 4,500 ships.

3.4 SUPPLY SIDE CHARACTERISTICS

Although the analysis of the available databases presented in the previous section shows that the number of ship management companies is actually smaller than initial impressions suggest, the supply side of the ship management market is, nevertheless, a fragmented one. Indeed, the structure of the supply side can be portrayed as a broad based pyramid made up of three distinctive tiers. These are:

3.4.1 Top Tier

This tier comprises some ten companies which offer a comprehensive range of services to a diverse fleet of 75 or more vessels. These vessels operate under a variety of flags and are manned with many different crew nationalities. Services are offered from a network of offices worldwide located close to clients in the major maritime centres.

3.4.2 Middle Tier

Some 30 or so companies comprise the middle tier. Each company serves a managed fleet of between 10 and 75 vessels typically from one or two office locations. Specialization in terms of vessel type, crew nationalities utilized, flag of operation and region of client base is evident.

3.4.3 Lowest Tier

Some 100 to 200 small-sized companies populate the lowest tier. These companies serve ten or fewer vessels perhaps owned by one or two clients from a single office location. Although many such companies claim to offer full management services the majority are thought to actually provide a limited range.

Although this three-tier pyramid structure is somewhat impressionistic given the lack of any meaningful time-series data, it has, nevertheless, been evident for some time. This picture of stability can be explained by a closer examination of why shipmanagers lose ship management contracts and the general business environment for ship management companies in recent years.

3.4.4 Why do Shipmanagers Lose Business?

Basically, contracts are lost for a number of reasons many of which are beyond the control of the shipmanager and indeed its ability to influence. These reasons include the simple fact that ships under management are sold for further trading or demolition which triggers, invariably, termination of the management contract—typically on three months' notice.

What might best be described as strategic factors also exert a powerful influence. These include an owner's desire to exert greater control over the day-to-day management of a vessel or, in the case of an owner using a number of shipmanagers, perhaps, for different ship types, the decision to rationalize operations by working with a lesser number of external managers.

Aside from the above factors, which are essentially beyond the shipmanager's control, contracts are terminated if a shipowner is dissatisfied with a shipmanager's performance or, conversely, the shipmanager may decide to terminate a contract if a client continually refuses to dedicate sufficient funding to ensure a vessel's continuing safe operation or funding is persistently late to the extent that the shipmanager, in effect, enters the shipping finance business. In both cases, however, actual instances of this kind are relatively few and far between. In the former case because shipowners in the past have been reluctant to incur the cost penalties involved in terminating a contract and, have, therefore, been prepared to put up with a poor standard of service over a lengthy period—particularly in firm freight markets which generate higher margins. In the latter case, the intensely competitive nature of ship management means that in a buyer's market shipmanagers have been reluctant in the past to give up or refuse business in the certain knowledge that a competitor will step in. Erosion of market share has tended to overrule the profitability of individual contracts in the shipmanager's decision-making.

3.4.5 What is the General Business Environment?

As alluded to in various sections of the book, shipmanagers have faced a difficult business environment in recent years typified by the erosion of management fees in real terms, intensive competition and the rising cost of service delivery. In the all too familiar absence of detailed financial information (most shipmanagers are privately owned and do not publish financial results), any analysis must rely on statements made by a number of the industry's leading practitioners.

Two recent examples worthy of mention are Petter Larsen, Senior VP of Barber International, and Captain Peter Cooney, Managing Director of Acomarit UK Ltd.

Mr Larsen was interviewed by Tradewinds in late 1993 in connection with an article examining the fees charged by three shipmanagers (Barber, Denholms and

Wallem) working for Benor Tankers. He estimated at the time that due to increasing environmental regulations, the work involved in managing a tanker was 30 to 40 per cent more than a conventional vessel without a commensurate premium in management fees. This situation was attributed by Mr Larsen to intense competition between shipmanagers who stressed that:

"The market gives you the same fees whether you spend 1,000 or 10,000 hours a year on a ship."

He also confirmed that in the light of this predicament Barber was endeavouring to cut costs by being more selective in the ships it takes into management.

Captain Cooney was quoted in an article published in *Lloyd's List* in 1997 as saying that:

"Twenty to 30 years ago, shipmanagement companies in Glasgow were earning in pounds what we are earning in dollars now. Over two decades, revenue has gone down by half."

He went on to address the following question in the same article:

"If I say to owners, I need more money to manage your ship, they give you one of two answers. Either I am not making enough money to give you more money or there are any number of shipmanagers who will do it cheaper."

Taken together, the net effect of the vulnerable position which shipmanagers find themselves in with regard to contract retention plus a difficult business environment explains why so few companies have entered the market in recent years. Three notable exceptions to this rule are Sea Praxis Shipmanagement, Dobson Fleet Management and Ganymed (Malta) Ltd which reflected the growth of the ship management community in the Mediterranean region in the 1990s.

Sea Praxis was set up in Cyprus by local business interests headed by Zenon Katsourides and Vassos Mavreas in late 1992 and Dobson the following year by privately-owned UK interests. Both ventures were started with owned tonnage with the intention of marketing services to third party clients. Ganymed was set up in Valletta in October 1995 on the strength of a full management contract awarded by the Swiss-based containership company Norasia.

What these market forces do not explain is the fact that there have been so few casualties. A number of shipmanagers have ceased trading in recent years for various reasons. Notable examples are:

NORWEGIAN SHIP MANAGEMENT
Oslo-based NSM closed in late 1992 following the decision of its parent company, Norwegian American Line, to transfer its vessels back into in-house management.

ORIENT SHIP MANAGEMENT
This Hong Kong bulk carrier and OBO specialist ceased trading in May 1995 in the face of the mounting costs required to secure compliance with ISM and ISO. Acomarit took over the 14 Orient managed vessels from its Glasgow offices.

CARDIFF SHIP MANAGEMENT

This wholly-owned subsidiary of Mexico's Transportation Maritima Mexicana (TMM) closed in May 1996 with the transfer of the management of its five remaining vessels owned by TMM to Mexico.

HUDSON STEAMSHIP CO

In 1995 this Brighton-based company was put up for sale by its owner, Mosvold. Without a seller found, the company closed the following year. In July 1997, however, the former management team started a new company, Euroship Services Ltd based in Purfleet UK.

What has not taken place, however, is the wholesale market shake-up as predicted in the early 1990s. At that time, the widely-held view, at least among the larger ship management companies, was that persistently difficult trading conditions would inevitably result in casualties among the smaller players. The mood at the time was reflected by comments made by David Underwood, the late CEO of Denholms, who was one of the first to publicly comment on what he saw as deteriorating business conditions for shipmanagers. In an interview in September 1992 he identified various factors which he believed would trigger a major shake-up in the ship management sector with a number of companies leaving the business either voluntarily or involuntarily. He identified these factors as the decline in real terms in ship management fees since 1979, overcapacity in the market place, the weak dollar and the effect of new legislation like OPA 90 in raising the cost of service delivery. However, at the same time he did identify what was described as a saving grace of this worsening situation through the fact that at least higher barriers to entry would prevent "five guys in a room together with a fax" from calling themselves shipmanagers.

Underwood's comments have been reflected by other commentators in recent years. For example, Jan Lissow, Managing Director of Interorient Navigation was quoted in *Containerisation International* in 1995 as stating:

"The rates at present are low and they have to increase for companies to survive. However, the main trouble is that on top of a competitive market, we have the added burden of quality assurance (QA) systems and increasing investment in information technology. This makes it even more difficult. Rates have to be improved, there is no question about it, otherwise companies will go under or merge in the near future."

So why have there been so few casualties in the past five years? One reason is the fact that smaller companies have been very resilient to increasing financial pressures caused by high regulatory requirements. Another would appear to be that the ship management market is not a particularly rational one in so far as the most efficient players have not been able to dominate at the expense of the weaker which are still able to enjoy contracts based on reasons other than purely financial ones. Consideration should also be given to the fact that certain ship management companies have been able to successfully diversify their interests into shipping-related and non-shipping areas to further strengthen their financial position.

Nevertheless, the pressures on shipmanagers are unrelenting and the market may well still witness the kind of market shake-out that David Underwood referred to and others have echoed but that it is taking longer to come to fruition than originally envisaged. In the meantime, the ship management sector is continuing to witness various initiatives designed to strengthen competitive standing. Three recent initiatives of note are:

BARBER INTERNATIONAL

In an effort to dramatically reduce its cost base, Norway's leading shipmanager relocated its head office from Oslo to Kuala Lumpur in 1995. Barber International claim that this initiative, which was also motivated by its desire to move closer to its major Asian manpower supply sources, has resulted in major savings.

CELTIC MARINE

In 1996, Celtic Pacific Shipping merged with Marine Management Services to form the Isle of Man headquartered Celtic Marine, which operates from a network of seven offices.

BIBBY HARRISON MANAGEMENT SERVICES

In October 1997 two long-established UK shipping companies, Bibby Line and Thos & Jas Harrison joined forces to create a 50:50 joint venture ship management company Bibby Harrison Management Services. This company based in Liverpool started trading on 1 October 1997 with 35 staff seconded from the two shareholding partners designated to look after a managed fleet of 22 vessels. Scale economies were reportedly a significant driving force in the merger of the two companies.

UNIVERSAL MARINE

In November 1997 two independent Japanese ship management companies, Universal Marine and Techno Marine, announced their intention to join forces in an attempt to enhance their competitive standing. The newly-merged company will control a fleet of 60 ships including ten under technical management.

To illustrate the importance of scale economies, Table 3.10 presents three hypothetical scenarios of how potential profitability is enhanced as the ratio of staff to ships under management diminishes. In Scenario A, a ratio of 2:1 sees the company generate a net loss unless additional revenue can be secured, say, through agency or other ancillary activities. In Scenario B, the company starts to generate a profit at a ratio of 1:4 given that eight additional staff can handle a net increase of eight ships. In Scenario C, at the same ratio as B, profits increase due to only a marginal increase in company overheads.

Whether further initiatives of this kind will emerge remains to be seen. For while the attractions of growth *via* acquisition or merger as opposed to the organic route remain attractive in many ways, a number of problems must be overcome. In the case of acquisitions, it is difficult to obtain an accurate valuation of a ship management company where the intrinsic worth is locked into existing contracts which for reasons already described may not be driven by purely financial considerations. Certainly, it is possible for two parties to agree an amicable consideration, perhaps based on a multiple of average earnings over the previous three years or a cent on the dollar percentage of current business turnover. Nevertheless, the potential loss of business post transaction is a constant threat even though such losses can be dealt with *via* price adjustments. Furthermore, blending two management systems (if that is the aim) is never easy although greater use of formal management disciplines and information technology may make the task easier.

Table 3.10: Scale economies in ship management

	SCENARIO A	SCENARIO B	SCENARIO C
Fleet:	6 Vessels	14 Vessels	19 Vessels
Income (@ US$110,000/Vessel)	US$660,000	US$1,540,000	US$2,090,000
Staff:	12 MD Secretary Technical Director Accountant S&Q Superintendent Crew Manager plus 1 × FLEET TEAM 2 × Superintendents Technical Controller Purchasing Manager Fleet Accountant Fleet Secretary	20 (As Scenario A plus: Insurance Manager Assistant Crew Manager 1 × FLEET TEAM)	27 (As Scenario B plus: Assistant S&Q Supt. 1 × FLEET TEAM)
Total Staff Cost:	US$575,000	US$887,000	US$1,274,000
Office and General Overheads[1]	US$190,000	US$287,000	US$386,000
Total Income	US$660,000	US$1,540,000	US$2,090,000
Total Costs	US$765,000	US$1,174,000	US$1,660,000
Profit/(Loss)	(US$105,000)	US$366,000	US$430,000

Note: 1—comprising office rent, rates, maintenance, communications, audit, insurance, travel, entertainment, training, stationery etc.

3.5 DEMAND SIDE CHARACTERISTICS

The diversity on the supply side of the ship management market equation is also witnessed on the demand side. Just as the providers of ship management services show diversity in terms of size, the services they offer, ownership and geographical presence, so do the users vary in a number of respects as do their requirements.

Size is certainly one of the most important distinguishing factors. Obviously, the attractions of contracting out the ship management function to a specialist offering reliable and cost effective services are greater for a smaller shipowner than a larger one. Smaller companies include private investors who from time to time are attracted by specialist opportunities, including contra-cyclical asset plays for which funds are made available for a limited period. Typically all day-to-day management functions are outsourced in the case of private investors including the preparation of corporate accounts.

Related to the private investors are the shipping funds which use the public and private equity markets (primarily US and Norwegian institutional investors) to provide financing for specific business ventures. Typically, these funds have been directed towards the tanker sector and have involved the delegation of day-to-day ship management to the sponsoring company or a company associated to it. The second half of the 1980s saw the rapid growth of such equity funds (B&H Bulk Carriers, Anangel American, MC Shipping).

Banks and other providers of debt finance represent a further category, the importance of which is directly related to the health of particular freight markets over time and the availability of cheap debt. In the second half of 1997, concern was growing in the marketplace over the health of certain (especially dry bulk) ship-owners and the prospect of widespread foreclosures. In the event of the banks choosing to pursue such a course of action, shipmanagers are available to manage tonnage on behalf of temporary shipowners until better trading conditions permit resale.

What might be best described as traditional shipowners represents the largest category of shipmanager clients. Such companies may use the services of a ship-manager on a highly selective basis (perhaps for one or two specialist ships) or, indeed, choose to outsource technical and crewing (and on fewer occasions) commercial management services. Such owners include publicly-quoted and privately-owned shipowners, as well as shipowners from developing countries who need to import technical expertise before home-grown skills can be developed. A good example of the latter type of client is Saudi Arabia's leading tanker owner Vela International which uses a number of shipmanagers to provide technical and crew management services but it is pursuing a programme of full integration which it hopes to complete in 1998.

A final category of shipowning clients can be collectively referred to as specials. These are companies which for particular reasons use the services of a shipmanager. The largest source of business in the specials category are East European ship-owners who have established joint venture type relationships with a number of the leading ship management companies including Columbia, Acomarit and V Ships as a way of marketing surplus domestic seastaff to Western third party owners and as a way of raising Western bank finance for fleet renewal based on the flagging out of ships to offshore registers.

Another important characteristic of the demand side of the ship management market equation is the type of ship which shipmanagers have been successful in winning over. From the early days when the unsophisticated vessel types were the principal sources of business, demand has spread to most vessel types to the extent that there are few sectors of the shipping market where shipmanagers do not have a presence.

Nevertheless, the degree of market penetration does vary from one sector to another as illustrated by the following three examples.

3.5.1 Tanker Sector

Shipmanagers have been present in the tanker market for many years. Despite mounting criticism in the late 1980s and early 1990s over the future role of the shipmanager in tanker management, shipmanagers have maintained a high profile. As Table 3.11, which is based on Lloyd's List's 1997 *Green Tanker Guide & Directory*, illustrates, shipmanagers manage a diverse array of vessel types ranging from large crude carriers to small short-sea trading products and chemical carriers. Shipmanagers provide services both to oil companies which have retained a direct presence in the tanker market and independent companies including shipowners representing the state-owned companies for the major oil producing countries.

Table 3.11: Shipmanagers in the Tanker Market

Vessel Type	Manager
Aframax Crude	Northern Marine Management
	Acomarit
	France Shipmanagement
	Anglo-Eastern
	Hanseatic
	Wallem
	Thome Ship Management
	Barber Ship Management
	Interocean Ugland Management
Suezmax	Acomarit
	Barber Ship Management
	Unicom Management Services
VLCC	France Shipmanagement
ULCC	Mideast Ship Management (Acomarit–NSCSA)
	Northern Marine Management
	Norbulk Shipping Ltd
	Wallem
	Barber Ship Management
Chemical/Products	Denholm Ship Management
	Northsouth Shipmanagement
	Thome Ship Management
	Latmar Columbia
	V Ships
	Singa Shipmanagement
	Ahrenkiel
	ASP Ship Management
Specials	
Methanol	Mideast Ship Management (Acomarit–NSCSA)
Caustic Soda	Northern Shipmanagement
	Singa Shipmanagement
	Denholm Ship Management
	Unicom Management Services
	Thome Ship Management
Fruit Juice	Acomarit
Asphalt/Bitumen	Northern Marine Management
Molasses	MMS

Table 3.11—cont.

Vessel Type	Manager
OBO, O/O	Jahre-Wallem
	Acomarit
	V Ships
	MMS
	Barber Ship Management
Small Products	Cambell Maritime
	Hanseatic
	V Ships
Handy Size Crude/Products	MMS
	Interorient Navigation
	Unicom Management Services
	Hanseatic
	V Ships
	Denholm Ship Management
	Latmar Columbia
	Univan Ship Management
	MMS
	Dorchester Maritime
	Norbulk Shipping UK
	Thome Ship Management

Source: Lloyd's List *Green Tanker Guide & Directory 1997*

3.5.2 Container Sector

Shipmanagers have been less successful in winning business from containership companies. Part of the reason for this is that traditionally many liner companies have within the conference system chosen or been required to maintain national flags rather than switch to cheaper flags of convenience. Furthermore, the major liner companies, many of which operated in consortia, have chosen to retain full control over all aspects of shipboard and landside operations.

Nevertheless, opportunities have arisen from time to time for shipmanagers to make inroads into the containership sector. The primary route has been through the close relationships forged between the extensive container feedership fleet built for German tax partnerships and a number of German shipmanagers. Also, opportunities have arisen from time to time for shipmanagers to take vessels into management for strategic reasons—notably joint venture type relationships between shipmanagers and shipowners in East Europe, South America and the Middle East.

A breakthrough in the market came in 1995 when two of the major US lines, APL and Sea-Land decided to contract out crew management to three shipmanagers (Columbia, Hanseatic and V Ships). In that year, a survey conducted by *Containerisation International* revealed that 17 of the major third party ship management companies controlled a combined fleet of some 281 containerships with a further 145 vessels served under part management contracts.

Against this background and in spite of the fact that the ownership of container vessels is consolidating through mergers and acquisitions, ship management companies hope that the containership sector will be a source of more business with the Japanese majors, under pressure to reduce vessel operating costs but cautious to date in their use of independent shipmanagers, a specific target.

3.5.3 Cruise Shipping

Cruise shipping is one of the fastest-growing sectors of the shipping industry which offers potential for ship management companies. It is, however, a specialist sector requiring particular skills into which only a few shipmanagers have been able to make inroads.

As in the containership market, the larger cruise lines have traditionally controlled all aspects of shipboard operation. From time to time, however, ship management and catering companies have been able to win contracts for specific services (crewing, catering, technical supervision, safety and quality management) from the major players and have been able to win full management contracts from new entrants to the market (principally tour operators) who have recognized the enormous potential that the cruise shipping sector offers but who lack the skills needed to ensure consistent on-board product delivery. Business has also been won from the management of ageing tonnage available on the charter market.

MARKETING SHIP MANAGEMENT

4.1 WHAT THE CLIENT WANTS

It was established in the previous chapter that marketing ship management is a difficult task for three main reasons. Firstly, the fundamental separation of the shipowning from the ship management function has not been universally accepted in the shipping industry for various reasons. These include the belief that the usage of ship management companies enables shipowners to take a short-term view of shipowning with little regard for maintenance and the protection of asset value. Consequently, ship management companies have faced an uphill task when trying to convince certain sectors of the shipping community that shipmanagers are able to manage ships to comparable standards to those achieved by the leading integrated shipowners.

A second reason concerns the fact that the low barriers to entry to the ship management sector and the apparently attractive rewards on offer have given rise to a persistently over-supplied market. As a result intensive competition has characterized the ship management sector for a number of years making marketing a difficult task on factors other than the level of management fees quoted or vessel operating budgets submitted.

Thirdly, a lack of market statistics and in-depth analysis of who manages what in the shipping industry means that there is little accurate data on which to base marketing strategy, i.e. to explain precisely how and why the market is moving.

Despite the difficulties outlined, the basic objective of marketing ship management services is a straightforward one and no different to any other service industry. That is, a ship management company must understand what the shipowning client wants and do its utmost to deliver a service which meets client requirements on a consistent basis and at a competitive price.

But what does the client want? Somewhat surprisingly, this seemingly simple question has not attracted a significant amount of attention in the trade press or at shipping conferences. This may be explained by the fact that shipmanagers serve a varied client base characterized by shipowning companies with differing needs and requirements. It may also reflect a widespread assumption on the part of many shipmanagers as Rajaish Bajpaee, Managing Director of Eurasia, stated at the LSM Ship Management Conference in 1996 (Bajpaee 1996):

"We as corporate executives do not usually see what exactly customers want. We only predict and judge the needs and behaviour of customers based on experiences and perspectives."

For this reason Bajpaee advocates the use of various techniques including regular interviews with customers to prevent situations arising where "dissatisfied customers, very often do not say anything but just walk out".

A useful insight into the needs and requirements of customers was provided by the Riley Williams Associates (RWA) study referred to in Chapter 3. Conducted in the mid 1980s, the study noted that while commercial and employment linkages were important in the selection of a shipmanager, the harsh realities of squeezing even more effectiveness out of assets, for improved profitability or survival, were rapidly assuming much greater importance. However, as stated in an article in *Lloyd's Ship Manager* in March 1987 which reviewed the RWA study (LSM 1987):

"Price and cost sensitivities have increased, but not necessarily to the point of lowest 'price-cost' acceptance in all market segments. In many there has been a growing tendency for an owner to establish a better definition of the relationship between, on the one hand, budget and fee structure, and, on the other his expectations in respect of management performance."

A more recent insight into client requirements is provided in a paper presented by Paul Kerr, Marketing Manager of V Ships, to the 1996 LSM Ship Management Conference (Kerr 1996). His paper identified seven main market wants in terms of:

1 global coverage and a 24-hour/day on call service;
2 a diverse range of personalized services;
3 a person-to-person office-next-door mentality;
4 more attention paid to formal management methods and systems;
5 good (well qualified/experienced) people;
6 a solid reputation;
7 cost effectiveness—tight cost control.

These seven factors were derived from an independent research study commissioned by V Ships in 1991 and undertaken by London-based Stamford Research Group. The study was based on telephone and personal interviews with 50 primary and secondary clients (banks, charterers, insurance companies) of ship management companies to address such questions as the image of shipmanagers, why shipmanagers are used, how shipmanagers are selected and likely future trends.

The main findings of this research study are worth considering as they reflect the challenges faced by shipmanagers in the early 1990s and how the market has developed since then. The ten most notable study findings were that:

1 Shipmanagers faced an image problem but were seen as taking tangible steps towards raising professional standards through the introduction of formal (safety and/or quality) management systems.

2 Shipmanagers were used in many instances when the owner's fleet was too small to sustain a cost-effective in-house operation and when an owner required specialist expertise for a certain ship type.

3 Shipowners favoured the use of more than one shipmanager whenever practical to do so.

4 The process through which a shipmanager is selected was essentially an informal one where personal contacts and recommendations were very influential.

5 Shipowners tended to be loyal to their shipmanager(s).

6 Quality accreditation was becoming a more important factor in selecting a shipmanager.

7 Personal contact on a regular basis, perhaps by way of an account manager, was an important factor in client retention as was the shipmanager's understanding of the shipowner's particular business needs.

8 Many shipowners never considered using a shipmanager because of a fear of loss of control.

9 There was a reluctance by many shipowners to use smaller and newly-established shipmanagers due to a lack of confidence in the ability to control costs and/or technical know-how.

10 The location of the shipmanager's office was not an important consideration in shipmanager selection.

With the possible exception of the last finding listed and the absence of price, these ten main findings show few surprises. Taken together they reflected the conservatism of shipowners in the early 1990s and the fact that the decision-making process lacked sophistication. The study also shows that shipowners were very reluctant to switch shipmanager because of the cost penalties involved and due to a preparedness to tolerate poor performance. This latter finding challenged the belief expressed in the earlier RWA study that in the face of a pessimistic outlook in many shipping markets, shipowners were becoming more cost conscious and more willing at least to consider different options as and when ship management contracts came up for renewal.

If a similar study was conducted today, in all probability, important changes would be evident in certain key areas. For example, likely findings might include:

1 Despite the continuing importance of personal contacts and recommendations, the use of a more systematic and formalized selection process would be evident, including greater use of tendering, together with much more diligent performance monitoring.

2 Access to experienced and well-qualified seastaff would carry considerably more weight in the selection process particularly for certain specialist ship types where shortages are apparent.

3 Accreditation to a recognized safety and/or quality management standard is of greater importance due to the mandatory requirement for ship operating companies to comply with the ISM Code.

4 In the face of increasing regulatory pressures, the level of management fees charged is less of an issue compared with the standard of services delivered. However, as one marketing manager contacted by the author during the preparation of this chapter commented:

> "What we are finding in the market today is that owners want more for the same price not more for a higher price. Instead of a contract being negotiated over a short period of time based on cost alone as was often the case in the past, many owners today want meetings to discuss our abilities, to see our systems, meet our staff and to tell us how money does not matter. After all of this has happened, we then start to talk money and end up, in most cases, finding out that money matters very much to the owner who insists that we charge less than what we think is fair."

5 Greater importance is attached to the use of information technology (IT) and the willingness of the shipmanager to tailor systems and procedures to meet specific customer requirements.

A number of these points are revisited later in this chapter.

4.2 MARKETING STRATEGY

It is against the background of changing customer requirements described above that individual ship management companies shape their marketing strategies. In doing so the following important questions must be addressed:

(a) How to differentiate the company from the competition?
(b) How to achieve a profile in the marketplace?
(c) What sales message should be delivered to clients and potential clients?
(d) Who should be responsible for selling?

4.2.1 Differentiation

Various opportunities for differentiation exist. In recent years these opportunities have included:

1 Safety and Quality Management

This is perhaps the single most important opportunity for differentiation particularly since the largely intangible benefits offered during the early days of quality assurance gave way to the importance of mandatory compliance to the IMO's ISM Code.

2 Globalization

The ability of a shipmanager to offer a consistent service from various geographical regions is an opportunity for differentiation which has been grasped by a number of the larger ship management companies which are now represented by offices located in at least three continents—the Americas, Europe and Asia.

3 Service Diversity

This method of differentiation involves the shipmanager leveraging its brand by offering a one-stop shop of services to the client base. However, this approach has not been without criticism on the grounds that diversification of effort detracts from focused commitment in the delivery of core services.

4 Information Technology (IT)

The effective use of IT is a fairly recent opportunity which is currently being grasped by a number of shipmanagers as an important competitive advantage.

5 Shipmanager–Charterer Relationships

In certain shipping sectors, notably the tanker market, a number of shipmanagers are taking the opportunity to forge close working relationships with the users of their clients' vessels as a way of cementing shipowner-manager bonds.

In reviewing the above opportunities, it should be remembered that all are transient in such a dynamic and competitive marketplace. A shipmanager must make every effort, therefore, to identify opportunities for differentiation as early as possible and to fully exploit competitive advantage before other shipmanagers recover lost ground.

4.2.2 Profile

Profile can be achieved in a number of ways. The primary and most important method is personal contact with clients and potential clients by way of regular visits. These personal contacts are an integral part of relationship marketing (see section 4.4). Such personal contacts can be reinforced by a number of secondary methods including the distribution of brochures, mailshots and press releases, advertising and miscellaneous PR activities such as presentations at conferences and stands at exhibitions. Collectively such initiatives help to keep the shipmanager's name visible in the marketplace. Arguably, a number of the larger shipmanagers have achieved a high degree of visibility in the marketplace through such initiatives.

4.2.3 The Sales Message

Of the various methods used by shipmanagers to communicate a sales message in the marketplace advertisements in the specialized trade press (notably *Lloyd's List, Tradewinds, Lloyd's Ship Manager, Seatrade Review, Lloyd's Shipping Economist, Fairplay*, etc.) are used on a consistent basis.

The use of advertisements by ship management companies was discussed by Spruyt in the previous edition (Spruyt 1994). In comparing the messages portrayed by ship management companies placing adverts in two important supplements in 1989 and 1993, Spruyt noted a major sea change in thinking reflecting the growing importance of safety and quality management in the ship management sector.

Spruyt's beliefs are supported by a senior advertising executive from one of the major maritime publishing houses contacted by the author in mid 1997. According to this executive, the basic sales message conveyed by shipmanagers has changed significantly over the past ten years. A fundamental change in fact took place around the time of the formation of the International Ship Managers' Association (ISMA) in 1991. Pre-ISMA, a large number of companies claiming to offer independent ship management services conveyed the basic message: "we manage your ships better than the next guy". Since the formation of ISMA, however, the message has changed to, "your ships are safe in our hands" with emphasis placed on terms such as responsibility and commitment.

Interestingly, this fundamental change has been accompanied by two related developments. Firstly, the overall advertising spend by shipmanagers has decreased with only a relatively small number of the larger ship management companies continuing to advertise on a regular basis. This decline may reflect a general disillusionment in the effectiveness of advertising. Secondly, greater sophistication is evident in terms of the visual images used to convey the sales message, i.e. a movement away from the traditional maritime images of sextants, flags, marine charts, ships and seascapes to images not directly related to the business of managing ships towards, for example, hot air balloons (Columbia), ocean-going yachts (Denholms), seagulls/otters (Acomarit) and dairy cows (Dobson)—the latter being one of the more imaginative offerings of recent years. Nevertheless, with one or two notable exceptions, shipmanagers in general still favour a traditional approach.

In providing an insight into current thinking, Table 4.1 presents the findings of an analysis of 30 advertisements placed by 24 shipmanagers in various shipping publications during the first nine months of 1997. This table shows that of the 61 messages conveyed in the 30 advertisements, 38 are categorized by the author to be primary messages with the remainder secondary (the distinction drawn between the two make on the basis of the point size and position of text and the use of visual images to reinforce written messages). The analysis shows that while the importance of safety and quality management was the most frequently used (17 instances), no

Table 4.1: Analysis of ship management advertisements

Message: P=Primary; S=Secondary

No. Company (No. of Ads)	Training	S&Q Mgmt.	Global Cover	Personal Service	Experience	Service Range	Specialization	Responsibility	Other (Specified)
1. ACOMARIT (3)	P	S/S	S/S						P(Environment) P(Information)
2. INTERORIENT		P							
3. OSTERR. LLOYD (2)		P/P		S					S(Europe)
4. RED BAND		P		S					
5. HANSEATIC		P			S				
6. SEASCOT				P					
7. ASP					P				
8. ANTHONY VEDER						P / S			
9. COLUMBIA		S					P	P	
10. NORTHERN MARINE	P	S	P						
11. AHRENKIEL			P						
12. BARBER		S						P	P(Asia)
13. THOME		P				P			
14. SUISSE-ATLANTIQUE					P				S(Cyprus)
15. HARMSTORF		S		S	S				
16. MTM				P			P		
17. ANGLO EASTERN	P	S			P			P	P(Motivation)
18. DENHOLM (3)		S	P/P						P(Location)
19. V SHIPS									
20. EURASIA			S			P			
21. WALLEM (2)		P/P		P	P				S(Size)
22. JEBSENS		S			P				
23. ROPNER					S				P(Relaunch)
24. DOBSON				S					P(Leadership)
PRIMARY TOTAL:	3	8	4	3	5	3	2	3	7
SECONDARY TOTAL:	0	9	3	4	3	1	0	0	3
GRAND TOTAL:	3	17	7	7	8	4	2	3	10

single message predominated reflecting the diversity of opinion among ship-managers as to perceived client requirements.

4.2.4 Responsibility for Selling

Two main schools of thought are evident. In the majority of cases, through either choice or necessity, the sales and marketing function is performed by the Managing Director (or equivalent position) as part of his overall duties assisted, as required, by other members of senior management. Support for this school of thought is based on the belief that not only is this the most cost-effective method but also that selling is best left to staff who have a thorough knowledge of all aspects of ship management especially the technical function. The drawback, however, as highlighted by Spruyt (1994), is that the resources needed to fulfil a pro-active marketing function are considerable, especially if regular visits to existing and potential clients are to be maintained.

The opposing school of thought supports the belief that marketing is best left to specialist staff who are able to tackle all aspects of sales and marketing i.e. what might be described as the "hard" and the "soft" elements. In the former case, this involves the preparation of quotations and budgets and the negotiation of management contracts. Although use of labour-saving computerized budget programs is now commonplace, the time needed to prepare, review and present pre-contract documentation is considerable and should be viewed in the light of the fact that in order to win ten new contracts during the course of a year, perhaps up to 100 quotations have to be prepared. Furthermore, as deals become more complex, the sheer volume of information which needs to be submitted increases.

In the latter case, so-called "soft" selling techniques include any PR, advertising, brochure production and related activities. These can, of course, be contracted out to media specialists. However, many of the larger ship management companies have at least one dedicated salesman/marketing manager who is responsible for all aspects of marketing and who is able to call on the expertise of various company specialists as the sale process develops.

Regardless of which school of thought is adopted, it is important to recognize that all company employees, both office and seastaff, have a role to play in sales and marketing. For example, although the MD is invariably the primary point of contact for the client, a superintendent is often in regular contact with the shipowning client's representative(s) and has, therefore, a responsibility for client relations. Furthermore, a well turned out and presented crew can speak volumes for a company during a ship visit by a potential client.

4.3 THE SALES PROCESS

Having discussed the marketing of ship management services in general terms it is useful to focus attention on the actual process through which the shipmanager takes on new business. While no two deals will be exactly the same in how they are conceived and/or how they develop, it is possible to describe the sales process in terms of a number of typical procedural steps.

Figure 4.1 depicts six such steps which are applicable to the takeover of a vessel from a shipowning client in the following way:

Step 1

This initial step involves the identification of the sales opportunity either during the course of or following on from a client visit, receipt of a tender invitation or other means. At this stage the primary task of the shipmanager is to collect as much information as possible about the potential client and the vessel(s) involved. Aside from the basic technical and operational (essentially vessel trading pattern) details, information is sought on what is and is not to be included in the budget quotation (for example an insured value is sought or estimated if insurance costs are to be included) and preferred crewing options. At this early stage, the shipmanager will also establish who are the key decision-makers involved, what are the likely time scales to be followed and whether the enquiry is a serious one or merely a "fishing" exercise.

Step 2

The second step involves the preparation and submission of an indicative budget quotation usually with a number of different crewing options. Typically, the figures produced show a 12-month projection although, occasionally, longer-term forecasts are submitted based on estimated annual inflation factors.

Indicative budgets are submitted with a number of provisos including, for example, the fact that insurance costs are based only on a desk quotation, purchasing costs on an assumed "normal" level of stores and spares on board, repair and maintenance costs on the assumption that the vessel has been maintained to date in a "good" technical condition with all equipment functioning, as well as other assumptions regarding the number of projected crew changes and communications expenses.

Step 3

At this stage the potential client reviews the indicative budget and, depending on circumstances and if not done so already, may seek a number of comparative quotations—typically between two and five. A preliminary (or follow-up) meeting is arranged at either party's premises at which the basic terms and conditions of the management agreement and any other matters concerning service delivery are discussed.

Figure 4.1: The ship management sales process

Step 1:   Initial identification of
                               the sales opportunity

Step 2:   S/M prepares and submits
                               indicative budget quotation

Step 3:   Prospective client reviews budget,
                               compares competitive quotes
                               and calls preliminary meeting to
                               clarify budget and terms of
                               management agreement

Step 4:   S/M conducts pre-takeover vessel
                               inspection and prepares/submits
                               report along with revised budget

Step 5:   Conduct of follow-up meeting to
                               review, discuss and finalize contractual
                               documentation. (Reference sought and
                               checked by prospective client and/or
                               S/M managed vessels visited)

Step 6:   Finalization and signature of management
                               agreement and commencement of
                               vessel takeover procedure

Step 4

A pre-takeover vessel inspection is undertaken at this stage during which the ship management company collects all the information needed to confirm or amend the figures presented in the indicative budget. The findings of this inspection are usually collated in the form of a short report which highlights any particular areas of concern regarding the vessel's technical and operational condition. Any outstanding deficiencies are identified and a timescale for rectification (either prior or immediately after takeover) is agreed.

Step 5

This, perhaps most critical, step involves the submission of the revised budget and pre-takeover inspection report the content of which is usually discussed at a further meeting. This same meeting will, typically, also discuss and resolve any clauses in the management agreement which the client and/or its legal representative have raised. Vessel takeover logistics are also discussed and any pre-delivery expenses confirmed. If the shipmanager is accredited to the quality standard ISO 9002 and/or ISMA's Code of Shipmanagement Standards, a contract review procedure will be performed during this stage. This procedure ensures that the shipmanager, as the supplier of the ship management services required by the client, is fully able to deliver the services according to the terms and conditions set out in the management agreement and according to the agreed vessel operating budget. In practice, this means that the various heads of department, specifically the technical and personnel directors, "sign off" the final budget and management agreement and a record to confirm this is generated.

During Step 5 the potential client may also seek references from the shipmanager's existing clients and also visit a vessel in the managed fleet.

Step 6

This final step sees the finalization of the vessel operating budget and signature of the management agreement. The vessel takeover procedure is commenced usually with the placement of two/three staff on board and notification of relevant authorities and interested parties.

It is important to stress that the process outlined above will vary significantly depending on circumstances. On important variable is the fact that certain shipmanagers insist that a vessel is inspected before a budget is issued. Another variable is time. Under normal circumstances, a typical sales process will span some two to three months. However, the process can be considerably longer if a formal tendering procedure is followed involving several ship management companies which must pre-qualify and be short-listed before standing a chance of winning the contract. Moreover, an initial sales visit yielding a possible sales opportunity may only bear fruit some two to three years later. Conversely, circumstances leading to the enforced sale of a vessel or a change in the shareholding of the shipowning company may condense the sales process to a period of just two to three weeks.

4.4 THE WAY FORWARD

Before looking ahead it is useful to refer back to the findings of the RWA study previously referred to in this chapter. This study was conducted a decade ago at a time when opinion was divided as to the future of the ship management sector. One school of thought believed that there was limited growth potential and that shipmanagers could only grow their managed fleets at the expense of each other. The opposing school held the belief that exciting new growth was possible.

The RWA study came down in favour of the high growth scenario. However, its authors stated that the successful shipmanagers would only be those who were prepared to radically rethink their marketing strategies. In specific terms the main study findings were:

1 Shipmanagers needed to commit far more resources to understanding what was described by *Lloyd's Ship Manager's* review of the study as "the systematic understanding of the market structure". Only in this way RWA argued could the shipmanager's own strengths and weaknesses be meaningfully assessed in comparison with its competitors.

2 It was no longer appropriate for the successful shipmanagers to think of themselves as merely suppliers of services but rather as "generators and facilitators of business; business that brings added value to others and hence to themselves". RWA argued that shipmanagers needed to be more pro-active in marketing and be prepared to work with banks and financial institutions in the development of new sources of business.

3 More effort was needed by shipmanagers to understand what were described as the broader aspects of client requirements rather than the narrow "first level" needs. RWA argued that in this way shipmanagers could improve customer satisfaction and generate fresh business opportunities.

4 Amid the mounting pressures in the marketplace at the time to reduce costs especially *via* the use of cheaper crews, the study warned that shipmanagers should not lose sight of the need for quality control if reputation in the marketplace was to be protected. In stating this belief, RWA recognized that this would cost money as considerable resources would be needed to improve systems and increase staff training to ensure that control over service delivery was maintained regardless of whether cheaper crews were utilized.

In conclusion, the LSM article stated:

"The ship management market is a maturing market that is still undergoing structural changes and delivering opportunities in its wake. It is also a more active market. There is little doubt that an opportunity exists for some management companies to take hold of the supply side. In so doing they can improve their own margins, generate new business for both their core and ancillary services, and place themselves in a strong survival and growth position."

Many of the points made by the RWA study ring true and, indeed, remain relevant in today's market. The successful shipmanagers have been those who have recognized that the shipping industry is a dynamic one which continues to undergo structural change and are prepared to be creative in marketing themselves as what RWA termed facilitators and generators of added value.

So with the RWA findings in mind, what of the future?

Although any attempt to forecast the future of the shipping industry and the marketing implications for the ship management sector is fraught with difficulties, three existing trends look set to continue to exert influence over how individual ship management companies shape their marketing strategy.

Firstly, despite increasing barriers to entry and the rising cost of service delivery, persistent oversupply in the ship management sector is likely to continue to under-pin intensive competition for the foreseeable future. As a direct result, ship management fees are unlikely to increase in real terms and the scope for shipmanagers being able to recover the rising cost of service delivery will be limited. The structure of the industry is likely to remain fragmented, therefore, with none of the major ship management companies able to command a significant market share.

Secondly, the decision-making process through which ship management companies are selected by shipowners is likely to become more sophisticated and rigorous with, for example, the use of the formal tendering process more common-place. As a result, shipmanagers will be under increasing pressure to demonstrate their capabilities and proficiencies which will, in turn, encourage them to bench-mark their performance against their competitors. For their part, larger shipowning clients are likely to produce their own "White Lists" of approved shipmanagers organized by ship type and to maintain league tables of shipmanager performance where persistently low scores will lead to de-selection.

Thirdly, the movement towards more complex deals between shipmanagers and shipowners looks set to continue. Recent years have witnessed an increasing number of contracts based on joint venture type relationships where deal construction is based on the need for shipmanagers to meet very specific client requirements. Shipmanagers have, therefore, needed to be more flexible regarding service delivery including the areas of the world they are prepared to operate from.

Collectively, the three factors outlined above indicate that shipmanagers face a challenging marketplace in the future. In meeting this challenge, the successful companies will be those which are able to detect new opportunities in the market-place ahead of the competition and be in a position to deliver high service standards on a consistent basis and at a competitive price. For this reason shipmanagers must be pro-active rather than reactive.

4.4.1 Relationship Marketing

Future success will also depend on how well a shipmanager understands the changing nature of its relationships with existing clients and how well these relationships are managed. In recent years, the increasing concerns over the professional standards of ship management companies have given rise to greater emphasis being placed on the contractual aspect of manager-owner relations as well as service delivery based on safety and quality management disciplines. Furthermore, in the past two years strategic and administrative aspects (especially better communications) have come to the fore with the increasing propensity of joint venture type relationships.

Although these various factors have exerted considerable influence over the marketing strategies formulated by ship management companies in the 1990s, it is the personal aspect of shipmanager-shipowner relations which has continued to exert a strong influence over many deals. This personal aspect has received very little attention. However, Panayides (1996) discusses its importance in terms of what is described as relationship marketing whereby the service supplier obtains an in-depth knowledge of each client's business practice, creates a close relationship with each client which extends beyond a single discrete transaction and manages the relationship to deliver client satisfaction and enhanced profitability. This latter factor is based, in part, on long-term client retention given that the cost of obtaining a new customer is estimated to be at least six times as much as retaining an existing one. A further benefit of relationship marketing is the fact that the service supplier will be able to sell additional services to the same customer over time to the extent that the client values the convenience and simplicity of the one-stop shop approach.

Panayides and Gray (1997) identify the key characteristics of relationship marketing compared with the traditional transaction-based approach (see Figure 4.2). These characteristics, which include informal/social communication and psychological governance, emphasize the importance of commitment and trust as the basis of building long-term relationships. While it is true to say that the benefits of relationship marketing take time to materialize, it is also true to say that the personal factors which it encompasses enable the successful shipmanager to truly differentiate itself from the competition. While other factors such as safety and quality management, IT and location are transient and fairly easy to replicate, personal relationships are not and can, therefore, yield enormous marketing benefits.

Figure 4.2: A comparison of transaction with relationship marketing

	TRANSACTION	RELATIONSHIP
Shipmanager's orientation	obtain contract	build relationship
Shipmanager's focus	service	service and client
Communication	formal	formal and social (informal)
Commitment/trust/cooperation/ investments	limited	high
Length of relationship	short-term	long-term
Governance	contractual	contractual and psychological
Shipowner's orientation	"shop-around"	true loyalty

Reproduced from "A Relationship Approach for Marketing the Professional Ship Management Service", Panayides, P and Gray, R, Centre for International Shipping & Transport, University of Plymouth, UK 1997.

5

WHICH SHIPMANAGER?

5.1 THE RIGHT SHIPMANAGER

Choosing the right shipmanager is no easy task. This is not because the shipowner has limited choice. As the examination of the supply side of the ship management market equation in Chapter 3 revealed, there are numerous companies offering ship management services from many different locations worldwide. The difficulty is more to do with the numerous factors which influence the shipowner's decision-making. While some of these factors can be readily quantified, others are less tangible and must be assessed on a qualitative, judgemental basis.

It is, of course, as with any outsourcing decision, important to make the right decision regarding the choice of supplier. The decision is of strategic importance to the shipowner given that it will be reliant to a greater or lesser degree on the professionalism of the shipmanager not least its ability to control costs. The shipmanager will be required to maintain high service standards perhaps over a long period of time during which the employment of the ship may change many times, as might the deployment area and the general state of the market. During this period, the vessel will undoubtedly be subject to numerous inspections by flag state, port state, charterers, insurers, classification societies and other bodies. The shipowner's reputation will be continually on the line and, if the shipmanager fails to deliver, can be irreparably damaged.

This chapter addresses the question "which shipmanager?". It does so essentially from the shipowner's standpoint and by examining the various selection criteria which a shipowner may or may not take into consideration, the selection process itself, some golden rules which are useful to follow and post-decision management i.e. how to manage a shipmanager.

5.2 SELECTION CRITERIA

The criteria used by a shipowner to select a shipmanager will vary according to the experience of the shipowner including whether it has worked in the past with a ship management company. The selection of a manager and the process will also differ depending upon the background of the owner, and it is therefore relevant to look at the different reasons for employing a manager; it can be one or more of the following where the shipmanager:

- provides a function that the owner does not cover itself or provides a support to the owners for part of the management function;
- provides cost-efficient management with access to good and economical resources;
- provides other special advantages like tax, liability cushion, quality assurance system and the like.

In most cases, using a manager means that the owner does not itself have the knowledge and expertise in-house to run the ships, although it is not unusual for a company with a ship management function to use a manager for benchmarking a special section of its fleet. If we look at the first of the above-listed cases, where the shipowner does not have the relevant departments, we find that a situation exists where a detailed knowledge and understanding of a very important part of the business is missing.

It is often claimed that money in shipping is made by the asset-players and that it is not necessary to know anything about how the ships are run or employed. For some this might be the case, but for those who have been in shipping for a long time and also desire to make money from ship operation, knowledge of the ships and their management is important. It is the ship and the performance of the ship that is marketed and sold and it is the ship itself and its complement that is in the marketplace.

The argument for an integrated model, which includes ship management, becomes stronger as the operation gets more sophisticated. In the highly specialized sectors of shipping, a close relationship between all different sectors of the business becomes essential. This is valid both for the day-to-day interface between chartering, commercial operations and ship management, as well as the development and contracting of the right assets and the right investments. With more standard operations of simple ships this argument becomes less valid, and it is, of course, mainly in the larger general shipping market that one will find the asset players.

One can also look at it from another angle, the good experienced shipmanager will have expertise in running most types of ships. It can provide that specialized service to an owner or operator who wants to enter a new market segment or it can take care of a group of ships that falls outside the main business of an owner.

In addition to the shipowner's background, selection criteria will also vary according to the individual circumstances surrounding the decision—circumstances which include the number and type(s) of ships involved, how the vessel(s) in question will be employed and time pressures. The basic objectives of the shipowner will also have an important bearing—an aspect of the selection process which is addressed in section 5.3—while a number of the main selection criteria are reviewed below.

5.2.1 Competence

The fundamental question to be answered (and the starting point in the selection process) is: does a shipmanager have the necessary skills and experience to manage the vessel(s) in question? In practice, this question is broken down into:

(a) Does the shipmanager offer a successful track record of managing ships of the same or a similar type (including, perhaps, experience of a particular main engine type and cargo handling gear)?

(b) Does the shipmanager currently have the same or a similar type of vessel under management?

(c) Do the office staff offer the right skills and experience?

(d) Is the shipmanager consistently able to recruit seastaff with the relevant skills and experience and, importantly, to develop those skills further by way of relevant training programmes?

(e) Is the shipmanager aware of how recently-introduced and impending changes in national and international regulations, as well as technological developments in cargo handling, will affect the operation of a particular ship type?

(f) Does the shipmanager provide other services or benefits to the owners like the management of tankers in full compliance with OPA 90 requirements?

(g) Does the shipmanager have the capability to meet owners' special requirements in terms of reporting, documentation or other special functions?

Of course the number of shipmanagers capable of managing a specific type of vessel will vary according to the degree of specialization. For most ship types, there will be no shortage of available shipmanagers although a shipowner may decide to rule out certain managers if it is providing services to a direct competitor (even though assurances of impartiality and "Chinese walls" are given). Furthermore, a shipowner may decide at an early stage to work with a shipmanager that specializes in a certain ship type rather than a generalist.

5.2.2 Manning

A key part of ship management is the manning of the ship and it is therefore essential that the manager has adequate manning resources. It is of strategic importance to a manager to have access to a reliable source of manning. Being able to provide well-qualified, stable and economical officers and ratings is a main sales point for a manager.

The lack of a strong link between the owner and a manager is often mentioned as a negative point when a ship is given to a manager. The good manager will be better able to provide a stable, secure workplace for his employees than the owner buying and selling ships and consequently changing his demand for officers and crew. By providing such long-term employment prospects, the manager should be able to attract and keep good people.

A frequently discussed topic is whether the shipmanager, compared to the integrated management, is willing to spend money on training and long-term development of his seagoing personnel. This is very different from management company to management company as it is between different owner managers. The large and serious shipmanager will invest in training its personnel ashore and afloat and so will the good and serious owner. There will unfortunately always be poachers out there who spend nothing on training and those who will try to attract well-trained personnel from other companies by offering to pay higher salaries.

5.2.3 Costs

While costs may not always be the most important selection criteria they will invariably influence the shipowner's final choice of shipmanager. In practice, shipowners view costs in terms of two (possibly three) separate components: the overall vessel running cost (or, in the case of a crew management contract, the crewing cost); the management or manning fee; and any indirect costs which the shipowner perceives in terms of the impact that the choice of a shipmanager has on the owner's standing in the marketplace.

Probably the most common reason for selecting a manager is to cut the running costs. In most cases, a manager can achieve this but that might also have a cost. Aggressive cost cutting can have a number of negative consequences and if not monitored properly will almost inadvertently have long-term effects on the ship.

The positive sides of cost reductions are those resulting from the good manager's capability to buy cheaper, whether it is supplies, spares or insurance. It may be able to provide the same quality at a lower price based on better purchasing power and better systems.

Cost cutting only becomes a problem when maintenance is reduced below acceptable levels. This occurs when rules and regulations and, consequently, safety is sacrificed to reduce M&R and purchasing; or when the quality and training of officers and crew is not maintained to the level necessary for a safe and proper operation.

Insufficient maintenance is in itself a difficult thing to define. What is sufficient for day-to-day operation of the ship for a year or two might not, or will normally not, be sufficient for the long-term protection of the asset value. If you are in short-term asset play, this could be fine for you even if maintenance costs were minimum over a few years and then the ship was sold. It does not really matter because later the cost to bring the ship up to good standard will be more expensive. This is a main point of criticism and those buying ships that have been managed on a minimum budget are well advised to inspect thoroughly.

A manager is often entrusted with management of a ship without information on the duration of his assignment. The manager is normally selected on the basis of a low budget and will provide one without any long-term maintenance consideration, and in general without any margin.

Ask for quotations

One should ask for budget quotations from a selected number of managers and be sure to give relevant information. One can only expect to receive reliable budget quotations if proper and accurate information is given. Actually, the quote given before a ship inspection can be considered as an indication only, and when comparing different quotations it is important also to consider the assumptions the manager has used and any reservations specified. When comparing quotations some items are directly comparable while others are more subjective. Directly comparable items are:

- manning cost (with same complement)
- victualling
- insurance cost
- management fee

Insurance cost is a good indication of the manager's purchasing strength, but is also an indication of the quality of his operation. A good manager with a good loss record will be able to budget with low insurance cost.

Although the management fee is an item that is frequently focused on, it only represents 10 per cent of the total cost. The bottom line and the performance of a manager should count more than a few dollars on the fee.

Let one or two of the short-listed managers inspect the ship. Make the ship and its records available. Only after this can a budget be really reliable, and it also removes any excuse later from the manager's side if the budget is exceeded.

Indicative budgets

Indicative budgets are prepared by the shipmanager at the request of the shipowner at an early stage in the decision-making process in order to provide an indication of the likely running/manning costs which will be incurred over a specified period (normally one year). As stated in Chapter 2, indicative budgets comprise estimates which are often based on the disclosure of a limited amount of information by the shipowner and, therefore, should be treated with utmost caution. Nevertheless, given that many shipmanagers have considerable experience in operating certain vessel types and a good understanding of the performance and reliability of specific types of equipment and machinery, the quotations prepared are accurate in many respects and can be used by the shipowner to conduct a preliminary assessment of capability and cost competitiveness.

Indicative budgets also reflect a shipmanager's experience in managing certain vessel types as well as its buying power in the marketplace for items such as insurance and consumables including lubricating oils, paints and chemicals. In certain cases, the shipmanager's indicative budget will reflect the determination of the shipmanager to win the contract regardless of whether the vessel operating cost quoted is realistic or whether the fees charged will enable the shipmanager to make a profit.

Taken together, these various factors explain why indicative budgets often vary considerably. To illustrate this point, Table 5.1 presents a comparison of four indicative budgets which were prepared by four shipmanagers competing for a full management contract for a handy size products tanker. In this actual example from the early 1990s, the four shipmanagers were asked to submit a budget based on the basic specifications of an unnamed ship, its approximate insured value and its trading area. Each manager was also asked to submit its recommended manning level and favoured crew nationality.

Table 5.1: A comparison of indicative annual quotations

Example:	A mid 1980s built 40,000 dwt Products Tanker (1,000 US$)			
	COMPANY A	**COMPANY B**	**COMPANY C**	**COMPANY D**
No of Crew	25	22	25	22
Nationality	Indian	Korean	Indian	Korean
Total Manning				
Costs	731.2	720.5	616.0	776.2
Hull Insurance	196.3	175.3	246.3	222.4
P&I	134.4	62.2	58.4	52.6
Stores	75.5	66.9	60.0	60.5
Lub Oil	65.8	51.2	71.0	46.2
D/D	120.0	120.0	120.0	120.0
R+M	177.1	85.7	113.0	70.0
Administration	188.0	137.0	107.0	175.0
TOTAL	**1,688.3**	**1,418.8**	**1,391.7**	**1,522.9**
US$/Day	4,626	3,887	3,813	4,172

The numbers presented in Table 5.1 make interesting reading and also raise several questions. In addition to the US$813/day difference between the most expensive (shipmanager A) and the least expensive (C), closer examination of the aggregated numbers shows significant variation in the major cost components.

- Manning costs. Comparing A to C one would automatically ask whether they both include the same expenses like crew travel, victualling, sign on costs etc., and it must also be clarified whether the complement have ITF cover or are under any other arrangement. Similar questions would be asked when comparing B and D even though the differences are smaller.
- Insurance cost. There are large differences which can both reflect the purchasing power and the quality i.e. the loss record of the manager.
- Stores and M+R can only be considered indications at this stage, as they will indicate what good purchasing contracts the manager has, and good purchasing contracts are in general something an owner would seek in a manager.

One should also ask for contract prices on the consumption on which the quotation is based.
- The administration costs are directly comparable, but one should ask for a split between fee and other billed costs.

These and other items would merit further examination by the shipowner to ensure that it understands the basis on which the indicative budget was prepared including, importantly, what the figures include and do not include.

Despite their obvious limitations, indicative budgets can be used by the shipowner to rule in/out certain shipmanagers at an early stage of the decision-making process. Often, a shipowner will decide to rule out the cheapest offer(s) on the grounds that a shipmanager has failed to appreciate the complexity of the vessel(s) in question or because an unrealistic approach has been adopted. A shipowner may also decide to discount the most expensive quote because of lack of competitiveness.

Full quotations

It is only when the shortlisted managers are given the opportunity to inspect the vessel(s) in question that a more accurate and, therefore, meaningful estimate of vessel running costs can be prepared. Table 5.2 presents a comparison of two detailed quotations as prepared in the mid 1990s by competing managers seeking the full management contract of a mid 1980s built medium sized containership. In reviewing the two sets of figures the following points should be noted; in addition to the comments accompanying Table 5.1.

Table 5.2: A comparison of two shipmanagers' competitive quotes

Example: 10-year old, 15,000 dwt geared container vessel
1,000 teu, 16 KNOT, Sulzer (10,800 BHP)
Insured value = US$20 million

	MANAGER "A"	MANAGER "B"
PROPOSED COMPLEMENT – Recommended nationalities	24 – European officers – Filipino/Russian Senior/Junior officers – Filipino ratings	21 – Full Ukrainian
CREWING COSTS ($/Day) – Wages – Travel & expenses – Victualling	1,090 260 160	805 250 125
TOTAL CREWING (% of total)	**1,510** (37%)	**1,180** (34%)

Table 5.2—cont.

INSURANCE COSTS ($/Day)				
– H&M	360		260	
– P&I	105		125	
– Other (LOH, FD&D)	150		140	
TOTAL INSURANCE	**615**	(15%)	**525**	(15%)
STORES & SPARES ($/Day)				
– Deck	215		175	
– Engine	465		245	
TOTAL STORES & SPARES	**680**	(17%)	**420**	(12%)
LUBRICANTS ($/Day)	**245**	(6%)	**275**	(8%)
REPAIR & MAINTENANCE ($/Day)				
– Deck	85			
– Engine	270		265	
– Survey	55		55	
TOTAL R&M	**410**	(10%)	**320**	(9%)
D/D PROVISION ($/Day)	**220**	(5%)	**495**	(14%)
ADMINISTRATION ($/Day)				
– Management Fee	240		260	
– General	155		45	
TOTAL ADMINISTRATION	**395**	(10%)	**305**	(8%)
GRAND TOTAL	**4,075**		**3,520**	

1 In addition to the fact that shipmanager B is offering an apparent saving of US$555/day over manager A, significant variations are evident in virtually all of the main cost elements.

2 The biggest variation is in the area of manning costs both in terms of the number and nationality of the recommended complement. The additional three crew recommended by shipmanager A were a fourth engineer, an extra electrician (to cope with reefer boxes) and a deck cadet. This manning proposal also mentions European officers. For a total cost picture nationality and number must be known.

3 While P&I premiums are broadly comparable, the US$100/day difference in H&M may reflect shipmanager B's stronger buying power and use of different markets as well as the possibility that collision insurance is included (rather than under P&I cover).

4 Stores and spares should be evaluated together with repair and maintenance as different managers have different accounting practices under these headings.

There is a difference of US$350/day in favour of B, but this might in part be negated by the US$275/day higher drydocking provision. The higher drydocking provision could reflect the fact that many R&M tasks which shipmanager A will perform as routine will be entered on the drydock list by B, but a drydock reserve could also be just a rule of thumb estimate, thus not reflecting different maintenance policy.

A further question is whether both managers use the same intervals between dockings and whether they have foreseen dockings in the same geographical area.

5 In the case of administration costs, while the management fees quoted are similar, shipmanager A proposes a general expenses category equating to US$56,575/year.

The budgets submitted by the competing shipmanagers would prompt many questions seeking clarification and, importantly, would serve as the starting point of further negotiations. For example, if the shipowner has reservations about the use of a full east European crew then it might request shipmanager B to rerun its numbers on the basis of different nationalities (perhaps Indians and/or Filipinos). Conversely, the shipowner may request a reduction in shipmanager A's complement to bring it in line with shipmanager B's. Moreover, the shipowner may well be uncomfortable with shipmanager B's heavy reliance on drydocking particularly if the vessel is dependent on its cranes being fully serviceable at all intended ports of call. These discussions will be influenced by a number of factors including the historical performance of the ship and the shipowner's freight market expectations and debt financing commitments which will determine the size of the operating margin and, ultimately, the expected profitability.

In conducting these negotiations, the shipowner's basic aims are to ensure that it ends up with a budget which is both realistic and affordable. The shipowner must also be clear as to what the budgeted figures include and do not include. Some shipmanagers prefer to quote prices which will include all anticipated costs with the exception of an additional daily charge if a superintendent, for example, attends the ship on more days than the agreed allocation set out in the management agreement (typically six days/year). Other managers, however, will quote a lower budget but charge miscellaneous services as extra. For example, a safety audit may be charged out at US$4,000–5,000, the preparation of an oil pollution contingency/response plan at US$1,000 and even document storage at US$500/year.

5.2.4 Size

The relevance of size when choosing a shipmanager is an ongoing debate. Sterrett (1996), for example, provides a useful summary of the various pros and cons of using a small, medium or large size manager (see Table 5.3). In arguing the case for selecting a large ship management company, Gilbert (1995) and others refer to the increasing regulatory requirements which have been imposed on the shipping

Table 5.3: Large, medium and small shipmanagers compared (After Sterrett, 1996)

SMALL (<10)	MEDIUM (21–50)
Strengths	*Strengths*
* Every member of staff can be very focused on every ship * Creates possibility of "personalized" service * Improved level of "communications" (every staff member knows what's going on) * Bureaucracy can be minimized * Staff tend to be multi-skilled	* Loss of one or several ships is not fatal * Critical mass achieved * Greater buying power * Can establish own training regimes * Can specialize in more than one market
Weaknesses	*Weaknesses*
* Small revenue base * Susceptible to loss of one ship or client affecting viability * Lower buying power * Greater dependence on each member of staff * Loss of multi-skilled staff member may severely damage service delivery * Difficulty in maintaining a critical mass * Need to outsource some specialist input may cause greater financial pressure and lower profit margins * Can only operate from one or a maximum of two sites, so geographical coverage poor * Outsourcing crew supply can cause quality problems * Average cost of employee high * Difficult to market * Difficult to service more than one market	* Loss of control if expanding too quickly **LARGE (>50)** *Strengths* * "Household" name, business comes to you * Can create global structure * Own training regimes in each supply centre * Can support all specialist skills in-house * Immense buying power * Opportunities for diversification into related markets (value added services) * Not dependent on one source of manpower * Opportunity to create "specialist" mini-fleets *Weaknesses* * Potential loss of control * Need for rigid policies/procedures to ensure maintenance of standards in all disciplines * Can become distant for clients * Potential range of clients with differing standards/ideals

industry in recent years, notably OPA 1990, the ISM Code and the revised STCW, which necessitate a shipmanager being able to provide substantial resources to ensure that a shipowner fully complies with the prevailing regulations. Other considerations of importance are the ability to offer a comprehensive "product range", the availability of extensive back-up resources to cope with emergency situations and, in the interests of the shipmanager's ability to provide a cost effective service, the financial strength to invest in information technology and to exercise clout in the marketplace in the purchasing of insurance, stores, spares and the miscellaneous services required including drydocking and port agency.

The big-is-beautiful school of thought also cites the advantages that a large shipmanager can offer in terms of safety and quality management. To install a system is expensive but more cost effective the larger the organization involved. Furthermore, to maintain and continuously improve the system is also resource intensive and may require further downstream investment if the shipmanager wishes to exert tight control over the most important factor which impacts the quality of the service it provides to the shipowner—manpower.

The opposing view as argued by Campbell (1995) and others stresses that in spite of the growing regulatory pressures, small ship management companies do have a continuing role to play especially if available resources are focused on one or two specialized areas. This school of thought is further supported by the oft-cited view that only the smaller shipmanager can provide a personalized service tailored towards the specific needs of the individual client.

In the selection process the size of the shipmanager may or may not be an issue providing that the shipowner is satisfied that sufficient resources are available to meet its needs. In comparing budget quotations, the shipowner will invariably test the price competitiveness of the various goods and services to be supplied and make a judgement as to how important such savings are within the overall choice of shipmanager. It is debatable, therefore, as to the importance of this factor other than, perhaps, the question of compatibility, i.e. the size of the shipowning company in relation to the size of the shipmanager. For example, a small shipowner may feel that it can exert little influence over a shipmanager controlling a large managed fleet.

5.2.5 Location

The question as to how significant the location of a shipmanager's office is in the selection process is also debatable. In the past, proximity to the client was considered to be of major importance to most of the larger ship management companies hence the efforts made since the late 1980s to globalize their office organizations. Indeed, this process is an ongoing one whereby the larger shipmanagers are seeking to offer a comprehensive range of services from most of the major shipowning centres and close to the major maritime trading areas.

Advances in communications and the increasing use of IT in-service delivery particularly in the last five years has, however, made location less of an issue. It should also be borne in mind that not all of the services covered by a management agreement will necessarily be supplied from a single office location. For example, a shipowner may require the shipmanager to provide the technical superintendency function from an office close to its own but be willing to have the various support services (purchasing and accounting for example (so-called back office functions)) from a centralized location perhaps many thousands of miles away providing that the shipmanager can supply information and is available to talk to the client regardless of differences in time zones—so-called 24-hours ship management.

5.2.6 Safety and Quality Management

As in the case of location, the significance of safety and quality management in the shipmanager selection process has changed in recent years. In the late 1980s and early 1990s when the safety and quality management "movement" was still very much in its infancy it was true to say that very few shipowners attached much importance to whether a shipmanager provided services according to a recognized safety and/or quality standard and fewer still were willing or able to differentiate between the ISMA Code, ISO 9002 and DNV's SEP. At that time a certificated management system was seen by many shipowners as an optional extra.

The situation changed, of course, with IMO's formal adoption of the ISM Code in 1994 which necessitated shipowners of certain ship types to comply with its requirements from July 1998. In the past two years, therefore, with the ISM Code soon to become a mandatory licence to operate, the safety management question has been brought into sharper focus and has become an integral part of the shipmanager selection process. To a lesser extent, the shipowning communities' awareness of the importance of quality management has increased given that safety and quality management share many basic disciplines and principles and the fact that a number of major charterers are looking for their sub-contractors to achieve certification.

With the forthcoming deadline, a number of owners may indeed find that the only option for them to meet the ISM requirement will be to employ a certified manager and let this company implement the system on its behalf.

5.2.7 Personal

The hardest selection criterion to assess but often one of the most influential is the personal factor. The relationship between the shipowner and shipmanager will work and endure if it is based on mutual respect and trust. It has been argued also that cultural compatibility is another important ingredient but this aspect must be viewed dispassionately as different cultures can work together very well particularly if they bring complementary strengths to the relationship. For example, the disciplines brought to the table by a north European culture can benefit from the flexibility and innovation which is often evident in Latin companies. In other words, the personal factor must be taken into consideration when selecting a shipmanager but it is an extremely difficult one to quantify.

5.3 THE DECISION-MAKING PROCESS

The decision-making process through which a shipowner selects a shipmanager will vary according to the size of the contract to be awarded, the time available to make the decision and the primary objectives of the shipowner. These objectives may well focus on cost-cutting as the primary aim but may also involve the desire to import specialist skills or gain access to new sources of crew. In certain cases, the shipowner may seek a shipmanager which will be able to immediately enhance its competitive standing in the market-place.

The decision-making process will also vary according to the amount of resources the shipowner is willing or able to commit to selecting a shipmanager. In many cases, particularly those involving smaller shipowners, relatively few people will be involved in collecting the relevant information from the competing shipmanagers, in evaluating the various proposals and in making the decision which may only be made after several months of deliberation. Nevertheless, even in the event of these less formal decision-making processes, an effort will be made to separate the evaluation and the selection elements in the interests of objectivity. For this reason, a shipowner may elect to use the services of an outside consultant to collect the relevant information and conduct the preliminary assessment.

While many contracts are awarded after the conduct of an essentially informal process without rigid deadlines, recent years have seen the greater use of more formal techniques including competitive tendering which involves clearly defined tasks, responsibilities, evaluation techniques and deadlines. A typical tendering process applicable to ship management contracts is presented as Table 5.4. This table shows five distinct steps commencing with pre-qualification whereby the shipowner pre-selects those shipmanagers it believes to have the right skills and experience, which are able to supply good references and meet other basic criteria including financial stability (particularly important in the case of long-term contracts). Following pre-qualification, a formal invitation to tender is used to collect the required information according to a standard format (with technical and commercial information often submitted in two separate sets of documents). A tenderers' meeting is often held which gives the competing shipmanagers the opportunity to ask further questions and, on occasion, to inspect the vessel(s) in question.

Table 5.4: A typical tendering process

STEP	DESCRIPTION/COMMENTS
1	**Pre-qualification**
	Potential tenderers submit application to pre-qualify for the formal tender process. (Applications include 2–3 years of company accounts, a concise statement outlining relevant experience and capabilities, trade and bank references.)
2	**Invitation to Tender**
	Shipowner selects list of qualified tenderers and sends tender document for completion and return within specified deadline. In certain cases, qualified tenderers are asked to attend a tender meeting/ship visit when an opportunity is given to ask questions.
3	**Initial Selection**
	A "long list" of tenderers selected for further evaluation according to shipowner's selection criteria.

Table 5.4—cont.

STEP	DESCRIPTION/COMMENTS
4	**Short Listing**
	A short list of (typically 2 or 3) tenderers is drawn up. Shipowner makes visit to offices and/or ship(s) managed by the tenderers.
5	**Final Selection/Contract Award**
	Shipowner makes final selection on grounds of cost, capabilities, experience and other factors.

The evaluation of the competing bids ensues. This often involves the weighting or ranking of the information supplied. This evaluation can be a lengthy process although the task is simplified if a standard, tightly-worded format is used which negates or minimizes the need for the shipowner to seek clarification or supplementary information (which might disqualify the tenderer under certain circumstances). A "long-list" of tenderers may initially be drawn up according to technical information before a shortlist is produced on commercial grounds. The short-listed companies are, typically, visited by the shipowner (and, possibly, certain vessels under management) before the final decision is made.

If conducted professionally, the tender process should be a thorough and fair method of contract award (although in certain cases the final decision may not be to contract out or only in part). However, this method of selecting a shipmanager can be extremely time-consuming and may not be as thorough as the shipowner desires, if, for example, an insufficiently detailed examination of areas such as safety and quality management or the use of information technology ashore and afloat is conducted for whatever reason. The shipowner must also accept that using a competitive tender process can be inflexible which prevents the shipmanager from submitting a proposal which will include an attractive aspect ruled out by the shipowner at the outset. The shipowner should also consider the fact that the tender process is viewed with a degree of scepticism in the ship management sector because the process is often seen as a smokescreen to cover done deals i.e. with the shipowner only seen to be going through the motions to justify a decision already made. The shipmanager must decide at an early stage whether it has a realistic chance of winning the contract before the commitment of substantial resources is made.

5.4 GOLDEN RULES

Having described the selection process it is useful to identify what might be termed "golden rules" which the shipowner may find useful when selecting a shipmanager.

5.4.1 Shop Around

The first and perhaps most obvious rule for the shipowner is to compare different shipmanagers. Budget quotations should be sought from a number of different shipmanagers who should be given the same brief. This should contain as much relevant information as possible in order that the competing managers can provide accurate projections.

Typically for single ship contracts, a shipmanager will respond within two or three days (or notify the shipowner why a longer period is necessary). The appearance of the presentation submitted will give the shipowner a good idea of the professionalism of the company it is dealing with, as will the assumptions used and accompanying reservations. The better proposals are those which are sufficiently detailed and accompanied by clear explanations of how the numbers have been compiled and what they include or exclude.

Whilst the initial selection of who to request indicative quotations from will obviously be based on the shipowner's knowledge of the strengths and weaknesses of different shipmanagers, care should be taken not to prejudge (unless, of course, the reasons for doing so are clear). It may be beneficial for an owner to include a surprise choice if only for comparative purposes—although on occasion a strong bid by such an outsider may well lead to a contract award.

5.4.2 Visit the Shipmanager's Office

Ship management, like any other service activity, is a people business. A shipowner must have confidence in the people that it designates to look after its vessel(s) on a daily basis and, importantly, who will deal with problems as and when they occur. There is no substitute, therefore, for the shipowner visiting the shipmanager's office to meet key personnel in their own working environment. Such a visit will also afford the shipowner the opportunity to get a feel for how well organized the shipmanager is.

The quality of the office, the working environment and the whole atmosphere of an office gives an indication of the quality of the operation. The owner should not only meet with the top managers but also with relevant personnel in the office. This also serves as an introduction for future communication and cooperation if a management contract is concluded.

One should make sure that all relevant functions of management are adequately covered, both capacity-wise and also when it comes to quality of personnel. It is also interesting to inspect the filing system and record keeping as this tells a lot about the control and quality.

Management tools like computer systems and instructions must, of course, be evaluated, and last but not least one should ensure that the QA system is in place and implemented. Other systems employed in the management are important, both for quality and consistency as well as timely reporting and documentation. Looking at samples of ship reporting and agreeing on formats and time management of reporting are important items to include.

In addition to an office visit, a visit to a ship under management will also prove helpful. Such a visit will give the shipowner a clear idea of how well the shipboard management team function as well as an insight into standards of maintenance and housekeeping.

5.4.3 Investigate Safety and Quality Certification

Don't take a Safety and Quality Certificate at face value. A quality and/or safety management certificate only signifies that a shipmanager has been able to satisfy an external auditing body, which may have only conducted a superficial audit, at a particular time. In order to get evidence as to the effectiveness of the shipmanager's management system the shipowner should look for a simple, well-structured documentary system as used by office and seastaff which is easily understood. This will indicate that a serious effort has been made to improve the system since it was first implemented. Effectiveness will also be derived from a review of internal office audit reports and minutes of management review meetings together with evidence of follow-up actions. Particular attention should also be paid as to how well the shipmanager's system of accident/incident/near miss reporting and follow-up action is functioning. This is one of the hardest requirements of safety and quality management to comply with and will, therefore, give the shipowner tangible proof that the system is working.

Obviously, when assessing these and other elements of the management system the shipowner will have to take into consideration how long the system has been up and running. The shipmanager may also elect to restrict assess to this information on the grounds of confidentiality. Nevertheless, it will be possible at least to discuss trends and specific examples of how progress is being made. The most professional shipmanagers will in this respect be able to demonstrate how they assess their own performance over time and clearly show how seastaff are contributing to the improvement of the management system.

5.4.4 Ask for References

In any selection process the opinion of other parties relevant to the decision can be very useful and influential providing, of course, that care is taken to ensure that the information supplied is impartial. In practice, the information derived from references can be particularly useful at two distinct stages in the decision-making process. At an early stage a reference will be useful in identifying areas meriting further investigation or, indeed, maybe sufficiently serious to rule a shipmanager out of further consideration. At a later stage, the shipowner may be able to check on specific findings derived from the selection process.

Larger managers will have a certain reputation in the market-place, which may give an indication. However, the best way is to ask the potential manager for a list of clients and then contact some of these directly for proper references. One should select some that preferably have similar types of ships including at least one that has a similar business style and philosophy. This is important because different owners may have very different approaches to the business and may well judge a manager differently.

5.4.5 Vet the Management Agreement

The shipowner must thoroughly examine the draft management agreement in order to identify any contentious clauses. While the increasing use of BIMCO's standard format SHIPMAN has simplified this task, many shipowners will still elect to take legal advice to ensure that they are not exposed to unacceptable risks. Care should also be taken to ensure that the services required and agreed with the shipmanager are properly described as are the rights and responsibilities of the respective parties. An issue of importance is liability, and a lawyer might be consulted to see that liabilities are reasonably distributed and that the necessary insurance covers are in place protecting the different parties who are exposed to liability. There are a number of standard management contracts available and one or more of these might be consulted for reference. Termination clauses must also be clear as should the period of notices during which either party has the chance to remedy any reason for contract cancellation.

5.4.6 Everything's Negotiable

Well almost everything! Shipmanagers hardly need reminding that they operate in a highly competitive market-place which gives the shipowner considerable leverage on contract negotiations. In the majority of cases, for any single vessel which becomes available on the market, there will be many managers chasing the contract. Therefore, in order to secure a contract a shipmanager might need not only to reduce the management/manning fee but also to customize service delivery or provide additional services. However, as in any contract negotiation, the provider of the service will set a limit to how far it is prepared to compromise its position. For example, shipmanagers will on occasion refuse to accept restrictions placed on the vessel operating budget by an owner if in its professional judgement the safety of the vessel or its crew are jeopardized. Shipmanagers must balance, therefore, the need for a short-term increase in turnover and, hopefully, profit with the potential havoc and disruption caused by a problem ship or owner if an inordinate amount of time is spent sorting out problems to the detriment of other ships and clients. Persistent late payments or underfunding can seriously damage the shipmanager's reputation among suppliers and, more importantly, destroy the morale of seastaff.

5.5 MANAGING THE MANAGER

An in-depth assessment of competing proposals should provide the shipowner with a clear idea of the strengths and weaknesses of the various candidates and form the basis of a rational decision as to which shipmanager(s) to select. This decision is, in effect, the start of a partnership based on mutual trust and understanding and clear appreciation of the contracting parties' respective roles, responsibilities and objectives.

Invariably in such a high risk, problem intensive business as ship operation things can and do go wrong. Relationships will be severely tested not only if an emergency situation occurs but also when problems of a lesser magnitude arise. What might start as a fairly minor incident can develop quickly into something more serious if communication breaks down and one partner suspects that it is deliberately not being kept fully in the picture by the other, or one partner believes that the other is not acting in its best interests. A shipowner may feel aggrieved if it believes that the shipmanager is acting without authority.

Conversely, as previously mentioned, the late payment of fees or expenses will also give major cause for concern. Shipowner–shipmanager relationships therefore need to be managed. In addition to the routine flows of information supplied to the shipowner, the shipmanager may meet with its client on a regular basis—typically quarterly after the submission of the quarterly vessel operating report. This meeting will allow for discussion on variances against the budget and decide on corrective actions. Major events such as the selection of a drydock company or change of vessel employment/trading area may also merit face-to-face discussions in addition to regular telephone conversations.

One point where a third party management differs from the integrated management model is the link between officers, crew and the shipowner. The manager normally employs the whole complement, and the loyalty obviously then is to the manager, not the owner or operator. In a traditional, integrated system, there is a very close link between the officers and crew on a ship and the owner. This is especially true for the master, who also legally is in a special position as the owner's representative, and this split loyalty between manager and owner could potentially be a problem. It is important to be well aware of this difference, and the owner should properly monitor that its interests are not adversely affected by this dual or split loyalty.

The lack of connection between the ship's complement and the owner does, in general, mean that an officer or crew member might serve different owners from contract to contract. This is a disadvantage, but on the other hand a strong link to a good manager can create a highly professional and flexible manning arrangement with wide experience and diverse knowledge.

A shipowner may also elect to follow a more formal method of monitoring the performance of its shipmanager. Benchmarking techniques can be used whereby the shipmanager's performance is measured over time against set criteria, or the performance of an in-house technical department, or another shipmanager. A shipowner may seek competitive quotes from other shipmanagers from time to time as part of this benchmarking process.

One aspect of special importance is the setting and control of a maintenance standard. The cost-curbing efforts of a manager and possible negative effects have been mentioned but these negative consequences can be controlled. It is, indeed, the owner's instruction to the manager that governs the way a ship is run. It is the owner who after proper consultation and discussion with the manager shall set the operating policy and who shall approve the budget. Hence, it is the owner who decides on the quality of operation. The same owner could give the same instruction to his in-house ship management, with similar consequence—good or bad quality.

One could assert that a manager will be more willing to cut costs without considering the consequences, if a cheap operation is what he sells. An owner who wants a cheap, even substandard ship will get it whether the ship is in-house or externally managed, it is in any case his decision. In most cases it can be said that the efficient professional manager is able to provide the same quality of ship management at a lower cost than most smaller in-house management departments can obtain. This is a result of stronger buying power, but it is also a result of a shipmanager being focused on management. It is its business and he sees to it that his organization includes the expertise and experience which is necessary to perform this specific task in the most efficient manner. He will be able to perform the management function for a tailormade organization and with a specific goal to do it well.

The key to success, therefore, is a proper definition of the maintenance standard, both short term and long term. The expectation of the shipowner may vary, especially when it comes to the costs to maintain the long-term value of the asset, and it is, consequently, essential that this point is properly defined, and that adequate control mechanisms are established.

While certain performance criteria used in benchmarking are very straightforward and readily measured, for example the acceptance of a vessel by an oil major, budget variances, timeliness and accuracy of reporting, etc., others may not be so. The latter include factors which are of more important strategic benefit to the shipowner including the introduction of improved systems and procedures allowing, for example, greater access to the shipowner to information on vessel performance. In the case of cruise vessels external partners will be involved given that the shipowner will also benchmark the shipmanager's performance by way of passenger satisfaction levels. End-of-cruise questionnaires filled in by passengers provide valuable feedback on key areas of a shipmanager's performance including, in the case of hotel management, food and staff presentation and service. A minimum level of customer satisfaction level may well be agreed prior to vessel takeover with any fall in standards leading to penalties.

As a final comment it is worth pointing out three further aspects of shipowner–shipmanager relationships. Firstly, the shipowner must resist the temptation to "micro-manage" the shipmanager. While the shipowner should retain a high level of technical expertise in order to understand the implications of decisions taken by the shipmanager, care must be taken to avoid interference and duplication which will ultimately lead to confusion. Often owners may have very weak or non-existent technical expertise. This creates a different difficulty, and the manager must take due care to inform the owner properly and in simple terms on the background for discussions.

Secondly, a shipowner who has contracted out for the first time after many years of in-house management will invariably expect the shipmanager to match or even exceed the level of past performance. This might not be possible given financial restraints imposed on the shipmanager or may take time to deliver.

Thirdly, a shipowner's relationship with a shipmanager will change over time. New staff in the shipowner's or the shipmanager's office may have an affect on the relationship which may take time to get used to.

If all of the above are properly handled there should be no reason for negative surprises. To conclude, the right manager selected in a proper manner shall be able to provide a good and flexible service to the owner whether this is for the whole fleet, for a group of ships or solely for benchmarking to keep the in-house management department on its toes.

WHO IS RESPONSIBLE? WHO IS LIABLE?

6.1 THE RECENT HISTORY OF SHIPMANAGERS' LIABILITY

As the modern role of the shipmanager has become more clearly defined, so too have his responsibilities and liabilities. A shipmanager's responsibilities are regulated by contract (the ship management contract) but as recently as the early 1980s many of those contracts made no direct reference to liability, relying on their agency construction to regulate the responsibilities of the owners and the shipmanager.

The early unsophisticated contracts typically contained a *"force majeure"* clause which sought to prevent either party from claiming against the other for events outside their control (a largely illusory protection under English law) and a ratification and indemnity clause by which the owners undertook to ratify and confirm any contract entered into or any action undertaken by the manager and to indemnify the manager against all claims and liabilities arising from the *bona fide* performance of his duties.

The more sophisticated contracts (often drawn up after the model drafted by Basil Eckersley QC) contained a fairly wide exceptions clause which provided that the officers and crew appointed by the manager were to be the servants of the owners and that the manager would not be liable for their negligence except where the loss was caused as a result of the manager failing to exercise reasonable diligence in their selection and appointment.

The incidence of claims involving shipmanagers in the 1970s and early 1980s was rare, not because such contracts would necessarily have precluded claims for negligence, but because the relationship between the shipmanager and his client was a generally close one. Problems were likely to be sorted out privately between them.

The mid 1980s, however, saw a profound change taking place in shipping—a worldwide slump, numerous shipping company bankruptcies and an increase in the general climate of litigiousness. The liquidation of shipping companies coupled with the low resale value of their ships forced the mortgagor banks to continue to trade them until the market improved. The banks turned to the shipmanagers for whom this proved to be a lucrative market. Later in the decade a new breed of shipping investors—the K/S partnerships—having little knowledge of ships, also turned to managers to operate those purchased through their speculative funds. However it was not perhaps until *The Marion* [1984] 2 Lloyd's Rep. 2—a summary of the case appears in the case notes at the end of this chapter—still the most celebrated case in the shipmanagers' lexicon—that the issue of shipmanagers' liability began to be examined more closely. The House of Lords found that the manager had been guilty of actual fault and privity in the management of the *Marion*. As the manager was the agent of the owners, the court held the owners were responsible for the loss, including the loss of their right to limit liability under the 1958 Merchant Shipping Act (which incorporated the 1957 Limitation Convention).

This case came as a bombshell to most shipmanagers, who quickly began to take a much greater interest in their contractual and insurance arrangements. It also coincided with the formation of TIM—Transport Intermediaries Mutual—a specialist mutual insurer (TIM merged with CISBACLUB in 1992 to become ITIC (International Transport Intermediaries Club)) for the ship agency and ship broking sectors of the shipping industry. This new club observed that shipmanagers had a clear and growing exposure to claims and decided to apply its professional indemnity cover to these potential liabilities. Shipmanagers were further encouraged to review their professional standards by the case of *The Maira* (*Glafki Shipping Co. S.A.* v. *Pinios Shipping Co. No. 1*) [1986] 2 Lloyd's Rep. 12—see summary of the case at the end of this chapter—in which a shipmanager was held liable for the under-insurance of a ship which suffered a total loss.

6.1.1 BIMCO's Initiative

In 1987 BIMCO decided to establish a subcommittee to prepare the first standard ship management contract (BIMCO "SHIPMAN" available from the printers, FR. GE. Knudtzon A/S, 55 Toldbodgade, DK-1253 Copenhagen—Fax Number: +45 33 93 11 84). The sub-committee's members were drawn equally from the shipowning and ship management sectors of the industry and this reflected the growing awareness that contracts containing wide exemptions for negligence were no longer acceptable in a competitive market which demanded greater accountability. Nor, perhaps, were they acceptable under the UK's Unfair Contract Terms Act 1977. SHIPMAN was published in 1988 and quickly established itself as the basic ship management contract, although many of the established ship management companies continue to offer clients their "house" contract forms. The 1988 version of SHIPMAN is still current, but is being reviewed by a BIMCO subcommittee in the light of experience of its use, the criticism of its insurance clause (Clause 13) and the effect of the ISM Code. See pages 127, 128 and 129 for discussion on the insurance clause and the revision published by BIMCO on 22 January 1997.

SHIPMAN marked a turning point—the contract contained a responsibility clause (Clause 18) which provided for the shipmanager to be liable to the owner for his own or his subcontractors' negligence, but subject to a limit of ten times the annual management fee.

Over the past decade this standard of liability has become accepted as a realistic balance between the respective interests of owners and managers. The balance is based on the premise that a shipmanager earns only between $80,000 and $150,000 per ship per year as a management fee and does not share in the commercial profits (or losses) of the venture. "This underlying economic reality means that a shipmanager is quite unable to bear the same degree of exposure to risk as the shipowner and must limit his exposure either by fixing a specific monetary limit on the amount of his liability to claims, contract out of liability or set the gauge for the degree of negligence for which he is prepared to accept responsibility at a high level". "Liability and the Ship Management Industry", Hereward Lawford Transport Intermediaries Mutual, LLP International Ship Management Conference, London 1989.

Other forces have however been at work to keep the balance of responsibility between shipowners and managers under consideration during the past decade. The first is the inexorable rise in the size of claims—particularly the major casualties—and the other is a growing awareness of the underlying causes of shipping accidents coupled with the growing perception that all parties to the maritime adventure should bear their proper share of responsibility for it. This line of thinking is now being applied to those who until now have, for reasons of public policy, contract law, general jurisprudence or commercial reality, not borne the full weight of responsibility for their own negligence. In addition to the classification societies, these include ports and terminals, charterers (see for instance Peter Martyr on *"Responsibility in Chartering"*. Maritime Cyprus, October 1995) pilots and surveyors. It remains to be seen whether shipmanagers, now firmly fixed with responsibility for operating the ships under their management in accordance with the ISM Code, will find pressure on them to accept a greater level of responsibility than under the current BIMCO SHIPMAN form, or whether, in the light of potentially greater exposure, they will require more protection. This issue will be discussed further later in this chapter.

6.2 THE SHIP MANAGEMENT CONTRACT

The general contractual position of a shipmanager is based on the law of agency. The shipmanager is the agent of his principal, the shipowner. The general law of agency provides that the manager must:

(a) comply with the owners' lawful instructions;
(b) exercise due skill and care;
(c) not delegate his duties to another without express authority;
(d) act in good faith (this includes avoiding conflicts of interest, not taking "secret profits" or commissions and acting in a fiduciary capacity);
(e) keep proper accounts;

(f) keep the owners' funds separate from his own.

In return, the manager is protected by the owner (and has a right of indemnity against him) for all expenditure, losses, costs and expenses incurred on his behalf.

The fact that a shipmanager is known to be a manager is insufficient to create a proper agency relationship with third parties. In the well-known case of *Maritime Stores Limited* v. *H.P. Marshall & Co. Ltd.* [1963] 1 Lloyd's Rep. 602, the fact that Maritime Stores knew that Marshall were ship agents was "in no way determinative of the issue". The court found on the facts that Marshall, the agent, had not contracted as agent and was personally liable. A shipmanager must therefore act like any other agent and make it clear when contracting with a third party on behalf of his principal that he is acting "as agent only". This is usually done by confirming all contracts in writing and signing off "for [the manager] as agent for and on behalf of [the owner]".

Shipmanagers rarely issue bills of lading, and are, therefore, not likely to be at risk of setting up a contractual relationship between themselves and cargo interests. They do, however, make contracts on behalf of the owner with suppliers of all kinds—bunker suppliers, repair yards, chandlers and providers, stevedores and port authorities. If they fail to make it clear that they are acting in an agency capacity, not only will they be directly liable to the owner for any deficiency in, for example, the quantity of bunkers supplied, but also they will be responsible to the supplier for payment for his services. It is therefore unwise, to say the least, for a shipmanager to forego the protection of his agency status.

6.2.1 BIMCO SHIPMAN

The contract drafted by BIMCO in 1998 is now widely used. In particular, it has been almost universally adopted in the Japanese market—the strongest "new" ship management market of the past decade.

SHIPMAN comes in two parts. Part I is in BIMCO's preferred "box" layout in which can be inserted the name and place of business of the owners and managers, the time and date of the commencement of the agreement as well as its intended termination, the annual lump sum management fee and the sum agreed in respect of redundancy costs. The other boxes are used to indicate the management services contracted for including crewing, technical management, insurance, freight management, accounting, chartering, sale or purchase, provisioning, bunkering and operations.

When SHIPMAN was drafted, the leading shipmanagers preferred to supply their owners with crews on an agency or "cost plus" basis, and this determined the construction of the contract. As a result, it is not suitable for use in the event of the managers supplying crews as a principal on a "lump sum" basis. BIMCO CREWMAN, issued in 1993, is the correct form to use in the latter case.

Part II, the main terms of the contract, contains the following provisions:

Clause 2—Appointment of Managers—This clause defines the obligation of the managers who are obliged to " ... use their best endeavours to provide the management services ... in accordance with sound ship management practice ...". The phrase "best endeavours" is an onerous duty. It obliges the shipmanager to go to great lengths to ensure that the services are provided "in accordance with sound ship management practice", but the obligation is leavened by the provision, in Clause 16.6, that "the Managers shall in no circumstances be required to use or commit their own funds to finance the provision of the management services". The phrase "sound ship management practice" is a useful "self levelling" concept, which provides a yardstick against which the manager's actions may be judged. The standard is a high one. Although untested, it is likely to be defined by reference to the ISM Code adopted as Chapter IX of SOLAS in May 1994.

The clause also allows the manager the necessary right, which might otherwise be in conflict with the fiduciary duty imposed by the law of agency, to act for other shipowners. The managers:

"shall be entitled to have regard to their overall responsibility in relation to all vessels as may from time to time be entrusted to their management ... and shall be entitled to allocate available supplies, manpower and services in such manner as in the prevailing circumstances the Managers in their absolute discretion consider to be fair and reasonable".

The clause also contains the essential agency provision, providing that the managers shall carry out the designated functions "as agents for and on behalf of the owners" while giving a necessary general right to "take such actions as the managers may from time to time in their absolute discretion consider to be necessary to enable them to perform this agreement in accordance with sound ship management practice". Ship management is not a predictable occupation.

Clause 13—Insurance Policies—has given rise to most criticism of the 1988 SHIPMAN form. It reads:

"All insurances shall be in the joint names of the Owners and the Managers provided that, unless the Managers give their express prior consent, no liability to pay premiums or P&I Calls shall be imposed on the Managers, notwithstanding the restrictions on P&I Cover which would thereby result."

The problem with this clause is that it fails to relate to actual market practice, and in particular to the practice of the P&I Clubs when granting co-assurance to a shipmanager. It may also lead the shipmanager to believe that he may be able to obtain full co-assurance cover "in the joint names of the Owners and the Managers" without the corresponding liability for calls (premiums). (BIMCO published explanatory notes with the SHIPMAN contract and the position was fully explained in these notes. Nevertheless, the clause itself could be misleading.) Briefly, P&I Clubs within the International Group (which between them insure more than 90 per cent of the world's ocean-going tonnage for P&I liabilities) will not grant "full" co-assurance coverage to a shipmanager without the manager assuming a corresponding obligation to pay the premiums in the event that they are not paid by the owners. In the ordinary course of events, the premiums will of course be paid by the owners either direct or *via* the shipmanager. Problems arise, however, when the premiums are not paid and the manager's obligation is called in. A fuller discussion on this issue appears later in this chapter.

As has been noted earlier, a BIMCO subcommittee is currently working on revised versions of SHIPMAN and CREWMAN. This revision is taking place in the light of experience of their use, the criticism of the insurance clause in SHIPMAN already referred to, and the perceived effects of the ISM Code and STCW 95 on the balance of responsibilities as between the owner and the manager.

The BIMCO subcommittee has already published a revised insurance clause to replace Clause 13 of SHIPMAN (and subclause 4.7 of CREWMAN). The "new" Clause 13 of SHIPMAN is set out below.

6.2.2 SHIPMAN Clause 13—Insurance Policies

"The Owners shall procure that throughout the period of this Agreement:
   (a) at the Owners' expenses, the Vessel is insured for not less than her sound market value or entered for her full gross tonnage, as the case may be for:
       (i) usual hull and machinery marine risks (including crew negligence) and excess liabilities;
       (ii) protection and indemnity risks (including pollution risks); and
       (iii) war risks (including protection and indemnity and crew risks)
       in accordance with the best practice of prudent owners of vessels of a similar type to the Vessel, with first class insurance companies, underwriters or associations ("the Owners' Insurances");
   (b) all premiums and calls on the Owners' Insurances are paid promptly by their due date for payment;
   (c) the Owners' Insurances name the Managers and any third party designated by the Managers as a joint assured, with full cover, with the Owners obtaining cover in respect of each of the insurances specified in (a) above:
       (i) on terms whereby the Managers and any such third party are liable in respect of premiums or calls arising in connection with the Owners' Insurances; or
       (ii) if obtainable, on terms such that neither the Managers nor any such third party shall be under any liability in respect of premiums or calls arising in connection with the Owners' Insurances; or
       (iii) on such other terms as may be agreed in writing.

(d) written evidence is provided to complete satisfaction of the Managers of their compliance with their obligations under this clause within 30 days of the commencement of the Agreement and of each renewal date and, if specifically requested, of each payment date of the Owners' Insurances."

The revised Clause 13 of SHIPMAN now follows the thinking behind the insurance clause of CREWMAN, published in 1993.

The revised clause specifies the minimum insurances that must be placed either by the owner or by the shipmanager acting on the owners' instructions. These insurances include hull and machinery (with excess liabilities), P&I (including pollution) and war risks (including P&I war risks).

The clause also provides that owners' insurances should name the managers as joint assureds, with full cover, either on the basis that the managers are liable for the premiums or on terms which do not give rise to such corresponding liability. The clause now corresponds to market practice in that shipmanagers will almost invariably obtain full co-assurance with a corresponding liability for P&I premiums, but it allows for the practice of other P&I insurers outside the International Group of P&I Clubs who may not insist on the manager having this liability (but may, instead, insist on the broker being liable). A shipmanager may also obtain co-assurance cover from some P&I Clubs and the market on terms which are sometimes known as "misdirected arrow" cover. A fuller discussion of this practice appears later in this chapter at pages 133 and 134.

Clause 15—Management Fee—This clause includes a provision whereby all discounts and commissions obtained by the manager in the course of his management duties must be credited to the owners. This of course is part of the manager's obligation under the law of agency not to make a "secret profit".

Clause 17—Manager's Right to Subcontract—This clause provides that the manager shall not subcontract any of his obligations under the agreement to a third party without the consent of the owner. This is an important clause which reflects not only the manager's obligation under the law of agency, but also the very high degree of responsibility undertaken by him, and the care with which he will have been chosen by the owners. Owners rightly expect that the ship management services will be delivered "personally" so far as is possible, by the organization that they have chosen. They should not be faced by the manager subcontracting part or all of his responsibilities to a third party without their express consent. In practice, however, shipmanagers may contract certain of their duties, for example, in relation to crewing and training, and may not always appreciate the need to obtain the owner's agreement to this. Nevertheless a shipmanager would be wise to do so, preferably during the negotiations over the agreement.

Clause 18—Responsibilities—The structure of Clause 18, while appearing at first to be somewhat complex, is in fact relatively straightforward. The clause contains a traditional *"force majeure"* clause which purports to allow either party to avoid responsibility for events beyond their control—although it should be noted that under English law *force majeure* is the equivalent of "Act of God", and can only be relied on in the most extraordinary circumstances such as war or some natural disaster.

The balance of the clause provides that the manager shall be under no liability to the owners unless the loss has arisen from the negligence, gross negligence or wilful default of the manager or his agents or subcontractors, in which case the manager's liability for each incident shall be limited to a total of ten times the annual management fee. This limitation of the manager's liability will, however, not apply where the loss has resulted from the manager's personal act or omission committed with the intent to cause such loss or recklessly and with knowledge that such loss, damage, delay or expense would probably result.

The clause contains an indemnity from the owners to the manager (as would be expected in a contract based on agency) except to the extent that the manager may be liable in accordance with the liability provisions just described. Further, the clause includes a "Himalaya" or subcontractors' exception clause granting the manager's employees, agents and subcontractors the same contractual protection from liability as provided to the manager himself.

The effect of the clause is that the manager is responsible for his own and his subcontractor's negligence up to the limit of ten times his management fee (an average figure of $1 million), unless he is found to have acted with intent or recklessly in the meaning of the words borrowed directly from the 1976 Limitation Convention. The owners for their part must indemnify the manager against claims which may be made against him either where the manager has not been negligent or, if he has, the claim exceeds the limit of ten times his management fee. Needless to say, the indemnity from the owner to the manager will not operate if the manager has lost his right to limit to the owners altogether under the test imposed by the 1976 Limitation Convention.

It is not immediately apparent from the wording of this clause that the manager is not liable for the negligence of crew supplied by him. This is because the manager has supplied crew on an agency basis, and is responsible only to the extent that he has been negligent in the supply of "adequate and properly qualified Crew" i.e. they lack certification, appropriate training or the necessary degree of competence.

In practice, the clause has worked well. The manager's liability is insurable (a key consideration for the BIMCO subcommittee which drafted the contract), does not conflict with the Unfair Contract Terms Act 1977 and is sufficiently realistic to provide owners with a significant cushion of protection in the event of a claim. Criticism of the clause has centred not so much on the degree of liability undertaken by the manager but on the fact that the loss of his right to limit liability at all is probably co-extensive with the loss of his own professional indemnity insurance protection.

Clause 24—Law and Arbitration—This clause provides for disputes to be governed either by English or US law and to be referred to arbitration either in London or in New York. The choice selected will have been entered in the appropriate box (18) in Part I of the contract.

In practice, English law and arbitration are selected for most ship management contracts.

6.3 THE SHIPMANAGER'S INSURANCES

In this shifting world in which the manager must rely heavily on the protection afforded him by his principal, the issue of insurance is an important one. A shipmanager's insurance is a mixture of professional indemnity insurance and protection against third party and statutory liabilities and is best administered by an insurer who fully understands the interrelationship between the owners' insurances and those of the manager. Thus a manager's insurances must provide cover for his own and his subcontractor's negligence as well as insuring him against the risk of being found to have contracted as a principal, breach of warranty of authority and the fraud of his employees. He also needs cover in the event of claims by third parties succeeding against him in situations where the owners' indemnity is inoperative or the owners have gone into liquidation. Finally, he needs insurance against his costs both in defending claims brought against him and also in pursuit of his claims against his principal and others.

This insurance—the manager's own insurance—is however arguably less important than the insurance that he must receive from the owner's insurers—in particular the owner's hull and P&I insurers. It is crucially important for the manager to be named as co-assured with the owner on the owner's hull and P&I insurances. Why? The simple answer is that the manager has effectively taken over from the owner all the main tasks that an owner undertakes, except the commercial operation of the ship, and is responsible in practice for the seaworthiness of the ship, the competence of the crew and the safety of the ship's operations. As such, he has potentially almost as wide a range of responsibilities as the owner—and similar liabilities. If, however, the shipmanager was to seek his own independent insurances for these liabilities, the cost might exceed his annual management fee, often by a significant margin. He must therefore become co-assured with the owner whose interests are to all intents and purposes identical with his own. This co-assurance—particularly in respect of potentially huge third party liabilities—comes free, that is the insurance premium is paid by the shipowner who could not otherwise find a manager to undertake that role in the absence of being named as co-assured.

Being co-assured affords the shipmanager a most important additional benefit—he may not be sued in subrogation by the insurer for a claim which he has "caused" and for which the insurer has paid. This important principle of insurance law means that the manager has complete protection provided by the owners' insurances for the largest claim, even when caused by his own negligence. There are, however, occasions where the manager's negligence has been such as to void the owners and his own insurances, and that is the situation described in the following case. (A fuller description of the claim appears later on pages 151–152.)

"A shipmanager failed to notify the ship's classification society of corrosion in a tanker's permanent ballast tanks. While the ship was on a laden voyage across the Atlantic, the corrosion caused structural failure in the tanks and the ship had to put into the Azores. Her cargo was transferred and the ship returned to Europe for repairs. Claims totalled $16 million of which $7 million was claimed from the manager.

Surveyors acting for the club and hull underwriters discovered that the managers had prior knowledge of the corrosion problems in the ship's permanent ballast tanks, but had decided that they were not serious enough to warrant the immediate arrangement of repairs or the giving of notice to class.

Both the ship's hull and P&I underwriters declined to pay their respective shares of the claim. The hull underwriters argued that both the ship's repairs and their contribution to general average did not arise as a result of an insured peril. The ship's P&I Club declined to pay on the grounds that their classification rule required any matter likely to affect the ship's class to be brought to the attention of the classification society. Although the shipmanager argued that his contract gave him some protection, the claim against him was settled by payment of $4 million."

This case well illustrates the "nightmare scenario" for a shipmanager—that of his own negligence causing both the owners and himself to lose the protection of the owners' insurances. However, it might have been worse—on the same facts the shipmanager's own professional indemnity insurers might have taken the view that he was "privy" to the loss, in the terms of the Marine Insurance Act (the Marine Insurance Act 1906, is applicable to marine insurance policies issued by British and Bermudian insurers). Had this been the case, the shipmanager would almost certainly have been put out of business by an uninsured loss of this magnitude.

6.3.1 Full Co-assurance and the Liability for Calls

The issue of co-assurance has always been a thorn in the side of shipmanagers because of the P&I Club's insistence that this vital cover should carry with it a corresponding liability for unpaid premiums (calls). Recently it has been given much greater public prominence as the result of the case of the *Newcastle P&I Club v. V Ships* [1996] 2 Lloyd's Rep. 515. The judgment of the Commercial Court, favourable to the shipmanagers, is being appealed by the Newcastle Club but in fact the case does not add anything new to the debate as it turns only on the exact agreement reached between the club and the shipmanagers at the time the particular ships were entered and not on any guiding point of principle. Nevertheless it does illustrate the problem that shipmanagers' face in being treated as the "guarantors" of the shipowners' premiums—not least because of the sum involved—$4 million (the ships were passenger ships which attract high P&I premiums).

P&I Clubs essentially have three types of entry. In their rules the clubs distinguish between those who are members or joint owners on the one hand, and those who are simply co-assured. They also offer cover for "affiliates". The terminology is not exact and differs between clubs but, for the purposes of this chapter, the co-assurance required by shipmanagers and crew managers is synonymous with "joint ownership" and is referred to as "full co-assurance".

"Membership" is self-explanatory. Joint ownership arises when a ship is entered in the name of two or more owners or operators (one of whom may be the shipmanager). All joint owners on an entry qualify for actual membership of the club and enjoy all the rights of membership, including voting rights at the club's AGM and eligibility for a seat on the board. These rights are usually set out in the club's bye-laws or statutes. A joint owner therefore has the full independent benefit of the club's cover. This is the cover referred to as "full co-assurance".

The second type of entry is that of "ordinary" co-assureds. Co-assureds are not members of the club but are merely named insureds on a member's or joint-owner's certificate of entry. Co-assureds do not have the same rights as members. For example they have no voting rights and cannot have a director on the board. Their cover is restricted in that they are insured only for liabilities arising from operations normally carried out by an owner, and only for those risks for which the owner member himself has cover. For instance, if the owner has no cargo claims cover or a huge deductible, so will the co-assured. But the club does bear the risk of a multiple liability in respect of the same entry (i.e. has to reimburse the member and each and every co-assured the full amount of their claim).

The third type of cover provided by clubs is offered to affiliated companies where there is a degree of financial interest between the owner and the affiliated company. They are neither members of the club nor named as co-assureds on the certificate of entry. Unlike co-assureds and members, affiliates do not even have a contractual right to cover because they are not parties to the insurance contract. One type of co-assurance is also known as "misdirected arrow" cover. It is normally given to agents—typically crewing agents—who undertake only limited duties for their principals and because of their agency capacity are not normally sued direct. When they are, they should normally be indemnified by their principal. Since they do not hold themselves out as undertaking substantial services for their principal, they are usually only caught up in a liability claim more or less by accident or because they happen to be the only company in the same country as the claimant.

The drawback to all co-assurance cover except for full co-assurance or joint ownership is that the co-assured has no independent cover of his own and must show that, had the claim been brought against the owners instead of the co-assured, then the owners would have been held liable. Thus if the owners had a good defence to the claim, or if they could limit their liability to some low figure, the "ordinary" co-assured would find himself exposed to the "excess" over the amount the owners had to pay. Whereas "full" co-assurance protects the shipmanager from his own acts and defaults, "ordinary" co-assurance or "misdirected arrow" co-assurance only protects the co-assured from the owners' acts and defaults. And should the owners go into liquidation and be unable to pay the claim, this type of co-assurance will be worth nothing.

The differences between "full" co-assurance and lesser forms are shown in the following table:

Table 6.1: Full co-assurance and misdirected arrow cover compared

Joint Owner's Cover	Ordinary co-assurance
"Full" co-assurance	e.g. "Misdirected arrow" cover
The shipmanager has his own cover independent from that of the owner.	The shipmanager does not have independent cover.
The shipmanager will be covered even if the owner goes into liquidation (provided he pays any outstanding calls).	The shipmanager will not be covered if the owner goes into liquidation.
The shipmanager will be covered even if the owner can limit his liability to an amount lower than that of the manager.	The shipmanger can only recover from the club to the extent that the owner himself would have been able to recover. If the owner can limit his liability and the shipmanager cannot, the shipmanager may find himself uninsured for the amount of the claim above the owner's limit.
The shipmanager will be covered even if the owner has a good defence to the claim which the shipmanager does not.	The shipmanager will not be covered if the owner has a good defence to the claim.

A shipmanager may enter a club only as a joint owner (full co-assurance) or with "misdirected arrow" cover. If he is a joint owner he will be liable for the owners' premium. Only if he has "misdirected arrow" cover will he escape liability for premium. And so far as the P&I Clubs in the International Group are concerned, when the shipmanager has full co-assurance the obligation to pay if the owners do not is non-negotiable. The clubs' view is that the manager is obtaining substantial cover in his own name—for which he pays no up-front premium.

The position is different in the hull market and, it must be said, amongst some of the P&I Clubs outside the International Group. There the co-assured shipmanager is not expected to act as guarantor of the owners' premium, but usually the broker is instead.

So the shipmanager has a choice. He must at least be co-assured; if he is not, then the club would be able to turn round and sue him in subrogation for any claims which it had paid and for which he, as opposed to the owner, could be shown to be responsible. And if he chooses—and if the club allows him—to take only misdirected arrow cover, then his cover is seriously deficient. He could be left exposed to a uninsured P&I claim which could run into millions. And his own professional insurance cover would not be able to help; they do not cover the gap between misdirected arrow cover and full co-assurance. They and their reinsurers are not prepared to take on the risk of becoming primary P&I insurers and require as a term of their policy that the shipmanager to be fully co-insured.

In this situation it is essential that the shipmanager looks hard at the owners' financial security before entering into the management contract. He must also try either to become co-assured in a club which will give him full documentation about the owners' entry or place the owner's insurances himself—so that he has adequate warning if the owners begin to fall behind with his premiums payments.

6.4 IMPACT OF THE ISM CODE

The legal effect of the ISM Code has given rise to much debate. The aspect that is most relevant here is the degree to which the shipmanager may take on additional liability as a consequence of becoming the party responsible for compliance with the Code.

The ISM Code does not impose its own liability regime, but it does require the company to conduct the management of its ships in a particular manner. In the context of the Code the "company" means

"the owner of the ship or any other organization or person such as the manager or bareboat charterer who has assumed the responsibility for the operation of a ship from the shipowner and who, on assuming such responsibility, has agreed to take over all the duties and responsibilities imposed by the Code" (Article 1.1:1).

The implementation of the Code is achieved through the medium of the safety management system. The obligation to create and run the SMS lies with the person who has assumed responsibility for the operation of the ship. In the case of a ship given out to third party technical or "full management" this will mean the manager is the person who has "assumed responsibility for the operation of the ship".

One essential effect of the Code is the creation of a connection between the ship and its management through the role of the designated person. The designated person must have contact with "the highest level of the management". Who, in this scenario, represents "the highest level of management"—the owners or the shipmanager?

The answer lies partly in the legal position of the shipmanager. As we have seen, the shipmanager is the agent of the owner. He binds the owner by his acts or omissions but in consequence of his acting in an agency capacity any liability for the operation of the ship passing from the owners to the manager is private, and makes no difference to third parties who must continue to look to the owners as the principal, ultimately responsible for the safe operation of the ship.

The other part of the answer lies in the fact that there are certain important duties from which the shipowner cannot escape, no matter what contractual devices he employs and whether or not a manager is involved. The most basic is the obligation to exercise due diligence to provide a seaworthy ship under the Hague and Hague/Visby Rules. This is a "non-delegable" duty. Many commentators have suggested that the ISM Code will make it easier for claimants to prove initial unseaworthiness by providing a clear "audit trail" of reports relating to the event or events affecting seaworthiness, but the increased likelihood of initial unseaworthiness being proved or the difficulty of maintaining defences such as crew negligence still impacts directly on the shipowner. Of course, it is still open to the shipowner to seek to pass responsibility for "causing" unseaworthiness to the manager under the ship management contract, but this will not be the natural effect of contracts such as BIMCO SHIPMAN. Even if he is found to have done so, he should still have protected himself by being named as co-assured on the owner's insurances, with the consequence that whoever is responsible for losing the owner's defence to a claim, the owner's P&I insurance will still respond. And, by being co-insured, the manager is also protected against claims in subrogation from the owner's P&I Club.

The issue becomes rather more interesting, however, when the question of limitation is raised—particularly if the owner is able to limit but not the manager, or if neither the owner nor the manager is able to limit—and as a consequence of the degree of recklessness found, the owner's insurances also fail.

Article 4 of the 1976 Limitation Convention states:

"A person liable shall not be entitled to limit his liability if it is proved that the loss resulted from his personal act or omission, committed with the intent to cause such loss, or recklessly and with the knowledge that such loss would probably result."

On the face of it, if the shipowner can demonstrate that he had no actual knowledge of the events giving rise to the loss, his right to limit liability should be protected. The hope would be that the act or omission of the manager which, had it been that of the owner, would have resulted in the loss of the right to limit, would not in fact cause the loss of the shipowner's right to limit because there was no personal act or omission on his part, nor knowledge of such acts or omissions because the designated person was not reporting to the owner.

The flaw in this scenario is again illustrated by the case of *The Marion* ([1984] 2 Lloyd's Rep. 2) and the *Ert Stefanie* (*Société Anonyme des Minerals* v. *Grant Trading Inc* [1987] 2 Lloyd's Rep. 371; [1989] 1 Lloyd's Rep. 349). Both deal with the loss of the owner's (and manager's) right to limit as a result of actual fault and privity—not on the part of the owner but of the manager. In the *Ert Stefanie* the Commercial Court quoted with approval Mr Justice Sheen's comments in *The Marion* when he said

"When a ship is owned by a limited liability company and managed by another limited liability company, the first question which arises is: to which of those companies should one look to see whether the owners are guilty of 'actual fault'? It is not disputed, nor can it be disputed in this court that the answer to that question is that one looks to the managing company."

So the position seems to be that although it will be to the highest level in the management company that the designated person reports, and it will be the management company that will be aware of events giving rise to either lack of seaworthiness or more serious problems leading to loss of limitation, the owner will still bear ultimate responsibility. He cannot delegate to the manager his responsibility for seaworthiness, nor, in terms of limitation, can he avoid responsibility for the acts of the manager that cause him to lose his right to limit.

That is not to say, however, that increased risk will not fall on managers as a consequence of the ISM Code, but I foresee that the additional risks will lie more in the area of uninsured claims than third party liabilities. One of the consequences of the manager being the person who has "agreed to take over all the duties and responsibilities imposed by the Code" is that any breaches of the Code—and indeed breaches of STCW 95 and the related ILO Hours of Work Convention 1996—discovered by Port State Control and leading to the detention of the ship or fines on the operator, may be the responsibility of the manager.

The other area of increased risk for the manager is caused not so much by the ISM Code itself but by its conjunction with Institute Time Clauses (ITC) Hulls 1/11/95, which extends the obligation of due diligence to "superintendents or any of their on-shore management" in relation to claims arising from crew negligence. If hull underwriters do decline claims, it will be more likely than not that the act or omission will have been that of the manager and his crew. Even though the manager is not primarily liable for his crew's negligence, claims for which the owner is uninsured are likely to test the manager's defence severely. That is why it is absolutely necessary for a manager to ensure that his repair and maintenance policy is accepted by the owner and fully funded and in a timely manner, otherwise he could expose himself to serious claims. The worst effects of this scenario may of course not come about until the hull insurance market hardens and owners are obliged to agree ITC Hulls 1/11/95 terms.

6.5 CREW MANAGEMENT

Crew managers—those who employ crews in their own name as principals, and supply them to owners on a "lump sum" basis—are mainly based in Cyprus.

Shipmanagers elsewhere have tended to supply crews on an agency or "cost plus" basis. However, with the growing importance of crew management, BIMCO decided in 1992 to create a standard crew management contract. It was published in 1993 and is known as CREWMAN.

The crew management contract differs from a ship management contract in that the crew manager conducts his business as a principal, and not as the agent of the owner. It is largely for this reason that crew management was not dealt with as an appendix to SHIPMAN, but as a contract in its own right.

As with BIMCO SHIPMAN, CREWMAN comes in two parts. Part I is in the box layout in which are inserted the name and place of business of the owners and the crew managers, the time and date of the commencement of the agreement as well as its intended termination, the flag of the ship and its regular trading area. In addition the monthly lump sum crew management fee, crew overtime expenses, transportation costs and severance costs are all shown.

Part II, the main terms of the contract, contains the following provisions relevant to this chapter.

6.5.1 Clause 2—Appointment of Crew Managers

This clause defines the obligation of the crew managers who "will be the employers of the crew and in concluding contracts of employment with the crew they shall have no authority to act on behalf of the owners". In some countries local law requires that crews must be employed by the owners and in this case CREWMAN must be varied. In the majority of countries, however, no change need be made.

As with ship management, the crew managers "undertake to use their best endeavours" to provide the crew management services in accordance with "sound crew management practice". The quality of the obligation placed on the crew managers in this contract is the same as that for shipmanagers, in SHIP-MAN. As with shipmanagers, whose obligations are becoming more onerous as a result of the ISM Code, crew managers are being similarly affected, principally by STCW 95.

Crew managers may also supply crew for ships other than those named in the contract, and CREWMAN allows for the potential conflict of interest by providing

"the Crew Managers ... shall be entitled to have regard to their overall responsibility in relation to all vessels that may from time to time be entrusted to their Management and ... the Crew Managers shall be entitled to allocate available manpower in such manner as in the prevailing circumstances the Crew Managers in their absolute discretion considered to be fair and reasonable."

6.5.2 Clause 3—Crew Managers' Obligations

This clause is extremely detailed—much more so than the equivalent clause in the SHIPMAN contract. Under it the crew manager shall:

> "3.1: Select and supply the Crew for the Vessel each of whom shall be suitably qualified;
>
> 3.2: ensure that all members of the Crew have passed a medical examination with a qualified doctor certifying that they are fit for the duties for which they are engaged and are in possession of valid medical certificates dated not more than three months prior to the respective Crew members leaving their country of domicile for embarkation, and maintained for the duration of their services on board the vessel;
>
> 3.3: ensure that the applicable requirements of the law of the flag . . . are satisfied in respect of the following:
> (a) the rank, qualification and certification of the crew;
> (b) manning levels where a full crew is provided by the crew managers;
> (c) employment regulations; and,
> (d) crews' tax and social insurance requirements;
>
> 3.4: ensure that the crew shall all have a command of the English language of sufficient standard to enable them to perform their duties safely.
>
> 3.5: Instruct the crew to obey all reasonable orders of the owners, including, but not limited to orders in connection with safety and navigation, avoidance of pollution and protection of the environment;
>
> 3.6: ensure that the crews individual contracts of employment specify clearly that the Crew Managers are their employers."

The obligation to select and supply crew "each of whom shall be suitably qualified" and the obligation to comply with the requirements of the law of the flag are now becoming progressively more onerous as a result of the coming into force of STCW 95 on 1 February 1997. Further reference will be made to those obligations later in this chapter.

Clause 3.2 deals with the crew's medical condition. The issue of pre-employment medical examinations is becoming an increasingly important one. Owners and crew managers are recognizing that the supply of medically unfit crew can be a safety as well as a health hazard (to other crew members or passengers). In addition repatriation and medical treatment of crew members is becoming more and more expensive—either for the owners if the crew risks are ensured on their P&I policy, or for the crew managers if they have elected to insure their crew themselves.

Clause 3.4 requires the crew manager to "ensure that the crew shall all have a command of the English language of a sufficient standard to enable them to perform their duties safely". It should be noted that the standard is applied to all crew members, but is modified by the requirement that the crew's command of English need only be sufficient for the particular crew member to perform his duties safely. The standard of English required of, say, the cook will therefore be of a very different order to that required of the Chief Officer. This requirement will similarly be affected by STCW 95.

Clause 3.5 requires the crew manager to instruct the crew to obey "all reasonable orders of the Owners". This allows the owners to give orders directly to the individual crew member even though it is the crew manager who is his employer. It is the crew manager's obligation to ensure that such orders are obeyed.

Clause 3.8 contains the provisions relating to the insurances to be taken out by the crew manager. As we have seen in the discussion on SHIPMAN, the managers who provide crewing services as agents of the owners will insure the crew under the owner's P&I cover, with the shipmanagers (and the crew supplied by them) covered by the managers' co-assured status. However crew managers often prefer to take out a separate P&I insurance for "crew risks" either on the market or with certain of the P&I clubs who provide "stand alone" crew risks cover. Crew managers often prefer to handle crew claims direct with their own insurers rather than having to involve the owner and their P&I club.

When crew managers take out separate "crew risks" insurance, they should be aware that they are not insuring themselves against the full range of P&I liabilities that could occur as a result of the negligence of "their" crew. (For a discussion on the legal liabilities of the crew manager under CREWMAN, see pages 141, 142.)

Finally, the clause provides that the crew manager will operate his drug and alcohol policy at his own cost "unless otherwise mutually agreed". Some of the major clients of the crew managers will insist on their own drug and alcohol policy being applied.

6.5.3 Clause 4—Owners' Obligations

The owners' obligations mirror those of the crew managers and require them to provide a ship which complies with the law of its flag in relation to safety and health and manning levels, where the owners supply part of the crew. Where a full crew is supplied, this obligation rests with the crew managers.

Clause 4.7 deals with owners' insurances. The text was given careful consideration by the original CREWMAN subcommittee and as a result has required only slight amendment by the current subcommittee considering changes to both SHIPMAN and CREWMAN. The text of the revised Clause 4.7 can be found on page 145.

The issue of co-assurance also arises in CREWMAN, but is a less critical requirement than for shipmanagers. The reason is that Clause 8—Responsibilities, excludes the crew manager's liability for the negligence of his crew and should thus protect the crew manager in the majority of cases. However, the risk of a crew manager being sued, particularly after a major casualty, is sufficiently strong for the contract to provide that owners' insurances name the crew manager as co-assured.

6.5.4 Clause 5—Crew Management Fee

The only part of this clause relevant to this chapter is Clause 5.9 which provides:

"The Crew Managers and the Owners will, prior to the commencement of this Agreement, agree on any trading restrictions to the Vessel which may result from the terms and conditions of the Crews' employment."

This clause relates to the possibility of flags deemed "flags of convenience" by the ITF, which may require an ITF "blue card" before the ship can safely trade to certain countries where the ITF may be able to have the ship "blacked". The CREWMAN subcommittee found it impossible to regulate the position as between the owner and the crew manager by contract, as each case depended on the owner's requirements and the ship's trading patterns. The contract is therefore silent on which party bears responsibility should a ship be delayed or back payments required to be made as a result of ITF actions. In general such issues are dealt with privately between the owners and the crew manager.

6.5.5 Clause 7—Crew Managers' Right to Subcontract

The crew managers must obtain the consent of the owners to subcontract any of their obligations, although in this case the owners' consent "shall not be unreasonably withheld". This latter provision does not appear in the 1988 version of SHIPMAN.

6.5.6 Clause 8—Responsibilities

The liability provisions of CREWMAN are similar to those of SHIPMAN.

The clause provides that the shipmanager shall be under no liability to the owners unless the loss has arisen from the negligence, gross negligence or wilful default of the crew manager or his agents and subcontractors, in which case the crew manager's liability for each incident shall be limited to a total of six times the monthly lump sum fee (which, it should be noted, includes the crew's wages). This limit of the crew manager's liability will, however, not apply where the loss has resulted from the crew manager's personal act or omission committed with the intent to cause loss or recklessly and with knowledge that such loss, damage, delay or expense would probably result.

The clause also provides:

"Under no circumstances shall the Crew Managers be liable for any of the actions of the Crew even if such actions are negligent, grossly negligent or wilful."

This provision is necessary (while SHIPMAN is silent on the point) because the crew manager is supplying the crew as a principal, and is, therefore, fully responsible, but for contract, for the negligence of his crew.

The clause contains an indemnity from the owners to the crew manager except to the extent that the crew manager may be liable in accordance with the liability provisions just described. Further, the clause includes a "Himalaya" or subcontractor's exception clause granting the crew manager's employees, agents and subcontractors the same contractual protection from liability as provided to the crew manager himself.

The effect of the clause is that the crew manager is responsible for his own and his subcontractors' negligence up to the limit of six times the monthly lump sum fee, unless he is found to have acted with intent or recklessly in the meaning of the words borrowed directly from the 1976 Limitation Convention. The owner, for his part, must indemnify the crew manager against claims which may be made against him where the crew manager has not been negligent or, when he has, the claim exceeds the manager's limit. Needless to say, the indemnity from the owners to the crew manager will not operate if the crew manager has lost his right to limit to the owner.

Although the clause specifically excepts the crew manager from liability for any of the actions of the crew even if such actions are negligent, grossly negligent or wilful, this will not protect him from liability if the loss has been caused as a result of the incompetence of crew negligently selected or trained by the managers. As it was noted earlier in the discussion on insurances, it would be wise always for the crew managers to be co-assured on the owners' insurances in order to protect them both against direct claims, and claims from underwriters in subrogation.

6.5.7 Clause 11—Law and Arbitration

This clause provides for disputes to be governed either by English or US law and to be referred to arbitration either in London or in New York. The choice selected will have been entered in the appropriate box (13) in Part I of the contract, except that it should be noted that if no selection is made, English law and London arbitration will automatically apply.

6.5.8 The Experience of BIMCO CREWMAN

Claims involving crew management are extremely rare. The case note No. 9 set out on page 154 is the only one known to the author, and it should be noted that the threat of a claim in this case probably only arose because the crew manager was not co-assured on the owner's hull and P&I policies. Nevertheless it is likely that with the more onerous duties imposed on owners and crew managers under STCW 95, the incidence of claims will grow.

6.5.9 What is BIMCO doing about their SHIPMAN and CREWMAN contracts?

BIMCO constituted a new subcommittee to review both the SHIPMAN and CREWMAN contracts in 1996 and it has already recommended amendments to the insurance clauses of both contracts. Those amendments were published on 22 January 1997 and have been widely circulated. The clauses have been reproduced at pages 128, 129, 145, 146 and now include an additional amendment ("at the discretion of underwriters") required as a result of discussion with the International Group.

The subcommittee is now engaged in reviewing the remaining elements of both contracts in the light of the ISM Code and STCW 95.

As we have seen, under the ISM Code the obligation to create and run the Safety Management System lies with the person who has "assumed responsibility for the operation of the ship". In the case of a ship given out to third party technical management it is the manager who is the person who has "assumed responsibility for the operation of the ship" and is therefore responsible for ISM Code compliance.

As a consequence of this, the owner needs to be satisfied that:

(i) the manager will maintain his DOC, and an SMC in respect of the ship;
(ii) the ship is being operated in accordance with the SMS;
(iii) the owner (who will still be liable under commercial contracts concluded in his name or in relation to casualties or pollution incidents involving the ship) must have access to the records and related SMS documents which may be needed to prove ISM compliance or to defend claims brought against him.

The subcommittee needed also to give consideration to the enhanced liability of the managers themselves if, as a result of their conduct, the ship becomes ISM non-compliant, is denied port entry, is detained, or loses her SMS certification.

The BIMCO subcommittee are dealing with these requirements by creating a new agreement—to be known as SHIPMAN 98. The basic form of the contract will remain the same. The principal differences are as follows:

(i) At the beginning of Part II there are a number of additional definitions including severance costs, crew insurances, management services and of course the ISM Code and STCW 95.
(ii) Clause 3—Basis of Agreement—provides that the managers shall carry out the management services as agents for and on behalf of the owners. This fundamental principle of SHIPMAN was somewhat buried within Clause 2.3 of the original form.
(iii) Technical Management is not much changed from the clause in the original SHIPMAN except for an addition which requires the managers to be responsible for the development, implementation and maintenance of a Safety Management System in accordance with the ISM Code.
(iv) Managers' Obligations and Owners' Obligations mirror the form adopted in the original CREWMAN. The Managers' Obligations clause states that where the managers are providing technical management, they shall be deemed to be the "Company" as defined by the ISM Code, assuming the responsibility for the operation of the ship and taking over the duties and responsibilities imposed by the Code (where applicable).

There is a corresponding obligation on the owners where the managers are not providing technical management, that they shall be responsible for ISM compliance. The owners also remain responsible for STCW compliance if the managers are not supplying the crew.

An additional requirement now included—directly related to the manager's responsibility for ISM compliance—is the owner's obligation to pay all sums due to the managers punctually in accordance with the terms of the agreement.

(v) The Insurance Policies clause is now similar to that of CREWMAN and has already been agreed and circulated. There is a minor alteration to the circulated clause which relates to the refusal by the International Group Clubs to accept as co-assured "any third party required by the manager". It has now been made clear that additional co-assureds can only be added at the discretion of the underwriters.

(vi) The clause dealing with responsibilities and liabilities, formerly Clause 18, is now Clause 11. This was extensively considered, but the resulting changes are in fact for the purposes of clarification rather than creating any fundamental alteration in the division of responsibility as between owners and managers. It was agreed that, despite the obligations placed on the party responsible for ISM compliance i.e., the manager, the balance of responsibility as between owner and manager is not fundamentally altered; the risk that claims may be easier to prove being one that still remains primarily with the owner.

There is however one major change to the clause designed to make it clear that the manager is not responsible for the negligence of his crew, and that even if he does have responsibility for failing to exercise due diligence in their selection and employment, this responsibility is still limited in accordance with the terms of the clause. The following clause has been added:

"Notwithstanding anything that may appear to the contrary in this contract, shipmanagers shall not be liable for any of the actions of the crew, even if such actions are negligent, grossly negligent or wilful, except only to the extent that they are shown to have resulted from a failure by the shipmanagers to discharge their obligations under Clause 3.1, in which case their liability should be limited in accordance with the terms of Clause 11.2.1."

(vii) A further additional clause has been added to deal with documentation reading:

"Where the managers are providing Technical Management in accordance with Sub-Clause 3.2 or Crew Management in accordance with Sub-Clause 3.1, they shall make available upon Owners' request, all documentation and records related to the Safety Management System (SMS) which the Owners need in order to demonstrate compliance with the ISM Code and STCW 95 or defend a claim against a third party."

(viii) The Law and Arbitration clause has been amended to take into account BIMCO's latest standard form.

From this it will be seen that although the manager who provides technical management services is clearly acknowledged as the "Company" responsible for compliance with the ISM Code, the basic balance of responsibilities under SHIPMAN have not changed—nor has the manager's limit of liability which remains at ten times the annual management fee. The only change to the responsibilities clause simply clarifies that the shipmanager is not responsible for crew negligence. Since the contract requires him to supply the crew as an agent, in truth he has only ever been responsible for his failure to exercise due diligence in the supply of e.g., uncertificated incompetent or improperly qualified crew.

At the time of writing SHIPMAN 98 should have been approved by BIMCO's documentary committee at its meeting in May, and be available for use before the date on which the ISM Code becomes mandatory for phase 1 ships (July 1st).

CREWMAN is proving more difficult to update, not because of any changes in the degree of responsibility between the parties as the result of ISM or STCW 95, but because of the change in the way in which it is used. Originally drafted largely for the Cypriot crew management industry, it is provided for crew managers who employ the crew themselves and supply them to the shipowner on a lump sum basis as a principal contractor. The problem is that the industry apparently now also wants the contract to reflect the fact that the crew managers also supply crews on a cost-plus basis—which usually denominates agency—which is what is currently provided for under both the old and new versions of SHIPMAN. There are likely therefore to be two different contracts allowing for the supply of crew as an agent i.e. SHIPMAN and CREWMAN, and one for the supply of crew as a principal —also CREWMAN.

The subcommittee has not yet completed its deliberations as far as the revision to CREWMAN is concerned. This is not as time sensitive as SHIPMAN, as it is not affected in the same way as SHIPMAN by the ISM Code, and the requirements of STCW 95 are only a development (albeit a very significant one) of STCW 78 to which crew managers have already to adhere. The insurance clause, long criticized in SHIPMAN, was brought up to date when CREWMAN was first drafted and, in any event, the amended insurance clauses of both contracts have already been agreed and circulated.

In the revised contract the subcommittee is unlikely to recommend altering either the limit or the level of responsibility accepted by the crew manager. The main task will be to ensure that it reflects industry practice and usage—particularly in relation to its use as both a cost-plus and a lump sum contract.

6.5.10 CREWMAN Clause 4.7

"The Owners shall procure that throughout the period of this Agreement:
  (a) at the Owners' expenses, the Vessel is insured for not less than her sound market value or entered for her full gross tonnage, as the case may be for:

(i) usual hull and machinery marine risks (including crew negligence) and excess liabilities;

(ii) protection and indemnity risks (including pollution risks and diversion expenses but excluding crew risks if separately insured by the Crew Managers in accordance with sub-clause 3.8(a)); and

(iii) war risks including protection and indemnity and crew risks;

in accordance with the best practice of prudent owners of vessels of a similar type to the Vessel, with first class insurance companies, underwriters or associations ('the Owners' Insurances');

(b) all premiums and calls on the Owners' Insurances are paid promptly by their due date for payment;

(c) the Owners' Insurances name the Crew Managers and, subject to the underwriters' agreement, any third party designated by the Crew Managers as a joint assured, with full cover, with the Owners obtaining cover in respect of each of the insurances specified in (a) above:

(i) on terms whereby the Crew Managers and any such third party are liable in respect of premiums or calls arising in connection with the Owners' Insurances; or

(ii) if obtainable, on terms such that neither the Crew Managers nor any such third party shall be under any liability in respect of premiums or calls arising in connection with the Owners' Insurances; or

(iii) on such other terms as may be agreed in writing.

(d) written evidence is provided to complete satisfaction of the Crew Managers of their compliance with their obligations under this clause within 30 days of the commencement of the agreement and of each renewal date and, if specifically requested, of each payment date of the Owners' Insurances."

CASE NOTES

The Marion [1984] 2 Lloyd's Rep. 1

The *Marion* was managed by Fairfield Maxwell Management Services. When anchored in Tees Bay to await a berth, her anchor fouled and seriously damaged an oil pipeline on the seabed. Although there was an up-to-date chart on board showing the position of the pipeline, the master had in fact been navigating by reference to an out-of-date chart on which the pipeline was not shown.

The shipmanager had left it to the master to order such charts as he needed. The master was responsible for updating charts on board and he was supplied on a regular basis with all weekly Admiralty Notices to Mariners and chart correction tracings.

After the casualty it was found that there were a large number of obsolete charts on board which should have been disposed of. It was also established that a year before the casualty a ship safety inspection had been carried out by the Liberian Bureau of Maritime Affairs. The report of that inspection, a copy of which had been sent to the shipmanager, contained the following comment: "Navigational charts for trade or vessel corrections omitted for several years". The contents of the Liberian report were never seen by the managing director of the ship management company who, at the time in question, was abroad for long periods. Subsequently, the assistant operations manager of the ship management company wrote to the master instructing him to ensure that all charts and navigational publications were regularly corrected and a careful record of such corrections maintained.

The master was also instructed to compile, a soon as possible, a requisition for Admiralty charts and navigational publications which needed to be replaced, and to ensure that all obsolete charts were destroyed. A substantial number of new charts were requisitioned, but the master did not confirm that he had complied with the other instructions and it was subsequently proved that he had failed to do so.

The owners of the pipeline, who claimed $25 million from the shipowner for repairs and consequential losses, argued that there should have been a proper system for ensuring that the charts on board were corrected—or disposed of if obsolete or superseded—and that the responsibility for implementing that supervisory system rested with the managing director of the ship management company. They also argued that he should have ensured that, while he was absent from the office, a matter as serious as the Liberian report was referred to him.

The House of Lords found that the managing director of the ship management company had a duty to ensure that an adequate degree of supervision was exercised over the master and that he had failed to perform that duty. The court also found that during his absences from the office he had failed to give proper instructions to his subordinates concerning the matters on which he required to be kept informed.

The House of Lords accepted the view of Mr Justice Sheen in the Commercial Court when he said:

"When a ship is owned by a limited liability company and managed by another limited liability company the first question which arises is: to which of those companies should one look to see whether the owners are guilty of 'actual fault'? It is not disputed, nor can it be disputed in this Court that the answer to that question is that one looks to the managing company."

As the actual fault had been on the part of the managing director of the management company, the shipowner was consequently unable to limit his liability. Had he been able to, his limit of liability under the 1957 Limitation Convention would have been just under $1 million.

As a consequence of the loss of the right to limit, the owner, or rather his P&I Club, settled the claim more or less in full, for almost $25 million. Fortunately, the shipmanager was co-assured on the owner's P&I policy and was, therefore, protected both from the claim from the owners of the pipeline and also from a claim in subrogation by the club.

The Maira (Glafki Shipping Co. S.A. v. Pinios Shipping Co. No. 1) [1986] 2 Lloyd's Rep. 12

Glafki were the managers of *The Maira* appointed by the National Bank of Greece following the owner's default on payments to her builders. It was a condition of the mortgages on the ship that the owner should insure her "for the full insurable value of the vessel and in any event for not less than 130 per cent (one hundred and thirty per cent) of the total balance of the mortgage debt remaining unpaid and interest thereon".

The ship management contract provided that Glafki should:

"place all hull and machinery protection and indemnity war risk insurances and any other insurance which the agent may think fit on the vessel, crew, cargo or freight and pay all insurance premiums thereon, in accordance with the respective insurance clauses for the mortgage in favour of the bank."

The ship management contract also provided that:

"neither the agent [Glafki] nor the bank shall be under any responsibility or liability for loss or damage to the vessel or for loss of profits or otherwise to the owner arising out of any act or omission involving any error of judgement on the part of its officers or employees selected with due care or otherwise in connection with the management of the vessel or in the performance of the agent's duties under this agreement."

The ship was delivered to the owners in February 1977 and insured for $10 million, although her market value was then substantially less. Glafki took over the management of the ship in September 1977 and maintained the insurance on the ship at the same level. The policies came up for renewal on 1 April 1978 at which time the balance of the mortgage debt remaining unpaid was about $9.17 million. Glafki nevertheless renewed the hull insurances for an agreed value of $10 million. Ten days later the ship became a total loss.

The bank sued the managers on the grounds that they had failed to insure her for 130 per cent of the total balance on the mortgage debt outstanding, an obligation that was imposed on the bank under the mortgage. The High Court found in favour of the managers on a number of grounds but was clearly influenced by the fact that the ship's market value on 1 April 1978 was only about $4.875 million and to have insured the ship for more than $10 million would have been inconsistent with the basic principle of marine insurance: that of providing an indemnity in respect of the ship insured and not in respect of the debts of the owners secured by mortgages on her.

The Court of Appeal disagreed with the High Court judge and found in favour of the bank. They found no difficulty with the discrepancy between the ship's market value and her insured value, quoting with approval the arbitrator's finding that it was common practice to insure for 30 per cent above mortgage liabilities even when the value of the ship was below those liabilities.

The managers sought to rely on the exclusion clause in the management contract, arguing that their failure to insure up to the level required under the ship's mortgages was an act or omission involving an error of judgement on their part. The arbitrator and the courts all dismissed this argument, the arbitrator holding:

"The clause itself only excludes liability in respect of any error of judgement and does not, to my mind, go sufficiently wide so as to exclude liability for a breach of the duties owed by the manager under earlier clauses of the management agreement. Since I decided that the managers breached the duties required of them under the management agreement it follows that I am of the view that the exemption clause does not protect the managers."

The House of Lords also commented on the effect of this clause saying:

"It appears to [me] that, in order to enable the managers to bring themselves within the protection afforded by the exemption provision in Clause 10, they would have had to obtain from the arbitrator two findings of fact: first that they had applied their minds properly to, and exercised an informed judgement about, the amount for which they were obliged to insure the ship; and, secondly, that in doing these things, they had committed no more than an error of judgement.

The arbitrator, however, made no finding upon these lines at all: on the contrary, the whole tenor of the reasons for his award is inconsistent with any such findings."

The managers were thus found liable for the difference between the amount for which they had insured the ship and the amount for which she should have been insured under the terms of the mortgage, a sum of about $1.92 million.

McDermid v. *Nash Dredging & Reclamation Co. Ltd.* [1986] QB 965

McDermid was employed as a deck hand by Nash Dredging and was working on a tug in Sweden when he was badly injured as a result of the negligence of the tug's master. The master of the tug was employed, not by Nash but by Nash's parent company, Stevin. The Court of Appeal, reviewing the authorities, referred to the general rule that an employer is not liable for a tort committed by another person in the course of the performance of work for the employer, unless the tortious act was committed by someone who is the servant of the employer, or has been directly authorized by the employer. The problem in McDermid's case was that the master of the tug was not the servant of McDermid's employer, Nash. The Court of Appeal dealt with this by holding that, if an employer delegates to another person, whether an employee or not, his personal duty to take reasonable care for the safety of his employees, the employer is liable for injury caused through the negligence of that person because it is in the eyes of the law, his own negligence. They accordingly held Nash responsible for McDermid's injuries.

The question then arose as to whether Nash were entitled to limit their liability to McDermid under the Merchant Shipping Act 1958. The High Court had held that they were, but the Court of Appeal looked more closely at the Act which provided as follows:

"(1) The persons whose liability in connection with the ship is excluded or limited by Part VIII of the Merchant Shipping Act 1894 shall include any charterer and any person interested in or in possession of a ship, and in particular, any manager or operator of the ship.

(2) In relation to a claim arising from the act or omission of any person in his capacity as master or member of the crew or (otherwise than in that capacity) in the course of his employment as a servant of the owners or of any such person as is mentioned in subsection (1) of this section, (a) the persons whose liability is excluded or limited as aforesaid shall also

include the master, member of the crew or servant and in a case where the master or member of the crew is the servant of a person whose liability would not be excluded or limited apart from this paragraph, the person whose servant he is."

The lower court had held that Nash were entitled to limit their liability under subsection (2) quoted above because they were vicariously liable for the negligence of the master of the tug. The Court of Appeal, however, found that the master of the tug was not the servant of Nash. Nash could, therefore, not claim limitation under subsection (2). Furthermore, Nash, whether as dredging operators or manning contractors, were not able to bring themselves within the provision of subsection (1) as being "any manager or operator of the ship". They were accordingly held unable to limit their liability to McDermid.

Nash's exact status was not defined in the judgment, but clearly they were neither the manager nor the operator of the ship. This highlights the inability of parties providing services similar to managers, such as crewing agents and perhaps crew managers, to limit their liability.

Ert Stefanie (Société Anonyme des Minerals v. Grant Trading Inc.) [1987] 2 Lloyd's Rep. 371; [1989] 1 Lloyd's Rep. 349

The *Ert Stefanie* was managed by Sorek Shipping Limited and carried a cargo of ferrosilicon in bulk from Rijeka to Rotterdam. The ship was seriously unseaworthy. Her bottom plating was defective allowing seawater to leak into the holds. Furthermore, the ship was not designed to carry ferrosilicon which when exposed to water gives off poisonous gas. On the voyage in question one crew member was killed and another made seriously ill. The voyage was eventually abandoned.

In London arbitration the owner was allowed to limit his liability under section 503 of the Merchant Shipping Act because the loss and damage had occurred without his actual fault or privity. However, on appeal the Commercial Court quoted with approval Mr Justice Sheen's comments in *The Marion* when he said "When a ship is owned by a limited liability company and managed by another limited liability company the first question which arises is: to which of those companies should one look to see whether the owners are guilty of 'actual fault'? It is not disputed, nor can it be disputed in this court, that the answer to that question is that one looks to the managing company."

The Commercial Court had no difficulty in finding that the actual fault was that of a director of Sorek responsible for the technical management of the ship. They said:

"A director forms part of the head management of the company and if he is at fault then his fault for the purposes of the Merchant Shipping Act is the fault of the company . . . (the director's) position as an *alter ego* of the company does not depend on any special delegation or authorisation; it depends upon his position and status as a director. Therefore, in the present case, on the findings of fact made by the arbitrator, given that there was fault on the part of (the director) there is no ground for saying that the fault was not a fault of an *alter ego* of the company and, therefore, an actual fault of the company."

Safe Carrier (Seaboard Offshore Ltd. v. *Secretary of State for Transport)*
[1994] 1 Lloyd's Rep. 75

The *Safe Carrier* was an offshore standby safety vessel which left the River Tyne for Aberdeen at 7.50 pm. She carried a chief engineer who at first boarded the ship at 5.00 pm and so had only two hours 50 minutes with which to familiarize himself with the machinery. During the next 24 hours the ship's engines broke down on three occasions leaving the ship drifting at sea. Eventually she was taken in tow and brought back to the River Tyne.

Seaboard Offshore Ltd., the managers of the ship, were charged with an offence under section 31 of the Merchant Shipping Act 1988 which provided:

"(1) It shall be the duty of the owner of a ship . . . to take all reasonable steps to secure that the ship is operated in a safe manner . . .

(3) If the owner of a ship . . . fails to discharge the duty imposed on him by subsection (1), he shall be guilty of an [criminal] offence."

The House of Lords held that the argument that the manager was vicariously liable for a breach of duty under section 31 of the Merchant Shipping Act 1988, arising from an act or omission by any of the manager's servants or agents, was incorrect. To secure a conviction under section 31, the prosecution had to prove beyond reasonable doubt that the manager had failed to take all reasonable steps to secure that the ship was operated in a safe manner. The court said that it was not helpful to seek to categorize the offence as either being or not being one of strict liability; it consisted simply in failure to take steps which by an objective standard were held to be reasonable steps to take in the interests of the safe operation of the ships, and the duty which it placed on the managers was a personal one. The manager was criminally liable if he failed personally in the duty but was not criminally liable for the acts or omissions of his subordinate employees if he himself had taken all such reasonable steps.

Case Number 1: Managers not Liable for Damage to Reefer Cargo

In one notorious case dating from 1982, a shipmanager faced several years of litigation from the voyage of a ship carrying meat from the Argentine to Egypt. The claim, for the alleged poor maintenance of reefer machinery, was pursued by the shipowner's P&I Club following the settlement of heavy cargo claims against the owner. The case was never decided on its merits, but consisted almost entirely of interlocutory (preliminary) proceedings aimed at discovering the amount of insurance coverage held by the manager. The P&I Club's claim was eventually withdrawn after substantial costs had been incurred.

Case Number 2: The Manager's Negligence Leads to the Loss of the Owners' Insurances

Shortly before a tanker loaded a cargo in Europe for Canada, the master, while walking on deck near the number 3 starboard ballast tank, heard a creaking noise within the tank. He then carried out a limited internal inspection of the tanks and found corrosion including damage to stiffeners and other structural members. The master telexed the managers reporting the result of his inspection. The managers responded that they would revert with repair instructions in due course. However, repairs were not undertaken before the ship loaded her cargo nor was the ship's classification society notified.

Whilst on the voyage the tanker encountered heavy weather and began to take water into her number 3 starboard water ballast tank through a crack in her shell plating. The ship put into the Azores and after examination of the ballast tank it was decided to tranship her cargo and put back to Europe for repairs.

At the time of the casualty the owners' P&I Club sent surveyors to the ship and arranged for statements to be taken from the managers and the crew. On completion of their investigations the P&I Club advised the owners that in their view there had been a breach of the Club Rules in relation to the failure to notify the ship's classification society promptly of pre-existing corrosion and weakness in the ship's ballast tanks. The ship's hull underwriters also declined to contribute both to the cost of repairs and to their proportion of general average on the grounds that the loss was not the result of an insured peril.

The total loss, costs and expenses arising from this incident amounted to $16 million although the part directly attributable to the manager's negligence was about $7 million. The managers argued that their contract gave them some protection but were obliged to negotiate a settlement of the claim for $4 million.

Case Number 3: Pre-purchase Inspection

Many shipmanagers carry out surveys on behalf of clients prior to their purchase of a ship. This is known as pre-purchase inspection.

A pre-purchase inspection was carried out in Europe by the manager's senior superintendent surveyor. Following his inspection, in which he recommended that certain repairs should be carried out, the owners bought the ship and put her into dry dock for those repairs to be undertaken. While she was in dry dock the owners' P&I Club conducted a condition survey which found the hatch covers in poor condition. The extra expense of repairing the hatch covers put the cost of repairs well beyond the surveyor's original estimate—as a result of which the surveyor deferred the repair work on certain machinery items so that the overall bill would be within the range of the original estimate.

After leaving the repair yard the ship suffered a number of breakdowns and problems directly related to those items of machinery on which repairs should have been undertaken. The owners sued the shipmanager on the grounds that had the repairs been correctly estimated they would have been able to reduce the price which they had paid for the ship, or decide not to purchase it at all. The managers were obliged to settle the claim.

Case Number 4: Error in Payment of P&I Calls

A shipmanager responsible for dealing with his owners' insurances, received a release call from the shipowners' P&I Club following the sale of the ship under their management. The club advised that unless the debit notes were paid by a certain date, they would be substantially increased. The managers omitted to pay the debit notes by the date specified and were liable to the owners for the substantial difference between the sum originally debited and the increased amount.

Case Number 5: Engine Room Fire at Sea

While on a loaded voyage, fire broke out in the engine room of a tanker. The cause was subsequently established to be leakage from a fractured small-bore pipe leading off the generator fuel crossover to a fuel pressure gauge. There was considerable damage which resulted in complete loss of power. A tug was engaged on LOF terms and the ship was towed into harbour where the cargo was transhipped. The total claim in respect of general average, repairs, towage, transhipment etc., amounted to $8 million.

On examination it was found that the same pipe had leaked when the ship was undergoing repairs some months previously, and a small fire had been caused. The fire was extinguished by the crew and was reported to the manager's superintendent and the chief engineer. The second engineer informed them that the necessary repairs were straightforward and would be carried out by him. Neither the manager's superintendent nor the chief engineer inspected the fractured pipe or the subsequent repairs closely. The second engineer did effect the repairs but following a series of subsequent leaks he blanked off two ends of the T-piece to prevent further leaks. He then left the ship. It subsequently became clear that the blanks inserted by him had been removed some time prior to the fire when further work was carried out on the pipe. Although it was never established who had performed these last repairs, there was no doubt that they had been carried out in an unseamanlike manner.

Cargo underwriters declined to contribute their proportion of general average, which was very substantial. Although the ship's P&I Club alleged negligence or lack of due diligence by the manager, no claim was in the event pursued against him.

Case Number 6: Main Engine Failure

The managers acted for the owners of a cruise ship which suffered a breakdown of both main engines due to contaminated lube oil. The owners' claim against hull underwriters for engine damage, repairs and loss of hire amounted to $3 million.

Underwriters rejected the claim on the grounds that the damage had occurred as a result of poor maintenance and lack of proper procedures on board.

The claim went to trial in America, but was settled before judgment, the managers contributing $490,000.

Case Number 7: Damage to Boiler

The ship was fitted with an auxiliary boiler which had been in service for 12 years when the manager advised the owners that it needed extensive repairs due to leakages. It was found that a rainwater hood situated in the funnel designed to prevent rainwater entering the boiler, had failed due to corrosion. Although a temporary canvas hood was then fitted to the funnel, external corrosion was found to the lower part of the boiler tubes due to acidic attack caused by the combination of water and sulphur/soot from the boiler. Repair costs amounted to over $1 million.

The owners' hull underwriters rejected their claim on the grounds that the damage was caused by wear and tear. The owners then brought their claim against the manager.

An argument then developed between the manager's and the hull underwriters' average adjusters as to whether or not the failure of the hood was wear and tear or an "accident". The matter was never resolved but the manager settled the claim against him with a contribution of $225,000.

Case Number 8: General Average—Incorrect Operation of a Valve— Manager No Longer Co-assured

The management agreement had come to an end and the ship taken back into the owner's own management, when an engineer opened instead of closing a valve in the sea chest. This particular valve closed anticlockwise and in trying to close it more tightly he flooded the engine room. Cargo underwriters refused to contribute their proportion of general average on the grounds of unseaworthiness. The P&I Club then alleged that the manager should have warned the owners of the rogue valve and sought to recover from the manager in recourse. The managers were by then no longer co-assured on the owners' P&I policy.

Case Number 9: Crew Managers—Collision

Crew managers employed the crew of a tanker which anchored awaiting discharge. A storm blew up and the ship dragged its anchor and collided with another ship. The first ship was found to be to blame for the collision on the grounds that she should have started her engines during the storm and failure to do so was due to the negligence of the second officer who was on watch at the time.

The crew managers were not named as co-assureds on the owners' P&I policy and were thus potentially liable to a claim in subrogation from the ship's P&I and hull underwriters. In the event, the claim, for more than $5 million, was not pursued.

THE QUEST FOR SAFETY AND QUALITY MANAGEMENT

7.1 INTRODUCTION

Quality Assurance (QA) has been defined in a multitude of different ways. Probably the most often used definition is the over simplistic one: the application of common sense to creating a functional organizational structure. The International Standards Organization (ISO), the body responsible for the ISO 9000 series, the most widely adopted quality assurance standard for design and production, has the following definition:

"The totality of features and characteristics of a product or service that bear on its ability to satisfy stated or implied needs."

This definition is elaborated upon in the same document as:

"All those planned and systematic actions necessary to provide adequate confidence that a product or service will satisfy given requirements for quality."

The detail of QA will be developed later in the chapter but it is important to understand at the outset that the ISO 9000 series provides a logical framework for defining, controlling and correcting a product or service so that it consistently meets defined requirements. It is a general code and is not specifically developed for ship management.

Further, it is also important to note that nowhere in the definition is a relationship made between "high quality" and product or service quality.

Since the middle of the 1980s QA has entered almost every aspect of ship operation. In today's market it is becoming increasingly difficult to operate unless some form of quality assurance accreditation is in place. Charter Parties often have QA clauses, the "oil majors" all have their individual QA requirements, suppliers' find it increasingly difficult to get on a company's register without it and ship management companies are not taken seriously without a recognized certificate.

The development of QA from its ubiquitous ISO series into hybrid codes specifically targeted towards ship management has been relatively rapid when compared to traditional industry developments. Further, in their development the codes have each had a slightly different goal. The most important of these codes is the IMO's International Safety Management Code (ISM) which will become progressively mandatory for different ship types from 1998 through to 2002. The ISM Code will affect almost every ship operator in the world and, in theory, will progressively become the operator's licence to operate.

There is no one particular catalyst that has initiated the movement towards the implementation of QA schemes in ship management but several major accidents have each contributed significantly.

These accidents can be grouped in three distinct categories: firstly the *Herald of Free Enterprise* and *Scandinavian Star* passenger losses, secondly the *Exxon Valdez* and *Braer* pollution accidents and, thirdly, *The Marion* incident when the use of out-of-date charts resulted in the vessel fouling her anchor on an oil pipeline. Additionally, there was a climate in the industry at the time of defensiveness due to the high level of media attention given to the above incidents as well as a more general problem with poorly maintained VLCCs and bulk carriers.

7.2 THE REASONS WHY SAFETY AND QUALITY MANAGEMENT WERE ADOPTED

It has become normal practice to differentiate between the physical ship and its equipment, the so-called hardware, and the ship and shore management, the software or "human ware".

In each of the major contributory accidents mentioned in the previous section, the software received the major part of the criticism in the various report findings. The ship/shore management interface was identified as a serious weakness and, consequently, the focus of the operation requiring the most attention.

Chronologically the first major disaster of recent times influencing the development of systems designed to improve the management interface was the *Herald of Free Enterprise*. The Sheen Report highlighted major deficiencies in the overall management of the vessel as well as specific criticisms of particular practices affecting the safety of the operation.

The IMO responded to the safety management aspects of the inquiry by adopting a resolution to approve and recommend "IMO Guidelines for the Management of Safe Ship Operation and Pollution Prevention". These guidelines have progressed from voluntary adoption to become the International Safety Management Code, which will become mandatory for certain classes and tonnage of vessels as of 1 July 1998.

The actual implementation schedule is as follows:

1 1 July 1998—all passenger ships, and the following ship types of 500 gross tons and over: oil tankers, chemical tankers, gas carriers, bulk carriers and cargo high speed craft.

2 1 July 2002—all other cargo ships and MODUs of 500 gross tons and over (Mobile Offshore Drilling Units cover the majority of mobile drilling, production and storage vessels not regarded as permanently moored).

The grounding of the *Exxon Valdez*, the resulting pollution, environmental damage and compensation costs in a sensitive area of the United States of America led to the introduction of the Oil Pollution Act 1990 (OPA 90). The legislation introduced severe liabilities on the operators of tankers, in particular, bringing oil to the USA. The commercial damage inflicted on *Exxon*, and by association the other oil majors, caused them to review their whole strategy for shipping. The result was that several "majors" decided to exit shipping. However, the requirement for transporting oil still existed and for those operators prepared to take the risk of unlimited liability a method of demonstrating professionalism and sound management control was necessary.

The oil companies were familiar with quality assurance from their exploration, production and refining operations and consequently introduced oil company specific guidelines based on QA schemes already in use. Unfortunately, these guidelines tended to be unilateral and caused operators a certain amount of confusion since the detail changed depending on the particular oil company charter being operated. The implementation of the guidelines was enforced through the use of oil company inspectors and auditors.

The situation today is slowly improving with the harmonization of the oil major requirements in the Oil Companies International Marine Forum (OCIMF) guidelines and the growing trust in the use of their Ship Inspection Reporting Programme (SIRE) database for tankers. Nonetheless, such was the impact of the *Exxon Valdez* on the oil majors that they are still extremely cautious about general guidelines and still insist on their own specific versions and verification procedures.

The guidelines from the respective oil majors are reasonably similar in outline and cover the following headings:

health, safety and environmental policies;	cargo handling procedures;
personal safety;	records;
training programmes for staff and crew;	alcohol and drug abuse policy;
	management controls;
navigation and watchkeeping policy;	maintenance programmes;
	emergency/contingency procedures.

In order to demonstrate compliance with these guidelines is was necessary for a shipmanager to generate a management system that produced a trail of evidence capable of being audited by the oil major inspectors.

In many cases complying with the above requirements was a reasonably straightforward "formalization" of the existing management system. However, for other managers and operators, who had a more autocratic management style, the development and indeed the intrusiveness of such system requirements proved to be extremely problematic. The logical development was to introduce a QA programme based around the same standard as used by the oil companies. The standard tended to be based on ISO 9002.

The impetus to drive through the changes brought about by the *Herald of Free Enterprise* and the *Exxon Valdez* disasters was reinforced as a result of the *Braer* and *Scandinavian Star* accidents. In both these incidents the management structure was found wanting in vital areas of communication and responsibility.

The adoption of safety management initiatives and quality assurance was not solely driven by the major accidents already quoted. During the later 1970s and early 1980s the ship management market witnessed the entry of many new players. Often the new entrants would be small companies of two to three people operating a handful of ships. Thus the spectrum of services offered by shipmanagers was extremely wide and there was little differentiation by potential clients between the "two men and a fax" operation and the highly developed organizations offering a full range of services.

It became apparent to the professional operators and managers that their industry of low entry and exit cost operation and widely varying service standards would have to find a method of differentiation. The introduction of some form of QA was an obvious route to follow. Consequently, many companies opted for the implementation of ISO 9002 whilst a group of leading shipmanagers decided to develop their own specific industry code. The initial development of this code was undertaken by five of the leading managers: Barber, Columbia, Denholm, Hanseatic and Wallem together with three of the major classification societies; Det Norske Veritas, Germanischer Lloyd and Lloyd's Register. In 1991 this "Group of Five" expanded the membership to form the International Ship Managers Association (ISMA).

7.3 THE DIFFERENT CODES AND THEIR FUNCTION

As has been already stated the ISO 9000 series of quality assurance standards has spawned several purpose-built codes and a lot of debate as to their relative merits and functions. Essentially these codes can be split into two types, firstly safety management and secondly quality management.

7.3.1 Safety Management Codes: The International Safety Management Code (ISM)

The ISM Code is reproduced in full as Appendix 3 and consists of 13 short chapters as summarized below:

1 General
  A general section emphasizing administration policy regarding safety management, operation of ships, and protection of the environment which should be incorporated into the company and shipboard Safety Management System (SMS).
2 Safety and Environmental Protection Policy
  Safety and environmental protection policies as required to be established by the ISM Code, must be signed by the company's chief executive or other senior executive officer, and should be reviewed at regular intervals to ensure that they remain likely to achieve the objectives of the ISM Code.

3 Company Responsibilities and Authority

The owner of each vessel must provide the Office of the Maritime Administration with the name, address, telephone, fax and telex numbers of the company responsible for the operation of the vessel. If the entity responsible for the operation of a ship is other than the owner, the owner must identify the full name of such entity and submit details to the administration which establish that entity as the company.

4 Designated Person

The company must provide the Maritime Authority with current information sufficient to enable direct and immediate contact at all times between the administration and the company designated person or persons required by the ISM Code for matters relating to the SMS, maritime safety, and the protection of the environment.

5 Master's Responsibility and Authority

Any system of operational control implemented by company shore based management must allow for the master's absolute authority and discretion to take whatever action he considers to be in the best interests of passengers, crew, cargo, the vessel and the environment.

The company should provide the master with documentation of the specific duties delegated to the officers under the master's command.

6 Resources and Personnel

Company training, hiring, manning procedures, terms of employment, personnel record keeping and reporting procedures must be consistent with the requirements of the STCW Code and the regulations of the Maritime Authority in order to ensure the use of competent qualified personnel.

The company SMS should ensure that joining crew members have proper seafarers' certification including licences, special qualification certificates, seaman's identification and record books and training as required by international conventions, the law of the Maritime Authority and any special requirements issued by the Maritime Authority.

The shipboard SMS should include procedures for the transfer of command, documented handover notes, documented ship and duties introduction, familiarization training in accordance with Section A–I/6 of the STCW Code for joining officers and crew, and on board documentation retention.

7 Development of Plans for Shipboard Operations

A "Master's Port Arrival/Departure Safety Check List" should be included in the shipboard SMS incorporating pre-established company policy guidelines for "Go, No Go" situations and reporting requirements for the master's compliance.

The ship's operations documentation should include a statement that its contents do not remove the master's authority to take such steps and issue any orders, whether or not they are in accordance with the contents of the documentation, which the master considers to be necessary for the preservation of life, and the safety of the ship, and the environment.

8 Emergency Preparedness

The company SMS must provide that statutory, administration, or company required emergency plans will be periodically reviewed, updated, amended and, if necessary, re-approved by the administration.

9 Reports and Analysis of Non-Conformities, Accidents and Hazardous Occurrences

The SMS procedures for reporting accidents and incidents should incorporate the provisions of the relevant Maritime Authority with regard to the duties and responsibilities for the company, ship officers, and crew to report such events.

The company SMS and shipboard SMS must incorporate the provisions of the Maritime Authority regarding accident prevention and appointment of a safety officer.

The company and shipboard SMS should contain procedures for immediately reporting port state detentions to the administration.

10 Maintenance of the Ship and Equipment

The maintenance system established by the company and documented in its SMS should include systematic plans and actions designed to address all those items and systems covered by class and statutory survey and ensure that the vessel's condition is satisfactorily maintained at all times.

As part of the company initiated ship safety inspections, the shipboard SMS should include reference to the Maritime Authority's periodic safety inspection requirements.

The company SMS should also provide for the logging of actions or measures taken to rectify deficiencies and non-conformities noted during surveys and annual safety inspections and the giving of notification to the administration of the corrective actions taken.

11 Documentation

Documents should be easily identified, traceable, user friendly and not voluminous as to hinder the effectiveness of the SMS.

12 The Company Verification, Review and Evaluation

The company must conduct internal audits shoreside and on each ship at least annually to determine whether the various elements of the company SMS have been fully implemented and are effective in achieving the stated objectives of the Code. The internal audits are in addition to the annual, intermediate, and renewal audits carried out by the responsible organization appointed by the Authority.

The introduction of the ISM Code has brought with it a great deal of expectation with respect to the conduct of the industry. Many pundits are suggesting that as of the implementation date many of the substandard operators will be driven out of the industry. This scenario is unlikely and it is more probable that the adoption of the principles of the ISM Code will gradually take effect over many years and during that time the code will be amended and developed in response to specific incidents and to meet new challenges facing the industry.

The shipping industry faces several structural problems with regard to the drafting, implementation, and enforcement of regulations. Consequently the ISM Code suffers equally and in some respects more so since it is a "qualitative" regulation as opposed to quantitative. The flaws associated with the code and its implementation are:

1 The IMO implementation will be very slow and there is a sense in which their targeting of developed countries, large ships, and specifically hazardous sectors like passenger and gas vessels as priority code adherents, is not actually tackling the real substandard end of the fleets.

2 The IMO Code sets a plateau standard and does not help to direct money and enthusiasm into quality development.

3 Each flag state appoints its own audit body and consequently the scope for wide variations in the interpretation and standard of audits is ever present. Further, few of the auditors to be appointed will actually be true auditors.

Invariably many will be re-trained surveyors more used to dealing with objective decisions rather than the more subjective type required in auditing. This situation will need careful monitoring since it is the auditors who will form a vital link in the ISM process.

4 The implementation of the code is the flag state's responsibility. It is difficult to see how it could be otherwise, and although there is a growing mood in port state control systems to target for detention certain ships which are flying the flags of states which have not so far shown much enthusiasm to police existing regulations, there is little reason to suppose that a sloppy flag will be any more interested in strict interpretation of the safety management code than it is in inspecting the physical attributes of vessels flying its flag. Essentially the substandard flag will attract the substandard operator and be audited by a substandard authority leaving the entire burden on port state control.

5 Historically regulations are implemented in a minimalist fashion by a great many operators and the success of the ISM Code relies on operators adopting a positive attitude to its implementation.

7.3.2 Other Safety Codes

Prior to the adoption of the ISM Code as a regulatory requirement several classification societies launched their own version of a safety code covering virtually the same aspects of safety, pollution and the environment. Fortunately the alternative codes were not widely adopted and the only one that is still mentioned to any great extent is the SEP (Safety, Environment and Pollution) code from DNV.

It is probably fortuitous that these alternative safety codes were not widely adopted otherwise the industry would effectively be further adding to the general confusion surrounding differences between each of them and inevitably creating a similar situation as was experienced with the oil major guidelines.

The continued use of SEPs is most common amongst Scandinavian owners and operators but it is likely that its use will diminish as operators choose to confine themselves to a safety management system based on the ISM. In reality the differences between the ISM and SEP are not readily identified by the industry and certainly not by the clients.

7.3.3 Quality Assurance: EN ISO 9002—Model for Quality Assurance in Production, Installation and Servicing

The citation ISO 9002 is now found on the company literature of a vast range of businesses and enterprises both within the marine industry as well as others. This citation is usually associated with the accreditation authority. Currently, there is no control over who can accredit a company to an ISO standard. This means that in order to give credibility to the citation the good companies will use a respected accreditation body.

Within the marine industries this invariably means a classification society belonging to IACS.

A further requirement when assessing the value of the ISO citation is to establish what exactly has been accredited. The certificate issued to a company carries a description of the services accredited together with the valid dates.

Therefore when assessing a ship management company it is important to establish the scope of the certificate together with the accreditation authority.

The requirements of ISO 9002 are written in a general form with no specific industry in mind apart from being: production, installation or servicing. Therefore a lot of interpretation is required in order to make the code suitable for use in the ship management sector. Further, no guidance is available as to what level of detail and control is required. It is due to this general nature of the standard that difficulty is often experienced in trying to find the right level of detail required in the procedures. Consequently poorly-designed and implemented systems are often criticized for being "paper mountains" and overly bureaucratic.

There are several ways to approach the design and implementation of a quality system. The best and most often recommended is to retain control of the project in-house and if possible use a suitably qualified member of the existing management team. Bearing in mind that implementation of ISO 9002 is voluntary and expensive, commitment from the top management is essential. Although this statement has been somewhat overplayed it remains true that without the genuine support of the management the QA system has very little chance of succeeding.

The use of consultants is an option and they can be utilized in several ways. They can be used to assist the company's implementation under a narrow remit or they can be used to completely write and deliver the system assisting the company all the way through the audit. The latter option carries a major pitfall insofar as most consultants deliver edited versions of a standard package which may or may not truly reflect a company's *modus operandi*. Consequently the staff who have to work with the system have no affinity to it and will tend to disown it over a very short period of time.

The ISO 9002 standard is far more extensive than the ISM Code but it still has many overlapping areas. This is not surprising since the ISO standard has been used as the basis for most safety and quality standards.

The quality system requirements for the ISO 9002 standard are summarized as in the following (NB the numbering used corresponds to the actual reference system in the Standard):

4   Quality system requirements
4.1   Management Responsibility
4.2   Quality system
4.3   Contract review

4.4   Design Control (not required in ISO 9002 but included to retain consistent numbering with ISO 9001)

4.5   Documents and data control

4.6   Purchasing

4.7   Control of customer-supplied product

4.8   Product identification and traceability

4.9   Process control

4.10 Inspection and testing

4.11 Control of inspection, measuring and test equipment

4.12 Inspection and test status

4.13 Control of nonconforming product

4.14 Corrective and preventive action

4.15 Handling, storage, packaging, preservation and delivery

4.16 Control of quality records

4.17 Internal quality audits

4.18 Training

4.19 Servicing

4.20 Statistical techniques

7.3.4 The International Ship Managers' Association (ISMA) Code of Ship Management

The ISMA produced a code in 1992 designed to cover all the major aspects of ship management that could reasonably be required in order that a company could call itself a shipmanager. It also established a minimum level of service required.

The ISMA Code committee took as its starting point the ISO 9002 model for quality assurance and attempted to interpret the standard in a way that would be general for all shipmanagers thus avoiding many of the traps found in the bare interpretation of ISO 9002. It also took into account other requirements such as the IMO guidelines, Resolution A741(18) that later became the ISM Code, the "oil major" requirements, the functions of insurance and accounting. In addition to the basic needs, the code also attempted to outline the minimum expectations that a client might have of a shipmanager. These were outlined as the ethics expected of an ISMA member.

The introduction of the Code provoked widespread debate amongst the ship-management industry. The major part relating to whether or not the ISMA Code or a combination of ISO 9002 and/or ISM or SEPs were more comprehensive. The debate did little to convince the outside world that the industry was maturing and reflected equally badly on the members of ISMA as well as the non-members. It also served to highlight the lack of understanding in the industry as to how a level of quality could be achieved.

A comparison of the elements of the various codes is shown in Table 7.1.

Table 7.1: A comparison of the various safety and quality codes

Procedure	ISMA	ISM (IMO)	ISO 9002
Business ethics/policies	●	●	●
Organization	●	●	●
Personnel	●	●	●
Contingency planning	●	●	●
Operational capability	●	●	●
Maintenance/maintenance standard	●	●	●
Corrective action	●	●	●
Records	●	●	●
Document control	●	●	●
Internal quality audits	●	●	●
Safety	●	●	
Environmental protection	●	●	
Technical support	●	●	
Cert. and compliance rules/regs	●	●	
Cargo handling and cargo care	●	●	
Communication procedures	●	●	
Auditing body	●	●	
Cost efficiency/purchasing/contracting	●		●
Contract review	●		●
Management review	●		●
Quality system	●		●
Drug and alcohol policy	●		
Insurance	●		
Accounting	●		
	24/24	17/24	14/24

In essence the ISMA Code remains an excellent starting point for anybody contemplating quality assurance since it partly interprets ISO 9002 in a language understood by the industry with respect to the level of quality expected. The ISMA Code certainly remains one of the highest, but equally the same level could be achieved through the combinations mentioned previously, however it is harder for a potential customer to establish this fact.

The factors that differentiate the ISMA Code from the rest can be summarized as follows:

1 The code interprets the outline requirements of ISO 9002, ISM, oil company and charterers requirements in a consistent form so that achievement of the ISMA standard demonstrates quality to a known base line.

2 The scope of the accreditation is defined in the code itself and does not require to be checked as for example with ISO 9002.

3 The code goes to the extent that a company is accredited to manage certain ship types and therefore must have suitable procedures prior to being allowed to have a specific ship type endorsement on the Appendix to the certificate.

4 The body formed to carry out the accreditation consists of four major classification societies and ensures that audits are performed consistently and to a homogeneous standard.

When ISMA was launched it was intended to be an industry association for shipmanagers and operators. The entry requirement was, chiefly, compliance to the ISMA Code and a suitable honeymoon period was introduced in order to allow members to achieve this. Consequently a substantial number of shipmanagers signed up to join ISMA.

The reasons for companies joining ISMA were very varied. They ranged from genuine interest in complying with the code and contributing to a body which could represent the industry to companies which wanted to find out what it was all about and to be sure that they would not miss out on any competitive advantage accruing from membership.

Therefore, to retain its integrity the membership rules were eventually tightened and some companies which no longer saw the benefit in complying with the ISMA standard or quite simply were not able to meet the standard, left. As a consequence of this tightening of the criteria the association has now stabilized at about 35 members.

The ISMA is the only true ship management body which can claim to represent the views of the managers within the wider industry; however it cannot be claimed that ISMA represents a majority of the managers. They have been granted observer status at the IMO and this must be seen as a positive step in having ship management recognized as a separate interest group within the industry.

In an attempt to attract the few substantial ship management companies still choosing to remain outside ISMA discussions took place concerning equivalency criteria for membership. Whilst theoretically this should have been a straightforward process it proved to be extremely complex and was eventually abandoned. Therefore the original requirements of the association have been retained and membership will only be granted to companies prepared to be audited against the ISMA's own code.

The ISMA Code is reproduced as Appendix 4.

7.4 TOTAL QUALITY MANAGEMENT

Total Quality Management (TQM) is defined as:

"Harnessing the commitment of everybody to continually satisfying customers' needs and expectations at the lowest internal cost."

TQM is the final state of quality development and quite often the names of the different types of quality system are mixed and therefore people become understandably confused. In fact when we hear of companies adopting TQM they really mean quality assurance. Their ultimate goal might be to have a TQM system. However without first achieving a quality assurance accreditation it is unlikely that the company will have many of the structures in place that will allow a smooth progress to the advanced state of TQM.

When deciding whether to implement a TQM programme it has to be realized that there are no certificates, no external audits and no regulatory requirements to be considered. The achievement of TQM is measured against the above definition and relies on the results measured.

There are numerous business books about TQM. It is not confined to shipping and a host of industries and companies have introduced TQM programmes. The quality of the books written on the subject is as variable as the subject itself but the majority of them start off with a statement outlining what is involved in a TQM programme:

"a fundamental human and organizational transformation which requires the underpinning of all activities first and foremost by a Quality Culture."

The idea of TQM as a culture change is promoted in many would-be quality organizations. However, when we look closely, it becomes apparent that TQM often exists only as a set of espoused values (slogans, declarations, statements of intent) and is only taken seriously by a few "quality disciples".

The basic assumptions about business, customers, quality and people remain unchanged for the majority of organization members. Conversely, many good companies already operate efficient customer orientated services without producing slogans; further their culture does not need a fundamental human and organizational transformation.

The real challenge of TQM is to translate the espoused values into a taken for granted set of assumptions shared by everybody. This requires a shift in the focus of change, from the manipulation of systems, structures and overt behaviour to a fundamental shake-out in managerial thinking. Culture change means seeing things differently. The task facing managers pursuing TQM is to learn to see their world from the customers' perspective and effect changes that meet the requirements of these perspectives.

In every written work on quality assurance and TQM great emphasis is placed on the requirement for commitment from the leadership. In shipping more than any other industry this is true due to the fact that the majority of organizations still subscribe to the autocratic style of management. The shipboard management is autocratic in its design and since the majority of managers in the ship management sector have a seafaring background it is quite normal to see this style appear in the shore management. Unfortunately TQM systems and an autocratic style are "oil and water".

The leader of a company needs to have clarity of vision and purpose. Embarking on a TQM project will expose his own role in the organization to analysis and any leanings towards an autocratic style of management will hamper and ultimately cause a TQM programme to collapse. The personal qualities of the leader will be severely tested and he must appreciate that empowering subordinates is fundamental to the achievement of a decision-making organization.

The philosophy of customer satisfaction and producing a profit is definitely not new but the concept of constantly minimizing internal cost is. Normally internal cost is driven by profitability or more correctly a drop in profitability. In TQM we are constantly competing with ourselves to minimize internal cost. This means that a large number of internal and external variables have to be measured and analysed and a decision taken based on this information.

The rate of change of the variables brought about by customers, environmental pressure, political pressure, economic pressure, demographics and governments must all be considered and even anticipated. Organizations that can anticipate and adapt quickly enough will have a significant competitive edge.

The collection, collation and interpretation of information in a scientific way within ship management is still in its infancy. Despite the development of data acquisition techniques, analysis methods and management science these tools are seldom utilized. This lack of data collection and analysis has the effect of underpinning the autocratic management style and consequently hinders the implementation of a TQM system. Another problem relating to not having access to good quality management information is in the evaluation of risk. In a TQM environment risk requires to be managed, otherwise a lost opportunity can occur or the return is not being maximized.

It is assumed, quite correctly in the majority of cases, that the people doing the job are best placed to assess the risk and thereby manage it since it is expected that they have the best information. The accidents of the 1970s and 1980s have shown that the ship management industry does not always have the best management structures for assessing risk or managing it. The introduction of a QA system has led to companies starting to gather and interpret data. The serious development of TQM will require a major change in ship management organizations.

If companies are to be capable of satisfying customers and minimizing internal costs through comprehensive assessment of the risks involved in the business new skills and technology will be required.

It has to be understood that among the factors militating against the acceptance of change, is the existence of a structure appropriate only to an earlier phase of development.

7.5 THE SAFETY AND QUALITY DEBATE

Since the late 1980s an enormous amount of energy has been expended in debating the issues of safety and quality. The debate has been wide-ranging and shipping publications have produced an abundance of articles covering every conceivable point of view.

The main themes being debated cover:

- the cost versus the return on investment of implementing a system based around quality assurance;
- the perceived extra work that is imposed on individuals in order to comply with
- the system;
- the benefits of having a QA system;
- the rationale of using a quality based qualitative management system for safety management;
- the control and administration of the ISM Code;
- the suitability of quality assurance as a management tool capable of crossing both company and nationality based cultural borders.

7.6 COST VERSUS THE RETURN ON INVESTMENT

The issue of how much it will cost to implement and maintain a quality management system is extremely sensitive. Typically the amount quoted for implementing an ISM or QA management system is in the range $200,000 to $300,000. This is a considerable outlay for the larger players and is of course much more significant for the smaller ones. In fact for some smaller operators it might not be viable to bear this cost at all. Consequently there will probably be a decrease in the overall number of managers and/or there may be an increase in the number of partnership arrangements between smaller and larger companies.

The figures quoted above will inevitably cause some debate but there is a general consensus that irrespective of whether or not everything is done in-house or by external consultants the amount of work averages out to be the same. Therefore if the internal management time is properly costed then the above estimates are approximately correct.

The above highlights one of the problems with the introduction of QA based systems: they are not very cost sensitive to the size of operation. Certainly not when comparing the largest shipmanagers with the smallest since each operator will need to have approximately the same level of procedures and systems irrespective of whether he is operating five ships or 200 ships. The maintenance costs of a QA system are slightly more sensitive to the size of the operation. The number of man hours required annually tends to correlate with the size of the organization and the amount of auditing required. The factor which is not sensitive to size is the amount of effort required to maintain the procedure manuals.

The economic justification for QA systems is normally made around the fact that QA is not a cost but an investment—the theoretical assumption being that through the reduction of re-working, accidents, insurance claims and personal injuries the savings will more than offset the implementation and maintenance costs.

In practice the investment argument is not so straightforward. In order to verify the savings it is necessary to measure them. In ship management this can be extremely difficult; further the timescale involved for any particular ship can often be too short to record a meaningful result. The resources required to make a sensible comparison of the before and after situation would quite simply be too expensive and far beyond the pockets of most managers and operators. Therefore the management have to make broad assumptions about the savings side while the cost side can be accurately reported. The type of information available tends to come from insurance statistics and the reasons for a certain trend can be the source of long discussions between the proponents and detractors of QA.

A further problem with the investment argument is that the shipmanager is unlikely to receive any recognition from the client in terms of increased management fees for the extra costs involved in maintaining a QA system. If there is a reduction in insurance premiums or the amount of "below deductible" payments then the shipmanager will not receive any benefit from this under a normal "cost plus" management agreement. It will all go to the client.

It can always be argued that a manager providing this type of service is bound to attract a reward through increased business; however the complexities of ship management do not always substantiate such propositions. The reality is that the shipmanager must accept that he requires a verifiable management system built around QA in order to stay in business.

The ability to maintain a sufficient margin will have to be found in other ways.

7.7 THE PERCEIVED EXTRA WORK

The arguments surrounding the additional amounts of bureaucracy created through the use of a QA management system have been widely used by critics of QA. The argument however is actually irrelevant. While it is true that some QA systems have created a bureaucratic nightmare, closer inspection of such systems will usually show that it is a poorly designed system. The major cause of this is normally a company management which has adopted a hands-off approach to the system design and allowed the QA manager to create a "quality nirvana".

Another common reason for claiming that the QA system has created a bureaucratic paper mountain is that the checklists required to be completed and the reporting to be returned actually highlight the fact that previously the job was not being carried out properly or insufficient control was being exercised. Whatever the cause, the management system has highlighted a problem and the issue of whether the procedure as written is too burdensome or something more fundamental is wrong can now be resolved in a structured fashion.

The first issues of a QA management system tend to contain an element of "wish list" type procedures. Whilst it is acknowledged to be a common error in most new systems the apparatus is in place to rationalize the system down to a true reflection of the required working environment within one or two revisions of the procedures. The success of the revision process presupposes that the people having to comply with the procedures have sufficient ownership of the system that they want to improve and rationalize it to a form where it reflects sensibly what is actually being done.

7.8 THE BENEFITS OF A QA SYSTEM

The operation and management of ships is very much driven by routines and procedures both ashore and afloat. Consequently a management tool which helps create a working framework for such activities must be worthwhile. However, as has been commented on in the past, many successful shipowning companies had in place their own management systems which generated a similar working framework. The major difference between the two approaches is that the latter type of company relied on its reputation as an owner/operator and the visibility of its success could be seen through the ships' house flag or funnel markings.

In the case of ship management there is seldom any outwardly visible sign as to who actually manages a particular ship therefore strategic marketing benefits are sought for the company through highlighting the quality badge and the accreditation authority.

Whilst the ship management industry expected the introduction of QA to create a greater degree of differentiation in a maturing market-place the behaviour of clients and potential clients still suggests that the industry remains very much driven by bottom line cost, personalities and reputations. Therefore those companies which sought to achieve QA accreditation as a marketing device will probably be more and more disillusioned.

As the ship management industry gains experience of QA it is beginning to realize that the real benefits to the organization are through increased reliability within its operations. This is not surprising. A review of other industries which have used QA as part of their management system, for example, the nuclear industry, the oil and gas industry, shipbuilding and nearly the whole of "Japan Inc." have never promoted themselves as better because of their QA accreditation. It is for them just one more management tool used in their business.

7.9 THE RATIONALE OF USING A QUALITY-BASED QUALITATIVE MANAGEMENT SYSTEM FOR SAFETY MANAGEMENT

Historically the development of new regulations in shipping has been a reaction to events. The introduction of the ISM Code is an important first step towards pro-active solutions in safety management.

In almost every incident whether it is a fatal accident, an oil spill or an expensive machinery failure there is seldom one root cause. Invariably the major event is the culmination of several minor ones, the classical event chain. These types of minor event can often be eliminated through the correct implementation of a QA system; in essence operational reliability using agreed methods and procedures.

Industries such as nuclear, space and petro-chemical have advanced significantly with the science of safety management. Their efforts are currently focused on more sophisticated risk/reliability theories where the determination of event probability and consequence is at the heart of safety management.

Inevitably the new theories being developed will filter down to the shipping industry. Further, the data and records that will be collected by companies complying with the ISM Code will form part of the database required to give accuracy and authenticity to risk/reliability based systems.

Early signs of the adoption of some of the new safety management thinking can be found in progress reports covering "Formal Safety Assessment" (FSA).

Recently the Maritime Safety Committee (MSC 68) has accepted FSA as a methodology that can assist the IMO in the formulation of safety regulations.

The FSA philosophy is only one sub-set of a risk/reliability approach to safety management and it is certain that more and more discussion will take place around this subject as it becomes better understood by the wider industry.

7.10 THE CONTROL AND ADMINISTRATION OF THE ISM CODE

One of the major problems which has constantly plagued the shipping industry has been its inability to effectively regulate itself within the framework of the IMO, Flag State Authorities, Classification Societies and Port State Control.

It has been argued in the past that the major problem with shipping regulations is that there is no truly effective system for enforcement of the regulations, not that there are inherent weaknesses in the actual regulations. Therefore, without some form of improvement in the policing of regulations it is hard to see how the ISM Code can be effective.

The problem is exacerbated by the fact that the assessment of the ISM Code will be carried out on a qualitative basis and this will inevitably lead to large variations in the interpretation of what is acceptable and what is not.

The ISM Code is based around a quality assurance model and shares the fundamental requirement of all such codes, namely commitment together with a spirit within the company to actually make it work. It is therefore hard to see how a code such as the ISM can be successfully targeted against substandard operators.

The first few years of the ISM Code will be extremely interesting. The resources and ability of the responsible bodies charged with overseeing the implementation and continued development of the Code will be severely tested. The attitude of the industry as a whole and the support offered towards adoption of the Code will form a useful barometer for the health of ship management.

7.11 THE SUITABILITY OF QUALITY ASSURANCE AS A MANAGEMENT TOOL CAPABLE OF CROSSING BOTH COMPANY AND NATIONALITY BASED CULTURAL BORDERS

In modern times when we think about quality assurance other than in shipping terms the majority of people think about the successful Japanese corporations, their production lines and how they usurped the West in the post-war years. It seemed that QA was tailor-made for Japan Inc. but it was in fact an American who introduced QA as a management tool to Japan. During the early post-war years while Japan was a closed market it struggled with the science of reliable production much to the cost of its own Japanese customers who did not have a choice in buying the goods. Our memory of Japan really only starts when they launched themselves at the Western markets. The interesting paradox being that formal quality assurance remains relatively scarce in the USA, particularly within the shipping community, yet it seemed to suit the Japanese culture.

The above raises many questions regarding culture and quality assurance, the most interesting being: does quality assurance in the form currently prescribed in the "international" codes successfully cross cultural boundaries? The question can be addressed in two ways. Firstly, how do the various nationalities found on board ship react to the imposition of one company's operating systems which are designed and written around that company's own monoculture which includes elements of both its national and business roots? Secondly, does there exist a homogeneous interpretation of the spirit of quality assurance between various cultures and nationalities.

Little research has been done into how well a structured system such as quality assurance actually translates across boundaries. The normal assumption seems to be that it does. While the system fundamentals might translate, the wholesale export of quality assurance systems might not.

It has been earlier stated that many ship operators and managers can be described as being autocratic. Autocratic companies are typified by strong pervasive cultures which tend to turn organizations into cohesive tribes with distinctly clannish feelings. The values and traditions of the tribe are reinforced by private language, catch phrases and tales of past heroes and dramas. The way of life is enshrined in rituals so that rule books and manuals are almost unnecessary; custom and tradition provide the answer.

The shipping industry is attempting to transfer this autocratic culture, which is understood by the shore staff, into what has become a migrant seastaff. The majority of companies have created quality assurance systems which reflect their autocratic roots but fail to understand that through the introduction of quality assurance there is a natural process of empowerment which does not always cross the cultural boundaries in the way that was expected.

It appears that we require major cultural shifts. On the one hand we have the largely autocratic companies designing and implementing working systems which are supposed to transfer the company culture to people from widely diverging backgrounds. On the other hand the seastaff and to some extent the office staff have their interpretation of the requirements based on their own cultural roots.

Human resource consultants will often talk about a "change of culture". The reality is that culture cannot be changed quickly unless the people are replaced. In shipping, culture changes very slowly.

In discussing the influence of culture on quality assurance and *vice versa* the type of company being considered was more typically the Western model. Considering the East European and Far Eastern companies even more strongly based in the autocratic culture, it will be interesting to see how they interpret and implement quality assurance and in particular QA as it is described in the ISM Code.

7.12 THE FUTURE OF QUALITY ASSURANCE IN SHIP MANAGEMENT

The introduction of quality assurance to ship management has occurred over an extremely short time span. It is therefore natural that a great deal of debate has surrounded its introduction. Expectation has also been high for the results that the system should achieve. A lot of this expectation has to do with the commercially competitive nature of ship management and must be accepted as part of the reality of business.

Eventually, as more experience is gained about QA, the expectation and general furore will gradually subside until it is accepted as a normal part of the management framework.

When the various QA systems begin to mature they will not automatically turn poorly operated companies into successful ones. What the system will achieve is to highlight the weaknesses so that improvements can be put in place in a structured manner. The QA system will also highlight the fact that ship management is a people-based industry relying almost entirely on the human element. If the people involved do not exhibit the correct levels of training, experience, ability and attitude then the best designed management system will ultimately fail.

8

THE IT REVOLUTION

8.1 INTRODUCTION

History tells us that the early Mediterranean seafaring traders were among the first groups to address the need for a "technology" for recording and processing trading information. The trading pressures, even then, demanded not only methods of recording the commercial transactions made but extended into the realms of simple voyage and vessel management (Lee, 1997). It is not surprising that, thousands of years on, the demand for Information Technology (IT) in the shipping and ship management industry prevails. Modern commercial and legislative pressures conspire, in spite of all the advances, to make ship management one of the most global and complex businesses which functions in a hostile trading environment.

Today, of course, the array of available electronic information technology in the form of computer and communications systems is vast. IT has in itself become a highly complex arena. With this complexity, it has gained the ability to absorb and distract management from the real issues and objectives of the business. Managing the IT itself has become a real issue.

It is a fact that the rate of development of the technology of information far outpaces similar improvements in our ability to implement and manage the technology. As a consequence, what can be achieved with modern IT lags far behind what is actually being achieved and the gap is widening. In particular there has been a tendency, not exclusive to the shipping industry, to become sidetracked with the technology itself as opposed to the job it is employed to do.

Too much emphasis is placed on the technology of information rather than managing the information in the business.

Since the early 1960s, developments in IT have tended to come thick and fast. Not all carry a significant or lasting impact but two specific developments have brought the worlds of IT and ship management even closer together.

8.1.1 Ship-to-Shore Data Communications

Hardware and software systems to utilize global and regional satellite and radio communications for the exchange of message, data (including computer programs), image and video information between ship and shore.

The development of cost-effective and reliable ship/shore communications is probably the most significant contribution IT has made to ship management. It completes the corporate communications infrastructure, presenting the opportunity of linking vessels to shore-based management and systems. It establishes an essential platform of "enabling technology" that underpins the potential for a host of strategic, control, and operational applications that would otherwise be difficult or impossible to implement and sustain.

8.1.2 On-Board Computing

Vessel tolerant computers, personal computers (PC) and computer networks

The advent of computer systems and networks that are truly vessel tolerant has enabled the natural evolution of computing into onboard management and control activities. The opportunity for the "floating office" is now a reality and already creating demands for operational management and control of implementation.

IT potential that was once stifled by the remoteness of, and environmental conditions on board, vessels has now been opened up; potential that when employed and managed well and aligned with strategic business objectives will stimulate a major leap forward in crew vessel and cargo safety, quality of service, commercial and technical management and ship design/building. Vessels as floating remote offices can now be integrated into the corporate infrastructure and information services. Every aspect of ship management is now within grasp and can be managed: a whole new vision, a whole new era, of quality ship management.

The timing is impeccable. International pressure for quality in ship management is mounting and is unlikely to abate in the foreseeable future.

8.2. IT: THE SHIP MANAGEMENT CHALLENGE

The challenge facing shipmanagers is that IT will not happen by accident (Favre, July 1996). There are too many variables for the right IT business solutions to be arrived at by chance. IT has to be aligned with business objectives and its implementation measured against a strategic plan.

That requires not only a deep understanding of commercial and operational issues affecting the individual organization but also knowledge of the inherent and vital role of information in the business. Often forgotten in the heat of technological progress is the fact that IT is a strategic management decision that can only be directed from the highest management levels of the company and with a keen perception of the value and characteristics of the essential information assets.

The IT challenge comprises many issues that, in essence, form three management considerations:

    (i) understanding the role and characteristics of information in business;
    (ii) aligning it with business objectives;

(iii) managing the technology.

Each consideration is reviewed below.

8.2.1 Understanding the Role and Characteristics of Information in Business

The Information Assets

Figure 8.1 simplifies the role of information in business. It provides a model company showing how the basic types of work (physical work and decision-making work) vary with management level within the organization. It reflects the fact that senior management are generally engaged in more decision-making work than staff at the more operational levels in the company.

Decision-making work and physical work depend on an important third element, information provision. The information provision element provides all the information required to support the decision-making work process and directs the physical work activities. The information provision element includes all the aspects of capture, storage, manipulation, retrieval and communication of data inherent in meeting the information needs of the decision-making and physical work elements. Naturally, it is the information provision element of the business that is responsive to the application of IT. It is therefore a fundamental requirement to appreciate the characteristics of this element.

Role: Information is Control

In simple terms, control is the essence of management and can be viewed as three actions:

setting an objective,
measuring progress toward that objective,
taking corrective action to meet the objective (as required).

Information is totally inherent to the control (management) process. Information is required to quantify and communicate the objective, measure against planned progress and to quantify and communicate any corrective action. Information has quality attributes (accuracy, timeliness etc.) that impact effective control. In fact the overall quality and level of management that can be attained in an organization can be directly related to the quality of information it receives.

This fundamental and vital role of information and its relationship with management is often overlooked. The planning and development of information systems is often delegated to staff who cannot possibly appreciate the full strategic and commercial issues facing the company and the management emphasis required. As a consequence, computer systems are often elevated beyond their rightful position as tools, in a much more significant trade.

Magnitude: The Major Corporate Workload

Information systems research has shown that some 60 per cent to 80 per cent of the corporate workload is engaged within the information provision element. Naturally, this figure will vary with the type and size of organization, but the range is thought by many information technologists to be conservative. There are few, if any, modern businesses where the information provision element of the business is not the major part of the workload. The rule holds true for ship management, even considering the strong physical nature of the business.

This fact alone makes the information provision within an organization a prime focus for senior management attention. In the continual struggle for efficiency and economy in the business practice whilst improving client service, information provision and the associated IT must provide significant opportunity.

Extent: Company-wide

Information provision extends across all levels of management and operations within the company. Nobody escapes; it is an inherent part of all work activities. It is a corporate issue that benefits from a corporate approach. Traditionally, this has not always been the case due to mitigating historical circumstances. However, the recent development of PCs, PC networks and communications systems eliminates any excuses for not adopting a corporate strategy, driven from the top down by senior management as a key ingredient to success (Slesinger, 1997).

Concentration: Middle Management

The mass of information provision congregates around the middle management layers of the organization penetrating upwards into senior management circles and downwards into operational management. Middle management has long played the role of information providers (human computers) in organizations. As a consequence, it is this region that has seen most impact from the implementation of IT. Companies are tending to a move towards a leaner, flatter organizational structure as middle management human resources are replaced by IT systems. It is important to note that while the information provision workload has probably increased in every case, the model of information provision has not changed, simply the methods.

Status: Dynamic

The business situation is not static. The legislative and commercial pressures demand responsiveness and flexibility to short-term change that is, at the same time, underpinned by a natural evolution of the survival of the commercially fittest. By definition, the provision of information must be equally dynamic reflecting this requirement. Again, this has not always been a feature of traditional IT implementations. There can be inconsistency between the need for dynamics and the ability to develop and modify computer systems. Managing the technology hits directly at the need for dynamic information provision and should feature well in the list of strategic systems criteria.

Conclusion

Clearly, information provision is a strategic decision to be managed at the highest possible levels within the business. Equally significant, are the characteristics of information in the business: these provide clear pointers to successful implementation. Fundamentally, business information and the systems that provide it, are vital corporate assets and should be developed and managed as such.

8.2.2 Aligning IT with Business Objectives

Applications v. Infrastructure

Figure 8.2 employs the company model to reflect a typical traditional "applications" approach to the implementation of IT systems in the business. The slice across the company represents a given group of associated activities (e.g. invoicing, sales ledger) to which the technology is applied. The technology in the form of various data processing activities (capture, storage, manipulation, retrieval, communication) is applied to meet the specific information provision requirements of the physical work and decision-making work related to the application slice. This is repeated for each application (Figure 8.3).

In concept, this approach involves the piecemeal application of comparatively high levels of available technology to individual and contained areas of the business. This has associated financial and operational downsides. In general, the more deeply the application area is covered by the implementations the more complex the technology required. High technology costs significantly more than low technology and is much more costly to implement and manage. The law of diminishing returns appears to apply to application coverage and the more deeply into the application one extends the more quickly the costs rise. In addition, a systems "friction" is generated at the boundaries with non-technology areas (Figure 8.3).

Figure 8.4 summarizes the general situation. The "cost" curve indicates that the latest high technology usually costs disproportionately more; the "coverage" curve that you can achieve most of what you want to do with low-medium technology (therefore, the 80/20 rule applies i.e. that you can do 80 per cent of what you want to do with 20 per cent of the available technology). Although this is a simplification, the consolidation clearly indicates that peak return on investment (ROI) is not necessarily associated with high technology.

It is only fair to relate much of the popularity of the traditional applications approach with the evolution of computer systems. Until recently, the basic design of the computing technology tended to promote a more applications-based approach. It is an important management principle to separate the fundamentals of business information from the technology. The essence of the former changes very little, the latter changes all too fast. In recent years, the development of IT has moved closer to providing us with systems that more naturally complement the way we organize and work. This has provided the luxury of alternative more natural approaches to systems development and the consideration of "infrastructure" rather than applications (Figure 8.5).

Figure 8.1: The company (division of work)

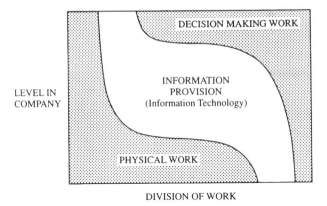

DIVISION OF WORK

Figure 8.2: The application slice

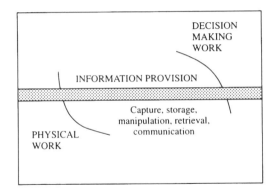

Figure 8.3: IT Implementation: the traditional approach

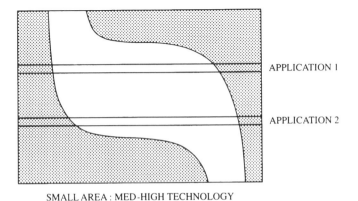

SMALL AREA : MED-HIGH TECHNOLOGY

Strategically, this is an important step forward that must be fully appreciated by senior management. Reports of poor return-on-investment from IT projects have always haunted the computer industry and the computer user alike, there is mounting evidence that this may have been directly related to the implementation approach taken.

As discussed, attempting to get a large return from a narrow area of the business will take a lot of technology and costs. Getting a small but significant return from across the entire company could be simple and inexpensive and strategically very sound. This makes the case for wide use of low technology as opposed to a narrow use of high technology. Computer systems evolution has now reached the point where both options, and some in between, are available for management consideration.

Figure 8.6 outlines the concept with reference to the prime example of communications. Instead of viewing each application and its specific data processing content as an individual entity, the data processing content of the information provision element is viewed on a corporate basis. Communication of data is a key constituent throughout all levels of the model and it is easy to perceive a communications infrastructure, an information pipeline, servicing the entire corporation. For those readers who are wondering at the popularity of Internet. Simply replace "the company" with "the world" in Figure 8.1 and you have the explanation.

The infrastructure approach not only has economies of scale but requires comparatively low cost, free availability and low level technology. Figure 8.7 takes the concept to its logical conclusion. Rather than information provision being seen as a number of business application slices, it is viewed as an overall corporate infrastructure. The infrastructure provides a base level of low cost technology (word processing, spreadsheets, database, e-mail, communications etc.) from which most local applications are derived.

As required and justified by cost, special applications can be superimposed on this infrastructure. The more comprehensive the infrastructure becomes, the less likely the need for special applications. Applications development will still be required for specialist technical and commercial areas but then the opportunity to interface with the infrastructure will considerably reduce effort and focus attention on the application objectives and ROI.

Compliance with the IMO ISM Code provides a good example of infrastructure versus applications. The 13 chapters of the IMO ISM Code are in reality a functional specification of the systems requirement. It is possible to take the view that IMO ISM Code compliance is an application and so build a specific application system to meet the specification. However, analysis of the requirement suggests that it is not complex in information systems terms, it calls for a broad based reporting and communications system (Vardakis, 1997). This is an ideal infrastructure project, improving the level of reporting and communications across the organization and absorbing the current IMO ISM Code requirement along the way.

Figure 8.4: Coverage/cost ratio

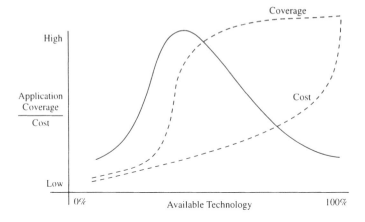

Figure 8.5: Implementation–infrastructure approach

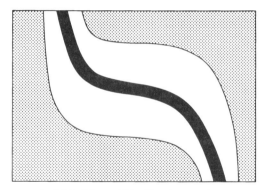

LARGE AREA : LOW-MED TECHNOLOGY

Figure 8.6: The information pipeline

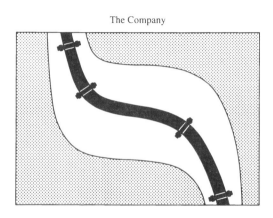

Figure 8.7: *Information provision as an overall corporate infrastructure*

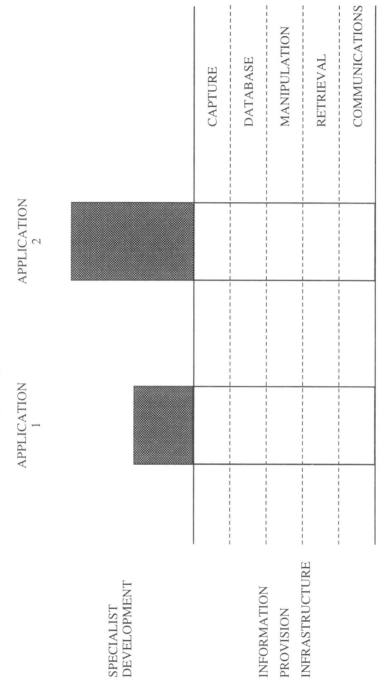

The infrastructure approach also has strategic advantages. The IMO ISM Code is not an isolated incident. It is another step in the continued strengthening of legislative pressures on marine safety and environmental issues. Already an inherent part of the ship management business, the momentum is such that the legislative and associated commercial pressures will conspire to make this a focus certainly in the short term but also for many years to come.

Ongoing compliance, safety and environment protection measures are a strategic issue. The IT solution must therefore reflect the long-term strategic nature of the requirement. Building another specific application for the next, and the next, raft of legislation is not the answer. Investing in an infrastructure approach addressing the current situation and laying foundations for future requirements is the strategic and cost effective solution.

Communications: The Key Infrastructure

We have seen that the fundamental role of information in business is control and that the ability to manage is directly related to the attributes of the information received. However, management is essentially a remote activity. It is not possible, even in the smallest of companies to be on the spot and fully integrated with every decision or process. In information terms, this remoteness introduces an imperfection in the system that it is essential to mitigate. It follows that an integral part of the control process is the communication of data to and from the management and operational centres within the business. It is not enough to capture the data or make decisions; these have to be communicated within the appropriate timescales to the point of relevance to be effective.

Next to the information itself, of all the data processing activities, communications stands supreme. The ability to communicate information freely and effectively consistent with management objectives is a prime essential. In a flexible and dynamic business situation it is not possible to predict fully the information content or routeing required or practical to react with *ad hoc* communication applications.

A communications infrastructure, underpinning the information requirement for the organization, is the only real solution and is strategically one of the most important IT investments that senior management can make. The model used in Figures 8.1–8.3 should be viewed in the context of the entire sphere of operations of the company including regional offices, agents, associated commercial and legislative bodies and, of course, vessels. The communications infrastructure must extend to all the points of management control required making it easy, cost effective and reliable to exchange vital information.

With many shipmanagers, the jury is still out on the question of ships as floating offices; with others it is a "no-brainer". From the information technologists viewpoint, the concept of oceangoing vessels equipped with integrated on-board computer and communications networks interconnected into corporate, regulatory and commercial land based systems is not an option; they are destined to become a necessary fact of ship management life. The current and emerging commercial and legislative pressures are building to the extent that almost by definition, to be both competitive and compliant, shipmanagers will require a managed on-board computer network and ship/shore communications system integrated into the corporate communications infrastructure.

IT Strategy: Senior Management Responsibility

An IT strategy is now an essential component in the business planning of any ship management company. The responsibility to provide for it falls to the senior management (Favre, September 1996). IT can only be well directed by addressing strategically the key business issues.

The prime source of this detailed strategic business knowledge, experience and expertise is senior management. Any approach that omits this body of expertise is doomed to fail.

The IT strategy provides the link between the real business issues to be resolved and the application and management of the technology. The senior management role can be summarized as:

  (i) identification of the key business issues that impact the business;
  (ii) understanding the role of information and information systems in managing the issues;
  (iii) evaluation of the infrastructure potential of the technology;
  (iv) building and managing the absorption of the technology.

It is not always that fate deals a good hand but currently shipmanagers can consider themselves a trifle lucky. They would do well to grasp the good fortune that has come their way. At the very time when the regulatory and business pressures within the industry are building to the point where significant improvements in operational and management standards are essential, help is at hand. The source of the help may not be obvious and it will not be a panacea to all problems, but IT will almost certainly feature in the solution. In recent years IT has come of age and now provides practical cost-effective solutions. The real question is whether the ship management industry is in a position to take advantage.

Conclusion

It is vital that senior management take on board the inherent role of information and information systems in the business and plan, develop and maintain them as corporate assets. They represent the lifeblood of the organization, create the personality of the organization, underpin control and provide competitive edge.

8.2.3 Managing the Technology

Managing Change

The analysis of the information provision element highlighted the dynamic nature of business information and, as a consequence, business information systems. This emphasized the need for flexibility and responsiveness in the information systems assets to meet the challenge of natural evolution and development within the business environment. Traditionally, there was a conflict here between long lead-times in computer systems development and the urgency of the business. Modern information systems tools and packaged solutions, as ingredients of an infra-structure-based approach, provide the opportunity for both delivering the systems foundations and absorbing dynamic development. Improving information provision capability and standards across a broad base will create latent potential for flexibility and dynamics in meeting information requirements.

The same evolutionary process is all too evident within IT itself, but the change is more rapid and sometimes revolutionary rather than evolutionary. Modern computer and communications systems have "shelf-lives" often measured in months with each new generation offering 2 or 3 times the price/performance. By contrast, the vision for business information and business information systems is one where the investment in precious data and systems assets is protected, underpinning the business and rolling forward for many years to come. The *status quo* for IT is rapid development and change (Barney, 1997). It is apparent that the natural frequency in the cycle of change for IT is much faster than, and therefore incompatible with, the more evolutionary cycle of business information and business information systems. This is not to say that there is no revolution in business; this is far from the case. However, the impact on information systems is rarely major and more rarely penetrates to infrastructure levels. The management challenge is how to handle this incompatibility taking full advantage of what IT offers today and at the same time planning to absorb the opportunities presented by future IT development. Change is inherent in IT and it is, therefore, imperative that it is accommodated in the technology management process.

Computer Systems Evolution

Implementing infrastructure platforms as opposed to applications is one approach to managing that change. The management objective is to protect the investment in the precious corporate assets of data and systems, including the intrinsic value of experience and expertise built up in the company management and staff ("warm-ware") while exploiting the technology to the full.

The conceptual vision is one of the precious and evolving information systems assets layered and cushioned from the dramatic vagaries of the volatile IT industry.

It is important to note that the evolution of computer systems now makes the concept a reality. More significant perhaps is the fact that the IT industry now acknowledges and embraces this requirement and direction in its R&D. This has not always been the case. Figure 8.8, shows the original blend for computer systems (early 1960) where the main system components of data, application system, operating system and hardware were proprietary to each manufacturer. These components were unique and "fused" together working only with each other when complete. When a component of the system was required to be replaced it was necessary to start all over again. If the computer hardware were to be updated, little or none of the data or systems assets could be preserved. This unacceptable situation was quickly addressed with the introduction of standard programming languages and data formats (COBOL *circa* 1964) that permitted migration of data and programs from one computer system to another. At first this was complex, time-consuming and inflexible but represented a considerable step forward. This established the traditional blend of computer systems (Figure 8.9) which prevailed for some 25 years. They still featured proprietary hardware and proprietary operating systems that were exclusive to the computer manufacturers.

A strategically significant shift in emphasis started in the early 1980s. The concept of an internationally standard operating environment for computer systems started to gain ground in some areas of the IT industry (not with the big manufacturers!). The change was relatively subtle but the impact eventually shook the entire IT industry to the roots and set the pattern for modern computing platforms. By establishing a standard operating environment (cf. UNIX, MSDOS), computer hardware would then be built to meet this operating standard. It would be evaluated on how fully and powerfully it achieved that standard. Strategically, the system layers above the hardware would be detached from the hardware insulated by the presence of the standard operating environment. For the first time computer hardware and operating systems were conceptually aligned with real business information systems objectives; with the protection and evolution of the information systems assets independently from hardware development. This was the era of Open Systems blend of computer system (Figure 8.10) and the foundation stone of modern commercial PC and Networking computing systems. Table 8.1 shows a consolidation of the typical layers of a modern information systems platform. Hardware is managed by reducing its role to that of a consumable, cycling below the insulation afforded by the standard Operating Systems Platform. The real corporate assets protected above Standards, whether *de facto* or official, play an important part in managing the technology and creating a "plug-compatible" computing resource.

Table 8.1: Consolidation of the typical layers of a modern information systems platform

ELEMENT	CHARACTERISTICS	STATUS
DATA	LONG TERM, EVOLUTION, DYNAMIC	CORPORATE ASSETS
APPLICATION SYSTEM	SPECIALIZED	
INFRASTRUCTURE SYSTEM	STRATEGIC, CORPORATE, EVOLUTION	
OPERATING ENVIRONMENT	PLATFORM, INSULATION	
HARDWARE	RAPID DEVELOPMENT, CHANGE	CONSUMABLE

Conclusion

Computer and communications technology have now evolved to the point where strategic infrastructure solutions are readily available. The way we strategise, manage and finance the systems has not evolved so quickly and remains firmly at the door of senior management.

8.3 SHIP MANAGEMENT IT IN ACTION

8.3.1 Introduction

As discussed, information provision in business represents the major part of the corporate workload. It follows that the opportunities for the application of IT in ship management are vast. However, the business potential from application will vary widely with the application and business circumstances. In many cases the real added value of an application may be cloaked in indirect benefits. This emphasizes the need for senior management involvement in defining the real business issues to hand, from which an IT strategy can be formulated and the IT building blocks established. It is a question of knowing the picture on the outside of the box before attempting to put the jigsaw puzzle pieces into place (Parker, 1997).

IT is individual to the business. There are no hard-and-fast rules on application choices or levels of expenditure; it is specific to each organization. Building infrastructure systems is a low-risk, flexible and diverse strategy. Infrastructure will underpin the essential business information requirements and provide an information systems foundation to build upon. Establishing a basic personal computing and communications infrastructure equates to completing the edges of the jigsaw first. It establishes a point of reference and an interface for additional development. Recognizing the general acceptance of the PC workstation, the most important infrastructure element is communications. Communications is a strategic application, an "enabling technology" connecting the information with the decision/operation. It is unlikely, and should not be implemented, to produce direct savings within itself but it will open up the opportunity for a whole range of cost-effective applications otherwise impractical to accomplish.

This section reviews the strategy and benefits of some of the many IT initiatives and implementations available to shipmanagers with specific focus on enabling technology, management decision support and strategy technology management.

8.3.2 Enabling Technology: The Communications Infrastructure

One of the most significant changes in the management perception of IT has taken place only in the last few years. The characteristics of traditional computers (and PCs) had left a legacy of the computer as the effective focal point of the system.

"Dumb" visual display units linked to a stand-alone processor were envisaged as "talking to the computer". It was the advent of Local Area Networking (LAN) and

Figure 8.8: Computer system evolution: the original blend

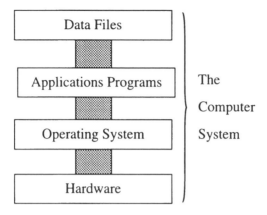

Figure 8.9: Computer system evolution: the traditional blend

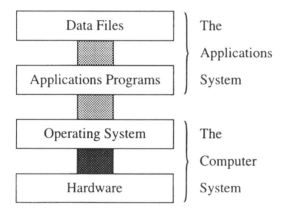

Figure 8.10: Computer system evolution: the "open systems" blend

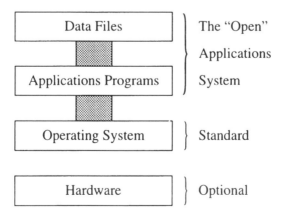

Wide Area Networking (WAN) technology, linking computer systems and PCs at high speed both locally (LAN) and *via* telecommunication systems (WAN) that began to change the actual perception into the information systems reality. All information systems should be perceived as "networks" integrating the decision making and operational work elements into an homogeneous, flexible, responsive whole.

Networking introduced other advantages. The finite power of stand-alone computers is diluted as users are added. After a given level the rate dilution is not linear but increases dramatically with each user added. Investing in bigger and bigger computers was not the answer (cf. Computer Systems Evolution). The "network alternative" allowed for the addition of appropriate processing resource (PC) along with each user, a measure of resilience to failure and workstation-to-workstation communication. In one technological step IT had moved closer to natural business information systems. Workstation-to-workstation communication was the key information systems prize. The technology was still dependent on focal point computers (servers) but the management perception could now change to one of a serviced and integrated workforce.

Electronic Mail

Some information technologists suspect that the acceptance of the term "electronic mail" by the IT industry has put networking back several years.

There can be no doubt that the choice of name did not inspire user management at the outset. This is indeed unfortunate because the concept and attributes of electronic messaging are at the root of a communications infrastructure, and as we have seen, the communications infrastructure is fundamental to the business. The backbone of an electronic mail network is the ability for each participating workstation to be individually addressed and receive information. It is the addressing, a combination of network hardware and software, that carries the power to get the information in the right place at the right time. In reality this is accomplished *via* a store-and-forward "Mailbox" on the server and the workstation accessing the server, but the result is workstation-to-workstation communications incorporating remote and remote mobile (vessels) offices. A corporate network can be extended to service communications requirements external to the company. Conventional telex and fax communications, e-mail *via* Internet (see below) or public/private networks can be linked *via* appropriate "gateways". Electronic messaging provides the delivery mechanism not only for text messages but for multi-media information (text, graphics, fax, video, sound) and is, therefore, the cornerstone of the communications infrastructure. When considering the corporate communications infrastructure an e-mail system will certainly present a low risk and highly cost effective initial step, even for the smallest organization.

Internet/Intranet

Senior executives and IT managers within ship management must cut through the marketing hype surrounding Internet and reach the core functionality. Internet is a very important infrastructure development that has a great affinity with the marine industry environment. Internet is a global business utility with two key attributes; a global communications network and a multi-media information resource. Both attributes provide the opportunity for integration into a corporate strategy and together can address a variety of operational, commercial and marketing objectives (Gilbertson, 1997).

As highlighted earlier, viewed one way, Internet is the world's equivalent of a corporate communications infrastructure. It is a worldwide group of computers linked by high speed communications networks. The function of the network is supported by systems technology that was originally designed to remain operational and deliver information following partial damage by nuclear attack. It provides PC-to-PC communications between participants anywhere in the world. It offers the choice between store-and-forward electronic messaging as described above, or direct communication. In addition to a conventional electronic mail network, the Internet backbone technology also has the ability to establish a "real-time" communications link between the participants, for the cost of a local telephone call. It is early days for commercial use of this functionality but this adds potential for new dimensions of applications. The global communications network capability of Internet is a natural consideration for integration into the corporate communications infrastructure to support multi-media electronic-messaging.

With impending developments in integrity and security of information on the Internet (see 5th Generation Messaging below) commercial use is destined to blossom and replace telex and fax traffic. Internet, as the international backbone for electronic messaging, therefore slides neatly into the corporate strategy and requires little justification. Already, some shipmanagers have set up electronic mail addresses for each of their vessels and are experimenting with a variety of communications uses.

Of course, the main claim to fame for Internet is not electronic messaging but the World Wide Web (WWW). The WWW provides a complete ready-made infrastructure for the storage of multi-media information and its content-related retrieval. When combined with the other Internet functionality, Internet presents an off-the-peg IT utility with considerable scope. The obvious compatibility between the international coverage of Internet and the truly international nature of the marine industry makes it hard to visualize a marine future devoid of Internet (Brightman, 1997). Understanding of, and experience with, the real functionality of the Internet is vital; it will certainly feature heavily in the future of the marine industry. The exploitation and marketing hype to date does not always serve to promote the infrastructure and strategic potential or, in contrast, the pitfalls. It is most important that shipmanagers acquire first-hand knowledge from which to make informed decisions.

The Internet technology can be adapted for use as an internal network for corporate information and applications. In this variant it is called Intranet and is promoted and supported by specialist suppliers with specifically developed hardware and software products.

Intranet presents a further partial or full infrastructure platform option that can only be fully considered within the context of individual corporate strategy and development. Again, there are no shortages of technology solutions if the strategy to exploit them is in place.

The simplicity and flexibility of the Internet, if not managed, will eventually lead to some misuse in terms of both information and time. The need to control the nature and frequency of access and optimize communications is already apparent in large implementations. The IT industry has responded with the development of an Internet Communications Controller or "Proxy Server". The Internet Proxy Server is a systems software that distributes, optimizes and controls all PC network access to the Internet. It allows several users to share an Internet link and can restrict access to relevant WWW sites. It logs all Internet activity for management review. The functionality of "Proxy Server" and similar developments in network fax and electronic messaging (including ship/shore satellite) suggest the technical evolution to an integrated corporate communications "hub" through which all such communications infrastructure connections are managed (cf. Rydex Industries Corp below).

Ship/Shore Communications

The nature of ship/shore communications endorses it as "the" classic example of enabling technology in the marine industry. Used well, it will almost certainly increase, rather than decrease, the expenditure on communications traffic and the real benefits will be gained only indirectly from associated "enabled" applications.

As such, it is difficult if not impossible, to justify cost without a clear strategic vision. The fact remains, a ship/shore communications infrastructure "enables" the floating office and is probably the most important single strategic IT investment that shipmanagers can make.

The technology has had to fight hard for acceptance within the marine industry, and in doing so, break down barriers both of tradition and commercial attitude. The owner/manager/charterer hierarchy has not been helpful in clarifying decision responsibility and apportioning benefits, when the reality is that all are winners. Until the advent of Inmarsat ship/shore satellite communications in 1982 (Gallagher, 1989), communication between ocean-going vessels and shore bases had been severely limited and, when available, strictly controlled. A legacy of minimal, authorized communication had been established, a far cry from the freedom of communication enjoyed in modern networks. The comparatively high cost of voice and telex satellite communications did not help with enlightenment and although the foundations of a ship/shore communications infrastructure had been set, the atmosphere was not right for rapid progress.

In the latter part of the 1980s marine computer systems suppliers were pioneering the application of PC hardware and software technology to Inmarsat satellite communications for the transmission of data ship/shore. The voice channel on the Inmarsat-A satellite communications system, when linked *via* a modem to a PC on both the vessel and shore, could be used to exchange data at high speed.

Telex equates to around seven characters per second and has a restricted character set, where a basic PC/modem system could achieve at least 30 times that speed (210 characters per second) with a standard ASCII character set. Further refinements in modems, transmission protocols, compression and communications management software, in conjunction with careful installation of Inmarsat-A, yield consistent effective data rates of between 5,000–10,000 characters per second depending on the mix of data exchanged. The building blocks for a practical ship/shore data communications infrastructure were apparent although the strategic vision was not yet in full focus.

In the early 1990s Rydex Industries Corporation (Supplier Reference 1, Appendix 5), a communications solutions and software development company specializing in corporate electronic messaging, commenced a project with Stolt Parcel Tankers. The project was to integrate the existing Rydex corporate electronic messaging system with the tanker fleet enabling the vessels to participate freely in the corporate electronic mail network that was available to the other offices of the company. To this point, much of the development of ship/shore communications had been tactical, focusing mainly upon traffic cost savings. The Stolt/Rydex view was a strategic initiative to provide an enabling ship/shore communications infrastructure. Rydex forged a strategic approach from these foundations; it recognized the attributes of three essential infrastructure layers:

(a) OPTIMIZATION
The inherent ability of the system to exploit the computer and communications technology to the full to automatically maximize the ship/shore throughput consistent with prevailing conditions, and with minimal or no operator intervention. (This had been the emphasis of much development to date but this was in isolation from the other layers.) (Note: Typically 60 per cent to 85 per cent savings on basic traffic can result.)

(b) INTEGRATION
The ability to connect and exchange messages and data end-to-end across the ship/shore network and corporate environment linking a variety of computer and communications systems features into a functional network. (This would encompass a variety of messaging types with delivery within the corporate network and beyond.)

(c) MANAGEMENT
The inherent functionality of the system to facilitate connection, automatic operation, monitoring, administration and support from land-based, possibly remote, central services. (The network management element had been missing from prior development and although generally relevant was specifically important to shipboard networks.)

The resulting Rydex Global Marine Communications Solution comprises;

(i) Rydex Exchange Protocol (REP-2). A powerful and sophisticated communications protocol that delivers the optimization requirement. It will function with Inmarsat A,B,C and M services as well as Cellular Telephone.

(ii) Rydex Mail System (RMS-PC). A user-friendly workstation messaging interface that provides shipboard and shore users with integrated messaging facilities (e.g. fax, telex, e-mail, graphics, Internet) and will interface with corporate messaging systems (e.g. cc.Mail, MCI Mail, AT&T Mail).

(iii) Rydex Mail Manager (RMM). A high availability server that concentrates and manages the ship/shore communications infrastructure and provides seamless integration with the shore based networks. The RMM can customize current capabilities and is configurable to encompass future growth.

The Rydex package not only provides a platform for advanced features but also additional services, for example;

Rydex Automated Message Exchange (AME) Developed in conjunction with Jo Tankers, AME allows for remote and automated management of shipboard systems and information. It can request automatic execution of remote programs based on given criteria. This is seen as a powerful ingredient in the effective management of developing shipboard technology and systems (see ISIT below).

Rydex Image Capture Facility (ICF) This feature not only revolutionizes ship/shore fax technology but addresses the growing need for high-resolution image capture and transmission.

Rydex Captain First Messaging This overlays the ship/shore communications infrastructure with an optional, simple and effective on-board message management function that allows the master to monitor and control communications activities as required.

Rydex Data Bulletin Boards This service allows for the request of data by the vessel in preference to automatic delivery and has many practical uses.

The Rydex Global Marine Communication Solution is an excellent example of the power and scope of a strategic, infrastructure approach to ship/shore communications. There are specific ship/shore communications requirements to be fully addressed and at the same time global and corporate *de facto* standards that need to be embraced. It is noticeable that the early adopters of on-board IT and ship/shore communications emanate mainly from "high-tech" and passenger vessel managers where the need for information is perhaps more obvious. The prevailing and impending pressures on ship management demand that, regardless of the type of vessel and trading, the basic requirement for information related to the safety, operational and commercial management of ocean-going vessels is such that a ship/shore communications infrastructure is an essential requirement.

Inmarsat

Naturally, no review of ship/shore communications would be complete without reference to the marine industry's unique and (as yet) the world's only, truly global communications provider, Inmarsat (Supplier Reference 2, Appendix 5). Commercial pressures in the global telecommunications marketplace have forced Inmarsat to consider more strongly the mounting non-marine opportunities in addition to its fundamental and traditional marine safety, navigation and communications role. At first sight this may appear to divert from Inmarsat's marine origins but in turn it will have spin-off in terms of products and services for the marine industry. Marine companies do have special ship/shore telecommunication requirements but they are also shore-based international traders with conventional commercial communications needs. The Inmarsat legacy should provide the marine sector with a head-start over other sectors in the use and benefits of global satellite communications.

Inmarsat-A and Inmarsat-C implementations currently make up the bulk of installed base, the latter being associated mainly, but not entirely, with GMDSS (Global Maritime Distress Safety System). Inmarsat-B and Inmarsat-M represent the new digital services that are establishing themselves both in new ship buildings and in the Inmarsat-A replacement market. Considering the length of time that Inmarsat-A has been available, the acceptance of the technology and subsequent infrastructure use has been poor. Many factors contribute to this. One can even point a finger at Inmarsat but the fundamental reason must revolve around congenital myopia with the shipowning, managing and chartering fraternity.

All the technology in the world will not compensate for the vision to use it to improve safety, quality and service.

Many of the Inmarsat services can make a viable contribution towards a ship/shore communications infrastructure (*Inmarsat Satellite Communications Handbook*). Inmarsat-B High Speed Data looks set to become the standard from which ship/shore foundations are measured. When considered over the life of a vessel with even the most modest projections regarding the increase of ship/shore data exchange during that life-cycle, it is likely to be one of the best investments shipmanagers can make. For many, there is perhaps an even more attractive, if short-term, proposition. With some reservations on older models, an existing Inmarsat-A system represents considerable infrastructure potential. When enhanced with ship/shore communications technology from suppliers such as Rydex Industries, Marinet Systems or SpecTec (Supplier References 1, 3 and 4, Appendix 5) this potential can be unlocked. Analysis suggest that over 60 per cent of Inmarsat-A shipboard installations are under-utilized. Subject to Inmarsat continuing to support Inmarsat-A as declared, it could represent an ideal initial step for many shipmanagers. There is much life in the old sea-dog yet.

5th Generation Messaging

5th Generation Messaging is a forum of leading companies from the fax and electronic messaging industry. Their aim is to promote and provide standards for multi-media messaging to integrate the technologies involved and provide commercial market needs such as integrity, security and legality.

The group is attempting to address the strategic requirement for compatibility of transfer of multi-media information between systems and at the same time enhance the legal and security status of fax and electronic messaging up to and beyond the status long enjoyed by telex. The marine environment is one of the few commercial areas where telex is still widely used. Although now comparatively slow speed and also restricted in character set telex does carry legal status and is frequently the only practical means of communication. Considering the flexibility and performance of modern communications, it is recommended that the progress of the 5th Generation Messaging forum is monitored for developments.

8.3.3 Ship Management Applications

The benefits of an infrastructure rather than an applications approach have been laboured. The role of specialist applications integrated into the infrastructure has been discussed (cf. Figure 8.7). The sourcing of such applications warrants further examination. The development of new computer applications programs is a time-consuming and expensive business. The support of suites of such programs over their lifetime is more costly. The raw power of modern computers has made application development tools a viable ingredient of the corporate infrastructure but the associated costs of systems design, programming and support expertise can still be prohibitive. The management of such projects is also a very specialist task. In the absence of an IT strategy that features the necessity for a significant and on-going programme of applications development and support, it is not likely to become a viable in-house alternative.

Packaged applications from IT suppliers offer a cost-effective alternative provided that the solutions offered are taken into context.

By definition, packaged IT applications software solutions are generalized solutions to specific application areas or an integrated group of application areas. Based upon relevant industry expertise and experience, they are flexible and configurable but it is rare that a perfect applications match will result. The integration with other applications and the IT infrastructure is a major consideration. Traditionally too much emphasis has been placed on the "good" provided in the application area(s) and too little on the "bad" in the surrounding organization. More significantly, as most packages have their origins in an applications approach, many are devoid of infrastructure integration elements. In the jigsaw puzzle analogy used earlier, application packages are large pieces that take the place of two or three smaller pieces and look as though they might fit. There will be "up-sides" in terms of speed of implementation and cost but there will also be "downsides" in terms of compromises in infrastructure and integration. The key to the successful exploitation of application packages once again resides in strategy. Against an IT strategy it is possible to measure and weigh the benefits and disadvantages and manage the latter.

In this context packaged applications solutions acquire the mantle of cost-effective strategic solutions and will be a certain feature of ship management implementations. It is a case of "if the application is worth doing, then it is worth doing a little badly", provided it is under control.

Integrated Ship Management

Modern ship management applications suites have evolved in conjunction with early adopters of the technology from the ship management industry. The pioneers and now major players with regard to integrated ship management packaged solutions are Marine Management Systems Inc. (MMS) (Supplier Reference 5, Appendix 5) and SpecTec (Supplier Reference 4, Appendix 5). The MMS Fleet Manager Enterprise is a fully integrated system and a good example of the teamwork between IT suppliers and shipmanagers. The MMS Fleet Manager enterprise suite comprises five comprehensive main modules:

- FleetWORKS: planned maintenance, inventory, ordering, recording, certification, budgets
- FleetLINK: ship/shore communications
- FleetCREW: personnel management and reporting, payroll
- FleetWATCH: vessel position, status and activities, weather, fuel/water management
- FleetREPORT: infrastructure report generator

The MMS strategy embraces the view that the integration of these functions is the key to ROI: integration underpins cost-effectiveness as it minimizes wasteful processes and functional interfaces. There are now sufficient implementations of such systems to begin to generalize on the benefits achieved. Figure 8.11, generalizes the IT benefits scenario.

The type of application reflects the benefits that can be expected. Operational applications (stock recording) will give rise to operational benefits (accurate stocks); management applications (inventory management) will give rise to management benefits (optimal stocks) and strategic applications (fleet procurement management) will give rise to strategic benefits (bulk purchasing). The opportunity for improved ROI increases with the level of application.

Strategic spares inventory management on an integrated fleet basis is reported to have achieved savings of up to 20 per cent through bulk ordering. Totem Ocean Trailer Express (TOTE) confirms savings of US$30,000 in the first six months of using MMS FleetWORKS and inventories that are now four times more accurate. A tanker company using the same software reports savings of US$250,000 per vessel by identifying minimum spare parts levels across the fleet and by bulk ordering. Strategically planned maintenance can have a massive impact on reducing vessel downtime. Several companies report vessel downtime reductions of between 40 per cent and 50 per cent (valued at over US$500,000) after the first year of installation

Figure 8.11: The IT benefits scenario

RICH PICKING

IT IMPLICATIONS?

of MMS FleetWORKS. One company reports savings of US$1.2 million in the first three years.

Some costs will rise. Ship/shore communications will enable many of the applications with resulting increases in traffic. However, this has been predicted and addressed by the many IT suppliers (see ship/shore communications above). The MMS FleetLINK module is typical with consistent operational savings of around 80 per cent on basic communications costs; strategically this is important as five to seven times more data can be sent for the same cost.

If managed well this can improve control and enable applications to release significant ROI.

These examples only indicate the specifics. Much (the best?) IT improvement, by its very nature, gets absorbed into the corporate infrastructure, becomes the *status quo*, and its specific contribution remains unreported. In many ways this is how IT should be, essentially a silent partner, reflected only in the overall success of the organization.

8.3.4 Decision Support

The ability for computer and communication systems to process, consolidate and display large amounts of data in easily assimilated graphical and numeric summaries is well known. The addition of key knowledge and decision parameters can introduce an "artificial intelligence" into the system and thereby suggest choices and preferences for management confirmation. In many cases the system can make simple decisions and more complex processes are feasible. Considerable R&D in the computer science surrounding these areas has taken place in recent years and the practical results are finding their way into everyday computer systems life.

The immediate objective is "Management Decision Support" providing management with easily absorbed summaries improving the knowledge of the total situation from which well-informed decisions can be made (cf. information is control).

The computer science techniques employed can range from simple accounting to complex mathematics, from basic visual display to multi-coloured high resolution graphics and video. Decision support needs not be complex to be effective. The fundamental objective is to access the vast pool of corporate information for relevant data, processing and presenting it in timely, understandable fashion. Decision support functions should be considered for inclusion in the corporate infrastructure. That way the decision-making work element is reviewed on a corporate wide basis and decision support is a natural part of systems.

On-board Decision Support

ORION On-board Ocean Routeing

On-board Ocean Routeing is a classic among ship management decision support systems. It not only demonstrates the computational and display power of modern PCs but confirms the vital enabling role of a communications infrastructure and specifically ship/shore communications. Although complex in many of its computational elements, it should be considered a model for many other similar and less complex opportunities.

It is rare these days for an ocean-going vessel to take to sea without some form of routeing advice, at the very least based on long-range weather forecasting. Crew and vessel safety always come first in the quest for optimal routeing so the choice of route can also have significant financial and commercial implications.

In a recent example using the Orion On-board Guidance Systems from WNI Oceanroutes (Supplier Reference 6, Appendix 5), a winter voyage from southern Chile to New Zealand *via* the "roaring 40s" was completed safely saving 40 hours of sailing time and 53 tons of fuel. The master, supported by the Orion system was not only able to ensure the safety of his charges but optimize commercial and operational factors.

Up to now much of the ocean routeing technology has been shore based. The computation and correlation required to integrate information from meteorology, oceanography, navigation, naval architecture and vessel economics being a major factor. Computers and routeing experts ashore would suggest an optimum route to the master prior to leaving port and this would be updated on route *via* satellite communications. Naturally, as much of the original and subsequent data was predictive the master and his shore based support work together to monitor the actual position and conditions. Appropriate ship/shore communications is vital to the exercise, returning actual position and local conditions in exchange for long-range (10 days) routeing. The master is best placed to handle the vessel through local conditions but the shore-based computation can provide vital long-range tactical information.

This application clearly demonstrates the decision-support potential of the combination of computing power and communications. However, the "ultimate" solution is seen as placing the ocean-routeing technology in the hands of the vessel master. Orion places the proven route-forecasting technology and the most up-to-date data at the perfect point of decision.

The vessel master now has the tools, the data and his expertise in the right place and at the right time. The shore-based support can still provide the long-range data but the master is capable of up-to-the minute fine tuning and "what if" simulations using his own personal onboard decision support technology.

IT has provided the solution in two key areas: cost effective ship/shore communications and powerful, ergonomic decision-support computing. The master has always had the final decision on vessel routeing; modern computing and communications can place the highest quality of information firmly in his hands.

8.3.5 Strategic Technology Management

The uncontrolled proliferation of PCs in the office is a technology management problem that most companies have to face sooner or later. The PC has many infrastructure computing advantages but these are not gained without some pain. Ship management companies have additional considerations when "the office" is afloat. A mass of mission-critical operational and control data exists on board. The PC has rooted this out, not only in "conventional" office data processing and communications, but in bridge, cargo and machinery control systems. Due to the divergence of the on-board applications, the variety of disciplines involved, and the arbitrary use of proprietary closed hardware/software solutions, it is often the case that the creeping proliferation goes unrecognized and unchecked. That is, until the systems become unmanageable.

On board, the IT opportunities are significant, but the associated management problems are magnified by the scope of systems, absence of IT support and remoteness of the "office".

Standing back from the immediate shipboard problem, it is readily apparent that the situation, if left to its own devices, can only get very much worse, and very quickly. The PC is now at home on board and, spurred on by eager suppliers, will creep into every available application area. The availability of useful data will increase and the need to standardize, manage and communicate ashore will surely follow. Early adopters of technology (e.g. Stolt Parcel Tankers, USA; Jo Tankers, Norway) have already met, and are addressing, the problem. Impending legislation will add to the information and communications workload. Proposals for ships data models and a vessel "lifecycle" database, with access by authorized parties, are well advanced and gaining support. Clearly there is a strong requirement for a consolidated and strategic approach to the subject of on-board information management including the acceptance of standards for hardware, systems and communications. This will be specifically relevant and inherent to newly-built vessels but due consideration must be given to the question of retro-fitting existing fleets.

ISIT: Strategic Initiative for Marine IT

The vision of a fully-integrated shipboard information technology has been pioneered by Eugene D. Story (President of Marine Management Systems Inc.) (Supplier Reference 5, Appendix 5).

As a naval architect by profession, Gene Story was able to visualize the on-board opportunities for IT at a very early stage and established MMS Inc. in 1968 to pursue that aim. From the vast shipboard IT experience and expertise gained in conjunction by ship builders and equipment suppliers, vessel owners and managers, computer and communications suppliers and the marine standards bodies the concept of "The ISIT Platform" was born in 1995. The Integrated Shipboard Information Technology (ISIT) Platform is now a reality and has been developed in conjunction with emerging international standards (cf. ASTM F1756, ISO TC8) (Figure 8.12).

The management of the ISIT Platform project is organized on three levels, the development team, an advisory board and a standards committee. ISIT participants total over 70 companies representing all areas of the ship design, ship building, navigation and ship management as well as classification societies and regulation bodies. Initial ISIT implementations during 1998 feature both new build and existing vessels (respectively; Eletson, Double Eagle and Coastal Marine, Corpus Cristi).

ISIT is an infrastructure approach to the integration and implementation of IT on board ships. ISIT provides a cost-effective, common computing environment for all potential shipboard applications within which they share data and communications

Figure 8.12: ISIT systems services

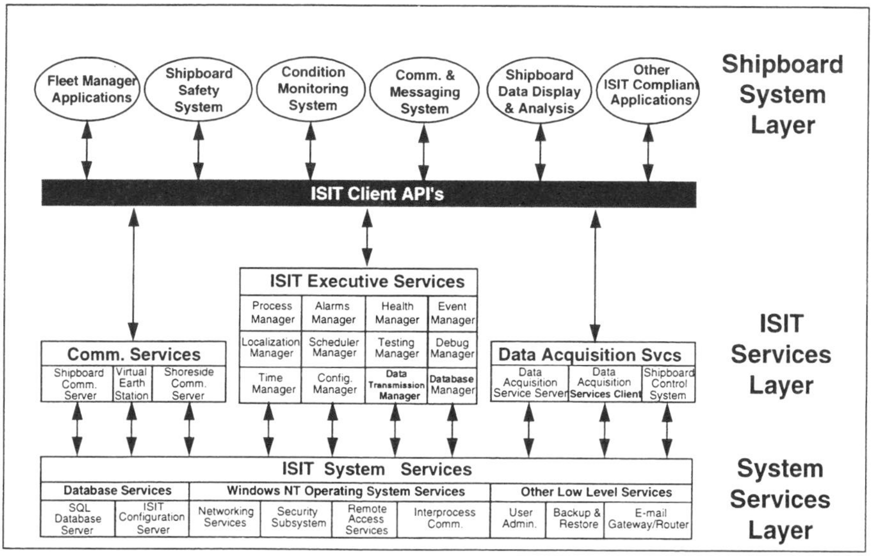

with shore-based management. It also enables remote administration and maintenance of the shipboard systems by shore-based operations and technology managers. ISIT mirrors for on-board systems the precise management requirements for all IT systems; protection and utilization of the IT assets and management of the technology.

ISIT is one of the most significant IT initiatives in ship management since Inmarsat satellite communications and the vessel-friendly PC. A benchmark by which to measure onboard ship management systems has been set. ISIT is infrastructure at work, it paves the way to the managed floating office of the future. ISIT provides enabling technology of huge strategic proportions that underpins all and every commercial and legislative issue facing modern ship management. The vision is not difficult to absorb; the reality is there; but making it an integral part of corporate strategy is down to the relevant senior management in ship management.

THE HUMAN ELEMENT

9.1 GENERAL SITUATION

It is relevant to start this chapter with a direct quotation from the first edition: "The real core capital of a ship management company is its people, its systems, its corporate leadership and its market image. Probably in that order of merit if . . ."

In the practice of managing ships, it is very easy to rely on the systems to carry an organization through. However, it would be very unwise to do this without looking hard at the unusual structure of the ship management sector. Typically, it is organized with one or more shore management centres each controlling a number of ships. So, we have a situation where those ashore believe that they are the first line of management, but in fact the potential for damage—whether to life, the environment, the ship, other ships, or the company—is most firmly in the hands of those on board.

Even in numerical terms, this is confirmed by the fact that the probable ratio of people afloat to people ashore involved in the direct management of ships is 10 to 1. It remains critical that we place a priority in recruiting, motivating, and retaining the best possible people within the shipping industry and within the ship management sector. Public pressure as well as international regulations insist on the highest standards of operation and performance and shipowners and managers are increasingly called to account if these standards are not met.

Over the past few years, we have been trying to match these standards in an atmosphere where it is apparent that there is certainly a possible future shortage of seafarers and increasingly apparent that there is a growing shortage of certain skills. It may seem surprising that there has never until recently been any attempt to quantify the number of people actually involved worldwide in the industry. The more developed seafaring nations, which until about 1980 were synonymous with the Western industrial nations, have long published national data, but there has not been anything on an international basis.

The need for something along these lines has become obvious with the increasing internationalism of the workforce and the first attempt came from the joint BIMCO/ISF Manpower Survey of 1990 (BIMCO/ISF 1990). This survey was updated in 1995 and the results of this updating are extremely interesting. Firstly, that the initial survey got it broadly right. Within survey errors, there are about 1.2 million seafarers or to put it into perspective, about 0.05 per cent of the global workforce. Secondly, that there is an imbalance between the areas which need to use seafarers and those which supply them.

The two sets of diagrams from the BIMCO/ISF Surveys which are shown as Figures 9.1, 9.2, 9.3 and 9.4 indicate this very clearly, particularly if the figures for Panama and Liberia are transferred from their geographical regions to the OECD area as it seems consistent and logical to do. The 1995 survey also came to the conclusion that there was a current shortage of officers, although not of ratings, and made several projections with varied assumptions on action which might be taken. Two of these are included as Figures 9.5 and 9.6. An empirical assessment leads one to believe that the industry has neither reduced manning scales nor increased training by as much as one third; consequently it is extremely probable that the gap between demand and supply has widened from the 4 per cent indicated in the survey under the benchmark scenario.

The surveys are not able to indicate where particular skill shortages will occur but it is not unreasonable to assume that it will be in the higher skills needed for specialized ships that shortages will first become evident. Evidence is now appearing to confirm this, and this of course has implications for training and recruitment standards.

Turning from questions of the quantity of seafarers it is necessary to look both at quality and at treatment of them. This is the so-called "hardware versus software" approach. It is over 20 years since there was a serious shortage of seafarers and there are many working in the industry today who cannot remember a time when this was so. In 20 years there has been an extremely long period of low freights, when cutting operating costs was the first, second and last call. Crew costs, including training, are one of the quickest acting cost-cutting measures in any business and they have certainly been used in shipping.

Unfortunately, the vast majority of attention paid to R & D over this period went into technical advancement rather than personnel and it is only in the last few years that attention has moved back into the people area. Two of the leaders in this have been the P and I Clubs and the United States Coast Guard. The United Kingdom P & I Club has carried out assessment of its members' ships for some years now and publishes the findings in its regular journals and also in a report "The Human Factor" (1996). Among the conclusions of this programme is the assertion that around 80 per cent of accidents and incidents on board ships are caused by human error—a statistic which has almost become notorious within the industry. One other conclusion is that ships operated by the independent ship management sector probably comprise about 27 per cent of the total, and are slightly more likely than an owner-operator to have an active management policy in force.

The United States Coast Guard has implemented an accident prevention programme with a very significant title. "Prevention through People" takes a very positive approach to the importance of people on board. One of its statements is even more definite than the 80 per cent rule; the Coast Guard claims that, taking

Figure 9.1: World demand for seafarers, 1990

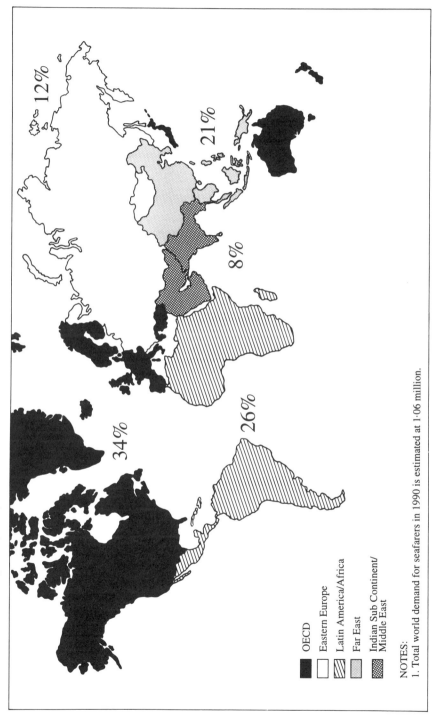

OECD

Eastern Europe

Latin America/Africa

Far East

Indian Sub Continent/
Middle East

NOTES:
1. Total world demand for seafarers in 1990 is estimated at 1·06 million.

Figure 9.2: World supply of seafarers, 1990

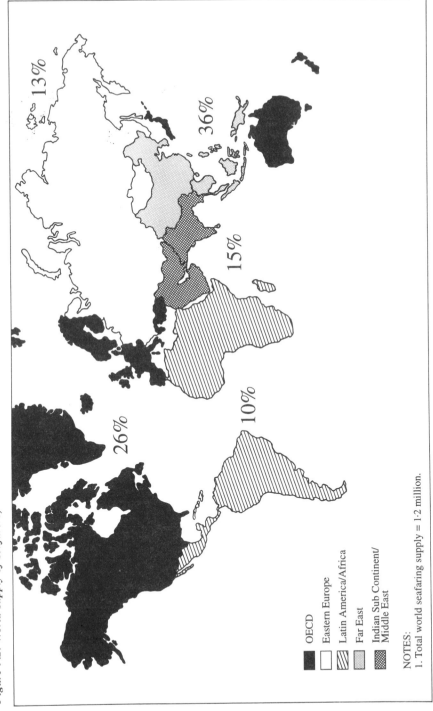

OECD

Eastern Europe

Latin America/Africa

Far East

Indian Sub Continent/
Middle East

NOTES:
1. Total world seafaring supply = 1·2 million.

Figure 9.3: World demand for seafarers, 1995

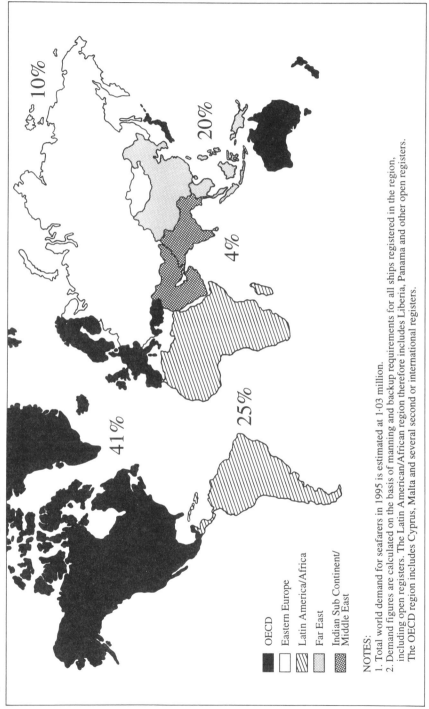

OECD

Eastern Europe

Latin America/Africa

Far East

Indian Sub Continent/
Middle East

NOTES:
1. Total world demand for seafarers in 1995 is estimated at 1·03 million.
2. Demand figures are calculated on the basis of manning and backup requirements for all ships registered in the region, including open registers. The Latin American/African region therefore includes Liberia, Panama and other open registers. The OECD region includes Cyprus, Malta and several second or international registers.

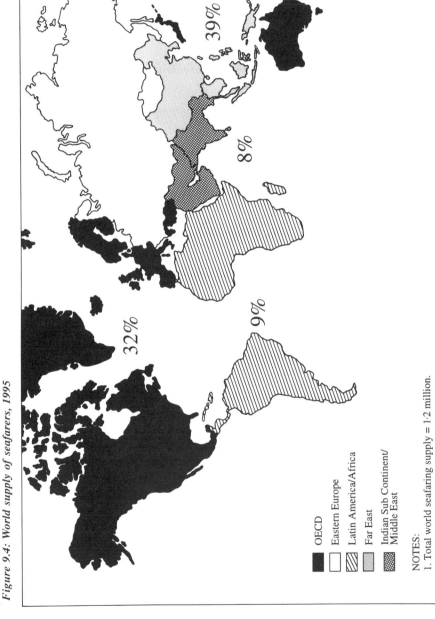

Figure 9.4: World supply of seafarers, 1995

13%

39%

8%

32%

9%

OECD

Eastern Europe

Latin America/Africa

Far East

Indian Sub Continent/
Middle East

NOTES:
1. Total world seafaring supply = 1·2 million.

Figure 9.5: Supply-demand gap for officers: sensitivity to supply assumptions

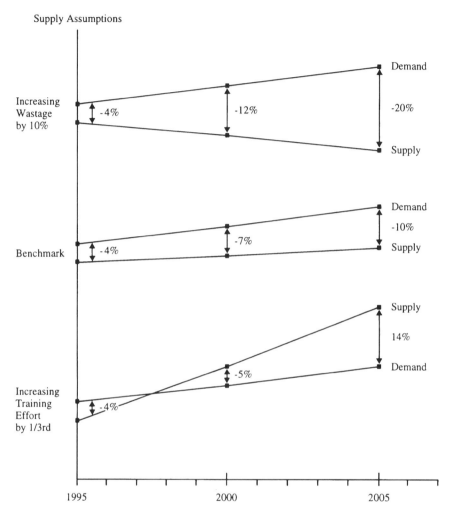

Source: BIMCO/ISF estimates based on computer model

management decisions ashore, design and build factors, into account much closer to 100 per cent of accidents and incidents are caused by human failings. The Coast Guard finds more than ever that it needs to focus on the human element in marine safety. As a Port State Control, as well as in its Flag State role, we find the USCG in the lead in checking the crew competencies of ships visiting United States ports.

Summarizing this section so far, the industry has a need to increase the numbers of seafarers to ensure that all seafarers meet acceptable standards of quality. We

Figure 9.6: Supply-demand gap for officers: sensitivity to manning assumptions

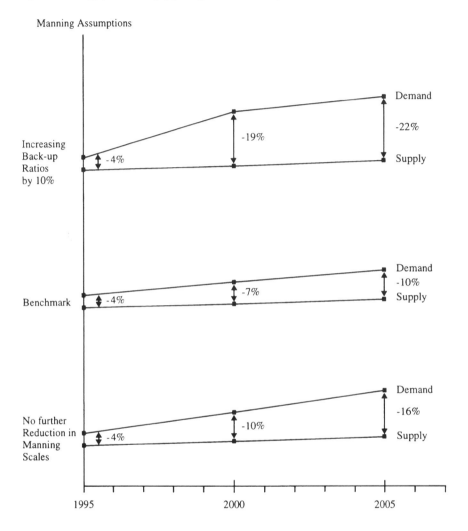

Source: BIMCO/ISF estimates based on computer model

have come back to the questions of recruitment, training and retention; and these three words will, in some sense, be a recurring theme throughout this chapter.

There will also be, of course, some subthemes:

– The question of numbers brings in alternative areas of supply, even revisiting former traditional areas. Should we be looking at a totally different internal operation on board ships?
– Why is it that only 1 in 40 seafarers is female?

- Training is dealt with in some detail further on.
- Retention brings in all the questions and comparisons; why is the wastage rate during cadetship 30 per cent in the United Kingdom, about 10 per cent in the Philippines and Eastern Europe and less than 5 per cent in India? Can we have a mixed shore-sea career structure pro-activated by the industry and not by the individual?

All of these questions will be brought into the equation during the chapter, and will I hope, cause some thought within the industry.

9.2 REGULATORY ENVIRONMENT

There are those in the industry who say that it is being stifled by regulation. It would be over-simplifying the matter to dismiss them as the sort of operators who consider all regulation to be bad. What is nearer to the truth is to say that the industry is being put in the position of having to digest a lot of new regulations simultaneously which could cause symptoms of indigestion in some areas.

Regulations are not new to this industry; we already have a sort of international alphabet soup in SOLAS, MARPOL, OPA 90, COLREGS, LOADLINE and so on. However, within this section, we shall concentrate on four very substantial and important sets of regulations. The International Safety Management Code (ISM Code), the International Convention on Standards of Training, Certification and Watchkeeping as amended (STCW 95) and the two ILO Conventions, Numbers 147—Merchant Shipping (Minimum Standards) and 180—Seafarers' Hours of Work and the Manning of Ships, all have a direct effect on the crew operation of shipping.

9.2.1 ISM: One Small Code . . .

The shortest of these is ISM. The Code itself, published by IMO, barely covers eight small A5-size pages, and traces its development through five earlier IMO resolutions. For the purposes of giving it a home and facilitating enforcement, ISM is Chapter XI of SOLAS. It will, however, have a huge effect on how shipping operates and on its approach to the safety culture within the industry. We have already seen above in the approach of the P & I Clubs and USCG how the culture change will depend on the attitude and actions of people to make it a success.

ISM asks—no, requires—everyone in the industry to take part in the creation of a culture of self-regulation of safety, where regulation goes beyond mere rules and regulations and requires the implement action of a Safety Management System (SMS). Each company and each individual become responsible for the actions to be taken to improve safety. This means that companies must develop specific systems for the company as a whole and for each individual operating unit; ships and shore offices.

The SMS does not arrive from above by some means of divine intervention. It has to be designed, implemented and owned by the people who will have the responsibility to make it work. And it will have to work; while the SMS itself is almost certainly the end result of a lot of extremely hard work, the system of regulating it is simplicity itself. The company is certificated by the flag state(s) of the ship(s), and the ship is certificated by its flag state (in the majority of cases, this will actually be carried out by an approved classification society). Port State Control will verify the fact that the necessary certification is in place and that it is being applied on board competently. The human element is involved in designing the SMS, in applying it, and in auditing it.

9.2.2 STCW: Classic Compromise

If ISM is short in words and long in implications, then STCW 95 is long in words and long in implications. STCW 95 is an amendment to the original convention which was defined in 1978 and came into force in 1985. Subsequent experience showed that it did not satisfactorily cover the ground that it was intended to and the route of amendment was chosen so that the work could be carried out quickly and without further delay in ratification i.e. a "fast track" process. The 1978 convention was in many ways a classic compromise between those countries which wanted the highest standards and those which had a genuine concern about their ability to implement it.

The 1995 amendments are intended to address three main concerns. In STCW 78 there are no precise standards of competence covering the abilities needed to perform the various shipboard functions. STCW 78 only sets out the knowledge requirements and the different interpretations had led to concern that there was indeed no uniform standard. In addition, it was found that there were no guarantees that the requirements had actually been implemented or were being enforced; in modern parlance, there was no effective audit trail and there was a growing belief in many flag states that STCW certificates issued by certain crew source countries were not reliable and were no guarantee that the convention was being applied. Finally, the 1978 convention only took account of traditional shipboard organization; it made no allowance for the changes which were taking place in modern training and the application of such things as dual officer certification—in essence it had become outdated.

The revised STCW 95 sets out new responsibilities for shipping companies; it sets out new uniform (and higher) standards of competence, new measures to ensure that governments actually implement the convention. In many ways it is a new set of rules dressed up as an alteration to the existing ones. The opportunity has also been taken to include the use of simulators for training, specific qualifications for instructors and assessors, hours of rest requirements, and alternative arrangements to permit dual certification. The convention began to come into force on 1 February 1997; 1998 will see its application to all new entrants to seafaring and all seafarers must comply by 1 February 2002.

There has been considerable confusion regarding these dates of implementation, with several countries either threatening to apply the entire convention to foreign flag ships in their ports at some date of their own choosing, or indeed applying it early to their own ships, However, over time, IMO seems to have persuaded the majority of countries to "march at the same pace". The convention requires governments to advise IMO of the steps which they are taking to implement the convention; and for countries which are substantial suppliers of seafarers to other flag states, this has meant a need for a certain openness on the standards of training which they apply. This is the origin of the so-called "white list" where IMO will list countries (as approved suppliers in quality assurance terminology) in compliance with the convention. Flag states also have the ability under the convention to physically assess the training establishments for seafarers who wish to serve in their ships. This has already led to certain administrations accepting graduates only from specified training establishments in other countries; and we can expect this sort of selection to continue for some time and, indeed, to increase if some countries do not improve or close unsatisfactory training establishments under their jurisdiction.

For those who are entering the area of STCW 95 for the first time, there is no substitute for reading the basic document thoroughly. It comes in a small but thick loose-leaf format. However, a newcomer should also obtain a copy of an ISF publication, "A Guide to the Revised STCW Convention" which will make his or her life very much easier.

9.2.3 ILO: Benchmark

Finally, we should look at the two ILO conventions. ILO 147 is a "blanket" convention covering accommodation standards, hospitals and medical scales, working and living conditions. As a means of enforcing minimum standards, it has largely been ignored. However, it is one of the benchmarks for Port State Control inspectors and it is increasingly being used against substandard ships. Regrettably, the practice of poor accommodation maintenance is one which is quite common and substandard operators should be aware of the increasing use of this convention to detain vessels.

The second ILO convention is No 180 which is intended to regulate both hours of rest on board ship and also hours of work. As ILO 180 is a new document, it will be brought into the Port State regime by incorporating it as a protocol to ILO 147. In addition, the European Union intends to implement the requirements of ILO 180 for all ships within EU waters. This convention will regulate the hours of all seafarers, not only watchkeepers who are covered by STCW 95. By the back door, almost, this could bring many changes to working practices on board merchant ships. There is a growing pressure, mainly from trade unions, that the hours worked are too long and that the pattern of work on board ships leads to high fatigue rates. Both NUMAST, the UK officers union, and ITF are conducting surveys in this area; and again the P & I Clubs have begun to investigate the implications. For the shipmanager, there are already situations where additional staff are required for certain trades, and there is a very real possibility that the work pattern on every ship will have to be reviewed.

9.3 CREWING COSTS

Crewing costs are probably the second or third highest part of the cost of owning and operating any ship, coming in the same area as finance charges and fuel. They are also the easiest to change quickly by various means such as reductions in numbers, extended tours of duty, reduced overtime, alternative sourcing, or by simply reducing wage rates. The preferred solution for some operators has been to delay payment of crew wages or ultimately to stop paying them at all, hoping that they can buy sufficient time to recover their cash flow and recognizing that in most jurisdictions crew wages have a priority claim on the value of the ship.

Several peripheral functions such as training can also be stopped quickly in case of need, and it is this result of the extended bad markets which has caused some of today's difficulties with poor crew training and upcoming shortages.

Crewing costs are comparatively easy to quantify and to compare. However, it is much more difficult to carry out any sensitivity analysis on a wide scale because so much depends on ship type, trade, speed and so on. Figure 9.7 has taken a standard crew cost expressed in US dollars which complies with the ITF Total Crew Concept (TCC) and inserted it into 1998 operating budgets for five vessel types.

The crew construction is 25 men in each case, and allowances have been made for any additional bonuses for ship types, and also for differences in tours of duty. So there are slight differences in the total dollar figures although the basis for the individual crew wages is the same in each case. For the purposes of this comparison total operating cost is made up of:

- crewing, including training and ISM compliance;
- stores and consumables;
- maintenance and repairs;
- insurance, including P & I;
- overheads; including communications, management fees/office overheads.

The results of this exercise, tabulated, are, in 1998 terms:

Ship type	*Crewing as a percentage of operating costs*
30,000 dwt Roll on/Roll off	34
40,000 dwt Bulk carrier	43
Panamax Bulk carrier	37
Suezmax tanker	35
VLCC	33

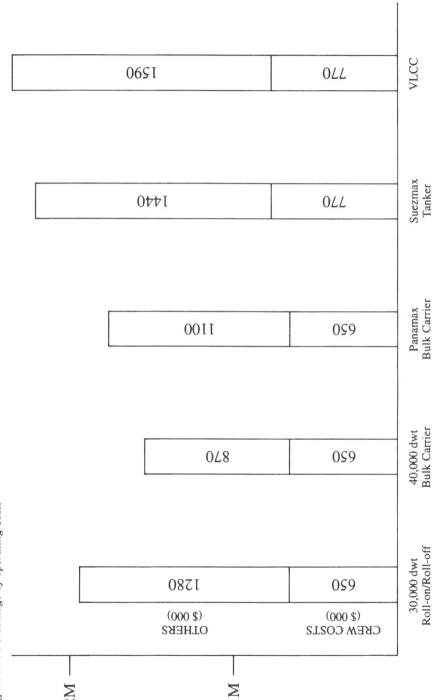

Figure 9.7: Percentage of operating costs

The basic rule of thumb is that crewing costs are a higher proportion of the smaller ship. Indeed, in the case of ships below (say) 5,000 dwt, then crewing costs will be the most critical factor overall.

We should now look at exactly what is included in crewing costs and for this, it is simple enough to set down exactly what has to be carried out to employ and make use of a crew.

First the crew has to be recruited. Many companies make use of manning agents and up to 30 per cent of crews are recruited contract-by-contract in this way. However, there is a definite shift, certainly by larger shipowners and by the larger independent shipmanagers—to move towards what is, in effect, permanent employment. While the legal framework is still in the majority a voyage-by-voyage contract, seafarers expect and are expected to return to employment with one company. In some cases, this return factor is as high as 92–95 per cent. Genuine permanent employment either in the form of salaried seastaff or in "back-to-back" voyages has returned in the United Kingdom, and never disappeared in places such as Japan or France. There have been attempts to introduce it in the developing countries but so far it does not seem to have caught on. It is difficult to see exactly why this is so, but part of the reason seems to be that there is no history of permanence. Permanence brings a certain amount of job security, but also introduces concepts such as notification to governments and the consequent tax payments, and commitment to returning early if required by rotation planning. So, there is a gain in security and a corresponding loss of freedom.

All quality assurance schemes cover the procedures to be completed at the recruitment stage; some of them such as checking certificates and licences are set down in STCW. After recruitment and allocation to a ship, medicals, working gear, briefing etc. have to be arranged. The crew has to be transported to the ship and arrangements for feeding made.

Once on board, a payroll system has to be in place, capable of coping with extra payments such as overtime, special bonuses and of coping with deductions like soft drinks, telephone calls, cash advances and remittances from wages.

A coding system to take care of all these items, both for budgeting and for control of crew costs, will look something like that set out in Table 9.1.

Table 9.1: Coding system for crewing costs

WAGES

Officers' Wages and Leave

Wages & Leave (to include Seniority, Wage Differentials, Trade Bonus, etc.).

Social Costs (including payments to all sources for Pensions, Medical Funds, Family Benefits, Social Security, etc.).

Table 9.1—cont.

Ratings' Wages and Leave

Wages and Leave
Social Costs

Overtime

Officers' Fixed
Officers' Additional
Ratings' Fixed
Ratings' Additional

Additional Wage Items

Standby Pay and Allowances
Study Leave
Extra Bonuses

VICTUALLING

Crew
Others

TRAVEL

Fares
Hotels/Local Transport at Port/Port Agents' Fees
Visas Immigration Costs
Home Country Travel

MANNING AND UNION COSTS

Union Dues (ITF/Local Unions)
Licences (Flag State)
Manning Fees and Expenses
Manning Office Communications

MEDICAL & SUPPORT

Medical/Insurances

Crew Insurances
Medicals (Pre-joining)

Table 9.1—cont.

Drug and Alcohol Testing
Medical Irrecoverable

OTHERS

Uniforms/Working Gear
Recreation/Welfare
Laundry Payments

TRAINING

In the time since the first edition of this book there have been several general moves in wage costs. Firstly, ITF has continued with its twin policy of working to abolish the free flag/flag of convenience system while also continuing with the approval of TCC agreements. There is a contradiction within these policies and it is fair to say that this contradiction is recognized by the ITF leadership and they are making attempts to open discussions with other sections of the industry. It is arguable that the free flag system is here to stay and should be officially recognized as permanent by the ITF but this will be some way in the future, if ever. By trying to regulate wages under free flag in return for the issue of a "Blue Certificate", the ITF has certainly increased the wage income of certain crew source countries, notably the Philippines, India and Eastern Europe. Without going into great depth, the TCC agreements are all based on a benchmark figure for an able seaman; which today is USS$1,200 per month, having risen from US$1,000 since 1993.

Table 9.2 is a very crude analysis of berth cost variations for chief officers and able seamen for certain major source countries in 1997. These figures are based on several surveys carried out during 1997 and should be taken as the result of an averaging process rather than as particular costs. No attempt has been made to take account of currency fluctuations.

Table 9.2: *Crude Analysis of berth costs for Chief Officer and Able Seamen, US$ per month*

	Chief Officer		Able Seamen	
Nationality	US$	Index	US$	Index
American	12,500	100	4,950	100
Norwegian	7,400	59	5,400	109
British	6,200	50	2,100	42
Australian	5,400	43		

Table 9.2—cont.

Nationality	Chief Officer		Able Seamen	
	US$	Index	US$	Index
Dutch	4,800	38	2,850	58
Croatian	3,500	28	1,400	28
Polish	2,950	24	1,000	20
Indian	3,400	27	850	17
Filipino	2,850	23	770	16
Bangladeshi	2,800	22	500	10
Chinese	2,200	18	480	10
Indonesian	1,900	15	514	10

Note: Particular distortions are likely in the Able Seamen figures for India and the Philippines, because of a combination of ITF and non-ITF wage structures.

If any conclusions can be drawn, then they might be:

1 Market forces are affecting officers' wages much more than ratings'. A three-tier effect is becoming apparent whereby wages in a middle group of Croatia, Poland and India are receiving a premium over other developing countries. These countries' officers are receiving a substantial premium over ITF TCC rates. In fact, as shortages become more apparent in specialized trades such as LPG, chemical and product tankers, a similar movement is becoming evident in the Philippines and in some other parts of Eastern Europe.

2 While substantial numbers of ratings from India, the Philippines and Poland are sailing under TCC agreements, these average figures lower than the benchmark certainly show that market rates in these countries are less than that figure. No major upward changes are being shown in the numbers of ratings employed from developed countries, so the major effect of benchmarking ratings' TCC wages so far as world trade is involved, is to increase, even if infinitesimally, the cost to the consumer of transportation.

Neither of these tentative conclusions is surprising and there is not time or space to develop them further in this forum. It is very much a case of "watch this space".

9.4 CREW SELECTION CRITERIA

At some stage a decision has to be made on what crew to man a ship with. It is not possible to talk of "best" or "worst" crews or, indeed, of "good" or "bad" crews.

The shipmanager is always working to obtain the "right" crew for any particular ship in a particular trade. In the case of the independent manager, it is not uncommon for the manager to begin by using a different set of criteria from his client. So, it is important, therefore, that there is a dialogue between manager and client before any final choice is made. Sometimes this is easier said than done as the client has his own prejudices and preferences which may or may not be made clear to his manager at the outset.

In the days of predominantly national flags, there often was no choice. National flag, national crew was the cry of governments and of unions. The existence of second registers and the growth of free flags has brought choice well to the forefront of the equation.

Today, the manager and his owner can usually make a rational choice based on:

- wage costs
- terms of employment
- experience/skills/training
- ITF status
- continuity
- availability

The largest managers are able to source crews from at least four or five places where they will have their own manning offices, or at least a long-standing relationship with a manning agent.

One of the first decisions to be made is whether to take the entire crew from one source or to employ a mixed crew. As owners from developed countries have flagged out, it was natural for them to want to continue to deal with senior officers with whom they could relate. In most cases, these would be the very same men they had previously employed in the home country. In some ways, this was a decision of necessity which suited all parties as there may not have been any availability of senior officers from the new crewing country. Nowadays, there are the complications of an ageing population of officers from developed countries, a history of no new blood from these areas, and an increased availability of seastaff who have become used to working with "Western" owners and operators.

The previous section gives us an indication of where the senior officers of the immediate future are being drawn from. Croatia, India, Poland are places where the barriers are dropping first, although there are many Western owners using full crews from the Philippines and the Former Soviet Union.

This decision is primarily one of cultural and professional confidence. However, it is sometimes forgotten that this confidence must be a two-way street; if an owner or manager shows this sort of confidence in a homogenous new world crew, he is more likely to have that confidence returned with a higher degree of motivation from that crew. This is one of the reasons why it is important for the future that STCW 95 is made to work successfully. It used to be said that a good homogenous crew works better than any mixed crew and it is quite possible that this maxim still applies.

STCW 95 is our official measure of competence. We may decide, however, that competence is more than a matter for IMO or a white list, and decide to involve ourselves more in measurement of competence which will be examined in the following section.

It is foolish to pretend that cost is not one of the most important factors in coming to this decision on what crew to use. However, it is necessary to look behind the direct wage costs at some of the indirect ones. For example, if tours of duty are shorter not only is there an increase in air fares; there is an increase in the cost of overlap (the extra time involved in a year in travel and handover); but in home travel, visas, port agents' charges and so on. The number of processing or recruitment fees incurred in a year will also be greater.

When we turn to the question of the direct wage and related costs, it is instructive to look again at Table 9.2. Wage-for-wage, British officers are over twice as expensive as Filipino and almost twice as expensive as Indian or Croatian. British ratings are almost two-and-a-half times as expensive as the (average) Indian or Filipino. If an owner is operating in the international market, how is he to be sure that this differential is worth it to him? At one time during the late 1980s and early 1990s, there was a great rush to cheap crews. Despite, or perhaps because of, the evidence from various surveys, it seems more and more true that there are no more truly "cheap" officers. Many of the so-called cheap crews came from countries which were rejoining the world economy after a period of absence. Now, they are working fully into this international market, and their remuneration is showing this. Again, as we have said many times, this is particularly true of the officers rather than the ratings.

For our officers, therefore, in order to obtain competent staff, we will find ourselves paying something around this market rate. Only in certain ship types and in certain trades, and perhaps if we go to one of the smaller and emerging source areas, and we will come back to these points, will we be able to drive officers' wages down below this figure.

For many years, when seafarer supply was greater than demand, it was common to say that if there were pressures to pay higher wages from some sources, it would be possible to go to another. This is no longer the case. Apart from the great enigma of China, there are no remaining untapped sources of substantial numbers of competent officers. There is no lost tribe. Myanmar, Indonesia, South and Central America are often quoted as potential sources; and perhaps they are in the future. For the present, however, there are no large numbers of unattached officers in these countries. All of this should lead us naturally to the conclusion that training in our existing source areas is necessary in the short and medium term.

For the ratings, the cost decision depends very much on whether either a national or TCC unionized agreement is required. In some cases, this decision will depend on the charter party; whether or not it contains an ITF Clause; or even if it imposes serious penalties on the owner if the ship is affected by a *bona fide* union dispute.

Alternatively, a decision to make such an agreement will result from the expected trading pattern of the ship. If the ship is flying a free flag and trading into Scandinavia, Australia, or North Europe and is likely to be in a public berth, it is a brave or foolhardy owner or manager who will not negotiate an ITF Agreement. If a TCC-based agreement is signed, then the ratings' wages are based on the AB benchmark of US$1,200 and other ranks will be calculated on a mathematical formula.

Finally, continuity is an important factor in the selection decision. There is no point in manning a ship from a source where we know that we cannot provide continuity of supply or continuity of employment. The second factor is as important as the first. While it is not possible for the independent shipmanager to guarantee employment—he has no idea if or when ships will enter or leave his managed fleet—it is not good practice to rapidly increase and decrease manning from one source. People, and seastaff are people, are demotivated by too rapid change.

9.5 CREW TRAINING

This is a subject worthy of a whole book to itself, and is one of the most critical areas in the success of any company. We have already seen how the regulatory framework in which shipmanagers work has gone through a recent period of great change. We have also touched on some of the results of a lack of training in the developed world and a low standard of training in the developing world.

What do we mean by training, and how do we define it? Training consists of:

- classroom work
- distance learning
- on-the-job training
- specialized external courses
- workshops
- attendance at conferences and seminars: interaction
- special assignments
- articles, books, videos
- simulation.

In order for our training to be successful, it must do at least three things. Firstly, it must have an objective; secondly it must be measurable; and thirdly it must satisfy the trainee's perceived needs if it is to motivate him. Training, almost by definition, has limitations. It can improve knowledge and instil or change behaviour. It cannot by itself alter attitudes; that requires education and experience. Our task, therefore, in arranging training within ship management is to cover a lot of ground, and also to match the manager's requirements to the needs of the seafarer.

STCW 95 has been one of the catalysts in changing the methodology and in introducing new training courses. The new amendments require a different approach both in the training establishments and in the companies. Familiarization immediately upon joining a ship, formally recorded, together with familiarization training before taking up duties is a new and sensible requirement. This familiarization upon joining must now include any supernumeraries, wives and families who are travelling on board.

There is a new requirement for a wider coverage of specialized cargoes, and indeed it appears that there will shortly be a specialized bulk carrier endorsement. Medical training for the ship's designated medical officer is now a must. Basic safety training for all seafarers and an advanced fire-fighting course for those taking charge of fire-parties is also required. All of these mean that companies have to give much more thought to their on-board systems.

The requirements for watchkeepers have altered quite considerably. While the cadet's minimum seatime requirements are reduced in the convention, the competence requirements are greatly enhanced and the need to complete an approved Record Book is fundamental to obtaining a certificate of competence/officer's licence. One of the unremarked consequences of STCW 95 is a reduction in the number of certificates. After 1 February 2002, there will be no certificates obtained through previous service. Both deck and engine departments will have a watchkeeper-in-charge certificate, a second-in-charge certificate and a Masters/Chief Engineer's certificate. These will be complemented by a ratings watchkeeper's certificate for each department.

The convention permits, indeed encourages, the use of simulation in various areas; and has stimulated a considerable number of simulation establishments as well as a large number of PC-based CD-ROM products. While these are still quite expensive and there are problems in making them accessible to all on board, there seems no doubt that this is a facility suited to training at sea. Similar programmes are available for assessment purposes and are used extensively by NIS authorities in Manila.

Qualifications for trainers and training establishments have been tightened quite considerably; all in pursuit of a common standard throughout the industry. One of the results of this activity has been that companies are making much greater use of company-led on-board training. The type of training that companies are carrying out in this way includes:

- Hazmat
- SMS training
- corporate induction
- Bridge Team
- simulated emergencies
- pollution prevention.

With the introduction of the GMDSS in February 1999, for a long time it was believed that there would not be enough approved training units to provide sufficient trained officers. However, many more came on stream in the second half of 1997 and thereafter, and it now seems that this prospective problem has been successfully overcome. This is through a mixture of public and private funding, and this may be a recipe for future cooperation. Certainly, the introduction on board ships of more powerful PCs has given an opening for many more PC/CD-ROM packages.

While the younger officers mostly have a familiarity with computers, many companies have found it necessary to introduce training packages for their older, more senior officers. Training of this type is usually carried out ashore shortly before an officer joins or rejoins his ship.

English language training is another area where attention has been concentrated. Within STCW 95, there has been identified a need to have a common language on board, and also a specific requirement for a certain competence in English. Unfortunately this level of competence has not been defined. However, the International Shipping Federation has introduced "Marlins", an objective test which can be used to give an immediate assessment. Some companies have taken this one stage further and are using the results obtained in the test to allocate English language training to seafarers within certain result groups.

9.6 FUTURE TRENDS AND CHALLENGES

Let me start this final section by repeating part of the quotation at the beginning of Section 9.1: "the real core capital of a ship management company is its people . . .". We are always looking to the future, we are always facing challenges and particularly so when we are considering people. The title of this section is partially an invitation to review the chapter and partially a challenge in itself to look into a crystal ball.

Earlier in the chapter, I said that the industry had to recruit, motivate, and retain its people. This is directed as much to the shore staff as to the seastaff. Ship management is a very specialized sector and traditionally a high proportion of senior and middle management has moved from sea to shore. If we are unable to attract and retain sufficient seastaff, then we have little hope of obtaining the people we will need for shore management in the twenty-first century.

Under recruitment, we have to look for both quantity and quality. Firstly, the question of quantity. Conventional wisdom has it that seafaring is no longer an attractive career in the developed countries and we have been complaining for many years that we have been unable to attract good candidates as potential officers. Yet, it now appears in Norway, Sweden and the United Kingdom that the problem has not been one of supply but more one of demand. David Livingstone of Clyde Marine Training in Glasgow has said on more than one occasion that he could place many more cadets if only the industry would take them and provide training berths.

In India, companies are regularly over-subscribed when they advertise for candidates. In the Philippines, one has only to visit the pre-sea training establishments to see literally hundreds of young people moving from one classroom to the next. Even in the Former Soviet Union, where the training infrastructure has been static since the end of the USSR, life is quickly coming back into the system and work at sea is still attractive to the young.

Our first new sources of supply must be the old sources. We know the standard of general education; we know the structure of the training establishments; we know the culture of the people; they are used to working with the industry and we are used to working with them. The situation is analogous to that of the salesman. The effort involved in keeping an existing customer is a fraction of the effort required to get a new one.

We also have to look at recruiting more females into the industry. In the United Kingdom, the level of female sea staff is roughly 2.5 per cent; in my own company's Russian fleet, it is almost exactly the same; in the Philippines we have two girls as cadets out of a total of 80. Even if, as wisdom has it, females stay at sea for a shorter period than males, it is still one quick and comparatively easy way to bring additional enthusiastic people into the industry as a pool for shore positions.

Only after these have been attacked, do we turn to the new sources; and by new sources I mean new to the international market. The most obvious country is China. Earlier, we noted that the seafaring population is 0.05 per cent of the labour force; in China alone, this would be about 450,000 people. China has been making great efforts to interest the international shipmanagers in its potential without a great deal of success. There is still a great scepticism about the standard of English language, motivation of the actual seafarer and the worry about continuity of service with the foreign company. After China must come the countries of Latin America; and here language is a definite concern as well as potential officer supply in countries where the poorest are likely to be illiterate and the middle classes are obviously not interested.

Any country wishing to be considered as a potential longterm supply source will need to meet certain criteria. It needs to have a sound general education system, accessible not only to the well-off; it preferably should have a tradition of seafaring which would be regarded either as socially desirable, or alternatively as financially so. English should be used either as a first or as a strong second language. Political and economic stability would be an advantage; superheated development which will price it out of contention in a short time is almost as bad as economic stagnation. Finally, there must be a reasonably-sized population, so that investing in the seafaring future of the country will have a better chance of success. A strong application of these criteria does not immediately lead to many additional places.

We are also able to make more effective use of the existing seastaff. However, this is not as good a solution as it would seem initially. Firstly, any further downsizing of crews will have a greater effect on ratings—the area where there is little or no shortage. Already it is quite common for ships to have more officers than ratings. Secondly, while in Russia, it might be possible to persuade officers to take less leave time, in the Philippines and India, most officers are looking for more leave, not less.

The wastage rate during cadetship is high, particularly in Western Europe. It is important that we take care to make sure that we recruit the right person. If we are losing 30 per cent of cadets in their first three years, then either there is something seriously wrong with our operations or with our selection process. From the beginning of 1998, a project on this subject is proceeding at Warsash, UK. Captain Colin Stevenson of Warsash College has highlighted this work, advocating further study of the personalities of successful seafarers and working to match this profile to new entrants, all as part of an increasing realization that unsuccessful investment in new entrants is worse than no investment.

Retention is a more difficult area to discuss. If we are selecting the right people, why are we losing them? In fact, we want to lose some of them—into shore employment within ship management. What we should be doing is investigating how best to cater within the industry for their changing needs. These changes can include marriage, boredom, frustration, children; as well as many others. We know that some will leave; in fact many of us left the sea for just these reasons, so why do we not prepare a programme which will assist both sides of the equation? As an industry, we have concentrated too much on the requirements of the industry without looking closer at the needs of the employee.

There has always been a certain amount of desire to treat ship management as a separate industry. In fact, it is simply a subset of ship operations; albeit a substantial sector as indicated by the UK P & I Club's estimate of 27 per cent. If we recognize this, it becomes easier to join forces with owner operators to tackle the crewing problems together. If the attitude is that we all take shares of a decreasing cake, then progress will be more difficult and more expensive. If we can work together to increase the size of the cake and/or to stop slices crumbling away, then life could be more pleasant. We see some signs of this co-operation in bodies such as IMEC (the International Maritime Employers' Committee) in Europe, and in FOSMA and MASSA in Mumbai.

Training initiatives include additions to the traditional vocation-orientated courses. Many companies are adding management training and culture differences to their corporate training schemes. Some items as comparatively simple as computer training are seen by the seastaff as at least a recognition that new skills are needed. There is a growing recognition that fatigue and stress are not simply a function of long hours, but that there are other motivational factors involved. STCW 95 itself includes moves away from the strictly vocational; IMO Model Course 5.04 is called "Human Resource Management" while the requirement for crisis management on ro-ro passenger ships is based on psychological principles.

As a summary of this subject, perhaps "trying harder than last term, showing willingness and could still do better" is a fair report. Several important building blocks, notably ISM and STCW 95 have been put in place. Ship management has genuinely accepted the importance of the human element where before there was a large element of lip service.

TOMORROW'S SHIPMANAGERS

10.1 THREE SCENARIOS REVISITED

In the second edition of this book John Spruyt put forward three scenarios for the future of ship management over the following six years. Given that half of those six years have now passed it may be useful to revisit the scenarios and examine which of the three has come to pass and at what stage the industry is in that scenario. However, it must be borne in mind that when Spruyt put forward these three scenarios the IMO ISM Code had not been fully formulated and its impact upon the shipping industry in general and ship management in particular was yet to be appreciated. Similarly, the revised STCW Convention was in its infancy and many in the industry did not appreciate the link between it and the ISM Code.

The three possible scenarios put forward were:

10.1.1 Scenario 1—Worst Case

- Shipmanagers fail to respond to calls for quality and go for least cost service.
- They try to avoid liability with devious corporate structures.
- They employ unqualified crew and are happy to run substandard vessels.
- Accidents and pollution are highly publicized.
- Responsible owners and charterers avoid managers.
- The concept of separate ownership and operation is devalued.
- Fleets shrink, supply prices go up and creditworthiness down.
- Management becomes a fringe and unscrupulous activity.

10.1.2 Scenario 2—Middling Case

- Shipmanagers are passive marketers and operators.
- They fall in with regulatory pressures as they arise.
- They are liable to attract only average quality people.
- They try to avoid trouble, like not taking on crude tanker business destined for the United States.

- They stick to easy vessels for reasonably reliable owners.
- They are not very profitable, so there are fewer competitive pressures.
- Fleet sizes fall or stay static and supply prices rise to put pressure on profits.
- It becomes a lack-lustre service business with no growth potential.

10.1.3 Scenario 3—Optimistic Case

- Managers are aggressive in acquiring the best crews.
- They focus their marketing on long-term business.
- They are innovators in technical and human resources.
- They pioneer systems of risk and error management and a pro-active approach to safety.
- In combination with cargo interests and finance houses they take a large share of the 1990s new buildings.
- They actively propose solutions to quality standards; this conditions the liability pressures which are responsive to good performance and intelligent insurance placing.
- Fleet growth in excess of 3 per cent per annum in sensitively placed, sized and managed units equivalent to 100 more ships by the year 2000.
- Profits growth is sufficient to fund long-term training and investment with some to spare.
- Increasingly recognized as a responsible and permanent part of the international shipping business, ship management grows.

Scenario 1 has clearly not come to pass, at least for the majority of shipmanagers. Most of the responsible ship management companies had some form of quality assurance (QA) certification long before the formulation of the ISM Code was completed and in doing so voluntarily opted to provide a higher quality of service. Indeed many of the major companies shed themselves of owners and vessels either unable or unwilling to settle for anything other than a least cost service.

Remarkably little manoeuvring has taken place to avoid liability issues, most companies choosing to take measures to control and manage risk. In doing so they have ensured, as a first priority, that they have access to well-qualified crew.

Accidents and pollution incidents will always be well-publicized no matter if a manager or an owner operates the vessel; this is unavoidable with the technology which is available to the media today. However, the very professional way in which Acomarit handled the grounding of the *Sea Empress* served to adequately demonstrate that a shipmanager has the resources and is capable of coping with such an emergency.

The client lists of most managers contain some very impressive and respectable names and there is no evidence that either owners or charterers are turning away from shipmanagers. Similarly most managed fleets are expanding with the credibility of shipmanagers and their services being increasingly recognized and accepted.

In looking at the middling case one has to recognize that all shipmanagers are not the same and, invariably, their philosophy and approach to business will vary. One must also be aware of the fact that there are now very few ship management companies which can be described as large whilst there are still very many small ones. It is, therefore, probable that whilst some will not fall into the middling category, others may well do so. This is an aspect of almost every type of business and ship management is no exception.

There are, therefore, those who have perhaps chosen to take a passive role and choose only to meet regulatory requirements as they arise. It is true to say that there are also some that have decided to concentrate on operating vessels that are perceived to be "low risk". These companies are not, however, representative of the vast majority of shipmanagers who, as we shall see later, are more representative of Scenario 3.

It is true however that ship management is an ever more competitive business requiring managers to be pro-active and innovative. Without these qualities *individual* companies may well conform to the majority of the conditions of Scenario 2 but it could be argued that this does not mean that the industry as a whole will become a lack-lustre service with no ambition.

In my view Scenario 3, the optimistic case, is far more representative of the position of the larger ship management companies as we approach the next millennium. The successful and profitable shipmanagers of today have access to the best-trained crews, manage fleets of ships on behalf of good quality clients and have some form of QA accreditation. Fleets are growing rapidly, in some cases at the rate of more than 10 per cent per annum and, whilst there is still some pressure on fees, respectable owners are prepared to pay for a quality and professional service.

Most shipmanagers conform to Spruyt's Scenario 3 with the exception of his assertion that they will take a large share of the 1990s newbuildings. There is no evidence that this is happening though equally there is no reason why it should not. David Underwood, the late Chief Executive of Denholm Ship Management, always maintained that shipmanagers would eventually turn themselves into shipowners and that the wheel would go full circle. There is some evidence of this happening, though not with newbuildings. Wallem has invested in handy-size bulkers and V Ships have invested through their fund MC Shipping in multi-purpose tween deckers and container ships.

There will inevitably be some fall-out of shipmanagers who cannot, or will not, meet the conditions of Scenario 3, but those who do and gain certification to the ISM Code will be part of the next phase of the development of the ship management industry.

So what will determine the shape and size of the ship management companies of the future and indeed what will the future hold for those who have already conformed to Scenario 3?

10.2 A QUESTION OF SIZE

There are undoubtedly several niche markets in ship management, for example those which specialize in the management of only one type of vessel, or manage vessels from one geographical area or flag (ASP is an example of a company that until very recently operated Australian flag tonnage almost exclusively). Such companies can and do operate very successfully and to a large degree conform to Spruyt's third scenario. They tend to attract good crews because their business tends to be stable, or as in the case of ASP, the crews are drawn from a country that has good standards of training and education. The relationship with their clients is usually long-term and a close relationship can develop between owner and manager.

Their experience in managing tonnage of a special type or in a special trade allows them to develop an expertise that is difficult for their competitors to equal and the business tends to be protected. This expertise also allows the shipmanager in the niche market to be technically innovative in his specialized field, developing techniques, operating practices and even participating in the design of equipment and ships. This, in turn, raises the entry barrier for the competition, thus further protecting the niche manager's business and client base.

The long-term difficulties that such a manager can face are significant and can even threaten his business. Niche markets, in any type of industry, are, by their nature, difficult to expand and develop and therefore the client base tends to remain small. As a result, if a client does leave or go out of business, the manager can lose a large proportion of his business—business that cannot easily be replaced.

The niche manager also faces the same problems in diversifying into other types of tonnage as its potential competitors do in penetrating his market: a lack of expertise. Shipmanagers, even the larger managers, tend to be "categorized" by owners and some will shy away from managers whom they perceive to operate a fleet that is biased towards tonnage which they—the owners—do not control. The niche manager who operates only reefer ships, for example, could experience extreme difficulty in obtaining the management of, say, tankers.

The smaller manager cannot easily meet the demand by the owners of today for the manager to have more than one geographical location. Owners now expect this as part of the service to be provided by the manager and are normally unwilling to pay extra for the facility. Geographical expansion is therefore difficult to achieve for the niche market shipmanager unless he is willing to fund it himself in the hope that by doing so he will attract new business and new clients.

Niche fleets tend to be small and require only the minimum of shore-based staff to keep the fleet operating efficiently. If this were not the case then small fleets would be uneconomic to manage. For such a manager to implement statutory legislation such as the IMO ISM Code represents a considerable strain upon his resources and he is faced with either bringing in a consultant or delegating the task to his own staff. In both cases the financial impact can be considerable and the disruption unwelcome.

Conversely the cost and impact of information technology may be easier for the niche shipmanager to cope with. He has a smaller fleet to equip with computers and satcom facilities and an "off the shelf" system will probably cope with the accounts and reporting requirements. The need for multi-user, multi-currency and multi-year end systems which drive the larger shipmanagers to ever more expensive and complex systems may not present itself to the smaller, niche player in the business.

The shipmanager seeking to expand must be prepared to manage a varied fleet of vessel types for a number of international clients. This will normally demand that the manager employ sea and shore staff with the skills to manage such varied tonnage and have more than one location from which he can manage the vessels. Additionally, he will have to invest in the latest in information technology in order to minimize his costs and maximize his efficiency by running his administration services as leanly as possible.

If such a manager operates tankers to the United States he will also have to maintain sufficient technical staff to deal with the latest changes in legislation as well as to assemble an emergency team capable of dealing with a serious accident or incident.

The bigger and more varied the fleet the greater the task and cost of implementing any quality assurance system. Multi-national crews and geographically diverse management locations will only serve to increase the cost of establishing such a system including the ISM Code.

The result of all the above factors is that it is possible in today's ship management business to survive either as a niche manager or as a large multi-national shipmanager, but it is extremely difficult for a mid-sized shipmanager to provide the services required to operate a varied fleet. Such a manager will experience difficulty in maintaining several management offices, to employ the staff required to effectively deal with emergency situations (whilst still running the remainder of the fleet), to develop effective QA systems and keep up with the latest developments in information technology.

As we enter the twenty-first century the demands upon shipmanagers will become even greater and size will become even more significant. The successful shipmanager will have to have the "critical mass" and financial ability to meet these demands and challenges and to continue to expand.

10.3 EXPANSION AND DIVERSIFICATION

A sure sign that any business or industry has reached maturity is its desire and ability to diversify into other activities. In the case of ship management the potential has always been there, inherent in the elements of the service already provided.

The basic service of "ship management" comprises four distinct elements:

    (1) Technical
    (2) Personnel
    (3) Purchasing
    (4) Accounts

Some elements, such as "personnel", can be provided independently whilst others, such as "technical" are capable of being split into further discrete parts:

- New construction/conversion supervision
- Purchase and other inspections
- Quality assurance consultancy

Most shipmanagers have provided these subservices for many years, generating much needed additional income whilst at the same time incurring very little extra overheads. These subservices have, however, only served to supplement full ship management fees and, with the possible exception of crew management, they have never been regarded as businesses in their own right.

Many of the larger shipmanagers have capitalized upon their strength in the market and their large pools of sea staff by offering "manning only" contracts to third party clients. The Cyprus-based companies, in particular, have exploited this market and have refined it to the extent that they frequently offer this service on a fixed (lump sum) price basis. Whilst it is very difficult to obtain statistics showing what proportion of their businesses constitutes manning-only contracts it is reasonable to assume that income from this activity is substantial for the companies which provide this service.

Whilst crew management and other services will continue to be provided by many shipmanagers they do not constitute development or diversification from the core business of ship management.

Major shipmanagers are now poised to diversify into other businesses and industries that utilize the skills gained through decades of ship management experience. Some of the more likely areas into which they may diversify are the management of:

- hotels and resort complexes
- ports and cargo handling complexes
- power stations (particularly floating power stations)
- offshore oil industry support vessels
- offshore production facilities
- shore bases for offshore support

Whilst some of these may appear to be major departures from the core business of ship management it should be borne in mind that some shipmanagers have already begun to enter these new fields.

At least one major shipmanager has used the skills he has developed in managing cruise ships to begin managing resort complexes. Others have entered the field of managing offshore oil industry tonnage—a very different business to that of managing deep-sea vessels.

Whilst many managers grew from shipowners, a few, pure third-party shipmanagers have entered shipowning on their own account. Wallem, for example, has entered into shipowning in a modest way whilst V Ships has been a shipowner for some time.

This represents a change from the perception that prevailed a decade ago that for a manager to own ships would be regarded as a conflict of interest. This has proven not to be the case and indeed many owners regard such an investment by a manager as a demonstration of his financial commitment to the shipping industry.

This conflict of interest perception was largely the view of the shipmanager, rather than the owner, and extended to providing other services such as commercial management, sale and purchase broking and other activities such as vessel operating. During the 1990s this view has changed and many shipmanagers, driven by the need to augment static or declining ship management fees, have begun to provide such services. Users of these services have not only been third parties, i.e. clients who do not use the same company as its shipmanager, but also owners who require the full range of marine services. Shipmanagers who have diversified in this way have seen their businesses grow and they have come to depend less on income from their core business of ship management.

10.4 WHO WILL OWN THE SHIP MANAGEMENT COMPANIES?

Almost all of the major ship management companies of today have developed from shipowning companies. Even Denholm who, probably correctly, claim to be the oldest of today's shipmanagers have been shipowners before and during their time as shipmanagers.

The questions that must however be asked are: "Will control of these companies continue to rest with their founders?" and if not "Who are likely to own the ship management companies of the future?"

Service companies and ship management companies in particular, are extremely difficult to purchase because they are difficult to value. Service companies, by their very nature, do not normally have very many fixed assets and the value is determined by previous profits, which in turn, are a product of "goodwill" i.e. the clients themselves. Unless the company is bought by an entity, which is regarded by the clients as completely neutral, there is always the danger that they will take their business elsewhere.

The choice of shipmanager by a shipowner can be a very personal one based upon any number of factors including:

- geographical location
- nationality of superintendents and line managers
- nationality of crew
- manager's client profile
- types of ship under management
- size of managed fleet

- recommendation from other owners
- manager's relationship with charterers
- manager's IT systems
- manager's operational structure and back-up services
- experience in operating a specific vessel type

All of the foregoing will influence the owner and can be easily verified by him, but one factor which will influence him more than anything is the "comfort factor" which he gets from the people he deals with in the management company. A long-term relationship in any business does not develop by accident. It is a product of many years of the client receiving the service he requires from people he likes and respects. Ship management is a prime example of this philosophy. If this important element does not exist then the relationship will be at best difficult and, more likely, end in acrimony.

Any prospective purchaser of a successful ship management company must therefore be very aware of these elements otherwise he may find that his client base will disappear and the price he has paid for the goodwill will have been wasted. This will be especially so if one shipmanager purchases another. After all if the owners chose manager "A" he probably has also considered but rejected manager "B". If "B" buys "A" and in doing so absorbs "A" and his systems the owner is bound to wonder if he will end up with his ships being managed by the people and under the systems he previously rejected. This may explain why, over the last 20 years, there have been very few cases where one shipmanager has purchased another.

Significantly there have been several cases where shipmanagers have merged or entered into "joint ventures". Examples of this have been Acomarit and American Automar Inc to form Osprey-Acomarit Ship Management and Ugland Ship Management with Interocean Management Corp. to form Interocean Ugland Management Corp. The success of these mergers has yet to be proven as in both cases there has been little or no increase in combined fleet size as a direct result of the arrangement.

It is interesting to note that both of these mergers involve American-based companies perhaps due to the fact that the American flag market has proven extremely difficult for European managers to break into. Denholm set up an office in Houston as early as 1980 and Barber and V Ships have both tried to break into the market, again without any obvious success. Those who have remained in the USA, notably Wallem, Barber and V Ships tend to manage non-US flag tonnage.

The American market is by no means the only one where mergers and joint ventures have seemed to be the best way to penetrate a particular market. Joint ventures, usually between shipmanagers and owners, have taken place in the Philippines, Indonesia and Saudi Arabia and these appear to have been successful.

It is extremely difficult to determine what the exact financial details of any specific transactions really are but there have been several examples of shipowners buying into shipmanagers in recent years. Perhaps the most decisive was the purchase by the Malaysian based owner Koncortium Perkapalan Berhad of Pacific

Basin, a shipowner who, in turn, had an interest in the Hong Kong-based ship management company, Anglo-Eastern. Koncortium Perkapalan purchased 100 per cent of Anglo-Eastern very soon after the purchase of Pacific Basin. A further example of an owner purchasing a shipmanager, or at least an interest in, is that of Osprey Maritime, a publicly-listed Singapore company, and Singapore-based Thome Ship Management.

It remains to be seen whether these companies will restructure themselves in order to enable them to still attract third-party ship management. Given that ship-owners have always owned some of the traditional ship management companies there is no reason to suppose that they will be unsuccessful.

It is notable, if not significant, that in both of the above cases the shipmanager already had his vessels managed by the manager in which he eventually took a financial interest. The purchase of a ship management company by an owner who does not use a shipmanager has yet to take place but the regulatory pressures now being felt by some owners could lead them to consider purchasing a shipmanager that already complies with the statutory requirements.

Expansion by franchising has always been a possibility for a major ship management company, though few have so far tried to do so. The downside of choosing the wrong franchising partner has always outweighed the attraction of expansion. An accident or incident occurring to a vessel in the fleet managed by the franchisee would be potentially catastrophic to the franchiser's reputation.

Managers have instead achieved a form of expansion (and extra income) by negotiating consultancy contracts whereby they implant their personnel, usually into an owner's organization, in order to develop quality assurance systems and to assist in establishing management systems. Several managers have already established such contracts and, as more owners begin to try to come to grips with the requirements of the ISM Code, the circumstances are right for the number of these arrangements to increase.

10.5 WHICH LOCATION?

As previously mentioned, most of the large international shipmanagers usually operate from a number of locations in order to be close to their clients or charterers or to be near the vessels usual trading areas. These satellite offices can be full ship management offices in their own right but more usually are "technical offices" which are manned by one or more superintendents with a minimum of back-up staff. Such offices will normally rely upon the head office to provide personnel, accountancy and purchasing services for the ships under their control.

The choice of location of the head office has usually been determined by the original location of the parent company though this is by no means always the case. Glasgow has always been the home of Denholm since the company was founded over 130 years ago but Acomarit, which is also Glasgow-based has its head office in Geneva.

The larger German shipmanagers such as Hanseatic and Columbia have chosen Cyprus as their base whilst Wallem, Univan and Anglo-Eastern have always been based in Hong Kong. Singapore has always been a popular location for ship management, particularly those companies of Scandinavian origin, whilst Barber have moved to Kuala Lumpur within the last five years.

It is worth while taking some time to examine why specific locations are attractive and why they are likely to remain so beyond the turn of the century.

The main Glasgow-based companies are Denholm, Acomarit, Northern Marine and Norbulk and several other smaller companies are also based there. The presence of these companies in Glasgow makes it, with the Isle of Man, one of the largest ship management centres in the UK. The reasons for choosing Glasgow are many but the main ones are:

- commercial property prices are amongst the lowest in the UK;
- staff salary levels are extremely competitive;
- relatively speaking there is a plentiful supply of technical staff;
- London is only one hour away by plane and there are direct flights to most North American cities and most European locations;
- staff can live outside of the city but still enjoy short commuting times.

The disadvantages of Glasgow as a ship management centre apply equally as well to any other UK location, i.e.:

- the bulk of the overhead of the operation is in pounds Sterling whilst the income is usually in US$, hence there can be significant exchange rate fluctuations which impact directly on the bottom line;
- UK corporate tax is high compared to some countries;
- it is difficult to employ non-EU staff.

The above disadvantages also apply to the Isle of Man though the tax regime there is much more benign than on the mainland. The exchange rate problem can be overcome to an extent by taking currency options or buying forward.

Despite the disadvantages of the UK, Glasgow in particular, is likely to continue to be a favoured location for the foreseeable future.

The Cyprus-based companies are, to a large extent, either "home grown" or trace their origins back to Germany. Reciprocal tax agreements between Cyprus and Germany have existed for many years serving to make Cyprus an ideal location for German companies. Low property prices, extremely competitive local staff salaries and the ability to employ expatriates with relative ease all combine to enhance its attraction as a centre for ship management.

The negative aspects of Cyprus as a location are few, though the political stability of the divided island is always questionable and air connections are not the easiest in the world. The companies based in Cyprus show no inclination to move and again it can be assumed that it will remain a popular location well into the next century.

Singapore has grown over the last 20 years to become one of the major shipping centres of the world. Its location at the edge of the rapidly expanding Pacific Rim, its use as a container hub, and its shipbuilding and shiprepair facilities make it an ideal location. Airline connections to almost anywhere in the world are excellent, it is extremely stable politically, and staff are able to commute using an efficient public transport system.

Unfortunately, however, until recently Singapore was becoming a victim of its own success in that property prices and staff salaries were escalating significantly whilst the Singapore dollar was also very strong. Staff are becoming increasingly difficult to retain and whilst it is possible to employ expatriates, work and residency permits are by no means guaranteed. It is largely due to these disadvantages that some companies are considering relocating to Johore Baru, just across the causeway from Singapore, in Malaysia. It is perhaps why Barber chose to set up ship management operations in Kuala Lumpur, one hour's flying time from Singapore, and with its own international airport.

Of the shipmanagers located in Singapore, Thome and Sembawang, are probably the largest and as the Singapore government owns the latter it is unlikely to move. Thome is now, if not completely, then significantly owned by Indonesian interests and as such Singapore is geographically a logical location.

It would not be unreasonable to assume that Singapore is unlikely to expand as a ship management centre and unless it is able to attract business from Hong Kong it may even decline or be used by managers as a "technical office" location.

Hong Kong has always been a popular location with shipmanagers such as Wallem, Denholm, Univan, Eurasia and Anglo-Eastern, to name but a few, having been established there for many years. Hong Kong's location has all the advantages of Singapore and is arguably better in that it is much closer to Japan and Korea as well as the increasingly important shipbuilding facilities in China. Air connections, both in the region and internationally, are excellent and commuting for staff is not too problematic.

The availability of local administrative staff is good and employing expatriates has, until now, not been difficult. A very benign tax regime and a currency pegged to the US$ combine to make it a commercially attractive location. The downside is that property prices are extremely high, both commercial and domestic, and wage inflation has only moved down from double digits in the past two years, largely due to employers simply resisting the pressure to award large increases.

The run up to the handover of Hong Kong to Chinese sovereignty in July 1997 was a period of uncertainty and some shipowners (though notably few shipmanagers) moved to other locations, with Vancouver and Singapore being the favoured options. (One year after the handover and little has changed that would affect or deter a shipmanager from choosing Hong Kong.) If Hong Kong can retain its present advantages and attractions and at the same time bring inflation under control (as it must do or risk losing its service sector to mainland China), then it stands a very good chance of retaining its status as a ship management centre for years to come.

It is not practical to cover all the locations from which ship management companies operate but the foregoing covers the major areas. There will of course always be others; V Ships is based in Monte Carlo, Ahrenkiel in Germany and the major American managers in various locations from New York to Houston. All have their individual attractions for the companies based there but few can be regarded as major ship management centres in the same way as Glasgow, Cyprus, Singapore and Hong Kong.

Certain other locations are either emerging as management centres or have the potential to do so, notably the Middle East (Dubai in particular), India, the Philippines and Vancouver which has attracted some Hong Kong shipowners.

10.6 THE INFLUENCE OF LEGISLATION

Shipping has always been subject to considerable government involvement, both in terms of economic control and regulation—epitomized by the British Navigation Laws. The move to free trade in the middle of the nineteenth century and the repeal of those Navigation Acts ironically saw an explosion of government legislation directed at the employment and qualifications of British seafarers. Indeed, a British historian, Sarah Palmer has stated: "It may be argued that no other group of nineteenth-century capitalists were so confined within a legal framework as were ship owners." Britain was not the only nation—Venetian laws regulating seafarers date from the Middle Ages. The USA, on becoming a major shipping force after its successful war of independence, rapidly introduced regulations governing the employment and qualification of seafarers. In Europe Germany, Holland and Norway certainly could not be accused of *laissez-faire* in this regard.

Shipping has been in the forefront of inter-governmental cooperation. The first international conference on Safety at Sea held in 1913 arose from the sinking of the *Titanic*. The ILO, which stemmed from the League of Nations, became involved in seafaring from 1920 but apart from recommendations on training in 1936, 1946 and 1970, which were of a general nature, it concentrated on employment issues.

In 1959 IMCO was formed under the auspices of the United Nations and in 1978 seafarers were addressed in the International Convention on the Standards of Training and Watchkeeping (STCW).

The present round of new legislation began with the American Oil Pollution Act of 1990 known as OPA 90 following the grounding of the *Exxon Valdez* in Alaska and the subsequent pollution. This far-reaching piece of legislation had a profound effect upon the way that both owners and managers conducted their business and significantly increased the workload and administration requirements of both.

The shipmanager who now operates tankers calling at US ports not only has to ensure that vessel response plans are prepared and submitted, and that emergency procedures are in place ashore but, more significantly perhaps, has to have the resources to deal with an emergency should it occur. An accident of the magnitude of the *Exxon Valdez* or the *Sea Empress* requires a rapid response with the deployment to the scene of the accident experts of various disciplines that can deal effectively with the situation. Typically (though no such accident is "typical") this may involve at least half-a-dozen people with technical, marine, naval architecture, purchasing and insurance skills plus at least one person to co-ordinate the operation. Additionally there must be one senior person who has the authority and skills to satisfy the requirements of the media.

If the accident occurs at a location which is not close to the manager's or owner's office, an emergency team in the office will have to man the emergency room whilst the emergency team are travelling to the scene of the accident.

When one considers that there also have to be sufficient people to run the rest of the fleet it can be appreciated that the vessel operator has to maintain a considerable resource of personnel. In the case of a shipmanager, both the owner and charterer have to feel comfortable that this resource exists and will be effective in an emergency situation. It can be argued that such personnel can be contracted in on an "as required" basis but this does not normally give the owner or the charterer the same confidence as it does if the personnel are the owner or manager's own staff. It is also not easy to ensure that such personnel are immediately available or that they will work together, or with the people on the ship, effectively as a team.

This requirement was the first to distinguish the advantage of having a vessel operated by a big shipmanager and although OPA 90 presented potential liability problems for the ship management industry it also presented opportunity for those who were prepared to meet the challenge. In the interim period since the legislation was passed, shipmanagers have improved their relationships with owners and charterers and have become respected and accepted as competent vessel operators with all the skills required to safely operate tankers to the United States.

The advent of the IMO ISM Code will also present problems and opportunities for the shipmanager. Maritime lawyers have been pointing out for some time that the potential liabilities for shipmanagers will increase if an accident occurs and the code has not been complied with to the letter. Similarly, if a vessel is delayed because the Safety Management Certificate (SMC) has been withdrawn, the owner may look to the manager for financial compensation.

That these liabilities will attach to the shipmanager is conjecture at the present time and will only be proven when such an incident occurs and the matter is tested through the legal system.

What is a fact is that many shipowners and shipmanagers may be hard pressed to meet the July 1998 deadline for code certification and therein lies the opportunity for the shipmanager who is already accredited. This is the opportunity for such a manager to offer the non-certified owner his management services and hence the opportunity to take into management entire fleets of ships, something which has rarely occurred since the heydays of the 1970s. Conversely, the shipmanager who is not code certified by the deadline of July 1998 will have little choice but to either merge with one who is certified or go out of business.

Once the ISM Code is mandatory there will be less inclination by the owner to change managers or to set up his own operation. The structure of the code dictates that the Document of Compliance (DOC), which certifies the shore-based operation, must be in place before the Safety Management Certificate (SMC) can be issued to the ship i.e. the two certificates are linked. This means that if a ship is sold or transferred to another manager a new SMC will have to be obtained by submitting the vessel to a further audit. This in itself is not a significant problem until one considers the implications of undergoing an audit with a new crew and new management systems. The problems may then become significant enough to make an owner think twice about moving from one shipmanager to another.

Following closely behind, and linked to the ISM Code, is the revised STCW Convention. The convention of 1978 has proven to be largely ineffective, with some flag states completely ignoring its requirements. The implications and potentially far-reaching effects of the latest revision are still not fully appreciated by many in the shipping industry and it once again presents an opportunity for the large, well established, shipmanager who controls his own pool of seastaff.

The requirements of the convention are complex but it basically requires that the staff on board the vessel are trained to a certain standard at a facility, which is approved for the purpose, and that the knowledge is updated on a regular basis. When linked to the ISM Code it is further required that the crew, upon joining a vessel, are familiar with its systems and equipment.

For the owner or manager who uses a third party manning agent and is not large enough to require that the agent provides him with a dedicated pool of seastaff, the STCW convention could present him with major problems. The onus will be on the vessel operator to ensure that the convention requirements are met to the satisfaction of Port State Control. Failure to do so will result in the vessel being detained with the operator probably having little or no recourse to the manning agent for compensation. Once again an opportunity is presented to the shipmanager who has a big pool of seastaff (or access to one) and is prepared to enter into manning-only agreements. Such a manager should be in a position to provide properly qualified and dedicated crews who are well versed in the requirements of the ISM Code and will thus be able to satisfy a Port State inspection.

Whilst new and changing legislation can present problems for shipmanagers those who are prepared to meet the challenges will potentially gain considerably. The effects of the legislation are to raise the entry barriers for those wishing to enter the business and provide major problems for those owners and managers who are unable or unwilling to meet the new requirements. It will, at the very least, cause manning agents to re-examine the comprehensiveness of the services they provide. All of these problems provide unique opportunities for the large, well-established shipmanager.

10.7 THE IMPORTANCE OF IT

There are few industries today which can afford to ignore the impact of Information Technology (IT) on the business world and the shipping industry is no exception. Furthermore, the impact has been felt and utilized to its maximum extent in the ship management sector and to appreciate why this should be we must go back to the middle 1980s and examine the intervening years.

In the 1980s the shipping industry was in a state of acute depression and the ship management sector of the industry felt the bite as great as any. Ship management fees had remained static or even declined since the heady days of the 1970s and shipowners were going out of business on an almost daily basis. For many shipmanagers costs were also rising rapidly, particularly shore staff salaries and other management related overheads.

Shipmanagers, therefore, found themselves in the classic dilemma of being trapped between rising costs, static management fees and a declining client base. The logical solution was, of course, to reduce costs by shedding staff but that is not an easy thing to do in a service business, particularly if the same staff will be unavailable if business subsequently improves.

Most managers at that time had some business processes that were computerized, usually the accounts system, but they tended to be rudimentary and could not be described as being people efficient. At that time very little software suitable for shipping operations was available "off the shelf" and many shipmanagers resorted to developing their own. This solution was both expensive and difficult, frequently actually adding to the overheads due to the large departments which were necessary to develop and maintain the systems.

It was not until the late 1980s that systems and software began to appear which offered the possibility of linking purchasing and accounts systems as well as subsystems for other functions such as report writing. By that time many shipmanagers had suffered financially for some years and it was quickly understood that efficient systems could reduce overheads and offer some respite. It also came at a time when many shipmanagers were beginning to develop quality assurance systems and to link this with a new, efficient IT system gave many the opportunity to radically overhaul their organizations.

The combined cost of these initiatives was to prove considerable and its magnitude was not appreciated by many at the time they embarked upon the programmes. Some shipmanagers, through no fault of their own, were poorly advised and once again tried to develop bespoke systems from basics only to find the task very complex and in many cases the end result was less than satisfactory. Others took advantage of established systems and either made minor changes to the software or changed their own systems to suit the software.

At the same time as the systems were being introduced for use ashore they were also being developed for shipboard use. Computerized systems for planning maintenance and stock control, portage bills and personnel administration, to name but a few all became available to the ship operator.

The catalyst, which brought all these systems together, was the introduction of faster, cheaper and more reliable communication systems, specifically e-mail.

It is now possible for a computer-generated spare gear requisition to be prepared on the ship from an inventory system and sent by e-mail direct to the purchasing department ashore. As a confirmed purchase order it can be entered into the accounts system where it becomes an accrual until the invoice arrives. Receipt of the goods by the ship can be confirmed electronically and, once matched to the invoice, payment can be made. The only paper in the whole system is the purchase order, which is sent to the supplier, and the end-of-month report for the owner.

E-mail or floppy disk can eradicate even these if the supplier has e-mail and the owner can receive his report in the same way or on a disk.

The foregoing is only one example of how advances in technology have allowed the shipmanager to be more efficient and manage more ships with considerably fewer staff. The same technology allows an office on one side of the world to download information from another on the other side of the world, even at night. Thus one good system can serve several offices around the world further reducing the number of people required in each office.

Those managers who have made the investment required in such systems have seen the margins per ship under management increase, even with today's low management fee levels. Those who have not made the investment will not only struggle to make ends meet in financial terms but will also face problems in meeting their client's expectations.

The importance of the Internet as an e-mail and information system is not yet fully appreciated by shipmanagers but it promises to have a profound effect upon their business. The Internet will allow access to information instantly. Everything from news reports to manufacturers', technical bulletins and spare-gear catalogues to ship suppliers will soon be available on the system. Many shipmanagers have already established their own web sites which update their clients and other interested parties on the range of services they provide and other items of interest.

10.8 ... AND WHAT OF THE FUTURE?

So what does the future hold for the ship management industry, what will be the size and shape of the companies involved in it and what services will they provide?

One of the best indicators of a business becoming mature is the gaining of recognition by others in the shipping industry. This recognition is as a result of the players in the business gaining credibility and, at long last, the ship management business as a whole and ship management companies individually gaining both recognition and credibility. This is best demonstrated by the fact that the International Ship Managers Association (ISMA) has been granted consultative status to the IMO.

The perceived shift in liability, to the potential detriment of the shipmanager, brought about by the introduction of the ISM Code has caused managers to look closely at how this problem can be addressed and, in particular, the terms of the ship management contract. The industry standard contracts are the BIMCO Shipman contract for full ship management and the BIMCO Crewman contract for fixed price crew management, both of which are currently undergoing the process of revision. This is being carried out with the input and assistance of ISMA.

Thus shipmanagers are now in a position to participate in and, therefore, influence, the formulation of legislation designed for the shipping industry.

The legislation that is already in place and that which will shortly be introduced will put both challenges and opportunities in front of the industry. It is likely that some will rise to the challenge and others will not, resulting in a reduction in the number of players in the business. This reduction will result in mergers, joint ventures and buy-outs with the larger companies being the beneficiaries of such deals.

Thus the industry will segment into the niche (but not necessarily small) players who will survive because they have dedicated clients and a small spread of vessel type and probably fewer than ten really large players.

Whilst the niche players may remain independent there is an increasing chance that the big players will not. The possibility that they will be either wholly or partially owned by shipowners is very real, the driving force behind this being the owners' desire to obtain compliance with legislation whilst gaining access to well-qualified crew. Those who do retain their independence will come under increasing pressure to enter into joint ventures with owners and operators for the same reasons.

Whilst the existing centres of ship management may not change they will be added to as other locations emerge as commercially viable competitors and as sources of technically competent shore staff. In this regard India and the Philippines must eventually be logical choices.

Success and recognition should also bring with it fees which are realistic for the services provided. This, in turn, will make the companies increasingly profitable. Investment in ship management companies by third parties will also take place purely for commercially speculative reasons or to provide capital for expansion and diversification.

Shipmanagers will add to their range of services in order to offer a complete suite of marine services. The larger companies will increasingly look for opportunities to diversify, the term "management" becoming more apposite than "ship management" to describe their business. In doing so they must be careful not to dilute their focus and attention on the ship management sector of their business otherwise they will find that it will decline rapidly. In this respect they must be very careful to structure themselves in such a way that they can still provide the individuality of service which owners and charterers have come to value so much.

Taking into account all factors it is reasonable to conclude that the ship management industry has a positive future. The growing acceptance of shipmanagers by owners, charterers and others in the shipping industry should now ensure the continued expansion of the business. The industry is therefore poised to fulfil the final factor in Spruyt's third scenario i.e. shipmanagers will be recognized as a responsible and permanent part of the International Shipping business as ship management grows.

PROFILES OF LEADING SHIP MANAGEMENT COMPANIES

Profiles of 20 leading ship management companies are presented on the following pages. Inclusion of a company in this appendix is based on responses to a questionnaire survey conducted in mid-1997.

The information contained in the profiles is derived from completed questionnaires and miscellaneous published sources. In addition to standard information on office locations, senior management, ownership, size, types of ships in the managed fleet and the range of services offered, details of recent and planned developments are also presented.

Profiles on the following companies are presented in alphabetical order:

1 Acomarit
2 Anglo-Eastern Ship Management Ltd.
3 ASP Ship Management
4 Atlantic Marine Ltd. Partnership
5 Barber International
6 Celtic Marine
7 Columbia Ship Management
8 Denholm Ship Management
9 Dobson Fleet Management
10 Eurasia
11 Hanseatic Shipping Company
12 Interocean Ugland Management Corp.
13 Marlow Navigation Company Ltd.
14 Midocean Maritime Ltd.
15 Navigo Management Ltd.
16 Thome Ship Management PTE Ltd.
17 Univan Ship Management
18 V. Ships
19 Vermillion Overseas Management
20 Wallem Shipmanagement Ltd.

The size of managed fleet categories the individual companies were asked to complete are: 0–50; 51–75; 76–100; 100–150; 151–200 and 200+.

ACOMARIT

Head Office: Geneva.
Other Offices: Glasgow, Bethseda (US), Dubai, Oslo, Hong Kong, Piraeus.
Senior Management (Name/Title): Giorgio Sulser/Group CEO; Peter Cooney/ Managing Director, MD Acomarit (UK) Ltd.; Lock Parker/Group Technical Executive; David Rodger/Group Manning & Training Executive.
Ownership/Shareholders: Privately owned. The company was founded in Geneva in 1967 and has since developed a global network of offices.
Other Group Companies: Manning offices have been established in Manila, Rijeka, Novorossiyisk & Riga.
Size of Managed Fleet: 151–200.
Safety & Quality Management Certification: DNV SEPS (1991) + ISO 9002.
Types of Vessel Managed: Most types of ships.
Services Offered: Full service range.

Recent/Planned Developments

Acomarit has enjoyed consistent expansion of its worldwide activities in recent years. In 1995 it established a joint venture company Acomarit-LPL (Hellas) in Piraeus with local shipowner LPL Shipping and the same year it took over the entire management fleet of Hong Kong-based Orient Ship Management which ceased trading.

In 1996 Acomarit was a co-founder of Osprey-Acomarit Ship Management Inc. which focuses on US-flag tonnage. Later the same year, the company established a joint venture company in Dubai, Mideast Ship Management Ltd., to manage part of the fleet of its shareholding partner in the venture, NSCSA.

Acomarit is viewed as an innovative manager which has invested heavily in computerized accounting and ship management systems. It was one of the pioneering companies in the introduction of safety and quality disciplines to shipmanagement.

ANGLO–EASTERN SHIP MANAGEMENT LTD.

Head Office: Hong Kong.
Other Offices: Singapore, Mumbai, Manila and Montreal.
Senior Management (Name/Title): Peter Cremers/Executive Chairman; Marcel Liedts/Managing Director; Richard Wong/Group Finance Director.
Ownership/Shareholders: Konsortium Perkapalan Berhad.
The company was established in 1974 by European shipowning interests including CMB. Shareholding changed in 1993 due to a management buy-out with Pacific Basin becoming a major shareholder. Malaysia's KPB acquired Pacific Basin in 1996 and acquired the remaining shares of Anglo-Eastern in March 1997.

Other Group Companies: Anglo-Eastern Technical Services Ltd., PNSL Shipmanagement SDN, BHD.

Size of Managed Fleet: 76–100

Safety & Quality Management Certification: Det Norske Veritas "SEP" (Safety & Environmental Protection) since 1991; International Shipmanagers Association (ISMA) since 1994; ISM "DOC" from various flag states.

Types of Vessel Managed: Bulk carriers, container ships, gas carriers, tankers, OBOs, multipurpose, self unloaders, ice breaker.

Services Offered: Technical ship management, crew management, commercial management, newbuilding, consultancy and supervision, technical consultancy, pre-purchase, cargo and all types of surveys, agency, consultancy for ISM/QA systems.

Recent/Planned Developments

Despite its acquisition by KPB, Anglo-Eastern will reportedly continue to function as an autonomous company offering independent ship management services to third party clients. Anglo-Eastern will, however, continue to manage Pacific Basin's fleet and will provide advisory services to KPB's subsidiary PNSL Ship Management SDN BHD in areas such as safety and quality management, crewing and communications.

Anglo-Eastern continues to be headquartered in Hong Kong but has expanded its office network to include Singapore, Bombay, Manila and Montreal.

The company has also made major investments in crew training facilities. Besides GMDSS, ship handling simulation and quality assurance training, the company has set up new facilities for electronics, electrical instrumentation and safety officer training. Furthermore, a new training course to upgrade the training provided to ratings has been started which includes safety and English language courses.

The company's technical services company has successfully completed newbuilding supervision contracts in Guangzhou, China and is involved in a four ship newbuilding project in Shanghai.

In December 1996, Anglo-Eastern upgraded its Montreal office to enable it to offer full management services. Activities commenced in 1997 with the management of two Canadian flagged vessels.

ASP SHIP MANAGEMENT

Head Office: Melbourne.

Other Offices: N/A

Senior Management (Name/Title): David J. Sterrnett, Managing Director & Chief Executive Officer.

Ownership/Shareholders: Marine Management Services Pty Ltd. (60%) ACN 050 244 061; Associated Steamships Pty Ltd. (40%) ACN 004 588 452.

Other Group Companies: Agencies have been established in South Africa, Indonesia, Japan and Singapore.

Size of Managed Fleet: 0–50.

Safety & Quality Management Certification:

ISO 9002.
Document of Compliance and Safety Management Certificates for Passenger Vessel Tankers & Bulk Carriers.

Types of Vessel Managed: Passenger, ro-ro, container, tankers (crude, product and LPG), bulk carriers and research vessels.

Services Offered: Full ship management, operations, superintendency, manning agency, ship inspections, newbuilding projects, chartering and post fixture, reconciliations, bunker broking, special projects, QA and safety management programmes.

Recent/Planned Developments

ASP is increasing its consultancy business and has a number of new projects in progress with large international shipping companies.

In 1997 the company set up an independent bunker booking service for vessels calling at Australian ports. In October 1997, it was announced that UK-based Seahorse Ship Management, part of the Pan Ocean Group, had been selected as the preferred buyer of a majority shareholding stake in ASP.

ATLANTIC MARINE LIMITED PARTNERSHIP

Head Office: Bermuda.

Other Offices: Cyprus, Isle of Man, Hong Kong.

Senior Management (Name/Title): Bruce Lucas/President; James Weedon/Fleet Manager.

Ownership/Shareholders: Bernhard Schulte, Hamburg.

Other Group Companies:

Dorchester Maritime Ltd., Isle of Man.
Eurasia Shipping & Management, Hong Kong.
Hanseatic Shipping Company, Cyprus.
Navigo Management Ltd., Cyprus.

Size of Managed Fleet: 0–50.

Safety & Quality Management Certification: ISO 9002, ISM.

Types of Vessel Managed: Containerships, LPG and LNG carriers, crude and product tankers, reefers, FPSO, floating power stations.

Services Offered: Crew and technical management, commercial and corporate management, consultancy, newbuildings supervision, superintendency, training; ship financing; equity sourcing.

Recent/Planned Developments

Attained ISO 9002 in 1995, ISM in 1996.

Developing both crew and technical management business in North and South America in addition to European business.

BARBER INTERNATIONAL LIMITED

Head Office: Kuala Lumpur.

Other Offices: Oslo, New Orleans, Dubai and Montreal.

Senior Management (Name/Title): Svein Sorlie/President; Per Steinar Upsaker/Vice-President; Richard John Binnington/Vice President, Organisation & Quality.

Ownership/Shareholders: Wilh Wilhelmsen ASA.

Barber is a wholly-owned subsidiary which manages vessels served by its parent and for third party shipowners.

Other Group Companies: Wilh. Wilhelmsen (Shipowning); Barwil (Agency); Barber Marine Consultants (Technical Consultancy).

Size of Managed Fleet: 151–200.

Safety & Quality Management Certification: ISMA, ISO 9002, ISM-DOC.

Types of Vessel Managed: Container, ro-ro, multipurpose, reefer, pure car carriers, tankers, chemical tankers, gas tankers (LPG), bulk carriers, OBE, ORE-oil carriers, various types, cruise vessels, FPSOs.

Services Offered: Technical ship management, crew management, commercial management, marine management, marine engineering, consultancy.

Recent/Planned Developments

In April 1994 Barber transferred its corporate headquarters from Oslo to Kuala Lumpur citing the benefits of proximity to its main manpower supply sources and the increasing importance of the Asian shipowning market as the main reasons. This move involved the relocation of senior management as well as the company's finance, marketing and IT functions.

In August 1995, Barber's activities in the Malaysian capital are further enhanced with the transfer of its Hong Kong office operation in a move designed to reduce overheads. The move also involved the establishment of a new company in Kuala Lumpur, Barber Ships Management to work in association with the group's local manning company, International Manning Services.

In early 1997, Barber created a new Kuala Lumpur-based senior management position, VP of Human Resources, Quality and Organizational Development to spearhead its drive towards TOM.

Allied to these various restructuring measures, Barber has invested in its major manpower supply countries—the Philippines, India and Poland. In 1993, the company established its own office, PMS, based in Szczecin. At the time of writing,

Barber was expecting to transfer its Mumbai office to a larger premises which will incorporate a training centre.

In recent years concerted efforts have been made to apply the company's in-house expertise to new sectors of the ship management market. These include cruise vessels, FPSOs and, latterly, a semi-submersible platform which will be used to launch rockets carrying communications satellites. This imaginative project is managed via a joint venture company with the Norwegian engineering group Kvaerner (Barber Kvaerner Marine Management AS).

CELTIC MARINE

Head Office: Isle of Man.
Other Offices: N/A.
Senior Management (Name/Title): Capt. D. Greenhalgh/Managing Director; Peter Evans/Finance Director.
Ownership/Shareholders: N/A.
Other Group Companies:

> Celtic Marine Ltd., Malta.
> Celtic Pacific (UK) Ltd.
> Celtic Marine LLC, UAE.

Size of Managed Fleet: 76–100.
Safety & Quality Management Certification: DNV SEP; ISO 9002; ISM – Doc.

Types of Vessel Managed: All types.
Services Offered: Technical, personnel and commercial management, consultancy, vessel inspection.

Recent/Planned Developments

Celtic Marine Response offering marine pollution contingency planning training, exercise, pollution equipment stockpile and maintenance and pollution response management.

COLUMBIA SHIPMANAGEMENT LTD.

Head Office: Limassol, Cyprus.
Other Offices: N/A
Senior Management (Name/Title): Dirk Fry/Managing Director; Erwin Koch/ Technical Director.

Ownership/Shareholders: Schoeller Group.
Other Group Companies:

Hanse Bereederung GmbH: Kajen 12, Hamburg.
Columbia Shipmanagement (Netherlands).

Size of Managed Fleet: 201+.
Safety & Quality Management Certification: ISMA, ISM.
Types of Vessel Managed: Bulk carriers, chemical carriers, containers, reefers, passengers, product tankers, gas carrier tankers, multipurpose.
Services Offered: Full (technical and crew) or partial management, chartering, insurance, newbuilding supervision, sale and purchase, purchasing, accounting, commercial operations, bunkering.

Recent/Planned Developments

ISMA Accreditation 1996.
ISM Accreditation August 1996.

DENHOLM SHIP MANAGEMENT (HOLDINGS) LTD.

Head Office: Glasgow.
Other Offices: Isle of Man, Hong Kong, Oslo, Singapore.
Senior Management (Name/Title): J.S. Denholm/Chairman; R.F. Speedie/Chief Executive; A. Cannon/Finance Director; M.M. Pride/Director; J.B. Hough/Director; D.J. Freeland/Director.
Ownership/Shareholders: J & J Denholm Ltd. (Denholm was founded in 1866 as a shipping agency: the company entered third party shipmanagement in 1959).
Other Group Companies:

Denklav Marine Services Ltd., Mumbai.
Denklav Maritime Agency Ltd., Manila.
PT Samudera Denholm Ship Management, Jakarta.
Denholm Shipping Services.
Denholm Seafoods.
Denholm Industrial Services.
Serco-Denholm.
Turner & Hickman Ltd., Glasgow.
(Representative offices in USA and Japan).

Size of Managed Fleet: 76–100.
Safety & Quality Management Certification: ISO 9002, ISMA and IMO Resolution A741(18), ISM.
Types of Vessel Managed: Dry bulk, chemical tanker, oil tanker, gas tanker, other cargo ships, OBO, oceanographic, PCC.

Services Offered: Crew management, technical management, commercial management, asset protection, marine consultancy, financial consultancy, technical consultancy, newbuilding supervision, project management.

Recent/Planned Developments

In 1996 Denholm established a joint venture company in Jakarta, PT Samudera Denholm Ship Management with the Samudera Group as its shareholding partner. This joint venture provides ship management and crew management services to Indonesian and third-party owners.

In 1997 the company established a London office to provide commercial management services to the Georgian Shipping Company's fleet of tankers, bulk carriers and chemical carriers.

In 1997 a new joint venture was established in Gdynia (Denpol) to handle the management of Polish seafarers.

Denholm is a group which has actively diversified into shipping-related and non-shipping services in recent years. Aside from its long-established interests in ship's agency, the group is active in fish processing, industrial services and, via a joint venture with the large UK-based facilities management company Serco, the management of small service vessels employed in the UK Ministry of Defence dockyards at Devonport, Portsmouth and Clyde.

In an effort to improve the standard of services in its core business area, the company is investing in a computer-based management system.

DOBSON FLEET MANAGEMENT LIMITED

Head Office: Limassol, Cyprus.
Other Offices: N/A.
Senior Management (Name/Title): Nigel D. Cleave/Managing Director; Laurence B. Williams/Technical Director.
Ownership/Shareholders: Privately owned (Dobson family).
Other Group Companies: All co-ordinated through DFM.
Size of Managed Fleet: 0–50.
Safety & Quality Management Certification: Processing ISM and ISO 9002 and expected to be accredited August 1997 by G.L.
Types of Vessel Managed: Reefers, bulkers, passenger, paper carriers, general cargo, container, multipurpose, supply vessel.
Services Offered: Full and crew management, vessel operations, chartering, ship finance, insurance, accounting, sale and purchase, crew travel, marine training, ship-owning, quality assurance, vessel and company registration, budgetary planning and control, newbuilding supervision, consultancy, reefer services, joint venture.

Recent/Planned Developments

At the time of writing Dobson was planning to:

(a) open various crewing offices,
(b) recruit additional staff to expand its full management portfolio,
(c) gain ISO and ISM certification.

EURASIA GROUP OF COMPANIES

Head Office: Hong Kong.
Senior Management (Name/Title): Mr R. Bajpaee/President & Group Managing Director.
Ownership/Shareholders: Reederei Bernhard Schulte Hamburg.
Other Group Companies:

Eurasia Shipping & Management Company Ltd.
Eurasia Shipping Services Ltd.
Eurasia Marine Consultancy Ltd.

Size of Managed Fleet: 51–75.
Safety & Quality Management Certification: ISMA; ISO 9002; ISM DNV; SEP LRS; ISM.

Types of Vessel Managed: Bulk carriers, log carriers, chemical tankers, crude oil tankers, pure car carriers container, product carriers.
Services Offered: Crew management, technical management, commercial management, technical consultancy, marine consultancy, quality assurance audit, newbuilding supervision, port agency representation of marine products and services, insurance services, marine catering, procurement and logistics, chartering and trading.

Recent/Planned Developments

A "one-stop-shop" of maritime and travel related services enterprise comprising a synergetic group of establishments in a responsibly independent and effectively interdependent structure, Eurasia Group of Companies provides global solutions through local presence and a customer focused personalized approach to quality services.

The group is represented by: Eurasia Shipping & Management Co. Ltd., specializing in full, crew and technical ship management services:

Eurasia Marine Consultancy Ltd.—the principal activities of which are new-building supervision and technical, marine and quality assurance audit consultancy; and

Eurasia Shipping Services Ltd.—specializing in port agency, marine insurance, marine catering (SeaChef), chartering and projects, procurement and logistics and representation of selected marine products and services.

Together they represent a broad-based maritime services enterprise comprising responsibly independent and effectively interdependent companies, providing a one-stop shopping opportunity for our customers.

Furthermore, we are associated closely with the following companies.

Eurasia Travel Network Limited Partnership—a specialized and licensed travel agency handling inbound and outbound tours and corporate and marine travel on a global scale.

Paramount Shipping & Management Private Ltd. in Mumbai, India which looks after the recruitment, training and travel services for seafarers from India.

We believe that the structure has a distinct appeal to our valued institutional customers to whom we aim to provide global solutions through local presence.

Backed with loyalty, dedication and enthusiasm of all our staff we have set our sights on creating a global maritime and travel related services enterprise, which brings together a diverse cross-section of people from different lands, with unity of purpose, to strive for harmony in elements with ingenuity of human spirit, through a principled and value-based approach. Our future business development plans focus towards realization of this vision in creating a truly global customer-focused and quality services organization.

Coming from all walks of life and working in every corner of the world, the Eurasia people stand committed to the singular goal of customer satisfaction.

We take pride in carrying on over a century old traditions of our shareholders, Reederei Bernhard Schulte.

HANSEATIC SHIPPING COMPANY LTD.

Head Office: Limassol, Cyprus.
Other Offices: Manila.
Senior Management (Name/Title): Capt. B. Behrans/Joint MD; Mr A.J. Droussiotis/Joint MD.
Ownership/Shareholders: Privately owned (Member of the Schulte Group; Hamburg). HSC was established in 1972.
Other Group Companies:

St George Insurance Services.
Telaccount Overseas Ltd.

Eurasia Travel (Cyprus) Ltd.
Other Schulte Group Members.
Philippine Hanseatic Ship Agency Inc.
HSC Asia Pacific Inc.
Hammonia Marine Services Inc.

Size of Managed Fleet: 101–150.
Safety & Quality Management Certification:

Safety & Quality Management Certification.
Accredited with the ISMA Code Quality Assurance Certificate.
ISMA Document for ISM.
ISM Documents for various flag states obtained.

Types of Vessel Managed: Bulk carriers, chemical tankers, coasters, crude oil tankers, full container, LNG/LPG, OBOs, product, semi-container.
Services Offered: Ship operations, manning, storage and maintenance, chartering, insurance, financial administration, cost control, management consultancy, superintendency, training, newbuilding supervision, brokerage, lay-up and reactivation.

Recent/Planned Developments

Hanseatic celebrated its silver anniversary in 1997. It played a pioneering role in the introduction of quality assurance disciplines into the ship management sector being a founder member of ISMA and the first company to receive ISMA QA Certification (in 1993).

Hanseatic's activities remain focused on Cyprus where separate businesses have been set up to provide specialist services (insurance, radio accounting, travel) and where the company established its own training school for ratings and junior officers.

Currently, Hanseatic's training school is being upgraded.

INTEROCEAN UGLAND MANAGEMENT CORPORATION

Head Office: New Jersey, USA.
Other Offices: Grimstad, Norway/London, UK.
Senior Management (Name/Title): Admiral J.W. Kime, Chairman/CEO; William Lockwood, Jr. President; Jorge Aguirre, Senior Vice President; James R. Brown II, Vice President, Finance.
Ownership/Shareholders: Totem Resources Corporation and Ugland International Holdings plc.
Other Group Companies:

Interocean Ugland Management AS, Norway.
Interocean Ugland Management AS, London.

Size of Managed Fleet: 0–50.
Safety & Quality Management Certification:

ISO 9002.
DNV Safe Ship Operations and Pollution Prevention (SEP).

Types of Vessel Managed: Tankers, bulkers, general cargo, heavy lift, container, ro-ro, vehicle carriers, coastal, offshore vessels.
Services Offered: Ship operations, vessel manning, storing and maintenance, insurance, financial administration, cost control, management consultancy, super-intendency, training, newbuilding, lay-up and reactivation.

Recent/Planned Developments

Acquisition of more third party business.

MARLOW NAVIGATION COMPANY LTD.

Head Office: Limassol.
Other Offices: N/A
Senior Management (Name/Title): Mr Andreas Neophytou, General Manager; Mr Hermann Eden, Managing Director.
Ownership/Shareholders: Privately owned
Other Group Companies: N/A
Size of Managed Fleet: 201.
Safety & Quality Management Certification: ISMA Certificate.
Types of Vessel Managed: General cargo vessels, passenger vessels, tankers.
Services Offered: Ship management in general.

Recent/Planned Developments

MIDOCEAN MARITIME LIMITED

Head Office: Isle of Man.
Other Offices: N/A
Senior Management (Name/Title): Axel van Hooven/Managing Director; Christos A. Ashiotis/Shipping Director; Peter C. Brammer/Director of Administration & Finance.
Ownership/Shareholders: Not named. Midocean is reportedly linked to German Shipowner Peter Döhle.

Other Group Companies:

Midocean Shipmanagement Ltd.
Midocean Carriers Ltd.
Midocean Properties Ltd.
Midocean Technical Services Ltd.

Size of Managed Fleet: 101–150.
Safety & Quality Management Certification: ISO 9002/ISM.
Types of Vessel Managed: Container, bulk carriers (conventional & self loaders), ro-ro, reefers.
Services Offered: Crew, technical and commercial ship management, insurance, chartering, consulting.

Recent/Planned Developments

The Midocean Group of Companies became, during last year, involved in ship-owning, chartering and time chartering of vessels. In 1998 it will expand its geographical spread of activities into the Americas.

In late 1998 Midocean will relocate its IOM offices to owned premises in Douglas.

Midocean at the time of writing was in the process of establishing its own office in Eastern Europe for recruitment of seafarers.

NAVIGO MANAGEMENT CO.

Head Office: Limassol, Cyprus.
Other Offices: N/A
Senior Management (Name/Title): Capt. L. Neubauer, General Manager; Andrew Airey, Business Development.
Ownership/Shareholders: Member of the Schulte Group.
Other Group Companies: Atlantic Marine, Dorchester Maritime, Hanseatic Shipping, Eurasia.
Size of Managed Fleet: 51–75.
Safety & Quality Management Certificate: ISMA Code (Cert no. HQS 30051), ISO 9002, IMO ISM (DOC LR0089D).
Types of Vessel Managed: Tankers (crude and products), container, ro/ro, bulk carriers, gas carriers, barge carriers, salvage vessels and multipurpose.
Services Offered: Full technical management, crew management, newbuilding supervision, ISM and management systems consultancy.

Recent/Planned Developments

THOME SHIPMANAGEMENT PTE LTD.

Head Office: Singapore.
Other Offices: N/A
Senior Management (Name/Title): Mr Olav Eek Thorstensen/Managing Director;
Mr Morton Jaer/Senior Manager.
Ownership/Shareholders: Mr Olav Eek Thorstensen, Osprey Maritime Ltd.
Other Group Companies:

> ISM Shipping (Phils) Inc.
> S&P Marine Consultants PTE Ltd.
> SPA-TSM Ship Management.

Size of Managed Fleet: 51–75.
Safety & Quality Management Certification: ISO 9002 Accreditation; ISMA
Code of Shipmanagement Certificate; DNV SEP Certification; ISM Code.

Types of Vessel Managed: Oil, chemical, product tankers, bulk carriers, container
vessels, log carriers.
Services Offered: Ship management, crew management, manning agency, ship
agency and technical consultancy/site supervision.

Recent/Planned Developments

A 50 per cent shareholding in Thome was acquired by Singapore's publicly traded
Osprey Maritime in 1994. Thome manages a number of Osprey vessels via its
Jakarta-based JVC with PT Samundra Petrindo Asia (SPA-TSM Ship Management)—a company which is looking to develop further business in the Indonesian
market.

UNIVAN SHIP MANAGEMENT LTD.

Head Office: Hong Kong.
Other Offices: Singapore, New Delhi, Manila.
Senior Management (Name/Title): Capt. C.A.J. Vandeperre, Managing Director;
Mr Sanjay Anand, Manager, Fleet Operations; Mr Jehanzeb Khan, Manager, Con-
struction & Maintenance Department.
Ownership/Shareholders: Bretton Limited, Liberia/China Inc. Panama; Univan
was established in 1973.
Other Group Companies:

> Univan Ship Management Ltd, Mumbai, New Delhi.

Univan Management Services, Philippines Inc. Manila.
Grandteam Management Services PTE Ltd., Singapore.

Size of Managed Fleet: 51–75.
Safety & Quality Management Certification: ISO 9002 certified by DNV since 1993; Certified Under the DNV SEP Rules since 1993; ISM Code Document of Compliance from DNV in 1993, Class NK in 1995; and LRS in 1996.

Types of Vessel Managed: Crude, chemical, product tankers, VLCCs, bulk carriers, reefer vessel, container vessels, woodchip carriers.
Services Offered: Third party ship management services, ship broking, marine asset valuation, ship breaking supervision, insurance, newbuilding consultancy, ship inspection, special projects, flagging out supervision, port agency, etc.

Recent/Planned Developments

In 1996 Univan established a joint venture ship management company with the Japanese trading house RAMS Corporation. The new company, Uniram Ship Management provides miscellaneous services from offices in Hong Kong and Japan.

V SHIPS

Head Office: Monaco.
Other Offices: Southampton, London, Limassol, Singapore, Dubai, Mineola USA, Miami, Oslo, Genoa.
Senior Management (Name/Title): Tullio Biggi, President; Hermann Messner, Head of Ship Management Division; Roberto Giorgi, Head of Leisure Division; Tony Crawford, Head of Commercial Division; Jerry Lees, MD V Ships (UK) Ltd.; Bob Wellner, President V Ships Marine; Even Ulving, MD V Ships Norway, AS; Lorenzo Malvarosa, Group Operations Director; Brian Martis, Group Crew Director; Manolo Veladini, Group Business Development Director; Guiseppe Ghiazza, Group Safety & Quality Director; Lous Carrell, MD V Ships Dubai; Daniel Chui, MD V Ships Asia Pacific.

Ownership/Shareholders: 40 per cent Vlasov Group, 40 per cent senior management, 20 per cent GE Capital.
Other Group Companies: Seamaster, Vanguard Adjusting, Marine Legal Services, Pegasus, Vita Marine, Viplex.
Size of Managed fleet: 200+.
Safety & Quality Management Certification: All offices hold or are in the process of securing ISM DOC. Oslo and Mineola offices are certificated also to DNV SEP and Monaco, Southampton and Limassol to ISO 9002.

Types of Vessel Managed: Dry bulk carriers, tankers, LPG, chemical carriers, multipurpose, OBOs, general cargo, ferry, ro/ro, containership, cruise.
Services Offered: Comprehensive range of management services.

Recent/Planned Developments

The group's network of offices continued to expand in 1996 with the opening of V Ships Asia Pacific in Singapore and the merger with IMC to form V Ships Marine. In 1997, the group opened offices in Florida and San Francisco.

Efforts are being made to expand the group's business activities in the Asian market and into leisure-related services.

VERMILLION OVERSEAS MANAGEMENT CO. LTD.

Head Office: Hong Kong.
Other Offices: N/A
Senior Management (Name/Title): Kenichi Iwakawa/Managing Director.
Ownership/Shareholders: Private
Other Group Companies:

> VOM (Manila) Corporation, Manila.
> Tokyo Liaison Office, Tokyo.
> Veritas Maritime Corporation.
> Sun Lanka PVT Ltd., Colombo.

Size of Managed Fleet: 0–50.
Safety & Quality Management Certification: DNV SEP for Shipmanagement for VOM Group; ISO 9002 for Manning (Veritas, Sunlanka).

Types of Vessel Managed: Bulker, container, multipurpose (general cargo).
Services Offered: Vessel management, operations, crewing, manning, newbuilding management, marine purchasing, superintendence, crew training, management consultancy, technical management.

Recent/Planned Developments

In July 1997, Vermillion completed implementation of DNV's SEP system on board all of its managed fleet.

WALLEM SHIPMANAGEMENT LTD.

Head Office: Hong Kong.
Other Offices: Singapore, London, USA.

Senior Management (Name/Title): R.G. Buchanan/Managing Director; U.C. Agarwal/Director; M.J. Sawyer/Director; D.K. Thakurta/Director.
Ownership/Shareholders: A.J. Hardy Ltd., Seattle Shipping Ltd., Mellaw Investments. Set up in 1971, Wallem Shipmanagement was sold to its present owners in 1992 by the UK financial services company, TSB.
Other Group Companies:

> Comprehensive International Freight Forwarders Ltd. (CIFF) Hong Kong.
> Electech Services Ltd., Hong Kong.
> Wallem Services Ltd., Hong Kong.
> Wallem Shipbroking (HK) Ltd., Hong Kong.
> Wallem Shipping (HK) Ltd., Hong Kong.
> Wallem Ltd. (Shipmanagement).
> Abbott House, 5/F, 1–2 Hanover Street, London W1R 9WB.
> Wallem Shipmanagement Inc.

Size of Managed Fleet: 101–150.
Safety & Quality Management Certification: Wallem Ship Management possesses the following Quality Management Certificates:

(a) ISO 9002 accredited by Det Norske Veritas (DNV).
(b) SEP Certificate, endorsed annually by DNV since 1992.
(c) ISMA since 1994.
(d) Safety Management, pre-convention, accredited by DNV and NK.

The company is in full compliance with the IMO, ISM code.

Major oil companies, among others, have audited our office and systems and we have always received a commendable overview of our operations and QA procedures.
Types of Vessel Managed: Bulk carriers, cement carriers, chemical tankers, container vessels, crude oil tankers (U/VLCC), FLASH vessels, floating production storage and offloading vessel (FPSO), floating storage and offloading vessel (FSO), gas carriers, general cargo vessels, LASH vessels, livestock carriers, log carriers, multipurpose vessels, OBO, off-shore vessels, passenger, product tankers, reefer vessels, ro-ro, survey vessels, tugs and barges, vehicle car carriers, woodchip carriers.
Services Offered: Full ship management, technical management, manning, training, newbuilding, conversion and repair planning and supervision, vessel audits, inspections and surveys, consultancy and projects in all marine sectors, power plant and machinery environments, cargo and port operations.

Recent/Planned Developments

The company plans to make further use of information technology to enhance all aspects of shipboard and shore operations.

Wallem will continue to expand its recruitment and training network to ensure continuity of supply of high calibre and well-trained officers and ratings. In July 1997 the company announced the opening of a new Singapore-based company, Wallem Manpower International PTE Ltd. Under the direction of Aswin Atre, formerly MD of Wallem's Hong Kong office, the new company will ensure that seagoing personnel employed on Wallem-managed vessels fully comply with ISM and STCW requirements.

APPENDIX 2

NATIONAL REQUIREMENTS FOR AN SMS

GENERAL

This section emphasizes administration policy regarding safe management, operation of ships, and protection of the environment which should be incorporated into the company and shipboard SMS. The national requirements are supplemental to the maritime regulations contained in the Combined Publication Folder (RL 300). The company and shipboard SMS should ensure compliance with both the national requirements and the maritime regulations.

SAFETY AND ENVIRONMENTAL PROTECTION POLICY

Safety and environmental protection policies as required to be established by the ISM Code must be signed by the company's chief executive or other senior executive officer, and should be reviewed at regular intervals to ensure that they remain likely to achieve the objectives of the ISM Code.

COMPANY RESPONSIBILITIES AND AUTHORITY

The owner of each vessel must provide the Office of the Deputy Commissioner of Maritime Affairs with the name, address, telephone, fax and telex numbers of the company responsible for the operation of the vessel. If the entity responsible for the operation of a ship is other than the owner, the owner must identify the full name of such entity and submit details to the satisfaction of the administration which establish that entity as the company.

DESIGNATED PERSON(S)

The company must provide the Office of the Deputy Commissioner of Maritime Affairs with current information sufficient to enable direct and immediate contact at all times between the administration and the company designated person or persons required by the ISM Code for matters relating to the SMS, maritime safety, and the protection of the marine environment.

MASTER'S RESPONSIBILITY AND AUTHORITY

Liberian Maritime Law expressly prescribes to the specific rights and duties of the master. The administration also acknowledges the importance of IMO Resolution A.443(XI), "Decisions of the Shipmaster with regard to Maritime Safety and Marine Environment Protection". The SMS should incorporate the elements of both A.443(XI) and the national requirements.

Any system of operational control implemented by company shore-based management must allow for the master's absolute authority and discretion to take whatever action he/she considers to be in the best interest of passengers, crew, cargo, the vessel and the marine environment.

The company should provide the master with documentation of the specific duties delegated to the officers under the master's command.

RESOURCES AND PERSONNEL

Company training, hiring, manning procedures, terms of employment, personnel record keeping and reporting procedures must be consistent with the requirements of the STCW Code and Liberian Maritime Regulations to ensure the use of competent qualified personnel.

The company SMS should ensure that joining crew members have proper seafarers' certification including licences, special qualification certificates, seamen's identification and record books and training as required by international conventions, Liberian Maritime Law, the Liberian Maritime Regulations and the specifics of the publication "Requirements for Merchant Marine Personnel Certification", RLM–118.

The shipboard SMS should include procedures for the transfer of command, documented hand-over notes, documented vessel and duties introduction, familiarization training in accordance with section A–I/6 of the STCW Code (as amended 1995) for oncoming officers and crew, and on-board documentation retention.

DEVELOPMENT OF PLANS FOR SHIPBOARD OPERATIONS

A "Master's Port Arrival/Departure Safety Check List" should be included in the shipboard SMS incorporating pre-established company policy guidelines for "Go, No Go" situations and reporting requirements for the master's compliance.

A vessel's operations documentation should include a statement that its contents do not remove the master's authority to take such steps and issue any orders, whether or not they are in accordance with the contents of the documentation, which the master considers to be necessary for the preservation of life, and the safety of the vessel and the marine environment.

The vessel's operations plans should include procedure to ensure the required Liberian annual safety inspection is conducted on time and in accordance with the maritime regulations and Marine Notice 7-191-2.

The ship's operations plans should incorporate the Maritime Regulations' requirement for weekly emergency drills and training sessions.

EMERGENCY PREPAREDNESS

The company SMS must provide that statutory, administration, or company required emergency plans will be periodically reviewed, updated, amended and, if necessary, re-approved by the administration or a recognized organization on its behalf.

REPORTS AND ANALYSIS OF NON-CONFORMITIES, ACCIDENTS AND HAZARDOUS OCCURRENCES

The shipboard SMS procedures for reporting accidents and incidents should incorporate the provisions of Chapter IX of the Maritime Regulations (RLM–108) which require the immediate notice and reporting of incidents to the administration and establishes duties and responsibilities for the company, ship officers and crew.

The company SMS should also incorporate the provisions of Article IV and Article X of the "Rules for Marine Investigations and Hearings" (RLM–260).

The company SMS should incorporate the provisions of Maritime Regulation 10.296 (7) on accident prevention and appointment of a safety officer.

The company and shipboard SMS should contain procedures for immediately reporting port state detentions to the administration.

MAINTENANCE OF THE SHIP AND EQUIPMENT

The maintenance system established by the company and documented in its SMS should include systematic plans and actions designed to address all those items and systems covered by class and statutory survey and ensure that the vessel's condition is satisfactorily maintained at all times.

As part of company initiated ship safety inspections, the shipboard SMS should include reference to the Liberian annual safety inspections required by Maritime Regulation 7.191, as more fully described in Marine Notice 7-191-2, and use of Form No. 338-6/93, the "Operational/Safety Checklist for SOLAS 74/78", as addressed in Marine Notice 7-191-3.

The company SMS should also provide for the logging of actions or measures taken to rectify deficiencies and non-conformities noted during surveys and annual safety inspections and the giving of notification to the administration and the designated RO of the corrective actions taken.

DOCUMENTATION

Documents should be easily identified, traceable, user friendly and not voluminous as to hinder the effectiveness of the SMS.

COMPANY VERIFICATION, REVIEW AND EVALUATION

The company must conduct internal audits shoreside and on each ship at least annually to determine whether the various elements of the company SMS have been fully implemented and are effective in achieving the stated objectives of the code. The internal audits are in addition to the annual, intermediate, and renewal audits carried out by the RO.

INTERNATIONAL SAFETY MANAGEMENT CODE (ISM CODE)

INTERNATIONAL MANAGEMENT CODE FOR THE SAFE OPERATION OF SHIPS AND FOR POLLUTION PREVENTION

Preamble

(1) The purpose of this Code* is to provide an international standard for the safe management and operation of ships and for pollution prevention.

(2) The Assembly adopted resolution A.443(XI), by which it invited all Governments to take the necessary steps to safeguard the ship Master in the proper discharge of his responsibilities with regard to maritime safety and the protection of the marine environment.

(3) The Assembly also adopted resolution A.680(17), by which it further recognised the need for appropriate organisation of management to enable it to respond to the need of those on board ships to achieve and maintain high standards of safety and environmental protection.

(4) Recognising that no two shipping companies or shipowners are the same, and that ships operate under a wide range of different conditions, the Code is based on general principles and objectives.

(5) The Code is expressed in broad terms so that it can have a wide-spread application. Clearly, different levels of management, whether shore-based or at sea, will require varying levels of knowledge and awareness of the items outlined.

(6) The cornerstone of good safety management is commitment from the top. In matters of safety and pollution prevention it is the commitment, competence, attitudes and motivation of individuals at all levels that determines the end result.

1   GENERAL

1.1   Definitions

1.1.1 *International Safety Management (ISM) Code* means the International Management Code for the Safe Operation of Ships and for Pollution Prevention as adopted by the Assembly, as may be amended by the Organisation.

---

* The International Management Code for the Safe Operation of Ships and for Pollution Prevention (International Safety Management (ISM) Code) comprises the annex to resolution A.741(18), the text of which is reproduced at the end of the Code (see page 272).

1.1.2 *Company* means the owner of the ship or any other organisation or person such as the manager, or the bareboat charterer, who has assumed the responsibility for operation of the ship from the shipowner and who, on assuming such responsibility, has agreed to take over all duties and responsibility imposed by the Code.

1.1.3 *Administration* means the Government of the State whose flag the ship is entitled to fly.

1.2 Objectives

1.2.1 The objectives of the Code are to ensure safety at sea, prevention of human injury or loss of life, and avoidance of damage to the environment, in particular to the marine environment and to property.

1.2.2 Safety-management objectives of the Company should, *inter alia*:

.1 provide for safe practices in ship operation and a safe working environment;

.2 establish safeguards against all identified risks; and

.3 continuously improve safety-management skills of personnel ashore and on board ships, including preparing for emergencies related both to safety and environmental protection.

1.2.3 The safety-management system should ensure:

.1 compliance with mandatory rules and regulations; and

.2 that applicable codes, guidelines and standards recommended by the organisation, administrations, classification societies and maritime industry organisations are taken into account.

1.3 Application

The requirements of this Code may be applied to all ships.

1.4 Functional requirements for a safety-management system

Every company should develop, implement and maintain a safety-management system (SMS) which includes the following functional requirements:

.1 a safety and environmental-protection policy;

.2 instructions and procedures to ensure safe operation of ships and protection of the environment in compliance with relevant international and flag state legislation;

.3 defined levels of authority and lines of communication between, and amongst, shore and shipboard personnel;

.4 procedures for reporting accidents and non-conformities with the provisions of this Code;

.5 procedures to prepare for and respond to emergency situations; and

.6 procedures for internal audits and management reviews.

2   SAFETY AND ENVIRONMENTAL-PROTECTION POLICY

2.1   The company should establish a safety and environmental-protection policy which describes how the objectives given in paragraph 1.2 will be achieved.

2.2   The company should ensure that the policy is implemented and maintained at all levels of the organisation both, ship-based and shore-based.

3   COMPANY RESPONSIBILITIES AND AUTHORITY

3.1   If the entity who is responsible for the operation of the ship is other than the owner, the owner must report the full name and details of such entity to the Administration.

3.2   The company should define and document the responsibility, authority and interrelation of all personnel who manage, perform and verify work relating to and affecting safety and pollution prevention.

3.3   The company is responsible for ensuring that adequate resources and shore-based support are provided to enable the designated person or persons to carry out their functions.

4   DESIGNATED PERSON(S)

To ensure the safe operation of each ship and to provide a link between the company and those on board, every company, as appropriate, should designate a person ashore having direct access to the highest level of management. The responsibility and authority of the designated person or persons should include monitoring the safety and pollution-prevention aspects of the operation of each ship and ensuring that adequate resources and shore-based support are applied, as required.

5   MASTER'S RESPONSIBILITY AND AUTHORITY

5.1   The company should clearly define and document the Master's responsibility with regard to:
.1 implementing the safety and environmental-protection policy of the company;
.2 motivating the crew in the observation of that policy;
.3 issuing appropriate orders and instructions in a clear and simple manner;
.4 verifying that specified requirements are observed; and
.5 reviewing the SMS and reporting its deficiencies to the shore-based management.

5.2   The company should ensure that the SMS operating on board the ship contains a clear statement emphasising the Master's authority. The company should establish in the SMS that the Master has the overriding authority and the responsibility to make decisions with respect to safety and pollution prevention and to request the company's assistance as may be necessary.

6 RESOURCES AND PERSONNEL

6.1 The company should ensure that the Master is:
.1 properly qualified for command;
.2 fully conversant with the company's SMS; and
.3 given the necessary support so that the Master's duties can be safely performed.

6.2 The company should ensure that each ship is manned with qualified, certificated and medically fit seafarers in accordance with national and international requirements.

6.3 The company should establish procedures to ensure that new personnel transferred to new assignments related to safety and protection of the environment are given proper familiarisation with their duties. Instructions which are essential to be provided prior to sailing should be identified, documented and given.

6.4 The company should ensure that all personnel involved in the company's SMS have an adequate understanding of relevant rules, regulations, codes and guidelines.

6.5 The company should establish and maintain procedures for identifying any training which may be required in support of the SMS and ensure that such training is provided for all personnel concerned.

6.6 The company should establish procedures by which the ship's personnel receive relevant information on the SMS in a working language or languages understood by them.

6.7 The company should ensure that the ship's personnel are able to communicate effectively in the execution of their duties related to the SMS.

7 DEVELOPMENT OF PLANS FOR SHIPBOARD OPERATIONS

The company should establish procedures for the preparation of plans and instructions for key shipboard operations concerning the safety of the ship and the prevention of pollution. The various tasks involved should be defined and assigned to qualified personnel.

8 EMERGENCY PREPAREDNESS

8.1 The company should establish procedures to identify, describe and respond to potential emergency shipboard situations.

8.2 The company should establish programmes for drills and exercises to prepare for emergency actions.

8.3 The SMS should provide for measures ensuring that the Company's organisation can respond at any time to hazards, accidents and emergency situations involving its ships.

9   REPORTS AND ANALYSIS OF NON-CONFORMITIES, ACCIDENTS AND HAZARDOUS OCCURRENCES

9.1   The SMS should include procedures ensuring that non-conformities, accidents and hazardous situations are reported to the company, investigated and analysed with the objective of improving safety and pollution prevention.

9.2   The company should establish procedures for the implementation of corrective action.

10   MAINTENANCE OF THE SHIP AND EQUIPMENT

10.1   The company should establish procedures to ensure that the ship is maintained in conformity with the provisions of the relevant rules and regulations and with any additional requirements which may be established by the company.

10.2   In meeting these requirements the company should ensure that:

.1 inspections are held at appropriate intervals;

.2 any non-conformity is reported, with its possible cause, if known;

.3 appropriate corrective action is taken; and

.4 records of these activities are maintained.

10.3   The company should establish procedures in its SMS to identify equipment and technical systems the sudden operational failure of which may result in hazardous situations. The SMS should provide for specific measures aimed at promoting the reliability of such equipment or systems. These measures should include the regular testing of standby arrangements and equipment or technical systems that are not in continuous use.

10.4   The inspections mentioned in 10.2 as well as the measures referred to in 10.3 should be integrated into the ship's operational maintenance routine.

11   DOCUMENTATION

11.1   The company should establish and maintain procedures to control all documents and data which are relevant to the SMS.

11.2   The company should ensure that:

.1 valid documents are available at all relevant locations;

.2 changes to documents are reviewed and approved by authorised personnel, and

.3 obsolete documents are promptly removed.

11.3   The documents used to describe and implement the SMS may be referred to as the Safety Management Manual. Documentation should be kept in a form that the company considers most effective. Each ship should carry on board all documentation relevant to that ship.

12   COMPANY VERIFICATION, REVIEW AND EVALUATION

12.1   The company should carry out internal safety audits to verify whether safety and pollution-prevention activities comply with the SMS.

12.2   The company should periodically evaluate the efficiency of and, when needed review the SMS in accordance with procedures established by the company.

12.3   The audits and possible corrective actions should be carried out in accordance with documented procedures.

12.4   Personnel carrying out audits should be independent of the areas being audited unless this is impracticable due to the size and the nature of the company.

12.5   The results of the audits and reviews should be brought to the attention of all personnel having responsibility in the area involved.

12.6   The management personnel responsible for the area involved should take timely corrective action on deficiencies found.

13   CERTIFICATION, VERIFICATION AND CONTROL

13.1   The ship should be operated by a company which is issued a document of compliance relevant to that ship.

13.2   A document of compliance should be issued for every company complying with the requirements of the ISM Code by the Administration, by an organisation recognised by the Administration or by the Government of the country, acting on behalf of the Administration in which the company has chosen to conduct its business. This document should be accepted as evidence that the company is capable of complying with the requirements of the Code.

13.3   A copy of such a document should be placed on board in order that the Master, if so asked, may produce it for the verification of the Administration or organisations recognised by it.

13.4   A certificate, called a Safety Management Certificate, should be issued to a ship by the Administration or organisation recognised by the Administration. The Administration should, when issuing the certificate, verify that the company and its shipboard management operate in accordance with the approved SMS.

13.5   The Administration or an organisation recognised by the Administration should periodically verify the proper functioning of the ship's SMS as approved.

Resolution A.741(18)

Adopted on 4 November, 1993

THE ASSEMBLY

RECALLING Article 15(j) of the Convention on the International Maritime Organisation concerning the functions of the Assembly in relation to regulations and guidelines concerning maritime safety and the prevention and control of marine pollution from ships,

RECALLING ALSO resolution A.680(17), by which it invited Member Governments to encourage those responsible for the management and operation of ships to take appropriate steps to develop, implement and assess safety and pollution-prevention management in accordance with the IMO Guidelines on Management for the Safe Operation of Ships and for Pollution Prevention,

RECALLING ALSO resolution A.596(15), by which it requested the Maritime Safety Committee to develop, as a matter of urgency, guidelines, whenever relevant, concerning shipboard and shore-based management, and its decision to include in the work programme of the Maritime Safety Committee and the Marine Environment Protection Committee an item on shipboard and shore-based management for the safe operation of ships and for the prevention of marine pollution, respectively,

RECALLING FURTHER resolution A.441(XI), by which it invited every State to take the necessary steps to ensure that the owner of a ship which flies the flag of that State provides such State with the current information necessary to enable it to identify and contact the person contracted or otherwise entrusted by the owner to discharge his responsibilities for that ship in regard to matters relating to maritime safety and the protection of the marine environment,

RECALLING FURTHER resolution A.443(XI), by which it invited Governments to take the necessary steps to safeguard the ship Master in the proper discharge of his responsibilities in regard to maritime safety and the protection of the marine environment,

RECOGNISING the need for appropriate organisation of management to enable it to respond to the need of those on board ships to achieve and maintain high standards of safety and environmental protection,

RECOGNISING ALSO that the most important means of preventing maritime casualties and pollution of the sea from ships is to design, construct, equip and maintain ships and to operate them with properly trained crews in compliance with international conventions and standards relating to maritime safety and pollution prevention,

NOTING that the Maritime Safety Committee is developing requirements for adoption by Contracting Governments to the International Convention for the Safety of Life at Sea (SOLAS), 1974, which will make compliance with the Code referred to in operative paragraph 1 mandatory,

CONSIDERING that the early implementation of that Code would greatly assist in improving safety at sea and protection of the marine environment,

NOTING FURTHER that the Maritime Safety Committee and the Marine Environment Protection Committee have reviewed resolution A.680(17) and the Guidelines annexed thereto in developing the Code,

HAVING CONSIDERED the recommendations made by the Maritime Safety Committee at its sixty-second session and by the Maritime Environment Protection Committee at its thirty-fourth session,

ADOPTS the International Management Code for the Safe Operation of Ships and for Pollution Prevention (International Safety Management (ISM) Code), set out in the annex to the present resolution,

STRONGLY URGES Governments to implement the ISM Code on a national basis, giving priority to passenger ships, tankers, gas carriers, bulk carriers and mobile offshore units which are flying their flags, as soon as possible but not later than 1 June, 1998, pending development of the mandatory applications of the Code,

REQUESTS Governments to inform the Maritime Safety Committee and the Marine Environment Protection Committee of the action they have taken in implementing the ISM Code,

REQUESTS the Maritime Safety Committee and the Marine Environment Protection Committee to develop guidelines for the implementation of the ISM Code,

REQUESTS ALSO the Maritime Safety Committee and the Marine Environment Protection Committee to keep the Code and its associated guidelines under review and to amend them as necessary,

REVOKES resolution A.680(17).

UNCONTROLLED COPY OF THE CODE OF SHIPMANAGEMENT STANDARDS
[herein also referred to as the ISMA Code]

ISSUED UNDER THE AUTHORITY OF THE EXECUTIVE COMMITTEE OF THE INTERNATIONAL SHIPMANAGERS ASSOCIATION

PREAMBLE

[P]1.0   SCOPE AND FIELD OF APPLICATION

The Code of Shipmanagement Standards is issued in three [3] parts as follows:

Part 1   General Services

Part 2   Crewmanagement Services

Part 3   Shipmanagement Services

A Crewmanager will require to comply with Parts 1 & 2 only.

A Shipmanager will require to comply with Parts 1, 2 & 3.

The Code of Shipmanagement Standards [ISMA Code] specifies requirements for quality assured ship and crewmanagement services.

Compliance with the applicable Parts [1 + 2 or 1 + 2 + 3] of the ISMA Code by a company will ensure that a company operates with quality assured systems for crewmanagement or shipmanagement.

The ISMA Code specifies those areas where systems and controls are essential to meet the objectives. The requirements of the ISMA Code apply to both shorebased and shipboard management.

Verification of compliance with the ISMA Code will be carried out by an independent body.

The requirements of the ISMA Code apply to all ships under management, where a Management Agreement does not require the Company to provide all of the services detailed in the ISMA Code, the Company shall, having received certification, apply the relevant requirements of the ISMA Code to the services it provides.

By the ISMA Code, International Ship Managers Association intends to establish quality assured systems within its scope and field of application. The ISMA Code is not intended to be read or construed as a product guarantee/warranty.

In the ISMA Code items with suffix "0" are a description of the underlying aims and general expressions of intent which fall outside of the scope of audit.

[P]2.0   OBJECTIVES

[P]2.1   To provide quality assured crewmanagement services, through the expedience of arranging employment of seafarers for the purpose of manning each ship, [in accordance with the conditions of limitation imposed by the individual Management Agreement]:

with qualified, medically fit and suitably experienced seafarers;

with adequate numbers of seafarers for the trade in which it is engaged;

in accordance with the requirements for Training, Certification and Watch Keeping Standards of the particular Flag State;

so as to provide for, but not be limited to, the human element of:

operating the ship safely and efficiently;

avoiding injuries to personnel and loss of life;

conserving and protecting the environment;

complying with all applicable National and International rules and requirements;

applying recognised industry standards when appropriate;

providing the client with sufficient, accurate and timely information about the status of the crew;

continuous development of skills and systems in the business;

preparing for emergencies.

[P]2.2   To provide quality assured shipmanagement services, which entails, but is not limited to:

operating the ship and transporting cargo safely and efficiently;

avoiding injuries to personnel and loss of life;

conserving and protecting the environment;

protecting the Owners' assets that are entrusted to the Company;

complying with Statutory and Classification rules and requirements;

applying recognised industry standards when appropriate;

providing the Client with sufficient, accurate and timely information about the operation and status of the ship;

continuous development of skills, systems and understanding of the business;

preparing for emergencies.

[P]3.0   REFERENCE

[P]3.1   Requirements of the following documents are incorporated in the ISMA Code:

ISO-9002 Quality Systems – Model for Quality Assurance in Production and Installation;

IMO – Resolution A-741[18]. International Management Code for the Safe Operation of Ships and for Pollution Prevention. **[International Safety Management (ISM) Code].**

*Note: The requirements of the **ISM Code** will not be applied to a company that only provides Crewmanagement Services*

[P]3.2   The requirements of the following documents are to be complied with in meeting the requirements of the ISMA Code:

appropriate **National and International** rules and regulations for the relevant ship;

appropriate **Classification Society** rules and regulations for the relevant ship;

appropriate **Industry Guidelines** *including codes, guidelines and standards recommended by IMO, Flag Administrations, Classification Societies and other Maritime Industry Organizations and as pertinent and relevant.*

[P]4.0   DEFINITIONS

[P]4.1   The **ISMA Code** means the Code for Shipmanagement Standards.

[P]4.2   **Quality**, *unless specifically stated otherwise, includes the requirements for Safety and Environment Protection Management.*

[P]4.3   The Company

[P]4.3.1   The Company is the organisation which controls and/or is responsible for the management of the ship. The Company may be:

The Shipmanager who is deemed to be the person or company or organisation to whom the client has entrusted the management of the ship by means of a legally binding document.

The division of the Owner which manages the ship.

The Company must consist of seagoing personnel to operate, maintain and control the ship [the Shipboard Management] and shore based personnel to establish, implement, verify and control policies, systems and procedures [the Shorebased Management].

or

[P]4.3.2   The Company is the organisation [Crewmanager] to whom the client has entrusted by contractual agreement responsibility for crewmanagement of a ship.

The Company must provide seagoing personnel to operate and maintain the ship and shore based personnel to establish, implement, verify and control policies, systems and procedures [Shorebased Management]. The Company must:

provide the full complement including the master for at least one [1] vessel trading internationally;

directly employ the crew or be responsible for the general administration processes for the selection and recruitment of crewmembers;

Note: the master and crew may be directly employed by the Company or as servants of the owner/client.

be responsible for the establishment and control of the crew's certification and qualification records.

[P]4.4   **The Client** is deemed to be the person or company who has the authority to entrust the management of a ship and/or crew to the Company.

The Client may be:

The Owner who is deemed to be the person or company who has the authority to entrust the management of a ship to the Company.

The Shipmanager who is deemed to be the person or company or organisation to whom the Owner has entrusted the management of the ship by means of a legally binding document wherein the Shipmanager is assigned responsibility for crewing the vessel.

[P]4.5   Shipmanagement Agreement is the legally binding document which defines the terms and conditions under which the Shipmanager agrees to provide services for the management of the owner's ship in return for agreed financial remuneration.

[P]4.6   Crewmanagement Agreement is the legally binding document which defines the terms and conditions under which the Crewmanager agrees to provide services for the crewmanagement of the ship in return for agreed financial remuneration.

[P]4.7   Shipmanagement means the rendering of services for ship operation and associated services.

[P]4.8   Crewmanagement means the rendering of services for the supply and management of crews for the ship and associated services.

[P]4.9   Procedures

Shipmanagement procedures means documented procedures promulgated by the Company to cover aspects of management and operation of the ship.

Crewmanagement procedures means documented procedures promulgated by the Company to cover aspects of crewmanagement of the ship.

Maintenance of Procedures requires that the Company shall [by means of internal & external audits] verify that established procedures are being observed.

PART 1

GENERAL SERVICES

INDEX – PART 1

[Part 1 Comprising Of Seventeen (17) Pages]

Chapter 01 [Part 1]   **BUSINESS ETHICS**

[1]1.0   The Company, by order of its Executive Management, shall expressly confirm its adherence to the requirements of the ISMA Code including the following points:

the Company's policy and aim shall be to provide services in compliance with the ISMA Code as applicable;

the Company acknowledges that both it and the client are carrying on business with a view to profit;

the Company shall not accept business for which it does not have the necessary capability and resources;

the Company shall allocate its resources so as to render equitable and faithful performance to each of its clients;

subject to all relevant provisions of the Management Agreement the Company shall advise clients of any conflict of interest;

the Company shall respect the confidentiality of each clients' business and activities;

the Company's policy shall emphasise its commitment to safety, protection of the environment and to safeguarding of Owners' property;

the Company shall, whenever possible, advise the client of any potentially dangerous or other unacceptable situations;

the Company shall not knowingly participate in activities or practices which it knows to be unsafe or illegal;

the Company's policy shall be to promote a healthy working environment including, but not limited to, the provision of safeguards against drug and alcohol abuse aboard ship always in conformity with internationally accepted standards;

the Company shall at all times adhere to sound principles with respect to the management of funds and cash;

the Company shall not continue or commit themselves to carry out business for a client and/or owner when the service to be provided may be used for the furtherance of illegal activities to the actual knowledge of the Company.

[1]1.1　The Company shall define and document its policies and objectives for and general commitment to quality.

The Company shall establish procedures to ensure that, this policy is understood, implemented and maintained at all levels in its organisation.

Chapter 02 [Part 1]　**MANAGEMENT AGREEMENT**

[1]2.0　The Company shall conduct its business in accordance with sound management practice.

[1]2.1　The Company shall sign with the client an Agreement accepting the [crew]management of a vessel.

[1]2.2　The terms and language of the agreement shall be clear, unambiguous and easily understood by the contracting parties.

[1]2.3　The Company's responsibilities, authorities, obligations and services shall be clearly defined in the Agreement.

[1]2.4　The Agreement shall further include financial aspects, reporting procedures and accounting system, suitable clauses for termination, proceedings in the event of default, arbitration and governing law, indemnities, liabilities and Force Majeure as well as official communication procedures.

[1]2.5　The client's responsibilities and obligations, including remuneration to be paid to the Company, shall be clearly defined in the Agreement.

[1]2.6　Nothing in the Agreement shall be contrary to or in violation of the applicable laws and regulations.

[1]2.7　The Company shall establish and maintain procedures for formal review of potential contracts or agreements which may be established with the client.

[1]2.8　The Company shall establish a contract review procedure to ensure that:

each Agreement is satisfactorily explicit and comprehensible in its terms;

the client's requirements of the Company are satisfactorily covered by the Agreement;

any requirements differing from the preliminary proposal are resolved;

the Company has the capability to discharge its obligations under the Agreement.

[1]2.9   *The Company shall identify how amendments to a Management Agreement are made and correctly transferred to the functions concerned within the Company organization.*

[1]2.10   Records of such reviews and amendments are to be maintained.

Chapter 03 [Part 1]   ORGANISATION

[1]3.0   A defined organisational structure for all applicable sectors of activity is necessary for the implementation of the ISMA Code.

[1]3.1   The Company shall establish and maintain a formal organisational structure which defines the responsibility, authority and inter-relation of personnel who manage, perform and verify work affecting quality.

[1]3.2   The Company shall identify in the formal organizational structure the personnel who are given the organizational freedom and authority to perform their inspection and verification responsibilities.

Such personnel shall verify compliance with the quality requirements and, when required, initiate necessary actions.

[1]3.3   The organisational structure shall give due regard to the Master's responsibility for all day to day onboard operations.

[1]3.4   The Company shall agree with the client and specify a designated command language and a working language for communication between Shipboard Management and Shorebased Management and the client.

[1]3.5   Shorebased Management

[1]3.5.1   Resources allocated to Shorebased Management shall be adequate to control and verify the effective implementation of the Company's procedures.

[1]3.5.2   The Company shall appoint a management representative who, irrespective of other responsibilities, shall have defined authority and responsibility for ensuring that the requirements of the ISMA Code and other matters affecting quality, are implemented and maintained.

[1]3.5.3   The appointed person shall have defined authority for reporting on the performance of the Management System, particularly for review and as the basis for recommending improvements to the system.

[1]3.5.3   The appointed person shall provide a link between the Company and personnel onboard ship to ensure adequate resources and shorebased support are applied as required and to monitor all aspects of the Management System operation onboard including safety and pollution prevention.

[1]3.6   Shipboard Management

[1]3.6.1   The Company shall recognise that the shipboard management personnel are to have detailed and specialist knowledge of their specific tasks. The Company's Management System shall make provision for this in their procedures.

[1]3.6.2   *The Master shall be the onboard manager of the Company/Client's Management System[s] as appropriate and relevant to the type of management.*

[1]3.6.3 Provision shall be made in the Management System to ensure the Master has overriding authority and the responsibility to make decisions regarding Safety and Pollution Prevention onboard the ship.

Chapter 04 [Part 1]   SHOREBASED PERSONNEL

[1]4.0 The Company recognises that human resources in shorebased management and their administration are a key element in quality operations.

[1]4.1 The Company shall establish and maintain procedures for the selection, recruitment and training of shore-based personnel which shall:

specify the minimum qualifications and experience of all personnel *who manage, perform or verify quality*;

specify the job description of *the aforementioned* personnel;

verify that persons employed meet the appropriate requirements for the position in which they are engaged;

verify that newly appointed personnel are properly briefed, given appropriate on the job training and are closely supervised during their probationary period[s];

specify an appraisal system to monitor and review the conduct and performance and to identify the training needs of personnel;

make provision for personnel to improve their knowledge and experience by attending appropriate courses, seminars and conferences;

administer the Company's training schemes;

ensure records are maintained of all qualifications, training undertaken including attendance at courses, seminars and conferences and also of identified training needs.

Chapter 05 [Part 1]   ACCOUNTING

[1]5.0 The structure of the Company's Accounting Department and the accounting system installed shall be such as to enable the accounting and funds management to be carried out in an orderly and efficient manner.

[1]5.1 The Accounting Department shall be supervised and controlled by competent qualified accountants.

[1]5.2 The Accounting Department shall follow generally accepted accounting principles in the preparation of accounts and, in particular, will follow recognised national accounting standards.

[1]5.3 The Accounting Department shall apply good accounting practices to ensure the security of client's singular funding and provide accurate records of all transactions.

[1]5.4 The Accounting Department shall have a formal organisational structure which defines and allocates authorities, responsibilities and identifies lines of reporting.

[1]5.5 The accounting and reporting systems of the Company shall be available to the other departments within the organisation and there shall be effective communication and cooperation between all departments, enabling the accurate recording of costs.

[1]5.6 The Company shall provide periodical financial reports as agreed with the client.

[1]5.7 Accounting records shall be made available for inspection by the client and/or his representatives at any time, subject to reasonable notice.

[1]5.8   The Company shall advise the client in adequate time if funds available are insufficient to cover financial commitments.

[1]5.9   The Accounting Department shall co-operate in formulating and preparing budgets.

[1]5.10   The Company shall retain all accounts relating to each ship for a period not less than the legal requirements of the country of incorporation and shall make these available to the client subject to reasonable notice.

Chapter 06 [Part 1]   *MANAGEMENT* SYSTEM

[1]6.1   The Company shall establish and maintain a documented *Management* System as a means by which stated policies and objectives are accomplished.

The documented management system shall incorporate, but not necessarily separately, a Quality Manual, Policies, Procedures and where appropriate Work Instructions to ensure effective implementation and control of the Management System.

If issued as a separate document, the Quality Manual shall reference procedures and outline the structure of the documentation used in the Management System.

[1]6.2   The documented system procedures and instructions are to be in accordance with the requirements of the ISMA Code *and any additional requirements defined by the Company.*

[1]6.3   The Company shall demonstrate by the provision of objective evidence that the documented Management System procedures and instructions are being effectively implemented.

[1]6.4   The Company shall conduct planned periodic management reviews of the Management System in order to verify or improve the effectiveness of the system.

Records of management reviews are to be maintained.

[1]6.5   The Company shall identify and plan activities and operations which directly affect quality and ensure that these are carried out under controlled conditions.

Controlled conditions shall include procedures, work instructions etc. where the absence of such would adversely affect quality.

[1]6.6   *The Company shall identify in the Management System procedures for inspection and checking, by suitable means, of services to and for the ship to verify the services meet specified requirements.*

Records shall be maintained to ensure the conformance or non-conformance of the service with regard to the inspections and checks.

[1]6.7   *The identification of inspection and check status shall be maintained as defined in the procedures from the time of introduction and throughout the entire period the service is in use, so as to ensure that only services that have passed the required inspections and checks [or released under consent—see [1]7.2 hereafter] are provided.*

[1]6.8   *The Company shall make provision in the Management System for the planned entry of new vessels and new types of vessel into management.*

The plan is to include procedures for implementation of the Management System and for Internal Audits on the newly managed vessel[s] and for External Audits of new types of vessels entered into the managed fleet.

[1]6.9   *The Company shall make provision in the Management System for withdrawal of the Management System from those vessels leaving the Company's Management.*

Chapter 07 [Part 1]   CORRECTIVE & PREVENTIVE ACTIONS

[1]7.0   The Company shall establish and maintain documented procedures to ensure that any service which does not conform to the specified requirements is prevented from inadvertent use.

Controls shall provide for identification, documentation, evaluation, segregation [where practical], disposition of non-conforming services and notification to all parties concerned.

[1]7.1   The Company shall identify plans for dealing with non-conformities which shall include procedures for applying preventive or corrective actions through an analysis of all processes, operations, concessions, records, reports and client/ship initiated complaints so as to detect and eliminate nonconforming management services.

[1]7.2   Review and Disposition

[1]7.2.1   Responsibility for review and authority for disposition shall be defined within the Management System, nonconforming services [including personnel and/or materials] shall be reviewed in accordance with documented procedures and may be:

 reworked [retrained] to meet specified requirements;

 accepted with or without modification/change by consent;

 regraded for alternative application;

 rejected or scrapped.

[1]7.2.2   Where required by contract, the proposed use of a non-conforming service is to be reported to the client for consent.

Reworked services shall be inspected in accordance with the quality plan[s] and/or documented procedures.

[1]7.3   Corrective/Preventive Actions

Corrective and/or preventive actions taken to eliminate the cause of actual or potential non-conformities shall be to a degree appropriate to the magnitude of the problem and commensurate with the risk[s] encountered.

The Company shall implement and record any changes to the documented procedures resulting from corrective and preventive actions.

[1]7.3.1   Corrective Action Procedures *shall include:*

 the effective handling of complaints from clients and other parties including reports of service non-conformities;

 investigation of the cause[s] of non-conformities relating to a service, a service process and the management system, the results of the investigation[s] shall be recorded;

 determination of the corrective action needed to eliminate the cause of nonconformity including the application of controls to ensure that corrective action is taken and that it is effective.

[1]7.3.2   Preventive Action Procedures shall include:

the use of appropriate sources of information such as processes and operations which affect quality, consents, audit results, quality records, service reports and client complaints to detect, analyze and eliminate potential causes of non-conformities;

determination of steps needed to deal with problems requiring preventive action;

initiation of preventive action and application of controls to ensure that it is effective including ensuring that relevant information on actions taken is submitted for management review.

[1]17.4   Shipboard/Master's Responsibility

[1]7.4.1   The Company's Management System is to incorporate procedures for ensuring that any non-conformities arising onboard and/or in services provided to the vessel are reported to the Company. Non-conformities shall include accidents and hazardous situations.

[1]7.4.2   The Company shall establish procedures for implementing corrective actions in respect of the reported non-conformities.

[1]7.5   Special Operations

These are activities, operations, tasks etc., where substandard performance/errors only become apparent after an accident has occurred or the quality of the service is significantly impaired.

Special operations are to be identified and continuous monitoring and/or compliance with existing documented procedures is required to ensure that intended service requirements are met.

[1]7.6   Near Miss Reporting

The Company shall establish a scheme for the vessels to report those events whereby a potentially hazardous situation endangering human life, the ship or cargo has occurred.

Chapter 08 [Part 1]   DOCUMENT CONTROL

[1]8.1   The Company shall establish and maintain procedures to control all documents and data that relate to the requirements of the ISMA Code *including, to the extent applicable, documents of external origin.*

Documents *and data* shall be examined for adequacy and approved by designated personnel before issue.

[1]8.2   All documents are to be controlled in order to ensure that the pertinent issue of appropriate documents are available at defined locations or to specified personnel.

[1]8.3   Obsolete documents are to be promptly removed from these defined locations or specified personnel.

Obsolete documents retained for legal and/or knowledge preservation/reference purposes shall be suitably identified and assured against inadvertent use.

[1]8.4   Changes to documents are to be reviewed and approved by the designated personnel before issue.

Changes are to be readily identifiable in the document.

[1]8.5   A suitable document control procedure is to be established and be readily available in order to ensure that the revision status of the documents can be easily identified and to preclude the use of superseded or invalid or obsolete documents.

The document control procedure may be a Master List or an equivalent procedure.

[1]8.6   *The Master List/control procedure shall contain all those external origin documents defined [see 8.1 above] as forming part of the Management System.*

The documentation control procedure shall also define the method of distribution and prescribed location or holder.

Chapter 09 [Part 1]   **RECORDS**

[1]9.1   Records shall be maintained to demonstrate the Company's achievements are of the required quality and give effective operation of the quality system.

[1]9.2   The Company shall establish, document and maintain procedures for identification, indexing, filing, storage, maintenance and disposition of quality records.

[1]9.3   All quality records shall be retained for a prescribed period and be easily available for such period.

[1]9.4   The records shall reflect the tasks undertaken and the results obtained.

[1]9.5   Storage conditions shall be adequate and *a back-up procedure defined* for computer records.

[1]9.6   Procedures for disposal of records shall be defined.

Chapter 10 [Part 1]   **INTERNAL AUDITS**

[1]10.1   The Company shall carry out internal audits to verify whether quality activities comply with planned arrangements and to determine the effectiveness of the quality system.

For those Companies requiring to comply with Part 3 of this Code, the requirements for internal audits shall include audits of all ships under management.

[1]10.2   Audits shall be scheduled on the basis of status and importance of the activity.

[1]10.3   The audits shall be carried out by personnel independent of those having direct responsibility for the work being performed.

[1]10.4   The audits and follow-up actions shall be carried out in accordance with the documented procedures.

[1]10.5   The results of the audits shall be documented and brought to the attention of the personnel having responsibility in the area audited.

The management personnel responsible for the area shall take timely corrective action on the deficiencies found by the audit.

[1]10.6   *Follow-up audit activities shall verify and record the implementation and effectiveness of corrective actions taken.*

Chapter 11 [Part 1]   **EXTERNAL AUDITS**

[1]11.1   Audit Body

External audits to verify compliance with the requirements of the ISMA Code shall be carried out by independent auditors.

The auditors comprise of members of the International Association of Classification Societies [IACS].

The auditors form an auditing body to ensure consistent application of the requirements for the ISMA Code.

[1]11.2   ISMA Code Requirements

The ISMA Code defines the requirements for quality ship and crewmanagement and includes the requirements of ISO 9002, as currently in force at the time.

Requirements for compliance with the **IMO – Resolution A-741[18]**. International Management Code for the Safe Operation of Ships and for Pollution Prevention **[International Safety Management (ISM) Code]** are included.

All requirements, *viz. Parts 1 & 2 for Crewmanagers and Parts 1, 2 & 3 for Shipmanagers*, of the ISMA Code are to be complied with.

[1]11.3   Certification

The initial assessment for certification will include all ship types under management by the Company.

On completion of a satisfactory audit, an appropriate and unique certificate shall be issued.

The certificates shall confirm compliance with ISO 9002 and for Shipmanagers will confirm compliance with IMO Resolution 741[18].

Partial compliance certification documents will not be issued.

[1]11.4   Validity

The certificate will be valid for a period of three years subject to annual intermediate audits.

PART 2

CREWMANAGEMENT SERVICES

INDEX – PART 2

[Part 2 Comprising Of Fifteen (15) Pages]

Chapter 01 [Part 2] **PERSONNEL**

[2]1.0   The Company recognises that human resources onboard each ship and their administration are a key element in quality operation.

[2]1.1   Selection and Recruitment and Employment of Ship's Personnel

[2]1.1.1   The Company shall arrange for the crew to enter into employment contracts.

[2]1.1.2   The Company shall establish and maintain procedures for the selection and recruitment of ship's crew which shall:

specify the qualifications and experience requirements for each position onboard that the Company is responsible for under the agreement;

ensure that the Master is properly qualified for command;

verify that each member of the crew that the Company is to supply has appropriate qualifications and experience and is medically fit when appointed to the ship;

verify that crewmembers can adequately understand key instructions in English and Native Language so as to be able to communicate effectively in the execution of their particular duties;

specify an appraisal system to monitor and review the ability and conduct of each crewmember supplied by the Company and which shall provide for identifying the training needs of the crewmember.

[2]1.1.3   The Company shall have a system to control the foregoing procedures for Selection and Recruitment when Manning Agents are used.

[2]1.2   Training of Ship's Personnel

[2]1.2.1   The Company shall make provision for:

maintaining regular contact with appropriate shore based training facilities;

encouraging crewmembers to improve and update their knowledge and understanding;

encouraging crewmembers to up-grade their current qualifications.

[2]1.2.2   *The Company shall establish procedures and maintain records for follow-up of training requirements identified/requested by the client.*

[2]1.3   Administration of Ship's Personnel

The Company shall have the resources including suitably experienced personnel designated to the administration of ship's personnel.

[2]1.3.1   The Company shall establish and maintain procedures to ensure:

the maintenance of records of all crewmembers in current employment;

applicants for employment onboard ship are interviewed;

that personnel appointed to the ship are issued with joining instructions and that suitable travel arrangements for personnel joining and leaving the ship are made;

the maintenance of a separate and current crew list for the Company's personnel onboard of each ship;

liaison with the ship, the appropriate persons in shore based management, the client and relevant third parties as necessary in matters concerning ship's personnel;

verification that arrangements for support, maintenance and repatriation for crewmembers who have to be landed ashore for any reason are made;

the establishment, review and advising of relevant parties of approved wage scales and conditions of employment;

administration of the Company's shore-based training schemes;

procedures for dealing with complaints and/or grievances arising from or about personnel supplied by the Company are implemented and maintained.

[2]1.4   Medical Examination

The Company will have in place procedures for medical examinations of Masters, Officers and Crew at the time of their employment in accordance with the requirements of the Administration.

Examinations shall include screening for drug and alcohol abuse which at least meets the standards of the Oil Companies International Marine Forum [OCIMF] guidelines on this subject in the form current from time to time.

The requirements of the client in respect of these examinations shall be complied with where these exceed the foregoing standards.

Chapter 02 [Part 2] SAFETY

[2]2.0 The Company places the highest emphasis on the safe operation of the ship and the safety of personnel.

[2]2.1 Company Safety Policy

The Company shall have a clear written statement of Policy concerning Safety.

The Policy shall be approved by the Executive Management of the Company and shall:

specify the importance the Company places on safety;

acknowledge the Company's responsibilities to safety;

designate Company Personnel in Shorebased Management who shall be given the Authority to implement the Company's Safety Policy and the responsibility to monitor safety matters;

detail the organisation to give effect to the Policy;

be explained to all Company personnel and copies of the Policy made readily available.

[2]2.1.2 *The Safety Policy is to be reviewed and amended as necessary to take account of relevant legislation, developments and occurrences.*

[2]2.2 Monitoring of Safety

The Company shall establish and maintain procedures for receiving reports of onboard personal accidents which shall:

review the Company's Safety Policy and make recommendations for revision of the policy as found necessary;

review any safety reports received from the client/ship and make recommendations *to the client* as appropriate;

implement action based on recommendations made/*as instructed by the client* and follow up/*liaise* such action.

Chapter 03 [Part 2] ENVIRONMENTAL PROTECTION

[2]3.0 The Company accords a very high priority to conserving and protecting the environment.

[2]3.1 Environmental Protection Policy

[2]3.1.1 The Company shall have a clear written Statement of Policy concerning Environmental Protection.

The Policy shall:

specify the importance the Company places on conserving and protecting the environment;

encourage personnel to be pollution conscious and have a positive attitude towards pollution prevention;

outline the organisation and arrangements to implement the Policy;

be explained to all Company personnel and copies of the Policy made readily available to them.

[2]3.1.2   The Environmental Protection Policy is to be reviewed and amended as necessary to take account of relevant legislation, developments and occurrences.

Chapter 04 [Part 2]   **CONTINGENCY PLANNING**

[2]4.0   The Company's response to an emergency incident must be coordinated, prompt and effective.

[2]4.1   The Company shall have a Contingency Plan for Shorebased Management to deal with emergencies which may have placed the lives of persons onboard at risk.

The purpose of the plan is to ensure that the Company responds to an emergency in a coordinated, prompt and effective manner.

[2]4.2   The Company shall ensure that relevant sections of the Contingency Plan are provided to *the client*.

[2]4.3   The Contingency Plan shall include the following:

the composition and duties of the Company Emergency Response Team who shall coordinate all Company activities to bring the emergency under control as soon as possible;

procedures to assemble the Emergency Response Team;

procedures for Emergency Response Team to follow;

procedures for establishing contact between the client and/or the ship and Shorebased Management;

check lists which will assist in systematic interrogation of the client and/or the ship appropriate to the type of emergency;

reporting methods for shore personnel;

lists of names and telecommunications numbers, including after hours telephone numbers, of persons and organisations who must be notified;

contact reference data for companies and organisations who may be required to assist;

procedures for notifying and liaison with the next of kin of employed personnel onboard the ship;

briefing the selected spokesperson and public relations personnel to answer queries from the media;

back-up arrangements in the event of a prolonged emergency.

In fulfilling these responsibilities, the Emergency Response Team Members shall be relieved from all routine duties and may call upon other Company personnel and specialists as required.

[2]4.4   The plan shall be exercised regularly and, *whenever possible, with the client[s]*, so as to provide for testing the viability of the plan and to reinforce required knowledge and ensure an adequate level of preparedness by individuals with responsibilities under the plan.

Chapter 05 [Part 2]   COST EFFICIENCY, PURCHASING AND CONTRACTING

[2]5.0   The Company shall be cost effective in providing crew and associated services of the required quality.

[2]5.1   Cost Efficiency

The Company shall at all times be diligent in exercising economic management in accordance with established practices of financial and cost control.

Such procedures and practices shall be documented and shall include:

the provision of an annual budget;

periodic monitoring of the agreed budget;

reviews of the actual cost compared to budgeted costs;

planning of cash outlays for the operation and for controlling cash flow and disbursement accounts.

[2]5.2   Sourcing and Provision of Manpower and Associated Services

[2]5.2.1   The Company shall establish and maintain procedures for:

ensuring that relevant documents clearly describe the service [seaman/associated supplies] ordered;

making routine and emergency requisitions;

evaluating cost effectiveness in providing crew personnel, goods and services in accordance with specified requirements;

providing timely and cost effective transport of crew personnel and delivery of goods and services to the ship;

acknowledging receipt and condition by the Shipboard Management;

checking, authorising and timely payment of invoices according to payment terms;

verifying that supplied personnel, goods and services meet the agreed quality;

dealing with non-conformities which shall include procedures for applying corrective actions through an analysis of all processes, operations, *consents*, records, reports and client/ship initiated complaints so as to detect and eliminate nonconforming crew-management services.

[2]5.2.2   *The Company shall review and approve purchasing documents for adequacy of the specified requirements before their release.*

Specified requirements are taken to include the following as applicable:

number required, source of supply and point of delivery;

type, class, grade or other precise identification;

title or other precise identification and issue of standards and experience, processing requirements, examination and certification instructions and other data relevant to

*requirements for approval or qualification of the seaman or services including proce-
dures for the foregoing;*

*where relevant, the title, number and issue of the management system standard to be
applied.*

[2]5.3   Sub-Contracting

The Company shall establish and maintain procedures to:

select sub-contractors to provide services required in respect of the crew of the ship;

the selection shall be based upon the ability of the sub-contractor to meet sub-contract
requirements, including quality requirements;

maintain records of performance of sub-contractors providing important services;

inspect and evaluate the sub-contractor's records pertinent to the Company's Management System and define the retention time of the pertinent records.

In establishing the above procedures due regard shall be paid to the significance of the item
or service and the availability of sub-contractors.

[2]5.4   Contracting

The Company shall, when found beneficial, endeavour to influence the conclusion, variation
and termination of contracts for supply of crew, stores, agencies and other services to the ship
in respect of the crew in a prescribed manner always with the intent to negotiate the best cost
consistent with quality and service for the benefit of the client.

[2]5.5   *Verification*

[2]5.5.1   *Where the Company requires to verify the services provided by a subcontractor at
the subcontractor's premises, the Company shall specify the verification arrangements and
method of release of the services in the purchasing documents.*

[2]5.5.2   *Where specified in the Management Agreement, the client or his representative
shall be afforded the right to verify at the subcontractors premises or the Company's premises
that the subcontracted service conforms to specified requirements.*

*Such verification shall not be used by the Company as evidence of effective control of quality
by the subcontractor.*

[2]5.5.3   *Verification by the client shall not absolve the Company of the responsibility to
provide acceptable services, nor shall it preclude subsequent rejection by the client.*

Chapter 06 [Part 2]   SUPPORT

[2]6.0   The Company recognises the importance of adequate and efficient support from the
Shorebased Management.

[2]6.1   The Company shall have suitably experienced personnel to provide assistance and
support to Shipboard Management.

[2]6.2   The number of personnel shall be adequate for the number and type of Agreements
entered into and for the number of crew employed.

[2]6.3 Each vessel must be assigned to be the responsibility of a designated person, with another person designated as backup.

[2]6.4 The Company shall have available in the office relevant reference documents.

[2]6.5 Effective communication shall exist to enable distribution of feedback and information within the Company.

[2]6.6 The Company shall ensure that outside specialist support as required can be made readily available and maintain a list of such specialists for easy access.

[2]6.7 Support shall also include the review of new rules and regulations to determine the scope and application to ships under management and for prospective agreements that the Company may enter into.

[2]6.8 The company shall establish and maintain procedures whereby newly appointed office personnel shall familiarise themselves with the details of the assigned ships when accepting responsibility.

Chapter 07 [Part 2]   **INSURANCE**

[2]7.0 The Company and the client shall ensure that adequate insurance cover is provided.

[2]7.1   Insurance Placing

[2]7.1.1 The Company shall have access to insurance expertise and who shall be well acquainted with the relevant types of insurance cover.

[2]7.1.2 The Company shall identify the insurance cover required for the crew and agree with the Owner/Client on the actual coverage.

The minimum cover with adequate security shall be as follows:

P&I – Crew Liabilities
War Risk – Crew Liabilities

[2]7.1.3 Where insurances are placed by the Owner/Client, confirmation of the cover shall be *requested* by the Company from the client and as such the Company shall safeguard its position regarding the crew in the Management Agreement.

[2]7.1.4 The Company shall ascertain that the agreed cover remains current and valid at all times their crew are onboard. The Company shall have procedures to follow up with respect to such cover.

[2]7.1.5 The Company shall ensure that proper documentation is made available to the ship, and other parties as required.

[2]7.2   Claim Handling

[2]7.2.1 The Company shall establish and maintain office procedures for reporting and handling any incident that might possibly result in a claim.

[2]7.2.2 The Company shall establish and maintain office procedures to respond to any type of incident report and for further handling of a claim.

The procedure must include:

ship's immediate reporting;

reporting to the P&I Club;

Company's response and support plans;

collection of all required documentation for presentation of the claim;

timely claim collection;

monitoring the progress of the claim;

proper and timely communication and consultation with the Owner/Client.

Chapter 08 [Part 2]   COMPLIANCE WITH RULES AND REGULATIONS

[2]8.1   The Company shall establish and maintain procedures to obtain information about local or international rules, legislations or regulations that affect the manning requirements of the ship and changes thereto and arrange efficient compliance.

Due reference shall be made to recognised and appropriate industrial guidelines including codes, guidelines and standards recommended by IMO, Flag Administrations and other pertinent Maritime Industry Organizations.

[2]8.2   Copies of rules and regulations and *pertinent industrial guidelines* relevant to the crewmanaged vessels shall be maintained in the Company's Offices.

Chapter 09 [Part 2]   COMMUNICATION PROCEDURES

[2]9.0   The Company recognises that effective communication at all levels is of prime importance in carrying out Quality Crewmanagement.

[2]9.1   The Company shall establish and maintain communication procedures *necessary for the Company to effectively render services in accordance with the terms of the Management Agreement* including, but not limited to the following:

port arrival and departure advice;

emergencies;

the distribution of routine information to and from the ship;

the identification of verbal communications that require to be recorded and/or confirmed in writing.

[2]9.2   The Company shall define lines and methods of communication within its Shore-based Management and between that management and the client and/or the ship, including those for weekends, holidays and after office hours.

[2]9.3   The Company shall establish and maintain communication procedures between the Company and the client, which shall ensure that the client receives in respect of the supplied crew:

all information that affects the operation or availability of the ship;

routine reports and documents as agreed with the client.

[2]9.4   The Company shall establish and maintain procedures for *identification, traceability* and for the prompt despatch of crew mail to each vessel.

The procedures will allow for unique identification of crew mail and for recording of the identification from receipt by the Company up until acknowledgement of receipt by the ship.

APPENDIX 4

PART 3

SHIPMANAGEMENT SERVICES

INDEX – PART 3

[Part 3 Comprising Of Twenty Three (23) Pages]

Chapter 01 [Part 3]   PERSONNEL

[3]1.0 *In recognising that a Shipmanager will have responsibilities beyond those of a Crewmanager in respect of personnel onboard ship*, in addition to the requirements under Chapter 01 of Part 2, the Company shall comply with the following requirements.

[3]1.1   Selection and Recruitment and Employment of Ship's Personnel

The Company shall establish and maintain procedures to:

determine the total manning requirement for the ship and verify that the ship is manned accordingly;

clearly specify the master has authority and responsibility with regard to:

* implementing the safety and environmental policy of the Company;

* motivating the crew in the observation of that policy;
* issuing appropriate orders in a clear and simple manner;
* verifying that specified requirements are observed;
* reviewing the Company's Management System and reporting its deficiencies to the shorebased management.

verify that crewmembers can adequately understand key instructions in the designated Command Language *where this language is not English or the native language of crewmembers*;

verify that the Master is conversant with Company Safety and Environmental Protection procedures;

verify that the Master and Chief Engineer are adequately briefed at the time of joining the ship.

[3]1.2   Training of Ship's Personnel

The Company shall establish and maintain procedures to:

ensure appropriate onboard familiarisation with the ship's machinery, equipment and systems including that essential information that shall be given prior to the vessel sailing;

verify that the crew have received relevant information on safety and environmental matters in a language understood by them;

ensure that a programme of training drills and exercises is carried out *to prepare for emergency actions and in particular to respond to potential hazards, accidents and emergency situations which the ship may encounter.*

[3]1.3   Administration of Ship's Personnel

In addition to the requirements under Section [2]1.3 of Part 2 of the ISMA Code, the Company shall establish and maintain procedures to:

make travel arrangements for personnel joining and leaving the ship;

arrange for support, maintenance and repatriation for crewmembers who have to be landed ashore for any reason.

[3]1.4   Drug and Alcohol Policy

The Company will have in place a Policy on Drug and Alcohol Abuse which at least meets the standards of the Oil Companies International Marine Forum [OCIMF] guidelines on this subject in the form current from time to time.

The Policy shall include suitable screening of Masters, Officers and Crew at the time of their employment and during service onboard. It shall also incorporate the need for the Master to exercise control over the issue of alcoholic beverages and maintain records of consumption.

Chapter 02 [Part 3]   SAFETY

[3]2.0   The Company places the highest emphasis on the safe operation of the ship and the safety of personnel.

[3]2.1 Company Safety Policy

The Company shall have a clear written statement Policy concerning Safety which shall at least comply with the requirements of **IMO Resolution A.741[18] – the ISM Code.**

The Policy shall be approved by the Company's Executive Management and shall:

specify the importance the Company places on safety;

acknowledge the Company's responsibilities to safety;

designate personnel in Shorebased Management and Shipboard Management, who shall be given the Authority to implement the Company's Safety Policy and the responsibility to monitor safety and pollution prevention and to ensure that adequate resources are provided;

the designated person[s] shall have access to the highest level of management to provide a link between the Company and those onboard. The responsibility and authority of the designated persons[s] shall include monitoring of the safety and pollution prevention aspects of the operation of each ship and to ensure that adequate resources and shore based support are applied, as required;

define that the Master has overriding authority and the responsibility to make decisions with respect to safety and pollution prevention and that he is to request the Company's assistance as may be necessary. It shall also ensure that the onboard Safety Management System contains a clear statement emphasising the Master's authority;

detail the organisation to give effect to the Policy;

be explained to all Company personnel and copies of the Policy made readily available;

specify that the Master has the responsibility to review the onboard safety procedures.

[3]2.2 Safety Of Personnel

The Company shall establish and maintain shipboard procedures to protect and secure the safety of personnel which shall include:

standards of safe working practices for general shipboard application and for application to the specific type of ship, type of cargo or any other aspect which may be a potential hazard;

maintenance procedures to maintain machinery, equipment and fittings in safe working condition;

emergency procedures, identification of potential emergencies, contingency plans and training for emergencies;

maintenance procedures to ensure that fire and life saving appliances are available for immediate use;

security procedures as appropriate to combat acts of terrorism or sabotage;

procedures to protect and preserve the health of seafarers.

[3]2.3 Safe Ship Operation

[3]2.3.1 Navigational Safety

The Company shall establish and maintain navigational and shipkeeping procedures to secure the safety of the ship and third party property which shall include:

allocation of bridge and engine room watchkeeping duties and responsibilities for navigational and machinery procedures;

procedures for voyage planning and prosecution;

correction procedures to maintain charts and nautical publications up to date;

procedures to ensure that all essential navigational equipment and main and auxiliary machinery is available.

[3]2.3.2 Integrity of the Ship

The Company shall establish and maintain onboard procedures to verify:

the watertight and weathertight integrity of the ship;

that the ship is not overloaded or overstressed;

that the ship has adequate stability.

[3]2.4 Safety Of Cargo

The Company shall establish and maintain onboard procedures to safeguard the condition and security of cargoes likely to be carried regularly by the ship during loading and discharge and throughout the voyage.

[3]2.5 Monitoring Of Safety

[3]2.5.1 Shipboard Monitoring

The Company shall establish and maintain procedures which shall include:

investigation of accidents to personnel and reporting of the circumstances and findings to the Company;

investigation and reporting of near misses;

immediate reports to the Company of significant safety deficiencies or defects which cannot be rectified by ship's staff;

conducting safety inspections at scheduled intervals and to record and report the results of these inspections;

verification of compliance with the specified safety procedures.

[3]2.5.2 Shorebased Monitoring

The Company shall establish and maintain procedures to:

review the Safety Policy and make recommendations for revision of the Policy as found necessary;

review all safety reports from the ship and make recommendations as appropriate;

review, collate and analyze accidents and near misses and distribute the findings as relevant;

monitor by onboard inspection the standards of safety being maintained and make recommendations based on findings;

implement action based on recommendations made and follow up recommended action;

detail reasons why recommendations are not implemented.

[3]2.6 Master's Responsibility And Authority

[3]2.6.1 The Company's Management System is to clearly define and document the responsibility of the Master in respect of:

implementing the Company's Safety Policy onboard;

motivating the ship's crew in the observation of the Company's Safety Policy;

issuing orders and instructions in a clear and *concise* manner in a language understood by the crew;

verifying all specified requirements are met;

reviewing the Management System with particular attention to Safety matters and reporting any deficiencies to the shorebased management.

Chapter 03 [Part 3]   ENVIRONMENTAL PROTECTION

[3]3.0 The Company accords a very high priority to conserving and protecting the environment.

[3]3.1   Environmental Protection Policy

[3]3.1.1 The Company shall have a clear written Statement of Policy concerning Environmental Protection which shall at least comply with the requirements of **IMO Resolution A.741[18] – the ISM Code**. The Policy shall:

specify the importance the Company places on conserving and protecting the environment;

acknowledge the Company's responsibilities to undertake all possible actions for preventing all kinds of pollution;

specify that the most important means of preventing pollution is to ensure safe ship operation as detailed in the Company's procedures;

encourage personnel to be pollution conscious and have a positive attitude towards pollution prevention;

outline the organisation and arrangements to implement the Policy;

define that the Master has overriding authority and the responsibility to make decisions with respect to safety and pollution prevention and that he is to request the Company's assistance as may be necessary;

specify that the Master has the responsibility to review the onboard environmental protection procedures.

[3]3.1.2 The Environmental Protection Policy is to be reviewed and amended as necessary to take account of relevant legislation, developments and occurrences.

Copies of the current Environment Policy shall be made available to all Company personnel.

[3]3.2   Environmental Protection Procedures

[3]3.2.1   The Company shall establish and maintain procedures for the prevention of all kinds of pollution. The procedures shall be appropriate to the type of ship and cargo.

In general pollution prevention procedures shall be provided for:

bunkers and oil transfer operations;

cargo handling operations and cargo stowage;

bilge and ballast handling operations;

sludge, sewage, garbage and other waste disposal;

handling of dangerous cargoes;

emissions to the atmosphere.

[3]3.2.2   The procedures shall also include:

contingency plans to minimise pollution from accidental occurrences;

immediate reports of all pollution incidents or near miss occurrences which could have resulted in pollution;

provision to investigate all reported accidents and near miss occurrences and make recommendations as necessary;

provision to review, collate and analyze reported incidents and near miss occurrences;

the action to be taken to implement recommendations.

[3]3.3   Master's Responsibility & Authority

The Company's Management System is to clearly define and document the responsibility of the Master in respect of:

implementing the Company's Environmental Policy onboard;

motivating the ship's crew in the observation of the Company's Environmental Policy;

issuing orders and instructions in a clear and simple manner in a language understood by the crew;

verifying all specified requirements are met;

reviewing the Management System with particular attention to Environmental matters and reporting any deficiencies to the shorebased management.

Chapter 04 [Part 3]   CONTINGENCY PLANNING

[3]4.0   The Company's response to an emergency incident must be coordinated, prompt and effective.

[3]4.1   The Company shall have a Contingency Plan for Shorebased Management to deal with emergencies which may put the lives of persons onboard at risk or the safety of the ship or cargo at risk or seriously pollute or threaten to pollute the environment. The purpose of this plan is to ensure that the Company responds to an emergency in a coordinated, prompt and effective manner.

An exercise of the contingency plan shall be carried out by office staff at regular intervals.

[3]4.2   The Company shall ensure that relevant sections of the Contingency Plan are provided to Shipboard Management.

[3]4.3   The Contingency Plan shall include the following:

the composition and duties of the Company Emergency Response Team who shall coordinate all Company activities to bring the emergency under control as soon as possible;

procedures to assemble the Emergency Response Team;

procedures for the Emergency Response Team to follow;

procedures for establishing contact between the ship and Shorebased Management;

check lists which will assist in systematic interrogation of the ship appropriate to the type of emergency;

reporting methods for both ship and shore personnel;

procedures to obtain details of personnel onboard ship;

lists of names and telecommunications numbers, including after hours telephone numbers, of persons and organisations who must be notified;

contact reference data for companies and organisations who may be required to assist;

procedures for notifying and liaison with the next of kin of persons onboard the ship;

briefing the selected spokesperson and public relations personnel to answer queries from the media;

back-up arrangements in the event of a prolonged emergency.

In fulfilling these responsibilities, the Emergency Response Team Members shall be relieved from all routine duties and may call upon other Company personnel and specialists as required.

[3]4.4   The Company shall establish and maintain procedures for the Shipboard Management to prepare and have available Contingency Plans to deal with emergencies. These plans shall take account of the various types of emergency which may arise on the particular ship and shall include:

the allocation of duties and responsibilities;

the action to be taken to regain control of the situation;

communication methods to be used on the ship;

procedures to notify the Company;

procedures to notify relevant authorities;

procedures to request assistance from third parties;

procedures for dealing with the media.

[3]4.5   *The Company shall establish procedures for regularly exercising the shorebased and shipboard Contingency Plans. The procedures will specify drills and exercises for responding to emergency situations, including the recording of drills and exercises when activated.*

The aim being that the shorebased and shipboard organizations can respond at any time to hazards, accidents and emergency situations involving the ships.

Chapter 05 [Part 3] **OPERATIONAL CAPABILITY**

[3]5.0 The Company shall endeavour to have the ship available and ready in all respects with regard to manning, equipment, maintenance and supplies for the intended trade and service.

[3]5.1 The Company shall establish and maintain procedures to ensure that the vessel will perform with minimum delays, damages, off-hire or losses.

[3]5.2 The Shorebased Management shall have sufficient qualified personnel to follow up the day to day operation of the vessel and monitor the efficiency and performance.

[3]5.3 The Company shall establish and maintain procedures with the view to verify that the ship is technically sound and in a condition to fulfil designated operations in respect of the cargo and the trade the ship is employed in.

The Company shall further be prepared on request to furnish technical information to the Shipboard Management regarding the operational requirements of particular and special cargoes to be carried.

[3]5.4 The Company shall establish and maintain procedures to:

  have the ship report at scheduled intervals on the operational capability;

  maintain the operational condition and performance of the ship;

  report operational problems which may arise on the ship to the client;

  initiate action to correct operational problems;

  confirm to the Client of the ship, condition and possible limitation as to intended trade as well as changes in operational parameters;

  provide guidance to the Client as necessary regarding improved performance, upgrading the ship and compliance with new Rules and Regulations to meet the requirements of specific intended trade;

  verify that corrective action has been taken;

  respond to the Master's request for assistance;

  assist the Master to obtain all relevant operational and commercial voyage information.

Chapter 06 [Part 3] **COST EFFICIENCY, PURCHASING AND CONTRACTING**

[3]6.0 The Company shall be cost effective in providing goods and services of the required quality.

[3]6.1 Cost Efficiency

The Company shall at all times be diligent in exercising economic management and operate the ship in accordance with established practices of financial and cost control. The procedures and practices shall be documented and shall include:

  the provision of an annual operating budget;

periodic monitoring of the agreed operating budget;

reviews of the actual cost compared to budgeted costs;

planning of cash outlays for the ship's operation and for controlling cash flow and disbursement accounts.

[3]6.2 Purchasing

[3]6.2.1   The Company shall establish and maintain procedures for:

ensuring that relevant documents clearly describe the goods, materials, parts or service [hereinafter goods and [or] services] ordered;

making routine and emergency requisitions;

evaluating cost effectiveness to provide goods and services in accordance with specified requirements;

providing timely and cost effective delivery of goods and services to the ship;

acknowledging receipt and condition by the Shipboard Management;

checking, authorising and timely payment of invoices according to payment terms;

verifying that supplied goods and services meet the agreed quality;

dealing with non-conformities which shall include procedures for applying corrective actions through an analysis of all processes, operations, *consents*, records, reports and client/ship initiated complaints so as to detect and eliminate nonconforming services.

[3]6.2.2   *The Company shall review and approve purchasing documents for adequacy of the specified requirements before their release.*

Specified requirements are taken to include the following as applicable:

source of supply and point of delivery;

type, class, grade or other precise identification;

title or other precise identification and issue of specifications, drawings, process requirements, inspection and certification instructions and other technical data relevant to requirements for approval or qualification of the goods or services including procedures, process equipment and personnel;

where relevant, the title, number and issue of the management system standard to be applied.

[3]6.3   Sub-Contracting

The Company shall establish and maintain procedures to:

select sub-contractors to provide services required for the ship;

maintain records of performance of sub-contractors providing important services.

In establishing the above procedures due regard shall be paid to the significance of the item or service and the availability of sub-contractors.

[3]6.4   Contracting

The Company shall, when found beneficial, endeavour to influence the conclusion, variation and termination of contracts for stores, lubricants, equipment, parts, agencies and other services to the ship in a prescribed manner always with the intent to negotiate the best cost consistent with quality and service for the benefit of the Client.

All negotiated and contracted discounts and rebates obtained by the Company will be allocated in accordance with the terms of the Management Agreement.

[3]6.5   *Verification*

[3]6.5.1   *Where the Company requires to verify the goods or services provided by a subcontractor at the subcontractor's premises, the Company shall specify the verification arrangements and method of release of the goods or services in the purchasing documents.*

[3]6.5.2   *Where specified in the Management Agreement, the client or his representative shall be afforded the right to verify at the subcontractors premises or the Company's premises that the subcontracted goods or service conform to specified requirements.*

Such verification shall not be used by the Company as evidence of effective control of quality by the subcontractor.

[3]6.5.3   *Verification by the client shall not absolve the Company of the responsibility to provide acceptable goods or services, nor shall it preclude subsequent rejection by the client.*

Chapter 07 [Part 3]   **MAINTENANCE AND MAINTENANCE STANDARD**

[3]7.0   The Company's maintenance objective is to protect the asset value and to have the ship in effective service with the minimum off-hire/stoppages at an economical cost level consistent with safety, availability and performance.

[3]7.1   The maintenance standard will be agreed between the Company and the Client. However, the standard shall be such as to ensure compliance with applicable Rules and Regulations and requirements of the ISMA Code.

[3]7.1.1   *The Company is to establish procedures in the Management System to identify equipment and technical systems the sudden failure of which may result in hazardous situations.*

The Management System is to provide for specific measures aimed at promoting the reliability of such equipment and systems.

The measures are to include regular testing of stand-by arrangements and equipment and/or technical systems that are not in continuous use. Due reference shall be taken of the requirements under Part 1 [1]7.5 Special Operations.

[3]7.2   The Company shall have qualified personnel designated to monitor and provide adequate technical support to vessels and to provide all applicable technical feedback information available from relevant sources.

[3]7.3   The Company shall establish and maintain procedures for the repairs and maintenance of the ship and its equipment to:

achieve and maintain the agreed standard;

assign areas of responsibility for the implementation, follow up and review of these procedures.

In establishing the above procedures, due regard shall be paid to the instructions and recommendations of the equipment supplier or maker and the Company's operating experience.

[3]7.4 The Company shall establish and maintain procedures to verify that:

maintenance and repairs are carried out in conformity with the provisions of relevant rules and regulations and to any additional requirements established by the Company and that relevant surveys are carried out in a timely manner in respect of the ship's trade, cargo, crew and passengers;

routine ship inspections are carried out by Superintendents;

maintenance records and reports are available both onboard and in the Shorebased Management office;

there is timely support and availability of spares, materials and other resources to implement the maintenance procedures.

[3]7.5   Measuring and Testing Equipment

The Company shall analyze the importance of measuring and testing equipment and shall, depending on type of vessel, establish procedures for calibration of such equipment.

[3]7.5.1   *Measuring and test equipment shall be used in a manner which ensures that the measurement uncertainty is known and is consistent with required measurement capability.*

[3]7.5.2   *The Company shall establish the extent and frequency of calibration to control and maintain the measuring and testing equipment so as to demonstrate the conformance of the service[s] to specified requirements, the Company shall maintain records of such calibration.*

[3]7.5.3   *Where required by the client, technical data pertaining to measuring and testing equipment for verification that the equipment is functionally adequate shall be made available to the client or his representative.*

Chapter 08 [Part 3]   TECHNICAL SUPPORT

[3]8.0   The Company recognises the importance of adequate and efficient technical support from the Shorebased Management.

[3]8.1   The Company shall have suitably qualified and experienced personnel to provide technical assistance and support to Shipboard Management.

[3]8.2   The number of personnel and the range of special technical disciplines shall be adequate for the number and range of ship types operated.

[3]8.3   Each vessel must be assigned to be the responsibility of a designated person, with another person designated as backup.

[3]8.4   The Company shall have available in the office important plans and manuals for reference. The Company designated personnel shall have particular knowledge of the technical condition and aspects of the ship.

[3]8.5   Effective communication shall exist to enable distribution of technical feedback and information within the Company.

[3]8.6   The Company shall ensure that outside specialist technical support as required can be made readily available and maintain a list of such specialists for easy access.

[3]8.7   The Company shall establish and maintain procedures for monitoring the technical condition and performance of the vessel through regular reports, samples and information.

These shall be examined and evaluated by Shorebased Management procedures and required actions shall be taken.

[3]8.8   Technical support shall also include the review of new rules and regulations to determine the scope and application to ships under management.

The review shall provide appropriate recommendations for implementation and timely compliance.

[3]8.9   The Company shall establish and maintain procedures to ensure that newly appointed personnel shall familiarise themselves with the technical details of the assigned ship when accepting responsibility.

[3]8.10   The Company shall have procedures for evaluating all information to provide positive and effective assistance in case of major damage or casualties.

Chapter 09 [Part 3]   INSURANCE

[3]9.0   The Company and the Client shall ensure that adequate insurance cover is provided.

[3]9.1   Insurance Placing

[3]9.1.1   The Company shall have access to the relevant insurance expertise and be well acquainted with the different types of insurance cover and the insurance market.

[3]9.1.2   The Company shall identify the insurance covers available for the ship and agree with the Client on the actual coverage.

The minimum cover with adequate security shall be as follows:

H&M
P&I
War Risk

[3]9.1.3   The Company shall be named as assured or co-assured in all insurance policies. Where insurances are placed by the Owner/Client, confirmation of the cover shall be made available to the Company.

[3]9.1.4   The Company [when it places insurance] shall ascertain that the agreed cover remains current and valid at all times. The Company shall have procedures to follow up all relevant aspects with respect to such cover.

[3]9.1.5   When the Company does not place insurances it shall safeguard its position regarding insurance cover in the Management Agreement.

[3]9.1.6   The Company shall maintain relevant loss ratio statistics.

[3]9.1.7   The Company shall ensure that proper documentation is made available to the ship, the Owner/Client, Financial Institutions and other parties as required.

[3]9.2   Claim Handling

[3]9.2.1   The Company shall establish and maintain onboard procedures for reporting and handling any casualty that might possibly result in a claim.

[3]9.2.2   The Company shall also establish and maintain office procedures to respond to any type of casualty report and for further handling of a claim.

The procedures must include:

ship's immediate reporting;

Company's reporting to Underwriters;

Company's response and support plans;

collection of all required documentation for presentation of the claim;

monitoring the progress of the claim;

proper and timely communication and consultation with the Client;

timely claim collection.

Chapter 10 [Part 3]   CERTIFICATION & COMPLIANCE WITH RULES & REGULATIONS

[3]10.0   The Company's objective is to ensure that the ship is operated in compliance with applicable rules and regulations.

Reference shall be made to recognised and appropriate industrial guidelines including codes, guidelines and standards recommended by IMO, Flag Administrations and other pertinent Maritime Industry Organizations.

[3]10.1   The Company shall establish and maintain procedures to verify that the ship is always provided with valid statutory and classification certificates and/or other certificates which are necessary for the ship's intended trade.

[3]10.2   The Company shall ensure that routine inspections are performed in order to monitor ship condition to maintain compliance with rules and regulations *and with any additional requirements which may be established by the Company.*

Any nonconformity found shall be reported to the Company, with, if known, the possible cause.

Appropriate corrective actions shall be taken in respect of the nonconformity.

Records of the foregoing activities shall be maintained.

[3]10.3   The Company shall establish and maintain procedures for routine monitoring and controlling the validity of the certificates and planning of surveys or inspections.

[3]10.4   The Company shall establish and maintain procedures to obtain information about local or international rules, legislations or regulations and changes thereto and arrange efficient compliance.

[3]10.5   Publications and documentation shall be available onboard and ashore to ensure operational availability and compliance with rules and regulations.

[3]10.6   The Company shall establish and maintain procedures for the Master to report any deficiencies in connection with statutory and classification or other requirements and initiate corrective actions.

Chapter 11 [Part 3]   CARGO HANDLING & CARGO CARE

[3]11.0   The Company recognises that efficiency in all cargo related matters is the basis for profitable ship operation. The Company also recognises that many cargo related matters are not within its control, but it will nevertheless where possible act in liaison with other appropriate parties to promote efficient cargo carriage and operations.

[3]11.1   The Company shall have sufficient expertise to respond to questions regarding carriage of different types of cargo and the implications this might have on safety of ship or personnel and for environmental protection.

[3]11.2   The Company shall provide the ship with general reference information about cargoes regularly carried in the ship's trade.

[3]11.3   The Company shall assist the Master in obtaining special information about a particular cargo when so requested and shall advise him of any special precautions to be taken.

[3]11.4   There shall be onboard procedures for receiving, handling, carrying and delivering cargo as well as documentation procedures.

[3]11.5   The Company shall establish and maintain procedures to ensure that the ship is technically fit and prepared for the intended type of cargo.

[3]11.6   The ship shall have standing instructions for handling of cargo shortages or cargo claims, if such claims are handled by the Company.

Chapter 12 [Part 3]   **COMMUNICATION PROCEDURES**

[3]12.0   The Company recognises that effective communication at all levels is of prime importance in carrying out Quality Shipmanagement.

[3]12.1   The Company shall establish and maintain communication procedures including, but not limited to the following:

the periodic reporting of the ship's position at sea;

port arrival and departure advice;

emergencies;

the reporting of hazardous occurrences/incidents, accidents, injuries and near misses;

the distribution of routine information to and from the ship;

the commercial operation of the ship;

the identification of verbal communications that require to be recorded and/or confirmed in writing.

[3]12.2   The Company shall define lines and methods of communication within the ship and within the Shorebased Management and between the ship and the Shorebased Management, including those for weekends, holidays and after office hours.

[3]12.3   The Company shall establish and maintain communication procedures between the Company and the Client, which shall ensure that the Client receives:

information that affects the ship operation or availability;

routine reports and documents as agreed with the Client.

IT SUPPLIER REFERENCES

1. **Rydex Industries Corporation**
   Corporate Headquarters, 130–13111 Vanier Place, Richmond BC, CANADA V6V 2JI
   Tel: +1 604 279 3400
   Fax: +1 604 279 3456

2. **Inmarsat**
   99 City Road, London EC1 1AX United Kingdom.
   Tel: +44 (0) 171 728 1000
   Fax: +44 (0) 171 728 1044

3. **Marinet Systems Ltd**
   186 Century Building, Tower Street, Brunswick Business Park, Liverpool L3 4BJ United Kingdom.
   Tel: +44 (0) 151 709 2217
   Fax: +44 (0) 151 709 2331

4. **SpecTec Limited**
   The Dock Office, Trafford Quays M5 0BX United Kingdom.
   Tel: +44 (0) 161 8882288
   Fax: +44 (0) 161 8882287

5. **Marine Management Systems Inc**.
   470, West Avenue, Stamford, Connecticut 06902, USA.
   Tel: 001 203 327 6404
   Fax: 001 203 967 2927

6. **Oceanroutes UK Ltd**.
   Harbour Point, Rye Harbour, East Sussex TN31 7TU United Kingdom.
   Tel: +44 (0) 1797 225797
   Fax: +44 (0) 1797 225022

MANAGEMENT IT BRIEFINGS

Cambridge Academy of Transport
48 Whittlesford Road, Little Shelford, Cambridge CB2 5EW United Kingdom.
Tel: +44 (0) 1223 845242
Fax: +44 (0) 1223 845582

LLP Conferences
LLP Limited, 69–77 Paul Street, London EC2A 4LQ United Kingdom
Tel: +44 (0) 171 553 1000
Fax: +44 (0) 171 553 1100

INDEX